LATIN PROVERBS AND QUOTATIONS.

LATIN PROVERBS AND QUOTATIONS.

WITH TRANSLATIONS AND PARALLEL PASSAGES

AND A COPIOUS ENGLISH

INDEX.

BY ALFRED HENDERSON.

LONDON:
SAMPSON LOW, SON, AND MARSTON,
CROWN BUILDINGS, FLEET STREET.
1869.

(All rights reserved.)

CHISWICK PRESS:—PRINTED BY WHITTINGHAM AND WILKINS,
TOOKS COURT, CHANCERY LANE.

NAMES OF AUTHORS ABBREVIATED.

Ammian.	Ammianus Marcellinus.
Auson.	Ausonius.
Cels.	Celsus.
Cic.	Cicero.
Claud.	Claudian.
Col.	Columella.
Cor. Nep.	Cornelius Nepos.
Erasm.	Erasmus.
Flor.	Florus.
Hor.	Horace.
Juv.	Juvenal.
Luc.	Lucan.
Lucr.	Lucretius.
Macrob.	Macrobius.
Mart.	Martial.
Pers.	Persius.
Petron.	Petronius.
Phæd.	Phædrus.
Plaut.	Plautus.
Plut.	Plutarch.
Prop.	Propertius.
Quint.	Quintilian.
Sall.	Sallust.
Sen.	Seneca.
Stat.	Statius.
Suet.	Suetonius.
Syr.	Syrus Publius.
Tac.	Tacitus.
Ter.	Terence.
Vir.	Virgil.

IT is deemed right to state, and we state it with deep regret, that the compiler of this work did not live to see the fruition of his labour of love. He completed the whole of the body of the work, and died suddenly whilst the sheets were passing through the press. The concluding proof sheets, and the whole of the elaborate and valuable Index, have been carefully revised by a friend.

THE PUBLISHERS.

LONDON, *April* 5, 1869.

PREFACE.

FREED awhile from the duties of an active professional life, and seeking rest after a severe illness, it occurred to me to devote those long tedious days which were then my own to making a manuscript collection of Latin Proverbs, intending it, when completed, as a book of reference for my own private use. As I proceeded in the task my interest in the subject increased, and, impressed more and more with the value of an acquaintance with the proverbs of antiquity, I at length resolved to offer to others the result of my labours. After making considerable progress in the undertaking, I became aware that several compilations of Latin Proverbs and Quotations had been already published, and this, at first, made me waver a little in my project. A very little examination, however, sufficed to show me that there was still room for such a book as I had in contemplation. I observed that the works before me, while containing a mass of the same common and useful material, embraced a very considerable number of extracts and quotations, which, though beautiful in themselves, were not capable of application to the every-day occurrences of life.

Then it struck me that the practical use of such a work would be greatly enhanced by the introduction of English Proverbs and Quotations of kindred meaning to illustrate the Latin.

Lastly, the want of a good Index in the works which came under my notice seemed a very serious deficiency.

With the view of supplying, in some degree, the requirements above referred to, I have ventured to publish the present compilation.

To aim at anything original in a Book of Proverbs is simply absurd, and the only merit which the author of such a compilation can claim, is that of sheer labour and of judgment in the selection of materials. I have not strictly adhered to the literal rendering of the passages quoted. On the contrary, wherever I thought a quotation would strike the mind of the reader more forcibly when the form of expression was slightly altered, I have not scrupled to give a lax translation.

A. H.

IVYWELL,
July, 1868.

CORRIGENDA.

Page 260, *for* " Don Juan, 145," *read* " Don Juan, i. 145."
,, 289, *for* " Nugæ seria ducunt," *read*
" Nugæ seria ducunt
In mala." HOR.

A bove majōri discit arāre minor.—From the old ox the young one learns to plough.

"The young cock crows as he hears the old one."
"As the old cock crows so crows the young."
"As the old birds sing the young ones twitter."

A fronte præcipitium, à tergo lupus.—A precipice is in front, a wolf behind.

"Go forward and fall—go backward and mar all."
See "*Lupum.*" "*Ventus neque.*"

A magnâ non degenerāre culīnâ. JUV.—To keep up as good a *cuisine* as your father.

A mortuo tribūtum exigĕre.—To exact an offering from the dead.

"To draw blood from a stone."

B

A puro pura defluit aqua.—From a pure source pure water comes.

A risu effuso abstine.—Indulge not in boisterous mirth.
"He laughs ill that laughs himself to death."

Ab actu ad posse valet illatio.—From what has taken place we infer what is about to happen.
"From the straws in the air we judge of the wind."

"But shepherds know
How hot the mid-day sun shall glow
From the mist of morning sky." SCOTT.

Ab altero expectes, alteri quod feceris. LAB.—As you behave towards others, expect that others will behave to you.
"Do unto others as you would be done unto."

Ab asinis ad boves transcendere. PLAUT.—To rise to a higher position.

Ab equinis pedibus procul recede.
"Trust not a horse's heels."

Ab inopiâ ad virtutem obsepta est via.—Hard is the path from poverty to renown.
"A broken sleeve holdeth the arm back."
See "*Haud facile.*"

Ab ipso lare.—From home itself.
[To begin at home.]

Ab ovo usque ad mala.—From the egg to the apple.
[From the beginning to the end of a feast.]

Ab transennâ lumbrīcum pĕtĕre. PLAUT.—To snatch the worm from the trap.

Aberrāre a scopo.—To miss his mark.

Abeunt studĭa in mores. OVID.
>"Habit becomes second nature."
>"How use doth breed a habit in a man." SHAKS.
>See "*Usus est.*"

Abnormis sapĭens.—A man of good natural plain common sense.

Absens hæres non erit.—The absent one will not be the heir.
>"Out of sight out of mind."
>See "*Multas amicitias.*"

Absentem lædit, cum ebrĭo qui litĭgat. SYR.—He who quarrels with a drunken man injures one who is absent.
>"He that is drunk is gone from home."

Absentem qui rodit amīcum,
Qui non defendit, alio culpante,
Hic niger est. HOR.

He who speaks ill of an absent friend, or fails to take his part if attacked by another, that man is a scoundrel.

Absit clamor in collŏquio aut lusu.—Avoid bawling in conversation or in play.

Absque băcŭlo ne ingredĭtor.—Leave not your staff at home.

Abstinenda vis a regibus.—Use not coercive measures against those in authority.

Absurdum est, ut alios regat, qui seipsum regere nescit.—It is an absurdity that he should rule others who cannot command himself.

Abundans cautela non nocet.—An excess of caution does no harm.

"Take heed is a good reed."

"Safe bind, safe find." SHAKS.

Abundat dulcibus vitiis. QUINT.—He is full of sweet faults.

"E'en his failings leaned to virtue's side." GOLDSMITH.

Acceptissima semper Munera sunt, auctor quæ pretiosa facit. OVID. Those presents are the most acceptable which are enhanced by our regard for the donor.

Acerrima proximorum odia. TAC.—The hatred of relations is the most bitter.

"The wrath of brothers is fierce and devilish."

"The sweetest wine makes the sharpest vinegar."

"Cousin-germans—quite removed."

"The greatest hate springs from the greatest love."

"If that you have a former friend for foe." BYRON.

Acribus initiis, incurioso fine. TAC.—Zealous in the commencement, careless in the end.

Acta exteriōra indĭcant interiōra secrēta.—Our outward actions reveal our hidden intentions.
> " Out of the fulness of the heart the mouth speaketh."
> " Glowing coals sparkle oft."

Actum ne agas. CIC.—Do nothing twice over.
> " Overdoing is doing nothing to the purpose."

Actus, me invīto, factus, non est meus actus.—What I do against my will cannot be said to be my own act.
> " A man convinced against his will,
> Is of the same opinion still."

Actus non facit reum, nisi mens sit rea.—The act itself does not constitute a crime, unless the intent be criminal.

Ad assem omnia perdĕre.—To lose his last farthing.

Ad calamitātem quīlĭbet rumor valet. SYR.—Every accusation against a fallen man gains credence.
> " He who wants his dog killed has only to say he's mad."
> " He that hath an ill name is half hanged."
> " When the ox falls, there are many that will help to kill him."
> " When the tree is fallen, every one goeth to it with his hatchet."
> " All bite the bitten dog."
> See " *Dejecta.*" " *Invīso semel.*" " *Pudīca non.*"

Ad consilium ne accessĕris antĕquam vocĕris.—Do not give an opinion until it is asked for.
> "Speak when you are spoken to."

Ad finem ubi pervenĕris, ne velis reverti.—Having achieved your purpose, seek not to undo what has been done.

*Ad gĕnĕrum Cĕrĕris sine cæde et vulnĕre pauci
Descendunt reges, et siccâ morte tyranni.* Juv.

Few tyrants go down to the infernal regions by a natural death.

"Tyrants' fears
Decrease not, but grow faster than their years." Shaks.

Ad Græcas Calendas.—When the Greek Calends come round. [Never.]

"When two Sundays meet."

"When the frog has hair."

Ad incĭtas redĭgere.—To checkmate your adversary. To leave him not a leg to stand on.

Ad lætĭtĭam datum est vinum non ad ebriĕtatem.—Wine is given to bring mirth not drunkenness.

"Eating and drinking
Shouldn't keep us from thinking."

"Every inordinate cup is unblessed, and the ingredient is a devil." Shaks.

Ad mensūram aquam bibunt, citra mensuram offam comedentes.—They limit their expenditure where it is not needed, and are ever lavish of that of which they should be sparing.

"To save at the spigot and let it run out of the bunghole."

"To skin a flint for a farthing, and spoil a knife worth fourpence."

"A cough will stick longer by a horse than a peck of oats."

"A sooty chimney costs many a beef-steak."

See "*In minimis.*"

Ad perdĭtam secūrim manubrium adjicĕre.
    "To throw the helve after the hatchet."
        See "*Furor est.*"

Ad pœnitendum propĕrat, citò qui judĭcat. SYR.—Hasty conclusions lead to speedy repentance.
    "Marry in haste, repent at leisure."
        See "*Festīna lentè.*"

Ad præsens ova cras pullis sunt melīora.
    "Better have an egg to-day than a hen to-morrow."

    "One bird in hand is better far
    Than two that in the bushes are."

    "A sparrow in hand is worth more than a vulture flying."

    "He that leaves certainty and sticks to chance,
    When fools pipe he may dance."

    "A living dog is better than a dead lion."
        See "*Capta avis.*" "*Una avis.*"

Ad tristem partem strenŭa est suspĭcio. SYR. — A suspicious mind sees everything on the dark side.
    "Suspicion always haunts the guilty mind!
    The thief doth fear each bush an officer." SHAKS.

        "Trifles light as air
    Are to the jealous confirmations strong
    As proofs of holy writ." SHAKS.

    "All seems infected that th' infected spy,
    As all looks yellow to the jaundiced eye." POPE.

Ad unguem
Factus homo. HOR.
A man perfect to the finger tips.

Adeo in tĕnĕris consuescĕre multum est. VIR. — Of such importance is early training.

> "Train up a child in the way he should go, and when he is old will not depart from it."
>
> "What is learned in the cradle lasts to the grave."
>
> "Bend the willow while it is young."
>
> "Just as the twig is bent the tree's inclined. POPE.
> See "*Principiis obsta.*"

Adhibenda est in jocando moderatio. CIC.—Joking must have its proper limit.

> "A joke driven too far brings home hate."
>
> "Wit is folly unless a wise man hath the keeping of it."
>
> "The would-be wits and can't-be gentlemen." BYRON.
> See "*Cum jocus.*" "*Ludus enim.*" "*Tolle jocos.*"

Adhuc sub judĭce lis est. HOR.—The question is yet before the court.

> [The point in question is yet undecided.]

Adolescentem verecundum esse decet. PLAUT. — Modesty should accompany youth.

Adornāre verbis benefacta. PLIN.—To enrich a favour by a courteous manner in conferring it.

> "A civil denial is better than a rude grant."
>
> "Her pretty action did outsell her gift,
> And yet enriched it too. She gave it me and said
> She prized it once." SHAKS.
> See "*Dat benè.*"

Adsum, qui fēci, in me convertĭte ferrum. VIR. — Here I stand the perpetrator of the crime—turn then your sword on me.

Ædĭficant domos et non habitābunt.—They build houses but shall not inhabit them.

Ægrescit medendo. VIR.—His sickness increases from the remedies applied to cure it.

> "The remedy is worse than the disease."

> "He is the more obstinate for being advised."

Ægrōtat anĭmo magis quam corpŏre.—His illness is more mental than bodily.

*Ægrōtat Dæmon, monăchus tunc esse volēbat;
Dæmon convăluit, Dæmon ut ante fuit.*

> "When the Devil was sick the Devil a monk would be,
> When the Devil got well, the devil a monk was he."

> "The danger past, and God forgotten."

> "When it thunders the thief becomes honest."

> "Vows made in storms are forgotten in calms."

> See "*In morbo.*" "*Quum infirmi.*"

Ægrōto, dum anĭma est, spes est.—While there is life there is hope.

Æmulātio alit ingenĭa.—Emulation is the whetstone of wit.

Æmulātio æmulatiōnem parit.—Emulation begets emulation.

> "For emulation hath a thousand sons
> That one by one pursue." SHAKS.

Æquālem uxōrem quære.—Choose a wife from among your equals.
>See "*Nube pari.*"

Æquālis æquālem delectat.—Like likes like.
>"Birds of a feather flock together."
>"Likeness is the mother of love."
>>See "*Similes.*"

Æquam memento rebus in arduis
Servāre mentem, non secus in bonis. HOR.

In hard times, no less than in prosperity, preserve equanimity.
>"A full cup must be carried steadily."

Æquam est
Poscentem veniam peccātis reddĕre rursus.

It is but fair that he who requires indulgence for his own offences should grant it to others.

Ærūgo anĭmi rubīgo ingenii. SEN.—The rust of the mind is the destruction of genius.
>"Practise not your art, and 'twill soon depart."
>"The used key is always bright."
>"Still water breeds vermin."

>"To have done, is to hang
>Quite out of fashion, like a rusty mail
>In monumental mockery." SHAKS.

>"A sword laid by,
>Which eats into itself, and rusts ingloriously."—BYRON.
>>See "*Doctrīna sed.*" "*Neglectis.*"

Æs debitōrem leve, grave inimīcum facit.—Small favours conciliate, but great gifts make enemies.
>"A little debt makes a debtor, a great one an enemy."
>
>"Excess of obligations may lose a friend."

Æstāte penŭlam detĕris.—Why wear out your great coat in summer?
>"Fie upon a cloak in fair weather!"

Æstimātor sui immŏdĭcus.—A self-conceited fellow.
>"Buy him at his own price and sell him at yours and you'll make no bargain."

Æstŭat ingens
Imo in corde pudor, mixtōque insanĭa luctu. VIR.
Passion and shame torment him, and rage is mingled with his grief.
>"Chaos of thought and passion all confused." POPE.

Ætāte prudentiōres reddĭmur.—We become wiser as we grow older.
>"Old foxes want no tutors."
>
>"Time flies, as he flies, adds increase to her truth,
>And gives to her mind what he steals from her youth."
>   MOORE.

Æthiŏpem dĕalbāre.—To make a black man white.
>"He is washing the crow."
>
>"Wash a blackamoor white."
>
>"Wash a dog, comb a dog, still a dog remains a dog."

Æthiŏpem lavāre.—To wash the Ethiopian.
> [Labour in vain.]
>> " To lather an ass's head is only wasting soap."
>> " Crows are never the whiter for washing themselves."

Age, libertāte Decembri,
Quando ita majōres voluĕrunt, utĕre. Hor.
Come, let us take a lesson from our forefathers, and enjoy the Christmas holyday.

> " At Christmas play, and make good cheer,
> For Christmas comes but once a year." Tusser.

> " Each age has deemed the new-born year
> The fittest time for festal cheer." Scott.

> " 'Twas Christmas broached the mightiest ale,
> 'Twas Christmas told the merriest tale." Scott.

> " Heap on more wood! the wind is chill!
> But let it whistle as it will,
> We'll keep up Christmas merry still." Scott.

Age quod agis.—What you are doing do thoroughly.

Agentes et consentientes pari pœnâ plectuntur.—Wrongdoers and assenting parties are equally punishable.
> " He who holds the ladder is as bad as the thief."
> See " *Cui prodest.*"

Agĕre consideratè pluris est quam cogitāre prudenter. Cic.
Prudence in action avails more than wisdom in conception.

Agnīnis lactĭbus alligāre canem.—To bind a dog with the gut of a lamb.
> "A mad bull is not to be tied up with a packthread."
> "Bolt a door with a boiled carrot!"
> "A rope of sand."

Agnum lupo erĭpĕre.—To snatch the lamb from the wolf.

Agri non omnes frugĭfĕri. Cic.—All soils are not fertile.

Ait latro ad latrōnem.—A rogue says "Yes" to what a rogue says.
> See "*Novi Simonem.*"

Albāti ad exsequias, pullāti ad nuptĭas procēdunt.—They attend a funeral robed in white, and a wedding in mourning.

Albæ gallīnæ filius.—Born of a white hen. [A lucky fellow.]
> "Born with a silver spoon in his mouth."

> "She was one of those who by fortune's boon
> Are born, as they say, with a silver spoon
> In her mouth, not a wooden ladle." Hood.

Ale lupōrum catŭlos!—Nourish the whelps of a wolf!
> "Breed up a crow, and he'll pick out your eyes."
> See "*Pasce canes.*" "*Tigrĭdis.*"

Alĕas fuge. Avoid gambling.
> "The devil leads him by the nose,
> Who the dice too often throws."

> "The best throw of the dice is to throw them away."

Aleātor, quanto in arte est mĕlior, tanto est nequior. Syr. The more skilful the gambler, the worse the man.

Aliă aliis placent.—Different men like different things.
> "All feet tread not in one shoe."
> See "*Mores dispāres.*" "*Non omnes.*"

Alia res sceptrum, alia plectrum.—A sceptre is one thing, a ladle another.

Aliâ voce psittăcus aliâ coturnix lŏquitur.—The parrot utters one cry, the quail another.

Alĭam ætātem alĭa decent.—Different pursuits suit different ages.

Alienâ in miseriâ cruciātum proprium metuit.—From the miseries of others he fears for his own position.
> "When your companions get drunk and fight,
> Take up your hat, and wish them good night."

> "When the next house is on fire, 'tis high time to look to your own."
> See "*Tua res.*"

Aliēna ne concūpiscas.—Covet not the property of others.
> "Enjoy your little while the fool seeks for more."

Aliēna negotia curat,
Excussus propriis. Hor.
Having no business of his own to attend to, he busies himself with the affairs of others.

Aliēna nobis nostra plus aliis placent. Syr.—The property of others is always more inviting than our own; and that which we ourselves possess is most pleasing to others.

Aliēna opprobrĭa sæpe
Absterrent vitiis. Hor.
We are often saved from crime by the disgrace of others.

Alienâ optĭmum insaniâ frui.—It is best to learn wisdom from the follies of others.

"Wise men learn by other men's mistakes, fools by their own."

"The folly of one man is the fortune of another."

"Happy is the man whose father went to the devil."

See "*Felicĭter sapit.*" "*Optĭmum est.*"

Alienâ vivĕre quadrâ. JUV.—To eat off another man's plate.

[To live at another's expense.]

Alienam mĕtis messem.—You reap the crop of another.

See "*Alii sementem.*"

Aliēni appĕtens, sui profūsus. SALL.—Covetous of another man's, prodigal of his own.

Aliēno nutu vīvĕre.—To live at the beck and call of another.

Alii sementem făciunt, alii messem.—Some sow, others reap.

"One beats the bush, another catches the bird."

Aliis lingua, aliis dentes.—One man uses his tongue, another his teeth.

Alio relinquente fluctus alius excipit.—When one wave leaves, another succeeds.

"The tide will fetch away what the ebb brings."

Aliōrum medĭcus, ipse ulcerĭbus scates. PLUT.—A healer of others, himself diseased.

"The devil rebukes sin."

"Physician, heal thyself."

See "*Clodius.*

Aliquando qui lusit, iterum ludet.—He who has once used deception will deceive again.

"A liar is not believed when he speaks the truth."

"Trust not him that hath once broken faith." SHAKS.

Aliquid consuetudini dandum est. CIC.—Something must be allowed to custom.

Aliquid mali propter vicinum malum.—An evil comes from a neighbouring evil.

"One scabbed sheep will infect a whole flock."

See "*Corrumpunt bonos.*" "*Grex totus.*"

Alitur vitium vivitque tegendo. VIR.—A fault is fostered by concealment.

Aliud aliis videtur optimum. CIC.—One man thinks one thing best, another another.

See "*Mores dispares.*"

Aliud est ventilare, aliud pugnare.—It is one thing to boast, another to fight.

"Brag's a good dog, but Holdfast's a better."

Aliud in titulo, aliud in pyxide.*—The title is one thing, the contents another.

"Don't rely on the label of the bag."

Aliud noctua sonat, aliud cornix.—The owl has one note, the crow another.

---

* Pyxis. A gallipot which does not contain that which is named on the outside.

Aliud stans, aliud sedens.—Whilst standing he holds one opinion, whilst sitting another.

    See "*Quo teneam.*"

Aliud vinum, aliud ebrietas.—Wine is one thing, drunkenness another.

Alius aliis in rebus præstantior.—One man excels in one thing, another in another.

    See "*Mores dispăres.*"

Alter ipse amicus.—A friend is a second self.

Alter remus aquas, alter mihi radat arenas. PROP.—Let me skim the water with one oar, and with the other touch the sand.

    [Go not out of your depth.]

Alterâ manu fert aquam, alterâ ignem.

    "He carries fire in one hand, water in the other."
    "He braks my head, an' syne puts on my hoo."
    "The cow gives good milk, but kicks over the pail."
    "He looks one way and rows another."
    See next sentence.

Alterâ manu fert lapidem, alterâ panem ostentat. PLAUT. He carries a stone in one hand while he holds out bread in the other.

    "He gives him roast meat and beats him with the spit."
    "He covers me with his wings, and bites me with his bill."
    See above.

Alterâ manu scabit, alterâ fĕrit.—With one hand he scratches you, and with the other he strikes you.

Alterius non sit, qui suus esse potest.—Let no man be the servant of another, who can be his own master.

*Alterĭus sic
Altĕra poscit opem res, et conjūrat amīce.* Hor.
Thus one thing requires assistance from another, and joins in friendly help.

"Claw me and I'll claw thee."
See "*Gratia gratiam.*"

Altissĭma quæque flumĭna minĭmo sono labuntur. Curt.
The deepest rivers flow with the least sound.

"Have a care of a silent dog and a still water."

"Smooth runs the water where the brook is deep." Shaks.
See "*Cave tibi.*" "*Ne credas.*"

Ama tanquam osūrus; odĕris tanquam amatūrus.—Treat your friends as if hereafter they will become your enemies, and your enemies as if they will become your friends.

Amantes amentes sunt.—Lovers are madmen.

"But who, alas! can love and then be wise?" Byron.
See "*Delīrus.*"

Amantĭum iræ amōris integratio est. Ter.—The quarrels of lovers lead but to the renewal of love.

"Cold broth hot again, that loved I never;
Old love renew'd again, that loved I ever."

"Old pottage is sooner heated than new made."

"By biting and scratching cats and dogs come together."

Amāra bĭlis amāris pharmăcis proluĭtur. One poison is cured by another.
> "Poison quells poison."
> "Desperate cuts must have desperate cures."
> "Knotty timber requires sharp wedges."
>> "One fire burns out another's burning,
>> One pain is lessen'd by another's anguish;
>> Turn giddy and be holp by backward turning;
>> One desperate grief cures with another's languish." SHAKS.
> See "*Malo nodo.*"

Amāre et sapĕre vix deo concēdĭtur.—To be in love and act wisely is scarcely granted to a god.
> "Love's mind of judgment rarely hath a taste:
> Wings and no eyes figure unheedy haste." SHAKS.
> See "*Amantes.*"

Amāre juvĕni fructus est, crimen seni. SYR.—To love is a pleasure of youth, a sin in old age.
> "Gray and green make the worst medley."
> "May and December never agree."

Amāre simul et sapĕre, ipsi Iovi non datur.—Even Jupiter himself cannot be in love and wise at the same time.
> See "*Amantes.*"

Amicĭtia avārōrum complexus sphœrārum.—When spherical bodies can unite and embrace, then there will be friendship amongst the avaricious.

Amīci vitĭum ni feras, prodis tuum. SYR.—You betray your own failing if you cannot bear with the fault of a friend.
> "A friend should bear a friend's infirmities." SHAKS.

Amīco ne maledixĕris.—Never malign a friend.

Amīcorum est admonēre mutuum.—It is the duty of friends mutually to correct each other.

Amīcus certus in re incertâ cernĭtur. Ennius.—A true friend is tested in adversity.

> "A friend in need is a friend indeed."

> "No man can be happy without a friend, or be sure of his friend till he is unhappy."

Amīcus omnium, amīcus nullōrum Cic.—Every man's friend is no man's friend.

> "He makes no friend, who never made a foe." Tennyson.

Amissum quod nescītur, non amittĭtur. Syr.—A loss, of which we are ignorant, is no loss.

> "What loss feels he that wots not what he loses?" Broome.

> "He that is robb'd, not wanting what is stolen,
> Let him not know it, and he's not robb'd at all." Shaks.
>   See "*Certe ignorantia.*" "*In nihil.*" "*Ingens malorum.*"

Amor fit irâ jucundĭor.—Quarrels enhance the pleasures of love.

> "Love's quarrels oft in pleasing concord end."

Amor non patĭtur moras.—Love brooks no delay.
> See "*Amare et.*"

Amor tussisque non celantur.—Love and a cough cannot be hidden.

> "They do not love that do not show their love." Shaks.

Amor, ut pila, vices exĭgit.—Love is like a shuttlecock.

> "Love cannot be bought or sold, its only price is love."

Amōto quærāmus serĭa ludo. Hor.—Joking apart, now let us be serious.

Amphŏra cœpit Institui: currente rotâ cur urceus exit? Hor. It was intended to be a vase, it has turned out a pot.

Amphŏra sub veste rarô portātur honestè.—A cup concealed in the dress is rarely honestly carried.

An dives sit, omnes quærunt, nemo an bonus.—All ask if a man be rich, no one if he be good.

An nescis longas regĭbus esse manus ?—Know you not that kings have long arms?

"He who sups with the devil must have a long spoon."

"Great men have reaching hands." Shaks.

Anĭmæ dīmĭdium meæ.—My better half.

"The life blood streaming thro' my heart,
Or my more dear immortal part,
   Is not more fondly dear." Burns.

Anĭmæ esurienti etiam amāra dulcia videntur.—When the soul hungers, even bitter things taste sweet.

Anĭmasque in vulnĕre ponunt. Vir.—Their own death accompanies the wound they inflict.

Anĭmi morbi a musĭcâ vel curantur vel inferuntur.—The diseases of the mind are either caused or cured by the power of music.

Anĭmo ægrotanti medĭcus est oratio.—Conversation ministers to a mind diseased.

*Anĭmum rege, qui nisi paret
Impĕrat.* Hor.
Govern your temper, which will rule you unless kept in subjection.

Anĭmus conscius se remordet.—A mind conscious of guilt is its own accuser.

>"A guilty conscience needs no accuser."

>"The mind that broods o'er guilty woes
>Is like a scorpion girt by fire." Byron.
>See "*Hi sunt.*"

Anĭmus homĭnis semper appĕtit agĕre alĭquid. Cic.—The human mind ever longs for occupation.

>"Pleasure and action make the hours seem short." Shaks.

Anĭmus in pedes decĭdit.—His heart fell down to his heels.

>"His courage oozed out at his fingers' ends."

*Animus quod perdĭdit optat,
Atque in præterĭtâ se totus imāgine versat.* Petron.
The mind still longs for what it has missed, and loses itself in the contemplation of the past.

>"Can a mill go with the water that's past?"

Annōsa vulpes non capĭtur laqueo.—An old fox is not caught in a snare.

>"Old birds are not caught with chaff."
>See "*Vetŭla vulpes.*"

Annŭlus aureus in nare suillâ.—A ring of gold in a sow's nostril.

Annus prodūcit, non ager.—It is the season not the soil that brings the crop.

Ante barbam doces senes.—A beardless boy would teach old men !

"Shall the gosling teach the goose to swim ?"
"Teach your grandam to spin."
See " *Aquĭlam volare.*"

Ante Dei vultum nihil unquam restat inultum.—Punishment awaits all offences.

"God permits the wicked ; but not for ever."
"The wages of sin is death."

Ante molam primus qui venit, non molat imus. He who has come to the mill first does not grind last.

"First come to the mill, first grind."
"For the last comer the bones."
"The early bird catcheth the worm."
See " *Sero venientibus.*"

Ante victoriam ne canas triumphum.—Sing not of triumph before the victory.

"Boil not the pap before the child is born."
"Don't cry till you are out of the wood."
"Sell not the bear's skin before you have caught him."
"Don't cry fish before they're caught."
"Don't snap your fingers at the dogs before you are out of the village."
"To swallow gudgeons ere they're catched
And count their chickens ere they're hatched." BUTLER.

Antehac putābam te habēre cornua.—Hitherto I gave you credit for having horns.

[I gave you credit for not being wanting in courage.]

Antīquior quam Chaos et Saturnia tempŏra.—More ancient than chaos and the reign of Saturn.

Antīquis debētur veneratio.—Antiquity is entitled to respect.

Anus saltat!—An old woman would dance!

"When a goose dances, and a fool versifies, there is sport."

Anus sīmia sero quidem.—The old monkey is caught at last.

Anus subsultans multum excĭtat pulvĕris.—An old woman dancing makes a great dust.

[Anything out of season is obnoxious.]

Apĕrit præcordia Liber. Hor.—Wine unlocks the breast.

"Wine wears no mask."

See "*In vino.*"

Apertè mala cum est muliĕr, tum demum est bona. Syr.—When a woman is undisguisedly bad, then indeed she is good.

[Comparatively speaking, as she at least lacks deception.]

Appārent rari nantes in gurgĭte vasto. Vir.—They appear but here and there swimming in the vasty deep.

[The portions of some books really worth notice are few and far between.]

Aquæ furtīvæ dulciores sunt.—Stolen waters are the sweetest.
> See "*Nitīmur.*"

Aquam e pumĭce postŭlas.—You seek water from a stone.
> "You can't take blood from a stone."

Aquam igni miscēre.—To mix fire and water.

Aquam in mortario tundĕre.—To pound water in a mortar.

Aquam plorat, cum lavat, profundĕre.—He even begrudges the water with which he washes.
> "He will not lose the parings of his nails."
> "He'd skin a louse, and send the hide and fat to market."
> "A goose cannot graze after him."

Aquĭla non capit muscas.—The eagle does not catch flies.
> "The eagle suffers little birds to sing,
> And is not careful what they mean thereby." SHAKS.

Aquĭlam volāre, delphīnum natāre doces.—Teach an eagle to fly, a dolphin to swim.
> "Teach your grandame to suck eggs."
> See "*Ante barbam.*"

Arbor natūram dat fructĭbus atque figūram.—It is the tree that gives its nature to the fruit.
> "A chip of the old block."

Arbor ut ex fructu sic nequam noscĭtur actu.—As the tree is known by its fruit, so is the wicked man by his deeds.

Arcădes ambo. VIR.—A precious pair of scamps.
> See "*Ait latro.*" "*Novi Simonem.*"

Arcānum demens detĕgit ebriĕtas.—Mad drunkenness discloses every secret.

> "When wine sinks, words swim."
> See "*In vino.*"

Arcānum neque tu scrutabĕris ullīus unquam,
Commissumque teges et vino tortus et irâ. HOR.

Pry not into the affairs of others, and keep secret that which has been entrusted to you, though sorely tempted by wine and passion.

Arcem ex cloācâ facĕre.—To make a palace of a pigstye.

> "To make a mountain of a molehill."
> See "*Murem pro.*" "*Parturiunt.*"

Arcta decet sanum comĭtem toga. HOR.—If you are only an underling, don't dress too fine.

Arcum intensio frangit, anĭmum remissio. SYR.—Straining breaks the bow, relaxation the mind.

> See "*Jocandum.*" "*Stare diu.*"

Arcus nimis intentus rumpĭtur.—A bow too much bent is broken.

> "Too to will in two."

Arēnæ mandas semĭna.—You are but sowing in sand.

Arēnam metīris.—You count the sand.

Argentĕis hastis pugna, et omnia expugnābis.—Fight with silver spears, and you will overcome everything.

> "Money will do more than my lord's letter."

Argentum versum est in scoriam.—The silver is become dross.

> *Argŭe consultum, te dĭlĭget; argŭe stultum,*
> *Avertet vultum, nec te dimittet inultum.*

Correct a wise man, and he will be grateful; correct a fool, and he will not only give a deaf ear, but send you off with a flea in your ear.

Argumentum baculīnum.—Club law.

Arrogantia non ferenda.—Arrogance is intolerable.

> "Arrogance is a weed that grows mostly on a dunghill."

Ars amat fortūnam et fortūna artem.—Fortune and the arts assist each other.

Ars compensābit, quod vis tibi magna negābit.—Skill will enable us to succeed in that which sheer force could not accomplish.

> "If I canna do't by might, I'll do't by sleight."
> See "*Dolus an.*" "*Si leonina.*"

Ars est celāre artem.—It is the perfection of art when no trace of the artist appears.

Ars longa, vita brevis.—Science is unlimited in its course; life is short.

> "The day is short, and the work is much."
> "Art is long, but time is fleeting." LONGFELLOW.

Ars portus inopiæ.—Education is the poor man's haven.

Artem natūra supĕrat sine vi, sine curâ.—Nature without an effort surpasses art.

>"God made the country, but man the town." Cowper.

Asĭni vellĕra quæris!—You seek wool from a donkey!

Asĭnum tondes!—Would you shear a donkey for wool!

Asĭnus asĭno, sus sui pulcher, et suum cuique pulchrum. An ass is beautiful in the eyes of an ass; a sow in those of a sow; and every race is attractive to itself.

>"A crow thinks her own bird fairest."
>
>"Every Jack has his Jill."
>
>"Like will to like."
>
>"What bird so white as mine? says the crow."
>
>"When yet was ever found a mother
>Who'd give her booby for another?" Gay.

Asĭnus esuriens fustem neglĭgit.—A hungry ass heeds not a blow.

>"A hungry dog is not afraid of a cudgelling."

Asĭnus in pelle leōnis.—An ass in the skin of a lion.

Asĭnus stramenta mavult quam aurum.—Hay is more acceptable to an ass than gold.

>"What should a cow do with a nutmeg?"
>
>"What's the use of putting honey in an ass's mouth."
>
>"A barley corn is better than a diamond to a cock."
>
>"Good hay, sweet hay, hath no fellow." Shaks.

Aspĕra vita sed salūbris.—A hard life but a healthy one.

> "Something attempted, something done
> Has earned a night's repose." LONGFELLOW.

> "Weariness
> Can snore upon the flint, when restive sloth
> Finds the down pillow hard." SHAKS.

Aspĕra vox, "Ite," sed vox est blanda, "Venīte."—Harsh is the voice which would dismiss us, but sweet is the sound of welcome.

Asperius nihil est humĭli cum surgit in altum. CLAUD. Nothing is more obnoxious than a low person raised to a high position.

> "Set a beggar on a horse and he'll ride to the devil."

> "The higher the monkey goes the more he shows his tail."

> "No pride like that of an enriched beggar."

> "The more riches a fool hath, the greater fool he is."

> "It is the bright day that brings forth the adder." SHAKS.

> See "*Licet superbus.*"

Aspĭce, quid faciant commercia! JUV.—See the effect of commercial intercourse.

Assidŭa stilla saxum excăvat.—Constant dripping wears away the rock.

> See "*Gutta cavat.*" "*Multis ictibus.*"

At suave est ex magno tollĕre acervo. HOR.—'Tis pleasant to have a large heap to take from.

Athenas noctuas!
> "Owls to Athens."
>
> "Coals to Newcastle."
>
> "Enchantments to Egypt."
>
> "Pepper to Hindostan."
>
> "Indulgencies to Rome."
>
> "Fir trees to Norway."

Atqui non est apud aram consultandum.—It is not at the altar that we should consider the course we would take.
> "Deliberate before you act."
>
> "Look before you leap."
>
> "Draw not thy bow before thy arrow be fixed."

Atria servantem postico falle clientem. HOR.—While your client is watching for you at the front door, slip out at the back.

Attritus galeâ.—Worn bare by the helmet.
> "I have been a soldier,
> Till the helm hath worn these aged temples bare." MILMAN.

Audaces fortuna juvat timidosque repellit.—Fortune smiles on the brave, and frowns upon the coward.
> See "*Audentes.*" "*Dii facientes.*" "*Tollenti.*"

Aude aliquid brevibus Gyaris et carcere dignum,
Si vis esse aliquis. JUV.
Have the courage to do something which deserves transportation if you want to be somebody.

Audendo magnus tĕgĭtur timor. Luc.—Great cowardice is hidden by a bluster of daring.

 "The dog that means to bite don't bark."

 "Timid dogs bark most."
  See " *Canes timidi.*"

Audentes fortūna juvat. Vir.—Fortune favours the bold.

 "Bold resolution is the favourite of providence."

 "Fortune gives her hand to a bold man."

 "Boldness in business is the first, second, and third thing."

 "He that dares not venture must not complain of ill luck."
  See "*Fortes fortuna.*" "*Timĭdi nunquam.*"

Audi altĕram partem.—Hear both sides of a question.

 "One tale is good till another is told."

Audi, quæ ex anĭmo dicuntur.—Listen to that which is openly and seriously spoken.

Audi, vide, tace.—Hear, see, and be silent.

 "Wider ears and a short tongue."

 "Nature has given us two ears, two eyes, and but one tongue."

 "Have more than thou showest,
 Speak less than thou knowest." Shaks.

Audiens non audit.—Hearing he hears not. He is deaf to entreaty.

 [*Aliter.* To feign deafness.]

 "He hath ears but hears not."

Audīre est obedīre. Isidor.—To hear is to heed.

Audītis alĭquid novus adjĭcit auctor. Ovid.—Every one who repeats it adds something to the scandal.

> [The rolling snow-ball.]

Audīto multa, sed loquĕre pauca.—Hear all, say nothing.

> "No wisdom to silence."

> "He that hears much and speaks not at all
> Shall be welcome both in bower and hall."

> "He that speaks, sows; he that hears, reaps."
>> See "*Est tempus.*" "*In garrŭlo.*" "*Non unquam.*" "*Quid de quoque.*"

Aulædus sit, qui citharædus esse non possit. Cic.—Let him play the second fiddle who can't play the first.

> See "*Si bovem.*"

Aurea ne credas quæcunque nitescĕre cernis.—Believe not that all that shines is gold.

> See "*Non omne quod.*"

Aureæ compĕdes.—Fetters of gold.

Aureo hamo piscāri.—To fish with a golden hook.

Auri sacra fames. Vir.—The accursed hunger for gold.

> "Gold! gold! gold! gold!
> Bright and yellow, hard and cold!" Hood.

Aurĭbus lupum tenĕo. Ter.—I hold a wolf by the ears.

> [I am in a dilemma.
> I have caught a Tartar.]

Aurīga virtūtum prudentia.—Prudence is the charioteer of all virtues.

See "*Nervi et.*"

Auro loquente, nihil pollet oratio.—Eloquence avails nothing against the voice of gold.

"You may speak with your gold and make other tongues silent."

"Where gold avails, argument fails."

Aurōra amīca musārum.—The early morn favours study.

Aurum igni probātum.—Gold is proved by fire.

"Prosperity discovers vices, and adversity virtue."

Aurum per medĭos ire satellĭtes,
Et perrumpĕre amat saxa, potentĭus
Ictu fulmĭnĕo. HOR.

Gold delights to walk through the very midst of the guard, and to break its way through hard rocks, more powerful in its blow than lightning.

"No lock will hold against the power of gold."

"Bribes will enter without knocking."

"The golden key opens every door."

"If the walls were adamant, gold would take the town."

"Yes! ready money is Aladdin's lamp." BYRON.

Ausculta et perpende.—Give ear and weigh the matter well.

Aut amat, aut odit mulĭer. SYR.—A woman either loves or hates.

F

Aut Cæsar, aut nullus.—Either Cæsar, or nobody.
> "Either a man or a mouse."
> "Success or ruin."
> "Neck or nothing."
> "Victory or Westminster Abbey." NELSON.

Aut dic, aut accĭpe calcem. JUV.—Speak, or be kicked.
> "He won't, won't he? Then bring me my boots." BARHAM.

Aut insānit homo, aut versus facit. HOR.—The fellow is either a madman or a poet.

Aut minus anĭmi, aut plus potentiæ.—Less malevolence, or more power to exercise it.
> "Anger without power is folly."
> "Don't show your teeth if you can't bite."

Aut navis, aut galērus.—Either a ship or a tuft of feathers.
> "'Tis either a hare or a brake-bush."

Aut non tentāris, aut perfĭce. OVID.
> "If thy heart fail thee, why then climb at all?"
> "Whatsoever thy hand findeth to do, do it with all thy might."

Aut numen, aut Nebuchadnezzar.—A deity or a devil.
> [Either greater or less than man.]
> "I dare do all that may become a man;
> Who dares do more, is none." SHAKS.

Aut potentior te aut imbecillior læsit; si imbecillior, parce illi; si potentior, tibi. SEN.—He who has wronged you is either stronger or weaker than yourself: be he weaker, spare him; be he stronger, then spare yourself.

Aut suadendo blandītur, aut minando terret.—He either wheedles by suasive means or terrifies by threats.

Aut victor, aut victus.—A king or a slave.
        See "*Aut Cæsar.*"

Avārus, nisi quum morĭtur, nihil recte facit.—A covetous man does nothing that he should till he dies.

Avĭde audīmus, aures enim homĭnum novĭtāte lætantur. PLIN. We listen with deep interest to what we hear, for to man novelty is ever charming.
        See "*Est natūra.*" "*Est quoque.*" "*Rarum carum.*"

Avĭdis natūra parum est. SEN.—The world itself is too small for the covetous.

Avīto viret honōre.—He flourishes by hereditary renown.

BALBUS balbum rectiŭs intellĭgit.—To understand a stammerer, you ought to stammer yourself.

"Set a thief to catch a thief."

Barbæ tenus sapientes.—Philosophers as far as the beard.

"With no more sign of wisdom than a beard."   TENNYSON.

"The beard does not make the philosopher."

"The hair that covers the wit is more than the wit, for the greater hides the less.   SHAKS.

Barbărus evāsit inter barbăros.—The rough manners of the vulgar are contagious.

"Harm watch, harm catch."

Beāti monŏcŭli in regiōne cæcōrum.—Happy are one-eyed men in the country of the blind.

"A triton among minnows."

"In Blindman's land your one-eyed man's a god."

"A giant among the pigmies."

Beatus ille qui procul negotiis,
Ut prisca gens mortālium,
Paterna rura bobus exercet suis,
Solūtus omni fænŏre. Hor.

Happy the man who, removed from all cares of business, after the manner of his forefathers cultivates with his own team his paternal acres, freed from all thought of usury.

"Far from gay cities and the ways of men." Pope.
See "*Nec otia.*" "*Si curam.*"

Bellum cum vitiis, sed pax cum persōnis. Isidor.—War with vices, but peace with individuals.

"Preserve the guns, but destroy the gunners."
"Condemn the fault, but not the actor of it." Shaks.

Bellum nec timendum nec provocandum. Plin.—War should neither be feared nor provoked.

Bene dormit, qui non sentit quod malè dormiat. Syr.—Well does he sleep who knows not that his sleep has been broken.

"He that is not sensible of his loss has lost nothing."
See "*Amissum quod.*"

Benè est cui Deus obtŭlit
Parcâ quod satis est manu. Hor.

Happy is the man to whom nature has given a sufficiency with even a sparing hand.

"The greatest wealth is contentment with a little."
"Much coin, much care."
See "*Is minĭmo.*" "*Lætus sorte.*"

Benefacta malè locāta, malefacta arbĭtror. CIC.—Favours out of place I regard as positive injuries.

"Praise undeserved is satire in disguise."

Benefĭcia dare qui nescit, injustè petit. SYR.—He who will not grant a favour has no right to ask one.

"Courtesy on one side can never last long."

Beneficia usque eo læta sunt, dum videntur exsolvi posse. TAC. Kindness, so far as we can return it, is agreeable.

"Little presents maintain friendships."

"A little debt makes a debtor, a great one an enemy."

"Excess of obligations may lose a friend."

Beneficii accepti memor esto.—Be not unmindful of obligations conferred.

"Gratitude is the least of virtues, but ingratitude the worst of vices."

"Blow, blow, thou winter wind,
Thou art not so unkind
As man's ingratitude." SHAKS.

Beneficium accipĕre, libertātem vendĕre est. LABER.—To place yourself under an obligation is to sell your liberty.

"Better buy than borrow."

"Begging a courtesy is selling liberty."

"He that goes a borrowing goes a sorrowing."

"See " *Emĕre malo.*

Beneficium invīto non datur.—A service done to the unwilling is no service.

"A wilful man maun hae his way." Scott.

Bestia bestiam novit.—One beast easily recognizes another.

"As leopard feels at home with leopard." G. Elliot.
See "*Æquālis æqualem.*"

Bis ac ter, quod pulchrum.—A good thing can be twice, nay, even thrice spoken.

"A good tale is none the worse for being twice told."

Bis dat, qui citò dat.

"He giveth twice who giveth in a trice."
"Unwilling service earns no thanks."
"Slow help is no help."
See "*Gratia ab.*" "*Tarde benefacĕre.*"

Bis est gratum, quod opus est, si ultro offĕras. Syr.—A kindness spontaneously offered to him who needs it, is doubly gratifying.

See "*Amīcus certus.*"

Bis interĭmĭtur, qui suis armis perit. Syr.—He dies twice who perishes by his own weapons.

"That eagle's fate and mine were one,
Who, on the shaft that made him die,
Espied a feather of his own,
Wherewith he wont to soar on high." Waller.

See "*Nostris ipsorum.*"

Bis peccāre in bello non licet.—War gives no opportunity for repeating a mistake.

Bis vincit, qui se vincit in victoriâ. Syr.—He is twice a conqueror, who can restrain himself in the hour of triumph.

> "He that is slow to anger is better than the mighty, and he that ruleth his spirit than he that taketh a city."

> "The noblest vengeance is to forgive."

Bona nemĭni hora est, ut non alĭcui sit mala. Syr.—No hour brings good fortune to one man without bringing misfortune to another.

> "Never morning wore
> To evening, but some heart did break." Tennyson.

Bona nomĭna mala fiunt, si non appelles.—Good debts become bad unless called in.

> "A man may lose his goods for want of demanding them."

Bonæ leges ex malis morĭbus procreantur. Macrob.—Good laws are the offspring of bad actions.

Bonārum rerum consuetudo pessĭma est. Syr.—The habitual living in prosperity is most injurious.

Boni pastōris est tondēre pecus, non deglubĕre. Suet.—It is the duty of a good shepherd to shear, not to skin his sheep.

> "Shear the sheep but don't flay them."

> "Friends are like fiddle-strings; they must not be screwed too tight."

> "The orange that is too hard squeezed yields a bitter juice."

Boni principii finis bonus.—A good beginning ensures a good ending.

> "Well begun is half done."

Boni venatōris est plures feras capĕre, non omnes.—It is the duty of a good sportsman to kill game freely, but not to kill all.

Bonis avĭbus.—With good luck.

Bonis nocet, quisquis pepercĕrit malis. SYR.—He who spares the wicked injures the good.

> "Pardoning the bad is injuring the good."
>
> "He who spares vice wrongs virtue."

Bonis quod bĕnĕfit, haud perit.—A kindness bestowed on the good is never thrown away.

Bonum est duābus niti anchŏris.—It is best to trust to two anchors.

> [Have two strings to your bow.]
>
> "Good riding at two anchors men have told,
> For if one break, the other yet may hold."

Bonum est fugienda aspicĕre in alieno malo. SYR.—It is prudent to learn what to avoid from the misfortunes of others.

> See "*Alienā optĭmum.*"

Bonum magis carendo quam fruendo sentītur.—A good thing is esteemed more in its absence than in its enjoyment.

"The ass does not know the value of his tail till he has lost it."

"It so falls out
That what we have we prize not to the worth
Whiles we enjoy it; but being lacked and lost,
Why, then we rack the value." SHAKS.

"Our rash faults
Make trivial price of serious things we have,
Not knowing them until we know their grave." SHAKS.

See "*Nostra intelligĭmus.*" "*Rem carendo.*"

Bonum servat castellum, qui custodiĕrit corpus suum.—He keeps watch over a good castle who has guarded his own constitution.

"Be old betimes that thou may'st long be so."

"Reckless youth makes rueful age."

See "*Maturè fias.*" "*Quæ peccāmus.*"

Bonus dux bonum reddit comĭtem.—A good leader makes a good follower.

"A good Jack makes a good Jill."

Bonus orātor, pessĭmus vir.—A good orator, but a very bad man.

"A grand eloquence, little conscience."

Bos aliēnus subinde prospectat foras.—The ox in a strange stall often casts a longing look towards the door.

"The frog cannot out of her bog."

"There is no place like home."

See "*Nescio quâ.*" "*Patriæ fumus.*"

Bos in stăbŭlo.—An ox [eating his head off] in the stall.

Bos lassus fortius figit pedem.—The ox when most weary is most surefooted.

"Slow and sure."

Bove venāri lepŏrem.—To hunt the hare with the ox.

"To catch a hare with a tabret."

Brevis esse labōro,
Obscūrus fio. Hor.

In trying to be concise I become obscure.

Brevis est magni fortūna favōris.—The favour of the great is not lasting.

"O how wretched
Is that poor man that hangs on princes' favours!" Shaks.

Brutum fulmen.—Harmless lightning.

[Impotent threats.]

"A blow with a reed makes a noise but hurts not."

"A tale
Told by an idiot, full of sound and fury,
Signifying nothing." Shaks.

Bubo canit lusciniæ.—The owl sings to the nightingale.

Bullātæ nugæ.—Empty expressions. Bombast.

CADIT quæstio.—There is an end of the matter.

Cæca invidia est, nec quidquam aliud scit quam detrectāre virtūtes. Livy.—Envy is blind, and is only clever in depreciating the virtues of others.

Cæci sunt ocŭli cum anĭmus res alias agit. Syr.—The eyes see not what is before them when the mind is intent on other matters.

Cæcus cæco dux!—A blind leader of the blind.

"He tells me my way, and knows not his own."

Cæcus iter monstrāre vult.—The blind man wishes to show the way.

"The blind would lead the blind."

"Cleaning a blot with blotted fingers maketh a greater."

"Like Banbury tinkers that in mending one hole make three."

Cædĭmur et totĭdem plagis consumĭmus hostem. Hor.—We get blows and return them.

"Tit for tat."

"Give and take."

Cædĭmus, inque vicem præbēmus crura sagittis.—We conquer and are conquered in our turn.

Călăbri hospĭtis xĕnĭa.—Presents more burdensome than profitable.

"A white elephant."

Calamitōsus est anĭmus futūri anxius. SEN.—The mind that is anxious about the future is wretched.

"Sufficient for the day is the evil thereof."

"Let to-morrow take care of to-morrow,
Leave things of the future to fate;
What's the use to anticipate sorrow?
Life's troubles come never too late." SWAIN.

"Round, round, while thus we go round,
The best thing a man can do,
Is to make it at least, a *merry*-go-round,
By — sending the wine round too." MOORE.
   See "*Carpe diem.*" "*Plus dolet.*" "*Quid sit.*"

Calcŭlo mordēre.—To pay off a grudge by a vote.

Călĭdum prandium comedisti. PLAUT.—You have eaten a meal dangerously seasoned. [You have laid up a grief in store for yourself.]

"Hot sup, hot swallow."

Caligāre in sole.—To be blind even in the light of the sun.

Calumniāre fortĭter, et aliquid adhærēbit.—Calumniate strongly and some of it will stick.

"Slander leaves a score behind it."

"Lay it on thick and some of it will stick."

"Even doubtful accusations leave a stain behind them."

"Slander! slander! some of it always sticks."

"If the ball does not stick to the wall, yet 'twill leave some mark."

"A blow from a frying-pan blacks, though it may not hurt."

Camēlus desīdĕrans cornŭa etiam aures perdĭdit.—The camel asking for horns lost also his ears.

[In grasping for things we need not, we often lose what we have. *Vide*, Fable of Dog and Shadow.]

"Much would have more, and lost all."

"Grasp all, lose all."
See "*Certa amittĭmus.*"   "*Duos qui.*"   "*Qui totum.*"

Camēlus, vel scabiōsa, complurium asĭnorum gestat onĕra. Even a mangy camel will carry more than a herd of asses.

Cancer lepŏrem capit.—The crab would catch the hare!

Cancros lepŏri compăras.—You compare the tortoise to the hare.

Candĭda pax homĭnes, trux decet ira feras.   OVID.—Honourable peace becomes men, fierce anger should belong to beasts.

Candor dat vīrĭbus alas.—Sincerity gives wings to power.

Canem excoriātam excoriāre.—To beat the dog already punished.

"To kick a man when he is down."

"To pour water on a drowned mouse."

Canes tĭmĭdi vehementius latrant quàm mordent. Q. CURT. Timid dogs more eagerly bark than bite.

"The greatest barkers bite not sorest."

"Dogs that bark at a distance bite not at hand."

"He threatens who is afraid."

"He who gives himself airs of importance, exhibits the credentials of impotence." LAVATER.

See "*Audendo magnus.*" "*Minĭma possunt.*" "*Vacuum vas.*"

Cani das palĕas, asĭno ossa.—You give hay to the dog and bones to the ass.

See "*Asĭnus stramenta.*"

Canis clancŭlum mordens.—A dog that bites silently.

[An insidious traducer.
He who would kill you with an air-gun.]

Canis festīnans cæcos partŭrit catŭlos.—The bitch in her haste brings forth blind puppies.

See "*Festīna.*"

Canis reversus ad vomĭtum.—A dog returned to his vomit.

[Going back to bad habits.]

"The sow that was washed is turned to her wallowing in the mire."

Cantābit vacuus coram latrōne viātor. Juv.—A pauper traveller will sing before a beggar.
> "The beggar may sing before the thief."
> "A thread-bare coat is armour proof against highwaymen."

Cantilēnam eandem canis. Ter.—You harp perpetually on the same string.
> "Still harping on my daughter." Shaks.

Capĭte gestāre.—To carry on the head.
> [*i. e.*, To love dearly.] *

Capta avis est pluris quam mille in gramĭne ruris.
> "A small benefit obtained is better than a great one in expectation."
> "A sparrow in hand is worth a pheasant that flieth by."
> "One hour to-day is worth two to-morrow."
> "I will not change a cottage in possession for a kingdom in reversion."
> See "*Ad præsens.*"

Captantes capti sumus.—While we would catch we are caught.
> "Subtlety set a trap and caught itself."
> "Dissemblers oftener deceive themselves than others."
> "Trickery comes back to its master."
> See "*Neque enim.*" "*Qui capit.*"

Captīvum impūnè lacessunt.—A captive they insult with impunity.
> "Even a child may beat a man that's bound."
> "Little birds may pick a dead lion."
> See "*Turpis in reum.*"

---

* From the custom of mothers and nurses carrying infants in a sort of cradle placed on the head.

Caput artis est decēre quod facīas.—It is the essence of good taste to do that which is consistent with our position.

"That suit is best that best fits me."

Caput lupīnum.—A wolf's head (on which a price was put).

[An outlaw. A Pariah.
Fair game for anybody.]

Caput serpentis contĕrĕre.—To bruise the head of the serpent.

Caput sine linguâ.—A head without a tongue.

Carent quia vate sacro. Hor.—(They are unknown) because they had no bard to sing their praises.

"Troy owes to Homer what whist owes to Hoyle." Byron.

"The present century was growing blind
To the great Marlborough's skill in giving knocks,
Until his late life by Archdeacon Coxe." Byron.

Caret perīculo, qui etiam tutus cavet. Syr.—He is the furthest from danger, who is on his guard even when in safety.

"He that is too secure is not safe."

"Though the sun shines, leave not your cloak at home."

"He that fears danger in time seldom feels it."

"The way to be safe is never to feel secure."

"Better to be despised for too anxious apprehensions than ruined by too confident a security." Burke.
See "*Citius venit.*"

Cari rixāntur, rixāntes concĭlĭantur.—Friends become foes, and foes are reconciled.

"Love-quarrels oft in pleasing concord end." MILTON.

Carĭus est carum, si prægustātur amārum.—Misfortunes make happiness more sweet when it comes.

"Pain past is pleasure."
"Pain is forgotten where gain comes."
"If there were no clouds we should not enjoy the sun."
"Sweet is pleasure after pain." DRYDEN.

See "*Forsan et.*" "*Jucunda est.*"

Carpe diem quàm minĭme crēdŭla postĕro. HOR.—Catch the opportunity while it lasts, and rely not on what the morrow may bring.

"Take time when time is, for time will away."
"Defer not till to-morrow what may be done to-day."
"One to-day is worth two to-morrows."
"Defer not till to-morrow to be wise,
To-morrow's sun to thee may never rise." CONGREVE.
"Let us crown ourselves with rosebuds before they be withered."
  WISDOM OF SOLOMON.
"But who would scorn the month of June,
Because December with his breath so hoary,
Must come? Much rather should he court the ray,
To hoard up warmth against a wintry day." BYRON.
"Then fill the bowl—away with gloom!
Our joys shall always last;
For Hope shall brighten days to come,
And Mem'ry gild the past." MOORE.
"We frolic while 'tis May." GRAY.

See "*Calamitōsus.*" "*Plus dolet.*" "*Quid sit.*"

Casta ad virum matrōna parendo impĕrat. Syr.—A virtuous wife commands her husband by obeying him.

"How gently glides the married life away,
When she who rules still seems but to obey."

"She stoops to conquer."

Casus dēmentis correctio fit sapĭentis.—The misfortune of the foolish is a warning to the wise.

"Think, ye may buy the joys o'er dear,
Remember Tam o' Shanter's mare." Burns.

See "*Alienâ optĭmum.*"

Casus plerumque rīdĭcŭlus multos elevāvit.—A ridiculous accident has often been the making of many.

"The race is not to the swift, nor the battle to the strong."

"Some are born great, some achieve greatness, and some have greatness thrust upon them." Shaks.

"Great actions are not always true sons
Of great and mighty resolutions." Butler.

"A lucky chance, that oft decides the fate
Of mighty monarchs." Thomson.

Catus amat pisces, sed non vult tingĕre plantam.

"Fain would the cat fish eat,
But she is loth to wet her feet."

Cauda de vulpe testātur.—A fox is known by his tail.
Caudâ tenes anguillam.—You hold an eel by the tail.
[You are dealing with a slippery fellow.]

Caudæ pilos equīnæ paulātim oportet evellĕre.—To remove the hairs from a horse's tail, one by one must be plucked out.

[Small persevering efforts succeed, when violent measures would fail.]

" Drop by drop the lake is drained."

" Feather by feather the goose is plucked."

See " *Gutta cavat.*"

Caudam păvĭtantem subjĭcĕre utĕro.—To put his tail between his legs.

Caudex, stipes, asĭnus, plumbeus.—A blockhead, a dolt, a donkey, a leaden-headed fellow.

Causa latet; vis est notissima. OVID.—The cause lies hidden; the effect is most notorious.

Cautus enim metŭit fovĕam lupus, accĭpĭterque
Suspectos lăqueos, et opertum mīluus hāmum. HOR.

The cautious wolf fears the pit, the hawk regards with suspicion the snare laid for her, and the fish the hook in its concealment.

Cautus homo cavit, si quem natūra notāvit.—A cautious man will observe the indications of character which nature reveals in others.

Cave canem.—Beware of the dog.

Cave ne quidquam incipias quod post pœniteat.—Have a care not to commence an undertaking of which you may repent.

"Consideration gets as many victories as rashness loses."

"Consideration is the parent of wisdom."

Cave ne titubes. Hor.—Take heed lest you stumble.

"He was slain that had warning, not he that took it."

Cave tibi a cane muto, et aquâ silenti.—Beware of a silent dog and still water.

"Still waters run deep."

See "*Altissima.*" "*Ne credas.*"

Caveat emptor.—Let the buyer be on his guard.

"Buyers want a hundred eyes, sellers none."

"Who buys hath need of eyes."

Cavendum est ne major pœna quam culpa sit. Cic.—Care must be taken that the punishment does not exceed the offence.

Cedant arma togæ. Cic.—Let the force of arms give place to law and justice.

Cede deo.—Yield to divine power.

"Who spits against heaven it falls in his face."

See "*In cælum.*" "*Ludere cum.*"

Cede repugnanti; cedendo victor abibis.—Give way to him with whom you contend; by doing so you will gain the victory.

Celāta virtus ignavia est.—Hidden valour is as bad as cowardice.

"Thoughts shut up want air,
And spoil like bales unopen'd to the sun." YOUNG.

See "*Paulum sepultæ.*"

Celerius occĭdit festināta maturĭtas. QUINT.—That which prematurely arrives at perfection soon perishes.

See "*Citò matūrum.*"

*Celsæ grăvĭōre casu
Decĭdunt turres.* HOR.

The higher the tower, the greater the fall thereof.

"The highest tree hath the greatest fall."

"Look high and fall low."

Certa amittĭmus, dum incērta pĕtĭmus. PLAUT.—In grasping at uncertainties we lose that which is certain.

"Catch not at the shadow, and lose the substance."

See "*Camēlus.*"

Certe ignoratio futurōrum malōrum utilĭor est quam scientia. CIC.—Ignorance of impending evil is far better than a knowledge of its approach.

"Where ignorance is bliss, 'tis folly to be wise." GRAY.

"What the eye sees not the heart rues not."

See "*Amissum quod.*" "*Ingens malorum.*"

Certis rebus certa signa præcurrunt. Cic.—Certain signs are the forerunners of certain events.

> "Coming events cast their shadows before." CAMPBELL.

> "Often do the spirits
> Of great events stride on before the events,
> And in to-day already walks to-morrow." COLERIDGE.

Certum pete finem.—Aim at a certain issue.

Cessante causâ, cessat effectus. COKE.—The cause ceasing, the effect ceases also.

> "Take away fuel, take away flame."

Cessit in proverbium.—It has become a proverb.

Chamæleonte mutabilior.—More changeable than the chameleon.

Cĭcāda cĭcādæ cara, formīcæ formīca.—The grasshopper is dear to the grasshopper, the ant loves the ant.

> See "*Æqualis æqualem.*" "*Similes simili.*"

Cĭcādæ apem compăras.—You compare the bee to the grasshopper!

Cithăra tollit curas.—The harp dispels care.

> "Little we heed the tempest drear,
> While music, mirth, and social cheer,
> Speed on their wings the passing year." SCOTT.

> "Where gripinge grefes ye hart would wounde,
> And dolefulle domps ye mynde oppresse,
> There musicke with her silver sound,
> Is wont with spede to send redresse." R. EDWARDS.

Citius elephantem sub alâ celes.—Sooner could you hide an elephant under your armpit.

Citius quam gradātim.—By speedy, not by slow measures.

"He that dallies with his enemy gives him leave to kill him."

"He that gives time to resolve, gives time to deny, and warning to prevent."

Citius terra æthĕra conscendet.—Sooner shall earth mount to heaven.

Citius venit perīculum cum contemnĭtur. SYR.—Danger comes on us more speedily when we treat it with contempt.

"Danger is next neighbour to security."

"Who looks not before finds himself behind."

"Good watch prevents misfortune."
See "*Caret periculo.*"

Citò matūrum, citò putrĭdum.—Soon ripe, soon rotten.

"A man at five may be a fool at fifteen."

"A man at sixteen will prove a child at sixty."

"There is an order
Of mortals on the earth, who do become
Old in their youth, and die ere middle age." BYRON.

"The ripest fruit first falls." SHAKS.
See "*Is cadet.*" "*Una dies.*"

Cito pede prætĕrit ætas.—Time flies with hasty step.

"My days are swifter than a weaver's shuttle."

"Time fleeth away without delay."
See "*Labĭtur.*"

Clamōsior lauro ardente. — More noisy than laurel when burning.

> "For as the crackling of thorns under a pot, so is the laughter of the fool."

Clausis thesauris incubāre. — To sit brooding over treasures, and enjoy them not.

> See "*Frustrà habet.*" "*Quo mihi.*"

Clodius accūsat mœchos! — Clodius impeaches the adulterers!

> "Thou art a bitter bird, said the raven to the starling."
>
> "The raven chides blackness."
>
> "Death said to the man with his throat cut, 'How ugly you look.'"
>
> "One ass nicknames another 'Long-ears.'"
>
> "The sooty oven mocks the black chimney."
>
> "The frying-pan says to the kettle, 'Avaunt, black brows!'"
>
> See "*Aliorum medĭcus.*" "*Quis tulĕrit.*"

Cochlĕa consiliis, in factis esto volŭcris. — Imitate the snail in deliberation, the bird in execution.

> "Deliberate slowly, execute quickly."

Cœlum, non animum, mutant, qui trans mare currunt. — HOR. In going abroad we change the climate not our dispositions.

> "Send a fool to the market and a fool he will return."
>
> "If an ass goes a-travelling, he'll not come home a horse."

Cœna brevis juvat. — A light supper is beneficial.

Cœpisti melius quam desinis; ultima primis Cedunt. OVID.

You began better than you have finished; the last act is not equal to the first.

Cogenda mens est ut incipiat. SEN.—To make a commencement requires a mental effort.

"The difficult thing is to get foot in the stirrup."
"The most difficult mountain to cross is the threshold."
See "*Dimidium facti.*"

Cogitāto quàm longa sit hyems.—Consider how long the winter will last.

"Winter finds out what summer lays up."
"Put by for a rainy day."
"Save something for the man that rides on the white horse."
"If youth knew what age would crave,
It would both get and save."
See "*Festo die.*" "*Ne quære.*"

Cognatio movet invidiam.—Relationship produces envy.

Collige, non omni tempŏre messis erit.—Fill your garners, harvest lasts not for ever.

"We don't kill a pig every day."
See "*Dum Aurora.*" "*Nosce tempus.*"

Colo quod aptâsti, ipsi tibi nendum est.—As you have arranged the thread so must you weave it.

"As you brew, so you shall bake."
"He that shippeth the devil must make the best of him.
See "*Faber compĕdes.*" "*Tute hoc.*"

Colŭbram in sinu fovēre. To nourish a serpent in one's breast.
> " Bring up a raven, and he will peck out your eyes."

Comĕdĕre beneficium. To forget a kindness.

Comes jucundus in viâ pro vehĭculo est. SYR.—A pleasant travelling companion helps us on our journey as much as a carriage.
> " Good company on a journey is worth a coach."
> " A merry companion on the road is as good as a nag."
> " And yet your fair discourse hath been as sugar,
> Making the hard way sweet and delectable." SHAKS.

Commissumque teges, et vino tortus et irâ. HOR.—Betray not a secret even though racked by wine or wrath.

Commūne naufragium omnĭbus est consolatio.—A common shipwreck is a consolation to all.
> See "*Solāmen misĕris*."

Communia sunt amīcorum inter se omnia.—Friends have all things in common.
> " Friends tie their purses with a spider's web."

Compendia, dispendia.—Short cuts are long ways round.
> " The farthest way about is the nearest way home."
> " Better go about than fall into the ditch."

Concĭliant homĭnes mala.—Misfortunes make friends.
> " Misfortunes make strange bedfellows."

Conciliat animos comitas affabilitasque sermonis. Cic.—Politeness and an affable address are our best introduction.

"Soft and fair goes far."

"Honey catches most flies."

See "*Persuasione cape.*" "*Pudore.*"

Concordiâ fulciuntur opes, etiam exiguæ.—Wealth is protected and poverty is assisted by concord.

Concordiâ res parvæ crescunt, discordiâ maximæ dilabuntur. Sall.—Small endeavours obtain strength by unity of action: the most powerful are broken down by discord.

Concors sic præstat uterque.—Both are the better for their mutual friendship.

Conjugium sine prole, dies veluti sine sole.—Married life without children is as the day deprived of the sun's rays.

Conscientia crimen prodit.—Conscience betrays guilt.

"A guilty conscience needs no accuser."

See "*Hi sunt.*"

Conscientia mille testes.—Conscience is as a thousand witnesses.

"My conscience hath a thousand several tongues,
And every tongue brings in a several tale,
And every tale condemns me for a villain." Shaks.

Consilium senum est sanum.—The counsel of the aged is sound.

Consŏnus esto lupis, cum quibus esse cupis.—You must howl with wolves if you wish to be one of their herd.

"When you are at Rome do as Rome does."
See "*Necesse est cum.*"

Constans et lenis, ut res expostŭlet, esto. CATO.—Be firm or mild as the occasion may require.

Consuetūdo est altĕra natūra. CIC.—Custom is second nature.

Consuetūdo peccandi tollit sensum peccāti.—Habit in sinning takes away the sense of sin.

Consuetūdo quovis tyranno potentior.—Fashion is more powerful than any tyrant.

"That monster, custom, who all sense doth eat
Of habit's devil." SHAKS.

Contingit et malis venātio.—The good fortunes of life fall to the lot even of the base.

"Into the mouth of a bad dog falls many a good bone."

"The worst pig often gets the best pear."
See "*Divitiæ non.*"

Contra lucrum nil valet.—Nothing prevails against wealth.

"Money makes the mare to go."

"Money will do more than my lord's letter."

"Beauty is potent, but money is omnipotent."
See "*Nihil tam firmum est quod.*"

Contra stimŭlum calcas. TER.—You kick against the goad.

"It is hard for thee to kick against the pricks."
See "*Si stimŭlos.*"

Contra vim mortis non herbŭla crescit in hortis.—There grows not the herb, which can protect against the power of death.

Contraria se mutuò commendant.—Contrasts mutually set off each other.

> "Lilies are whitest in a blackamoor's hand."

> "How far that little candle throws its beams;
> So shines a good deed in a naughty world." Shaks.

> "Her beauty hangs upon the cheek of night,
> Like a rich jewel in an Ethiop's ear." Shaks.

Contŭmēliam si dices, audies. Plaut.—If you say hard things you must expect to hear them in return.

> "What's sauce for the goose is sauce for the gander."

Cornīce loquācior.—A greater chatterbox than a raven.

> "Mere verbiage,—it is not worth a carrot!
> Why, Socrates or Plato—where's the odds?—
> Once taught a jay to supplicate the Gods,
> And made a Polly-theist of a Parrot!" Hood.

Cornix scorpĭum răpuit.—The crow has seized a scorpion.
 [The soldier caught a Tartar.]

Cornūtam bestiam petis.—You attack a horned animal.
 "You play with edged tools."

*Corpus onustum
Hesternis vitiĭs anĭmum quoque prægrăvat unà.* Hor.

The body, enervated by the excesses of the preceding day, weighs down and prostrates the mind also.

> "A drunken night makes a cloudy morning."

Corrumpunt bonos mores colloquia prava.
> "Evil communications corrupt good manners."
> "A wicked companion invites us all to hell."
> "'Tis meet
> That noble minds keep ever with their likes:
> For who so firm that cannot be seduced?" SHAKS.
> See "*Dum spectant.*" "*Grex totus.*" "*Si juxta.*"

Corrumpunt otia corpus. OVID.—Idleness ruins the constitution.
> "Idleness is the sepulchre of a living man."

Corruptio optimi pessima.—The corruption of the best things makes the worst.
> "The sweetest wine makes the sharpest vinegar."
> "For men at most differ as heaven and earth;
> But women, worst and best, as heaven and hell." TENNYSON.

Corvus ab aquilâ relictis cadaveribus vescitur.—The carrion which the eagle has left feeds the crow.

Corvus, absente graculo, pulcher.—The crow is a pretty bird when the jackdaw is not present.

Cotem secare novaculâ. FLOR.—To cut a whetstone with a razor.

Crambe bis cocta.—Colewort twice cooked.
> "Life is as tedious as a twice-told tale." SHAKS.

> *Cras amet qui nunquam amavit,*
> *Quique amavit, cras amet.*
> "Let those love now, who never loved before,
> Let those who always loved, now love the more." PARNELL.

Cras credēmus, hŏdie nihil.—To-morrow we will credit it, not to-day.

Credat Judæus Apella! Hor.—Let Apella the Jew credit it, if he will.

"Tell that to the Marines!"

Crede, quod habes, et habes.—Believe that you have it, and it is yours.

Credŭla res amor est. Ovid.—A credulous thing is love.

"The man who loves is easy of belief."

Crescentem sĕquĭtur cura pecuniam. Hor.—Care follows the increase of wealth.

"Much coin, much care."

"Who has land, has war."

Crescit amor nummi, quantum ipsa pecunia crescit. Juv. The love of money grows as money grows.

"It is not want but abundance that makes avarice."

"Poverty craves many things, but avarice more."

"The more we have, the more we want."

"Avarice increases with wealth."

See "*Quo plus.*"

*Crescunt divitiæ, tamen
Curtæ nescio quid semper abest rei.* Hor.

Wealth increaseth, but a nameless something is ever wanting to our insufficient fortune.

"Avarice is never satisfied."

"Covetous men's chests are rich, not they."

See "*Crescit amor.*" "*Multa petentĭbus.*"

*Creverunt et opes, et opum furiosa cupido,
Ut, quo possideant plurima, plura petant.* OVID.

Riches too increase, and the maddening craving for gold, So that men ever seek for more, that they may have the most.

See "*Quo plus.*"

Cribro aquam haurire.—To draw water in a sieve.

[To waste time.]

"He catches the wind with a net."

*Crimina qui cernunt aliorum, non sua cernunt,
Hi sapiunt aliis, desipiuntque sibi.*

Those who see the faults of others, and see not their own, are wise for others and fools for themselves.

"He is nobody's enemy but his own."

Crimine nemo caret.—No man is faultless.

"To err is human."

"If the best man's faults were written on his forehead, it would make him pull his hat over his eyes."

*Crine ruber, niger ore, brevis pede, lumine læsus:
Rem magnam præstas, ————, si bonus es.* MART.

Red-haired, black-lipped, club-footed, and blink-eyed; if you're a good man, you're a wonder!

Crocodili lacrymæ.—Crocodile's tears.

[Hypocrisy.]

Crœsi pecuniæ terunciam addĕre.—To add a farthing to the riches of Crœsus.

> See "*Athenas noctuas.*"

Crudēlem medĭcum intempĕrans æger facit. SYR.—An intemperate patient makes a harsh doctor.

Cucullus non facit monăchum.—The cowl does not make the monk.

> "The beard does not make the philosopher."
>
> "Reynard is still Reynard, though he put on a cowl."

Cui bono? Cui malo?—Whose interest was it? To whose prejudice was it?

> [Who might expect to derive benefit, or injury, from a crime committed?]

Cui multum est pĭpĕris etiam olerĭbus immiscet.—He who has plenty of pepper may season his food as he likes.

> "He who hath much peas may put the more in the pot."

Cui placet, obliviscĭtur; qui dolet, memĭnit.—He who has received a kindness forgets it; he who has been injured remembers it.

> [To benefit one and injure another at the same time is a losing game, for revenge is a stronger feeling than gratitude.]
>
> "Men are more prone to revenge injuries than to requite kindnesses."
>
> "The memory of a benefit vanisheth, but the remembrance of an injury sticketh fast in the heart."
>
> "When I did well, I heard it never; when I did ill, I heard it ever."
>
> "Benefits grow old betimes, but injuries are long livers."
>
> See "*Si quid juves.*"

Cui placet alterĭus, sua nīmīrum est odĭo sors. Hor.—When a man is pleased with the lot of others, he is dissatisfied with his own, as a matter of course.

"Men would be angels, angels would be gods." Pope.

Cui prodest scelus, is facit. Sen.—He who profits by a crime, commits it.

"The receiver is as bad as the thief."

See "*Agentes.*"

Cui puer assuescit, major dimittĕre nescit. The habits of our youth accompany us in our old age.

"He that corrects not youth, controls not age."

"He will go back to the old faith he learnt
Beside his mother's knee." A. Smith.

"A colt you may break, but an old horse you never can."

See "*Principiis obsta.*" "*Quo semel.*"

Cui sunt multa bona, huic dantur plurĭma dona.—To him that hath much, shall much be given.

"Every one basteth the fat hog, while the lean one burneth."

Cuilĭbet in arte suâ perīto est credendum. Coke.—You should trust any man in his own art provided he is skilled in it.

Cuivis dolōri remĕdium est patientia. Syr.—Patience is the remedy for every misfortune.

"Patience is a plaister for all sores."

Cujus vita despĭcitur, restat ut ejus prædicātio contemnātur.—When a man's mode of life is contemptible, it follows that his preaching is treated with contempt.

"The best mode of instruction is to practise what we preach."

"A good example is the best sermon."

Cujus vita fulgor, ejus verba tonĭtrua.—Whose life is as lightning, his words are as thunder.

Cujuslibet rei simulātor atque dissimulātor. SALL.—One who can ever assume to be what he is not, and to conceal what he is.

Cujusvis homĭnis est errāre nullīus nisi insĭpientis in errōre perseverāre. CIC.—To err is human, but to persevere in error is only the act of a fool.

"It is human to err, but diabolical to persevere."

Culex lychno se committens adurĭtur.—The gnat trusting itself to the flame is singed.

Culpam pœna premit comes. HOR.—Punishment follows close on the heels of crime.

"Where villany goes before, vengeance follows after."

"Where vice is vengeance follows."

"Gather thistles, expect prickles."

See "*Sequitur sua.*"

Cum amīco non certandum æmulatione.—Compete not with a friend.

Cum corpŏre mentem
Crescĕre sentīmus, parĭterque senescĕre. LUCR.
We notice that the mind grows with the body, and with it decays.

Cum donant, petunt.—They give, to find a pretext for asking.

>" To give an egg to get an ox."

>" Venture a small fish to catch a great one."

>" Give a loaf, and beg a shive."

>" One must lose a minnow to catch a salmon."

>" He who does not bait his hook catches nothing."

>" Giving is fishing."

Cum duplicantur lătĕres, venit Moses.—When the tale of bricks is doubled, then Moses makes his appearance.

>" When things are at the worst they sometimes mend." BYRON.

>" When bale is hext, boot is next."

>" When misery is highest help is nighest."

>" When the night's darkest the dawn is nearest."

>" Man's extremity, God's opportunity."

>" In man's most dark extremity
>Oft succour dawns from Heaven." SCOTT.

Cum fĕriunt unum, non unum fulmĭna terrent. OVID.—When the lightning strikes but one, not one only does it terrify.

Cum fortūna perit nullus amīcus erit.—When fortune deserts us, our friends are nowhere.

> "An empty purse frights away friends."
> See "*Fervet olla.*" "*Horrea formīcæ.*"

Cum grano salis.—With a grain of salt.

> [To accept a statement with doubt.]

Cum jocus est verus, jocus est malus atque sevērus.—When an observation by joke is true, it is out of place and ill-natured.

> "Play not with a man till you hurt him, nor jest till you shame him."
>
> "True jokes never please."
>
> "Whose wit in the combat as gentle as bright
> Ne'er carried a heartstain away on its blade." MOORE.
>
> See "*Adhibenda.*" "*Temperūtæ.*"

Cum larvis luctāri.—To fight with ghosts.

> [To speak against the dead.]
> "To fight with windmills."
> See "*Nullum cum.*"

Cum magna malæ supĕrest audacia causæ
Credĭtur a multis fidūcia. JUV.

When great assurance accompanies a bad undertaking, such is often mistaken for confiding sincerity by the world at large.

Cum muli pariunt.—When mules breed. [i. e. Never.]

> See "*Ad Græcas.*"

Cum prīncipe non pugnandum.—Avoid strife with those in power.

> "Who draws his sword against his prince must throw away his scabbard."

Cum vulpe habens commercium, dolos cave.—When you bargain with a fox, beware of tricks.

Cunīcŭlis oppugnāre.—To oppose by stratagem.

Cupias non placuisse nimis. MART.—Make it a point not to be over-fascinating.

Cupiditātes medĕri paulo.—To satisfy one's wants at a small cost.

Cupīdo domĭnandi cunctis affectĭbus flagrantior est. TAC.—The love of dominion is the most engrossing passion.

> "By that sin angels fell." SHAKS.

Cura esse, quod audis.—Try to deserve the reputation you enjoy.

Cura fugit multo diluiturque mero. OVID.—Grief is put to flight and assuaged by generous draughts.

> "Wine gladdeneth the heart of man."

> "Care, mad to see a man sae happy,
> E'en drouned himsel amang the nappy." BURNS.

> "Come, come, good wine is a good familiar creature if it be well used." SHAKS.

> "Inspiring bold John Barleycorn,
> What dangers thou canst make us scorn." BURNS.

Curæ laqueāta circum
Tecta volantes. HOR.
The cares that flutter batlike round fretted roofs.

>See "*Si curam.*"

Curæ leves loquuntur, ingentes stupent. SEN.—Light cares cry out; the great ones still are dumb.

> "The wound that bleedeth inwardly is the most dangerous."
> "That grief is light which is capable of counsel."
> "By telling our woes we often assuage them."
> "Fire that's closest kept, burns most of all." SHAKS.
> "Give sorrow words; the grief that does not speak
> Whispers the o'erfraught heart, and bids it break." SHAKS.
>
> See "*Illa dolet.*"

Curiosus idem et garrŭlus.—Inquisitive and prone to gossip.
>[A Paul Pry.]

Curiŏsus nemo est, quin idem sit malevŏlus.—A busybody is always malevolent.

> "Where curiosity is not the purveyor, detraction will soon be starved."

Currus bovem trahit.—The carriage draws the ox.

> "Putting the cart before the horse."

Cutem gerit lacerātam canis mordax.—A biting cur wears a torn skin.

> "Quarrelling dogs come halting home."
> "Snapping curs never want sore ears."

Da dextram misero.—Give a helping hand to a man in trouble.

"Help the lame dog over the stile."

Da locum melioribus. TER.—Give place to your superiors.

Da spatium tenuemque moram, malè cuncta ministrat Impetus. STAT.

Give time and permit a short delay, impetuosity ruins everything.

"Most haste, worst speed."

"Haste trips up its own heels."

"The hasty hand catches frogs for fish."

"Stay a little, that we may make an end the sooner." BACON.

See "*Festina lentè.*" "*Qui nimis.*"

Dæmon te nunquam otiosum inveniat.—Let the devil never find you unoccupied.

> "An idle brain is the devil's workshop."

> "Idle men are the devil's playfellows."

>> "Satan finds some mischief still
>> For idle hands to do." WATTS.

>> See "*Facito aliquid.*" "*Nihil agendo.*" "*Res age.*"

Dæmŏna dæmŏne pellit.—He drives out one devil by another.

> "Take a hair of the dog that has bitten you."

> "One fire burns out another's burning;
> "One pain is lessen'd by another's anguish." SHAKS.

> "Take thou some new infection to thy eye,
> And the rank poison of the old will die." SHAKS.
>> See "*Malum malo.*"

Damna minus consueta movent. The misfortunes to which we are accustomed affect us less deeply.

> "Eels become accustomed to skinning."

>> "In time the rod
> Becomes more mocked than feared." SHAKS.

Damnant quod non intellĭgunt. CIC.—They condemn that which they cannot comprehend.

Damnōsa quid non immĭnuit dies? HOR.—What has not wasting time impaired?

> "Time tries a'."

Damnum appellandum est cum malâ famâ lucrum. SYR.
That should be regarded as a loss, which is won at the expense of our reputation.

Danda venia lapso.—Mistakes are to be pardoned.

Dantur honōres in curiïs non secundum honōres et virtūtes.
Courts grant not their favours as men are good and deserving.

"Kissing goes by favour."

"Preferment goes by letter and affection." SHAKS.

Dat benè, dat multum, qui dat cum munĕre vultum.—He gives well and bountifully who accompanies the gift with a pleasing look.

"A forced kindness deserves no thanks."

"A cup must be bitter that a smile will not sweeten."

"A gift with a kind countenance is a double present."

"Rich gifts wax poor, when givers prove unkind." SHAKS.

"And with them words of so sweet breath composed
As made the things more rich." SHAKS.

See "*Adornāre verbis.*" "*Munĕrum.*"

Dat Deus immīti cornua curta bovi.—Providence provides but short horns for the fierce ox.

"Cursed cows have short horns."

"A cursed cur should be short tied."

Dat sine mente sonum. Vir.—He talks nonsense.

> "It is a tale
> Told by an idiot, full of sound and fury,
> Signifying nothing." Shaks.
>
> See "*Vox et.*"

Dat veniam corvis, vexat censura columbas. Juv.—Censure pardons the ravens but rebukes the doves.

> [The innocent are punished and the wicked escape.]
>
> "Pigeons are taken when crows fly at pleasure."
>
> "One man may steal a horse while another may not look over the hedge."
>
> "The frost hurts not weeds."

Data tempore prosunt. Ovid.—A gift in time of need is most acceptable.

De alieno corio liberalis.—Liberal enough of another man's leather.

> "It is easy to be generous with another man's money."

De alieno largitor, et sui restrictus. Cic.—Prodigal of the property of others, sparing of his own.

De asini umbra disceptare.—To dispute about a donkey's shadow.

De calceo sollicitus, at pedem nihil curans.—Anxious about the shoe, but disregarding the foot.

> [Careful about external appearances, but regardless of the culture of the mind.]

De cælo ad synagōgam.—From repose to tumult.

De duōbus malis, minus est semper eligendum.—Of two evils the least is always to be chosen.

> "Of two evils I have chose the least." PRIOR.

De fumo disceptāre.—To dispute about smoke.

De fumo in flammam.—From smoke to flame.

> "Out of the frying pan into the fire."

De gustĭbus non est disputandum.—There is no accounting for tastes.

> "Every one to his liking."

De malè quæsītis vix gaudet tertius hæres. JUV.—A third heir seldom profits by ill-gotten wealth.

> "What is gotten over the devil's back is spent under his belly."
>
> See "*Malè parta.*"

De mortuis nil nisi bonum.—Speak not against the dead.

> See "*Nullum cum.*" "*Pugna suum.*"

De omnĭbus rebus et quibusdam aliis.—About everything and something else.

> "Famed
> For every branch of every science known." BYRON.

De parvâ scintillâ magnum sæpe excĭtātur incendĭum.—
From a simple spark there will often be produced a great conflagration.

"A small spark makes a great fire."
"A little leak will sink a great ship."
"A spark may raise
An awful blaze."
"Despise not a small wound or a poor kinsman."

De parvis grandis acervus erit—From small things a great heap is made.

"Little by little the bird builds its nest."
"Little and often fills the purse."
"Drop by drop fills the tub."
"Sma' winnings mak a heavy purse."
"Many littles make a mickle."
See "*Minūtŭla.*"

*De paupertāte tacentes
Plus poscente ferent.* HOR.
Those who say nothing about their poverty will obtain more than those who turn beggars.

De pilo pendet.—It hangs by a hair.

De re amissâ irreparābili ne dolĕas.—Grieve not for that which is irreparably lost.

"Fear not the future, weep not for the past." SHELLEY.
"Never grieve over spilt milk."
"What's gone, and what's past help,
Should be past grief." SHAKS.
See "*Non luctu.*"

De se bene existĭmāre.—To have a good opinion of himself.
> "He does not think small beer of himself."
> "He does not think milk-and-water of himself."

Dēbĭle fundamentum tollit opus. — A weak foundation destroys the work.

Decies repetīta placēbit. HOR.—It will please though ten times repeated.
> "A good tale is none the worse for being twice told."

Decipĭmur specie recti. HOR.—We are deceived by the semblance of what is just.
> "Vice is most dangerous when it puts on the garb of virtue."
> "A fair face may hide a foul heart."
> "Springes to catch woodcocks." SHAKS.
> "For man may pious texts repeat,
> And yet religion have no inward seat." HOOD.
> See "*Fronte polītus.*" "*Habent insidias.*"

Decipŭla murem cepit.—The mouse is caught in the trap.

Decor inemptus.—Unbought grace.
> "Loveliness
> Needs not the foreign aid of ornament,
> But is, when unadorn'd, adorn'd the most." THOMSON.

Dedĕcus ille domi sciet ultĭmus. JUV.—He will be the last to discover the disgrace of his house.

Dediscit animus sero quod didicit diu. SEN.—The mind does not easily unlearn what it has been long in learning.

> "It is not easy to straighten in the oak the crook that grew in the sapling."
>
> "You can't teach an old dog new tricks."
>
> See "*Principiis.*"

Defendit numĕrus junctæque umbōne phalanges. JUV.—They are safe in their numbers and their close array.

Deficit ambōbus, qui vult servīre duōbus.—He falls short of his duty to both who tries to serve two masters.

> "You cannot serve God and mammon."
>
> "It's good to be off wi' the old love
> Before ye be on wi' the new."
>
> See "*Duos qui.*" "*Flare simul.*"

Deformius nihil est ardeliōne sene. MART.—There is nothing more revolting than an old busybody.

Degĕnĕres animos timor arguit. VIR.—Want of pluck shows want of blood.

Dejectâ arbŏre, quivis ligna colligit.—When the tree is fallen every one runs to it with his axe.

> "All the world will beat the man whom fortune buffets."
>
> "If a man once fall, all will tread on him."
>
> See "*Turba sequitur.*"

Delectando pariterque monendo.—By pleasing, while we instruct.

*Delenda est Carthago!** Carthage must be destroyed!
[Our greatest enemy must be subdued.]

Delībĕrando sæpe perit occasio. SYR.—By hesitation the opportunity is often lost.

"Take time when time is, for time will away."
"Be wise to-day; 'tis madness to defer." YOUNG.
"Defer no time; delays have dangerous ends." SHAKS.
See "*Tolle moras.*" "*Dum deliberāmus.*" "*Qui non est.*"

Delībĕrandum est diu quod statuendum est semel. SYR.—What is to be once resolved on should be first often well considered.

Delībĕrāre utilia, mora est tutissĭma. SYR.—That delay is our surest protection which enables us to deliberate on the merits of our intentions.

"Look before you leap."

Delīrus et amens dicātur amans.—A lover should be regarded as a person demented.

"He's a fool that's fond."
See "*Amantes.*"

Delphīnum natāre doces!—You teach the dolphin to swim!
See "*Ante barbam.*"

Delphīnum sylvis appingit, fluctĭbus aprum. HOR.—He paints a dolphin in the woods, a boar in the waves.

---

* The well-known conclusion of all the speeches of Cato.

Demitto aurĭcŭlas, ut inīquæ mentis asellus. Hor.—I hang my ears like an ass whose spirits droop.

Deo præeunte, nullus offĭcit obex.—Providence our herald, no barrier can oppose us.

Deōrum dona sæpe non dona.—The gifts of fortune (windfalls) do not always benefit us.

Deōrum injūriæ Dĭs curæ. Tac.—Sins against Heaven may be left to Heaven.

"Vengeance is mine, saith the Lord."

"Leave her to Heaven,
And to those thorns that in her bosom lodge,
To prick and sting her." Shaks.

Destĭnāta tantum pro factis non habentur.—Mere intentions are not to be esteemed as actions.

"Good words fill not a sack."
"Fair words butter no parsnips."
"Hell is paved with good intentions."
"There's no compassion like the penny."
"He is my friend that grindeth at my mill."
"Words are men's daughters, but God's sons are things."
"To promise and give nothing is comfort for a fool."

See "*Ex factis.*" "*Ne verba.*" "*Pleno modio.*"

Destĭtūtus ventis, rēmos adhĭbe.—If the wind will not serve, take to the oars.

Desunt inopiæ multa, avaritiæ omnia. SEN.—Poverty needs much, avarice everything.
>See "*Crescit amor.*"

Detur aliquando otium quiesque fessis. SEN.—Let ease and rest at times be given to the weary.

Dētur dignĭori.—Let it be given to the most meritorious.
>"Let him that earns the bread eat it."
>>See "*Palmam qui.*"

Deus ex māchĭnâ.—Providential aid at a critical moment.
>See "*Cum duplicantur.*"

Deus nobis hæc otia fēcit.* VIR.—We have to thank God for this retirement.

Deus omnĭbus quod sat est suppĕditat.—God sends enough to all.
>"Where God sends babbies he sends penny loaves."

Deus, quos dīlĭgit, castīgat.
>"Whom the Lord loveth he chasteneth."
>
>"Then happy those, beloved of heaven,
>To whom the mingled cup is given;
>Whose lenient sorrows find relief,
>Whose joys are chastened by their grief." SCOTT.
>>See "*Dolor hic.*" "*Est ipsis.*" "*Periisset.*" "*Tribulatio.*"

---

* Motto of the Chelsea pensioners.

Di tibi divitias dĕdĕrunt, artemque fruendi. Hor.—The gods have given you wealth and the means of enjoying it.

Dic, senior, bullâ dignissime. Juv.—Tell me, thou old man, worthy of a child's bauble.

> "Vain, froward child of empire, say,
> Are all thy playthings snatched away?" Byron.

Dicendo dicĕre discunt.—Men learn oratory by practice.

[Practice in speaking makes us eloquent.]

"Practice makes perfect."

See "*Doctrīna.*" "*Scribendo.*"

Differ, habent parvæ commŏda magna moræ. Ovid.—Take time: much may be gained by patience.

"Hastiness is the beginning of wrath, and its end repentance."

See "*Festina lentè.*"

Difficĭlè custodītur, quod plures amant.—That is with difficulty preserved which all hanker after.

"A good thing is soon caught up."

"Fair flowers do not remain long by the wayside."

Difficile est longum subĭto depōnere amōrem.—It is not easy suddenly to cast aside a fancy long indulged in.

Difficile est propriè communīa dicĕre. Hor.—It is no easy matter to say commonplace things in an original way.

Difficĭle est satĭram non scribĕre. Juv.—It is hard to abstain from writing satire.

"Satires run faster than panegyrics."

Difficĭlem oportet aurem habēre ad crīmĭna. SYR.—It is well not to lend too easy an ear to accusations.

Difficĭlia, quæ pulcra.—Beautiful things are secured with most difficulty.

"Fairest gems lie deepest."

Diffūgērĕ nives, rĕdĕunt jam grāmĭna campis,
Arbŏrĭbusque comæ. HOR.

The snow has at last melted, the fields regain their herbage, and the trees their leaves.

Diffugiunt, cadis
Cum fæce siccātis, amici. HOR.

Friends fly away when the cask has been drained to the dregs.

"In time of prosperity, friends will be plenty,
In time of adversity, not one amongst twenty."

See "*Fervet olla.*"

Digna canis pābŭlo.—A dog is worthy of his food.

"'Tis an ill dog that deserves not a crust."

"Thou shalt not muzzle the ox that treadeth out the corn."

"It is a poor horse that is not worth his oats."

See "*Quis enim virtūtem.*" "*Rota plaustri.*"

Dignus obĕlisco.—Worthy of a monument.

Dii facientes adjŭvant.—The gods assist the industrious.

"God helps those who help themselves."

"For a web begun God sends thread."

See "*Tollenti.*"

Dii labŏrĭbus omnia vendunt.—The gods sell all things for labour.

> "No mill, no meal."
>
> "Without pains no gains."
>
> "Plough deep whilst sluggards sleep,
> And you shall have corn to sell and to keep."
>
> "Nothing to be got without pains but poverty."
>
> "For, wake where'er he may, man wakes to care and coil."
>
> Scott.
>
> See "*In sudōre.*" "*Neque mel.*" "*Nil sine labōre.*"

Dii laneos habent pedes.—The avenging gods have their feet clothed in wool.

> [Noiseless is the approach of the avenging deities.]

Dilucŭlo surgĕre saluberrimum est.—Early rising is most conducive to health.

> "Go to bed with the lamb, and rise with the lark."
>
> "The morning hour has gold in its mouth."
>
> "God helps the early riser."
>
> "Too much bed makes a dull head."
>
> "An hour in the morning is worth two at night."
>
> "Early to bed, and early to rise,
> Makes a man healthy, wealthy, and wise."
>
> "At morn the blackcock trims his jetty wing,
>   'Tis morning prompts the linnet's blithest lay ;
> All Nature's children feel the matin spring
>   Of life reviving, with reviving day." Scott.

Dimidĭum facti, qui cœpit, habet.   HOR.

  "Well begun is half done."
  "A beard once washed is half shaven."
  "The hardest step is over the threshold."
    See "*Cogenda mens.*"

Discipŭlus est priōris posterior dies.—To-morrow is the pupil of to-day.

  See "*Dum deliberāmus.*"

Discĭte justitiam monĭti et non temnĕre divos.   VIR.—From my example learn to be just, and not to despise the gods.

Discordat parcus avāro.   HOR.—Frugality is one thing, avarice another.

Discordiâ fit cārĭor concordia.—Peace gains a value from discord.

Discum quam philŏsophum audīre mālunt.—The quoit attracts them more than philosophy.

  Discŭtit en tenĕbras roseis aurōra capillis
  Et sol astra fŭgăt perfundens omnia luce.

Morn with her rosy locks dispels the shades of night, and the sun puts to flight the stars, lighting up the world.

  "Night's candles are burnt out, and jocund day
  Stands tiptoe on the misty mountain-tops."   SHAKS.

Dissipat Evius
Curas edāces. Hor.
The bowl dispels corroding cares.
> "Give wine to them that are in sorrow."

Dissolve frīgus, ligna super foco
Largè repōnens. Hor.
Dispel the cold, bounteously replenishing the hearth with logs.
> "Bring in great logs and let them lie
> To make a solid core of heat." Tennyson.

> "The fire, with well-dried logs supplied,
> Went roaring up the chimney wide." Scott.

Diu delībĕra.—Ponder long before you act.

Dives aut inīquus, aut inīqui hæres.—A rich man is either a rogue or a rogue's heir.

Dīves eram dudum; fēcērunt me tria nudum;
Alĕa, vina, Venus; tribus his sum factus egēnus.
But now I was a rich man, three things have left me bare; dice, wine, and women, these three have made me poor.
> "God defend you from the devil, the eye of a harlot, and the turn of a die."
> See "*Nox et amor.*" "*Vina Venusque.*"

Dīves qui fiĕri vult,
Et citò vult fiĕri. Juv.
He who wants to get rich wants to get rich quickly.

Dives tibi, pauper amīcis.—Rich for yourself, poor for your friends.

Dīvĭde et impĕra.—Divide and rule.
  [Win by creating disunion among your adversaries.]

Dīvīsum sic breve fiet opus. MART.—This division of labour will lessen the task.
  See "*Multæ manus.*"

Dīvĭtiæ non semper optĭmis contingunt.—Riches fall not always to the lot of the most deserving.
  "Some rise by sin, and some by virtue fall." SHAKS.
  See "*Contingit.*"

Docendo disces.—You will learn by teaching.
  "Teaching others teacheth yourself."
  "Who teacheth often learns himself."

  Doctrīna sed vim promŏvet insĭtam,
  Rectique cultus pectŏra rōbŏrant. HOR.

Teaching brings out innate powers, and proper training braces the intellect.
  "Knowledge is a treasure, but practice is the key to it."
  See "*Ærugo.*"

Dolium volvĭtur.—It is easy to set a cask a rolling.
  [To influence a fool.]
  "Raw leather will stretch."

Dolor decrescit, ubi quo crescat non habet. SYR.—Grief diminishes when it has nothing to grow upon.
  See "*Cessante causâ.*"

Dolor hic tibi prodĕrit olim.—This grief will prove a blessing.

> "The far-off interest of tears." TENNYSON.

> "In poison there is physic." SHAKS.

> "Crosses are ladders which lead to heaven."

> "Vexations, duly borne,
> Are but as trials, which heaven's love to man
> Sends for his good."
> See "*Periisset.*"

Dolus an virtus, quis in hoste requirat? VIR.—In strife who inquires whether stratagem or courage was used?

> "If the lion's skin cannot, the fox's shall."

> "All's fair in love and war."

> "Some Cupid kills with arrows, some with traps." SHAKS.

> "I'll potch at him some way;
> Or wrath or craft may get him." SHAKS.
> See "*Ars compensābit.*" "*Si leonīna.*"

Dolus versātur in generalĭbus.—Fraud lurks in loose generalities.

Domi leōnes.—Lions at home.

> "Every cock crows best on his own dunghill."

> "To beard the lion in his den,
> The Douglas in his hall." SCOTT.

Domi manēre oportet belle fortunātum.—A prospering man should remain at home.

> "Leave well alone."
> See "*Si quâ.*"

Domi suæ quilĭbet rex.—A man is a king in his own house.

Dona præsentis rape lætus horæ.—HOR. Enjoy in happiness the pleasures which each hour brings with it.

> "Gather ye rosebuds while ye may,
> Old time is still a-flying;
> And this same flower that smiles to-day,
> To-morrow may be dying."—HERRICK.
>
> See "*Collige.*"

Donec eris felix multos numerābis amīcos,
Tempŏra si fuĕrint nūbĭla, solus eris. OVID.
In prosperity you may count on many friends: if the sky becomes overcast you will be alone.

> "Friends and mules fail us at hard passes."
> See "*Fervet olla.*"

Donum, quodcunque alĭquis dat, probā.—Ever receive a present with approbation.

> "Look not a gift horse in the mouth."

Dos non uxor amātur. JUV.—The dowry, not the wife, is the object of attraction.

> See "*Veniunt a.*"

Duābus sellis sedēre.—To sit on two seats.

> "To run with the hare and hold with the hounds."
> "To carry two faces under one hood."

Dubiam salūtem qui dat afflictis, negat. Sen.—He, who holds out but a doubtful hope of succour to the afflicted, denies it.

Dulce bellum inexpertis.—War appears pleasant to those who have never experienced it.

"Nothing so bold as a blind man."

Dulce est desĭpĕre in loco. Hor.—'Tis sweet at certain times to drop the sage.

"Every monkey will have his gambols."

"Though we may pluck flowers by the way we may not sleep among flowers."

See "*Misce.*"

Dulce et decōrum est pro patriâ mori. Hor.—It is sweet and meritorious to die for one's country.

Dulce pomum quum abest custos.

"Stolen fruit is sweet."

"Stolen waters are sweet, and bread eaten in secret is pleasant."

"Stolen kisses are always sweeter." Leigh Hunt.

Dulce resistens.—Coyly resisting.

"And whispering, 'I will ne'er consent,' consented." Byron.

"Yielded with coy submission, modest pride,
And sweet reluctant amorous delay." Milton.

Dulci mala vino lavĕre. Hor.—To drink away sorrow.

"Drink boys, drink boys,
Drive away your sorrow!" Old Song.

*Dulcis inexpertis cultūra potentis amīci;
Expertus mĕtuit.* Hor.

To the inexperienced it is a pleasant thing to court the favour of the great; an experienced man fears it.

"He that eats the king's geese shall be choked with the feathers."

"Put not your trust in princes."

"Sharp is the kiss of the falcon's beak." Bulwer.

Dulcis sæpe ex aspĕris.—Pleasure often comes from pain.

Dum Aurōra fulget flores collĭgĭte.—Gather flowers while the morning sun lasts.

"Make hay when the sun shines."

"Handle the pudding while it's hot."

See "*Dona præsentis.*" "*Nosce tempus.*"

*Dum bĭbĭmus, dum serta, unguenta, puellas
Poscĭmus, obrēpit non intellecta senectus.* Juv.

"Whilst we drink, prank ourselves, with wenches dally,
Old age upon's at unawares doth sally."

Dum căput infestat, labor omnia membra molestat.—When the head aches, all the members suffer with it.

See "*Vitiant artus.*"

Dum deliberāmus quando incipiendum, incipĕre jam serum est. QUINT.—While we are making up our minds as to when we shall begin, the opportunity is lost.

"He that lets his fish escape, may cast his net often yet never catch it again."

"By the street of 'By-and-by' one arrives at the house of 'Never.'"

"To-morrow, and to-morrow, and to-morrow,
Creeps in this petty pace from day to day,
To the last syllable of recorded time;
And all our yesterdays have lighted fools
The way to dusty death." SHAKS.

See "*Deliberando.*" "*Qui non est.*"

Dum Fata sĭnunt vīvĭte læti. SEN.—As long as the Fates permit, live cheerfully.

Dum lŏquĭmur fugit ætas.—While we discuss matters, the opportunity passes by.

See "*Dum deliberāmus.*"

Dum loquor, hora fugit. OVID.—While I am speaking the opportunity is lost.

Dum singŭli pugnant, universi vincuntur. TAC.—Fighting without concert, they suffer universal defeat.

"By uniting we stand, by dividing we fall." DICKINSON.

See "*Vis unīta.*"

Dum spectant læsos ocŭli, læduntur et ipsi.   OVID.—By looking at squinting people you learn to squint.

> "Mocking is catching."
> See " *Corrumpunt.*" " *Si juxta.*"

Dum spiro, spero.

> "While there's life, there's hope."

Dum tacent, clāmant.   CIC.—Their silence cries aloud.

> "With swimming looks of speechless tenderness."   BYRON.
> See " *Sæpe tacens.*"

Dum trahĭmus, trahĭmur.—While we draw we are drawn.

> [Mutual attraction.]

Dum vires annique sinunt tolerāte labōrem:
Jam veniet tăcĭto curva senecta pede.   OVID.

Work while your strength and years permit you; crooked age will by-and-by come upon you with silent foot.

> "Winter is summer's heir."
> See " *In secundis.*"

Dum vitant stulti vĭtia, in contrāria currunt.   HOR.—In avoiding one vice fools rush into the opposite extreme.

> "Flying from the bull he fell into the river."
>
> "To get out of the rain under the spout."
>
> "What boots it at one gate to make defence,
> And at another to let in the foe?"   MILTON.
> See " *In vitium.*" " *Incidit in.*"

Dum vīvĭmus, vivāmus.—While life lasts let us enjoy it.
> "I am sure care's an enemy to life." SHAKS.
>> See "*Carpe diem.*"

Duos pariĕtes de eâdem fideliâ dĕălbāre.—To whiten two walls from the same lime-pot.
> "To kill two flies with one flap."
> "To catch two pigeons with one bean."
>> See "*In saltu.*"

Duos qui sequĭtur lepŏres neutrum capit.—He who follows two hares loses both.
> "All covet, all lose."
> "Between two stools you come to the ground."
>> See "*Defĭcit ambōbus.*" "*Flare simul.*"

Dūrāte atque expectāte cicādes. JUV.—Hold on, and wait for the grasshoppers.
> [Wait for better times.]

Dūrāte, et vosmet rebus servāte secundis. VIR.—Endure the present, and watch for better things.
> "Bear with evil, and expect good."
> "Adversity's sweet milk, philosophy." SHAKS.

Durior ădămante.—Harder than adamant.

Durō flagello mens docētur rectius.—The mind is best taught with a sharp whip.
> "Wisdom is a good purchase, though we pay dear for it."
> "Wit's never bought till it's paid for."
> "What smarts teaches."
> "They say, best men are moulded out of faults." SHAKS.

Durum et durum non făcĭunt murum.—Hard things alone will not make a wall. [Some soft substance must unite them : and so with hard men—to fraternize they require some soft influence from others.]

Durum telum necessitas.—Necessity is a strong weapon.

"Need makes the old wife trot."

Dux fœmĭna facti. V<small>IR</small>.—A woman the leader of the enterprise.

E CANTU dignoscĭtur avis. — A bird is distinguished by its note.

> "As the sweet voice of a bird,
> Heard by the lander in a lonely isle,
> Moves him to think what kind of bird it is,
> That sings so delicately clear, and make
> Conjecture of the plumage and the form." TENNYSON.

E felīcitate invidia.—Happiness invites envy.

> "An envious man waxes lean with the fatness of his neighbour."

E flammâ cibum pĕtĕre. TER.—To pick out meat from the very funeral pile.

E multis paleis parum fructus collēgi.—Little grain have I collected from a mass of chaff.

E perforāto pocŭlo bibĕre.—To drink from a colander.

E squillâ non nascĭtur rosa.—An onion will not produce a rose.

E Tantăli horto fructus collĭgis.—You seek for fruit in the garden of Tantalus.

E terrâ spectāre naufragium.—To look at a shipwreck from the shore.
> "To see it rain is better than to be in it."

E veritāte odium.—Candour breeds hatred.
> "Truths and roses have thorns about them."

E vīpĕra rursum vīpĕra nascĭtur.—Viper produces viper.
> "Bad hen, bad egg."
>
> See "*Mali corvi.*"

Eâdem oberrāre chordâ.—To err again on the same string.
> "To stumble twice over the same stone."

Ebĭbĕ vas totum si vis cognoscĕre potum.—Empty the glass if you would judge of the drink.

Ebur atramento candefăcĕre.—To whiten ivory with ink. To spoil nature by art.
> "To gild refined gold, to paint the lily,
> To throw a perfume on the violet." SHAKS.
>
> See "*Solem.*"

Echīno asperior.—More prickly than a sea urchin.

Edentŭlus vescentium dentĭbus invĭdet.—The toothless man envies those who can eat well.

Edĕre oportet ut vivas, non vīvĕre ut edas.—We should eat to live, not live to eat.
> See "*Ad lætitiam.*"

Effūgi malum, invēni bonum.—In avoiding that which is evil I have found that which is good.

Ego apros occīdo, sed alter ūtĭtur pulpamento.—I kill the boars, but another eats the flesh.

> "One man beats the bush, another catcheth the bird."
>
> "Child's pig, father's pork."

Ego de alliis loquor, tu respondes de cepis.—I speak of garlic, you reply about onions.

> [I speak of one thing, you reply what is wholly irrelevant.]

Ego de caseo loquor, tu de cretâ respondes. ERAS.—I talk of cheese, you of chalk.

Eheu! fugāces labuntur anni. HOR.—Alas! the fleeting years, how they roll on!

> "Time rolls his ceaseless course." SCOTT.
>
> See "*Tempus fugit.*"

Eheu! quam brĕvĭbus pĕrĕunt ingentia causis! CLAUD. Alas, by what trivial causes is greatness overthrown!

> "What mighty contests rise from trivial things." POPE.

Elephantum ex mure facis.—You make an elephant of a mouse.

> "You make a mountain of a mole-hill."
>
> "All your geese are swans."
>
> See "*Parturiunt.*"

Elephantus non capit murem.—An elephant does not catch mice.

> "An eagle will not catch flies."

Emĕre malo quam rogāre.—I would rather buy than beg.

> "What is bought is cheaper than a gift."
> See "*Beneficium accipĕre.*"

Empta dolōre docet experientia.—Experience purchased by suffering teaches wisdom.

> "Bought wit is best."
>
> "Whom a serpent has bitten a lizard alarms."
>
> "Boys avoid the bees that stung 'em."
> See "*Piscātor ictus.*" "*Qui semel est.*"

Emunctæ naris homo. HOR.—A man of refined taste and judgment.

Ense cadunt multi, feriunt sed crāpŭla plures.—Many fall by the sword, but more from gluttony.

> "Men dig their graves with their teeth."
>
> "Hunger and thirst scarcely kill any,
> But gluttony and drink kill a great many."
> See "*Immodĭcis.*" "*Optĭma medicīna.*"

Eōdem bĭbĕre pōcŭlo.—To drink from the same cup.

> "To row in the same boat."

Eōdem collyrio mĕdēri omnĭbus.—To cure every one with the same ointment.

Eōdem in ludo docti.—Taught in the same school.

> "Hatched in the same nest."
>
> "Tarred with the same stick." SCOTT.

Eōdem labōrat morbo.—He suffers from the same disease.
>[He is in the same difficulty.]
>"Companions in misfortune."

Equi dentes inspicĕre dōnāti.
>"To look a gift horse in the mouth."

Equus, suo defraudātus pabŭlo, ignāvus.—A horse deprived of his food won't work.

Ergo pretium ob stultitiam fero. TER.—This is the reward of my folly.

>*Erĭpe turpi*
>*Colla jugo; liber, liber sum, dic age.* HOR.

Withdraw yourself from that vile bondage; Come say, "I am free," "I am free."

Erĭpĭte isti glădium qui sui est impos animi. PLAUT.—Leave not a sword in the hand of an idiot.
>"Children and fools
>Shouldn't play with edged tools."

Esse solent magno damna minōra bono. OVID.—Trivial losses often prove great gains.

Est etiam, ubi profecto damnum præstet făcĕre, quam lucrum. PLAUT.—There are games in which it is better to lose than win.
>"Gaming gains a loss." BYRON.

Est facies testis, quales intrinsĕcus estis.—You may judge a man by his countenance.
>"His face would hang him."

*Est in juvencis, est in equis patrum
Virtus.* HOR.
Even in animals there exists the spirit of their sires.
> See "*Fortes creantur.*"

Est in nobis assuescĕre multum.—We can accustom ourselves to anything.
> "Custom makes all things easy."
> "For use almost can change the stamp of nature." SHAKS.
> See "*Usus est.*"

*Est ipsis injuria passis
Utĭlis interdum.* OVID.
An injury may prove a blessing.
> "A stumble may prevent a fall."
> See "*Periisset.*" "*Tribulatio.*"

Est miserōrum, ut malevolentes sint, atque invĭdĕant bonis.
PLAUT.—It is the nature of the unfortunate to be spiteful, and to envy those who are well to do.
> "Base envy withers at another's joy,
> And hates that excellence it cannot reach." THOMSON.

*Est modus in rebus: sunt certi dēnĭque fines
Quos ultrā citrāque nequit consistĕre rectum.* HOR.
There is a medium in all things. There are certain limits beyond, or within which, that which is right cannot exist.
> "Keep within compass and you may be sure,
> That you will not suffer what others endure."

Est natūra homĭnum novitātis avĭda.   PLIN.—Man naturally yearns for novelty.

> "New dishes beget new appetites."
>
> See "*Est quoque.*" "*Jucundum.*" "*Rarum carum.*"

Est nulli certum cui pugna velit dare sertum.
The issue of all contention is uncertain.

> [Witness the glorious uncertainty of the law, and of the turf.]

Est proprium stultitiæ aliorum vitia cernĕre, oblivisci suorum.
CIC.—It is peculiarly a fool's habit to discern the faults of others, and to forget his own.

> "The hunchback does not see his own hump, but he sees his brother's."
>
> "Every clown can find fault, though it would puzzle him to do better."
>
> "Why beholdest thou the mote that is in thy brother's eye, but considerest not the beam that is in thine own eye?"

Est quædam flēre voluptas.   OVID.—There is a certain kind of pleasure in weeping.

> "Like summer tempest came her tears:
> Sweet my child, I live for thee."   TENNYSON.
>
> "With a smile on her lips, and a tear in her eye."   SCOTT.

Est quiddam gestus edendi.   OVID.
There is a good deal in a man's mode of eating.

Est quoque cunctārum novĭtas cārissĭma rerum. Ovid.—
Novelty in all things is charming.

"Want of variety leads to satiety."

"Variety's the very spice of life,
That gives it all its flavour." Cowper.

See "*Est natūra.*" "*Jucundum.*" "*Rarum carum.*"

Est tempus quando nihil, est tempus quando ălĭquid, nullum tamen est tempus in quo dicenda sunt omnia.—There is a time when nothing should be said, there is a time when some things may be said, but there is indeed no time in which everything can be said.

"No wisdom to silence."

"The loquacity of fools is a lecture to the wise."

"Speech is silvern, silence is golden." Carlyle.

See "*Audīto multa.*" "*Exigua est.*"

Est,
Vīvĕre bis, vitâ posse priōre frui. Ovid.
Twice does he live who can enjoy the remembrance of the past.

Esto mihi ; ero tibi.—Be mine ; I will be thine.

"Ca' me, ca' thee."

Esto quod esse vidēris.—Be what you appear to be.

[Act up to the reputation which you enjoy.]

"Be the same thing that ye wa'd be ca'd."

Esurienti leōni prædam exsculpĕre.—To wrest the prey from the hungry lion.

Esurienti ne occurras.—Oppose not a hungry man.

> "A hungry man, an angry man."

Et canis in somnis lepŏris vestigĭa latrat.—A dog as he sleeps barks as if on the track of the hare.

> "Like a dog he hunts in dreams." TENNYSON.

> "There are a kind of men so loose of soul,
> That in their sleeps will mutter their affairs." SHAKS.

*Et latro, et cautus præcingĭtur ense viātor;
Ille sed insĭdias, hic sibi portat opem.* OVID.

The robber and the cautious traveller alike are girded with the sword; the one uses it as a means of attack, the other as a means of defence.

> "One sword keeps another in its scabbard."

Et levis erectâ consurgit ad oscŭla plantâ. JUV.—She stands on tiptoe to be kissed.

*Et mea cymba sĕmel vastâ percussa procellâ,
Illum, quo læsa est, horret adīre lŏcum.* OVID.

My bark, once struck by the fury of the storm, dreads again to approach the place of danger.

> See "*Empta dolore.*"

Et mihi res, non me rebus, submittĕre conor. HOR.—I strive to mould circumstances to myself, not myself to circumstances.

Et mihi sunt vires et mea tēla nocent. Ovid.—I too am not powerless, and my weapons strike hard.

"Two can play at that game."

Et mĭnĭmæ vires frangĕre quassa valent. Ovid.—Very slight violence will break that which has once been cracked.

"It is not the burden but the over-burden that kills the beast."

"'Tis the last straw that breaks the camel's back."

"The last drop makes the cup run over."

Et neglecta solent incendia sumĕre vires. Hor.—Flames too soon acquire strength if disregarded.

"A small spark makes a great fire."

Et quâcunque potes dote placēre, place. Ovid.—Whatever charm thou hast, be charming.

Et, qui nolunt occidĕre quenquam,
Posse volunt. Juv.

Though they don't want to kill anybody, they like to have the power to do so.

Et scissâ gaudens vadit Discordia pallâ. Virg.—And there stalks Discord delighted with her torn mantle.

Etiam celerĭtas, in dēsīdĕrio, mora est. Syr.—Even speed, when we are anxious, seems like delay.

Etiam illud quod scies nescīvĕris:
Ne vīdĕris, quod vīdĕris. Plaut.
That which you know, know not; and that which you see, see not.

"'Tis wisdom sometimes to seem a fool."
See "*Qui nescit.*" "*Quod scis.*"

Etiam innocentes cogit mentīri dolor.—The rack can extort a false confession from the innocent.

Etiam mendĭcus mendīco invĭdet.—Even the beggar envies the beggar.

"'Tis one beggar's woe, to see another by the door go."

"One dog growls to see another go into the kitchen."
See "*Una domus.*"

Etiam oblivisci quod scis interdum expĕdit. Syr.—It is as well now and then not to remember all we know.

"The wise man does not hang his knowledge on a hook."

"Speech was given to man to disguise his thoughts."
See "*Etĭam illud.*" "*Qui nescit.*"

Etiam sanāto vulnĕre cicātrix manet. Syr.—Even when the wound is healed the scar remains.

Eum ausculta, cui quatŭor sunt aures.—Give ear to that man who has four ears.

"When silent men speak they speak to the purpose."

Ex abundanti cautēlā.—From excess of caution.

Ex abūsu non arguitur in usum. LAW MAX.—It is not to be argued that the abuse of a thing proves that it is useless.

Ex arēnâ funĭculum nectis.—You would weave a rope of sand.

Ex aurĭbus cognoscĭtur ăsĭnus.—A donkey is known by his ears.

Ex eōdem ore călĭdum et frigĭdum efflāre.—To blow hot and cold in the same breath.
    See "*Defĭcit.*" "*Vulpanīri.*"

Ex factis non ex dictis amīci pensandi. LIV.—Friends should be judged by their acts, not their words.
    "He is my friend that succoureth me, not he that pitieth me."
    "Good words and no deeds are rushes and reeds."
    See "*Destināta tantum.*" "*Non verbis.*" "*Pleno modio.*"

Ex inimīco cogĭtā posse fiĕri amīcum. SEN.—Consider that an enemy may become a friend.

Ex linguâ stultâ venĭunt incommŏda multa.—Many an injury comes from a fool's speech.

Ex magnâ cænâ stomăcho fit maxĭma pœna,
Ut sis nocte levis, sit tibi cœna brevis.

Great discomfort arises from too hearty a supper: if you would enjoy a tranquil sleep let your supper be a light one.

Ex matre filiam.—Judge of the daughter by the mother.

Ex minĭmis initiis maxĭma.—From trifling causes great results arise.

"A little stream drives a great mill."

"The greatest oaks have been little acorns."
See "*Neglecta.*"

Ex minĭmo crescit, sed non citò fama quiescit.—Rumour grows easily enough, but is not easily silenced.

"A false report rides post."

Ex natāli emortuālem facĕre.—To make a birthday a day of grief.

[To turn joy into sorrow.]

Ex nihĭlo nihil fit.—Out of nothing nothing comes.

"Nothing can come of nothing." SHAKS.

Ex pede Hercŭlem.—Judge of the statue of Hercules by the size of the foot.

Ex prætĕrĭtis præsentia æstimantur.—We judge of the present from the past.

[The boy and the wolf.]

Ex quovis ligno non fit Mercurĭus.—The bust of Mercury cannot be carved in every wood.

"You can't make horn of a pig's tail."

"You cannot make a silk purse of a sow's ear."

"Every reed will not make a pipe."

"All flowers are not fit for nosegays."

Ex ungue leōnem.—You may know a lion by his claw.

"To show the cloven foot."

Ex uno disce omnes.—From one you may judge of the whole.

Exactâ viâ, viatĭcum quærĕre.—When the journey is finished to lay up provisions for the journey.
>[Avaricious old age.]

Excusatio non pĕtīta fit accusātio manifesta. LAW MAX.—An uncalled-for defence becomes a positive accusation.
>"He declares himself guilty, who justifies himself before accusation."
>
>"An unasked excuse infers transgression."

Excŭte mihi ignem, et allucēbo tibi.—Strike me a light, and I'll light you.
>See "*Gratia gratiam.*"

Exēgi monumentum ære perennius. HOR.—I have raised for myself a monument more durable than brass.
>"The most lasting monuments are doubtless paper-monuments."

Exemplo plus quam ratiōne vīvĭmus.—We live more by fashion than common sense.

>*Exĭgua est virtus, præstāre silentĭa rebus;*
>*At contrā gravis est culpa tacenda lŏqui.* OVID.

It is but a small merit to observe silence, but it is a grave fault to speak of matters on which we should be silent.
>"More have repented of speech than of silence."
>
>"A wise head makes a close mouth."
>
>"He that keepeth his mouth keepeth his life; but he that openeth wide his lips shall have destruction."
>See "*Audīto multa.*" "*Est tempus.*"

*Exīlis domus est, ubi non et multa supersunt,
Et dŏmĭnum fallunt, et prosunt furĭbus.*—Hor.
It is but a poor establishment where there are not many superfluous things which the owner knows not of, and which go to the thieves.
"The back door robbeth the house."

Exĭmia est virtus præstāre silentia rebus. Ovid.—Reticence is a great gift.
"Talk much, and err much."
"A fool's tongue is long enough to cut his own throat."
See "*Audīto multa.*"

Exĭtus acta probat. Ovid.—The act is judged of by the event.
"The evening crowns the day."
"The proof of the pudding is in the eating."
"All is well ended, if the suit be won." Shaks.
See "*Finis corōnat.*"

Expĕrientia docet.—Experience teaches.
"By ignorance we mistake, and by mistakes we learn."
"One learns by failing."
"The man of wisdom is the man of years." Young.

Experientia præstantior arte.—Practice is better than theory.
"Experience without learning is better than learning without experience."
"An ounce of wit that's bought
Is worth a pound that's taught."
See "*Usus est optĭmus.*"

Experto crede.—Believe him who speaks from experience.

"Years know more than books."

Expertus metuit.—He who has tried it, is afraid of it.

See "*Empta dolore.*"

Explētur lachrymis egĕrĭturque dolor. Ovid.—Grief brims itself and flows away in tears.

"When the pot boils over it cooleth itself."
"A small tear relieves a great sorrow."

Expressio unīus est exclusio altĕrĭus. Law Max.—The naming of one man amounts to the exclusion of another.

Exstinctus amābĭtur īdem. Hor.—He will be beloved when he is no more.

"Not to know the good we have
Till time has stolen the cherish'd gift away,
Is cause of half the misery that we feel,
And makes the world the wilderness it is."

Extrā chorum saltāre.—To dance out of time.

[To say an irrelevant thing: a thing out of place.]

Extrā lutum pedes habes.—You have got your feet out of the mire.

Extrā olĕas fertur.—He goes beyond the bounds.

Extra scopum jaculāre.—To overshoot the mark.

Extra telōrum jactum.—Out of danger.

Extrēma gaudii luctus occŭpat.—Sorrow dwells on the confines of pleasure.

> "Joy surfeited turns to sorrow."
>
> "If you laugh to-day, you will cry to-morrow."
>
> "Excess of delight palls the appetite."
>
> "The holydays of joy are the vigils of sorrow."
>
> "Laughter
> Leaves us doubly serious shortly after." BYRON.

Extrēma primo nēmo tentāvit loco. SEN.—Extreme remedies are never the first to be resorted to.

Extrēmis malis extrēma remĕdia.

> "Desperate maladies require desperate remedies."
>
> "Restive horses must be roughly dealt with."
>
> "For a stubborn ass a stubborn driver."
>
> "Diseases, desperate grown,
> By desperate appliance are reliev'd,
> Or not at all." SHAKS.
>
> See "*Amāra bilis.*" "*Non opus est.*"

FABAS indulcat fames.

"Hunger gives a relish even to raw beans."

"Hunger is the best sauce."

See "*Jejūnus.*"

*Faber compĕdes quas fecit ipse
Gestet.* Auson.

Let the blacksmith wear the chains he has himself made.

"He who has shipped the devil, must carry him over the sound."

"Let him fry in his own grease."

See "*Colo quod.*" "*Tute hoc.*"

Faber quisque fortunæ suæ. Sall.

"Every man is the architect of his own fortune."

"Every man is the son of his own works."

See "*Nostris ipsōrum.*" "*Sui cuique.*"

Fabricando fabri sumus.—Work makes the workman.
> "By writing we learn to write."
> "Knowledge without practice makes but half an artist."
> "Despise school and remain a fool."
>> See "*Doctrīna.*" "*Scribendo.*"

Fac de necessitate virtūtem.—Make a virtue of necessity.
> [Claim credit for compulsory rectitude.]

Fac nidum unum unâ in arbŏre.—Build but one nest in one tree.

Facĭe majōris vīvĕre census. Juv.—To live with the show of a greater income than you have.

Facies, non uxor amātur. Juv.—The face, not the woman is the attraction.

Facĭlè consilĭum damus aliis.—We easily give advice to others.

Facĭle est inventis addĕre.—It is an easy task to improve upon an invention.

Facĭlè omnes cum valēmus recta consilia ægrotis damus. Ter.—When in good health we easily give good advice to the sick.
> "Every man can master a grief but he that has it." Shaks.
> "He jests at scars that never felt a wound." Shaks.

Făcĭli sævitiâ negat. Hor.—With winsome cruelty she refuses.
>> See "*Dulce resistens.*"

Făcĭlis descensus Averni,
Sed revocāre gradum, superasque evādĕre ad auras
Hoc opus, hic labor est. VIR.
The descent to the infernal regions is easy enough, but to retrace one's steps, and reach the air above, there's the rub.

> "It is easier to descend than ascend."

> "It is easier to run from virtue to vice, than from vice to virtue."

> "I have a kind of alacrity in sinking." SHAKS.

Facilĭus crescit quam inchoātur dignĭtas. SYR.—A position of dignity is more easily improved upon than acquired.

Facĭnus quos inquĭnat, æquat. LUC.—Villany reduces those whom it defiles to the same level.

Facit gratum fortūna quam nēmo videt. SYR.—A sly piece of good luck, which nobody knows of, is delightful.

> "Stolen waters are sweet, and bread eaten in secret how pleasant is it."

Făcĭto alĭquid opĕris, ut semper te diabŏlus inveniat occupātum. ST. JEROME.—Be ever engaged, so that whenever the devil calls he may find you occupied.

> "The devil tempts all, but the idle man tempts the devil."

> "If the brain sows not corn, it plants thistles."

> See "*Dæmon te.*" "*Nihil agendo.*" "*Res age.*"

Facta canam; sed erunt qui me finxisse loquantur. OVID.
I shall speak facts; but some will say I deal in fiction.

> "'Tis strange, but true: for truth is always strange;
> Stranger than fiction." BYRON.

Facta juvĕnum, consilia mediocrĭum, vota senum. HESIOD.—
Actions from youth, advice from the middle-aged, prayers from the aged.

Fallācia alia aliam trudit. TER.—Deception follows on the heels of deception.

> "One falsehood leads to another."

> "One lie makes many."

> "O! what a tangled web we weave,
> When first we practise to deceive." SCOTT.
> See "*Scelĕre.*"

Fallit enim vitĭum spĕcie virtūtis et umbra. JUV.—Vice deceives us when dressed in the garb of virtue.

> "A wolf in sheep's clothing."

> "Wickedness with beauty is the devil's hook baited."

Fallĭtur augŭrio spes bona sæpe suo. OVID.—Good hope is often beguiled by her own augury.

> "Not seldom clad in radiant vest
> Deceitfully goes forth the dawn,
> Not seldom evening in the west
> Sinks smilingly forsworn." WORDSWORTH.

> "So from that spring, whence comfort seem'd to come,
> Discomfort swells." SHAKS.

Falsa veris finitima sunt. CIC.—Falsehoods border on truths.

> "A lie that is half a truth is ever the blackest of lies."
> TENNYSON.

Falsum in uno, falsum in omni.—False in one respect, never trustworthy.

> "A cracked bell can never sound well."
> See "*Aliquando.*"

Falsus honor juvat, et mendax infamia terret,
Quem nisi mendosum et mendacem? HOR.
Whom does undeserved honour please, and undeserved blame alarm, but the base and the liar?

Famâ nihil est celerius. LIVY.—Nothing moves more quickly than scandal.

> "For evil news rides post, while good news baits." MILTON.
> See "*Ex minimo.*" "*Nihil est tam.*" "*Non est remedium.*"

Famem pellere satius quam purpurâ indui.—It is better to satisfy our hunger than to be clothed in purple.

Famem pestilentia sequitur.—A pestilence follows a famine.

Fames bilem acuit.—Hunger sharpens anger.

> "A hungry man, an angry man."
> "When the stomach is full the heart is glad."

Fames est optimus coquus.—Hunger is the best cook.

> "A hungry horse maketh a clean manger."

Fames et mora bilem in nasum concĭunt.—Hunger and delay raise up anger.

"A waiting appetite kindles many a spite."

Fames optĭmum condimentum.

"Hunger is the best sauce."

Fames præter seipsam edulcat omnia.—Hunger sweetens everything but itself.

Familiāris domĭnus fatuum nutrit servum.—By the familiarity of the master the servant is spoilt.

"Familiarity breeds contempt."

Fas est et ab hoste docēri. OVID.
It is good to be taught even by an enemy.

"It is always safe to learn, even from our enemies, seldom safe to venture to instruct, even our friends." COLTON.

"An enemy may chance to give good counsel."

Fastīdĭentis est stŏmăchi multa degustāre. SEN.—To taste many things bespeaks but a poor appetite.

[To engage in a multiplicity of studies shows but a weak mind.]

Fastus inest pulchris, sequĭturque superbia formam. OVID.—Pride is innate in beauty, and haughtiness is the companion of the fair.

Fata obstant.—The Fates will not permit it.

Fatētur facĭnus is qui judĭcium fugit. LAW MAX.—He confesses his guilt who flies from his trial.

Favōre et benevolentiā etiam immānis anĭmus mansuescit.—By good nature and kindness even fierce spirits become tractable.

"A soft answer turneth away wrath."
"A soft answer bids a Furioso to put up his sword."
"Smooth words make smooth ways."
See "*Frangĭtur ira.*" "*Sermōnes blandi.*"

Fecundi călĭces quem non fecēre disertum? Hor.—Whom has not the inspiring bowl made eloquent?

Felicĭter sapit, qui aliēno perīculo sapit.—He gets his wisdom cheaply who gets it at another's cost.

"Their harms, our arms."
"Wisdom rides upon the ruins of folly."
See "*Alienā optimum.*" "*Optĭmum est.*"

Felīcium omnes consanguinĕi.—All claim kindred with the prosperous.

"No longer pipe, no longer dance."
"When the wind serves, all aid."
"When good cheer is lacking, our friends will be packing."
See "*Cum fortūna.*" "*Fervet olla.*"

Felix crimĭnibus nullus erit diu. Auson.—No man will revel long in the indulgence of crime.

"It is hard to see an old tyrant."

Felix quem faciunt aliēna perīcula cautum.—Fortunate is he whom the dangers of others have rendered cautious.

    See "*Aliená optĭmum.*"

Felix qui nihil dēbet.—Happy is the man who is out of debt.

    "Out of debt, out of danger."

Felix qui non lītĭgat.—Happy the man who keeps out of strife.

    "Hell and Chancery are always open."

    "Physicians rarely take medicine."

    "Lawyers' gowns are lined with the wilfulness of their clients."

    "A wise lawyer never goes to law himself."

    "Fond of lawsuits, little wealth,
Fond of doctors, little health."

    See "*Nescis tu.*" "*Quum licet.*"

Felix qui potuit rerum cognoscĕre causas. VIR.—Happy is he who can trace effects to their causes.

Feras, non culpes, quod vitāri non potest. SYR.—You must endure, and not cry out against that which cannot be avoided.

    See "*Grave.*" "*In re malâ.*" "*Levius fit.*"

Feras quod lædit, ut id quod prodest perfĕras. SYR.—You must endure what is painful to secure that which is profitable.

    "He who would catch fish, must not mind getting wet."

    "He that will have the kernel, must crack the shell."

    "He that would have the fruit, must climb the tree."

    See "*Dii laborĭbus.*" "*In sudōre.*" "*Nil sine.*"

Ferè libenter homines id, quod volunt, credunt. CÆS.—Men freely believe that which they wish to be the truth.

"Thy wish was father, Harry, to that thought." SHAKS.
See "*Quod quisque.*"

*Feriuntque summos
Fulmĭna montes.* HOR.

Lightning strikes the tops of the mountains.

"High winds blow on high hills."

"High regions are never without storms."

"They that stand high have many blasts to shake them." SHAKS.

"Who aspires must down as low
As high he soar'd." MILTON.
See "*Tolluntur.*"

*Ferre quam sortem patiuntur omnes,
Nemo recūset.*

Let no man refuse to endure that which is common to the lot of all.

Ferrĕus assĭdŭo consūmĭtur annŭlus usu. OVID.—Even a ring of iron is worn away by constant use.

"Constant dropping wears the stone."
See "*Gutta cavat.*"

Ferrum, cum igni candet, tundendum.

"Strike while the iron is hot."

"Make hay when the sun shines."
See "*Nosce tempus.*"

Ferrum ferro acuĭtur.
"Steel whets steel."

Ferrum natāre doces!—You are teaching iron to swim!

*Fertĭlior seges est aliēno semper in arvo,
Vicīnumque pĕcus grandius uber habet.* OVID.

Our neighbour's crop is always more fruitful and his cattle produce more milk than our own.

Ferto, ferēris.—Bear with others and you shall be borne with.
"Give and take."

Fervet olla, vivit amīcĭtia.—Friendship lasts as long as the pot boils.

"Poverty parteth friends."

"When poverty comes in at the door, love jumps out at the window."

"Now I have got a ewe and a lamb,
Every one cries, 'Welcome, Peter.'"

"A fu purse never lacks freends."

"Men shut their doors against the setting sun." SHAKS.

See "*Cum fortūna.*" "*Diffugiunt.*" "*Felicium.*" "*Horrea formīcæ.*"

Festīna lentè.—Hasten gently.

"Make no more haste than good speed."

"Good and quickly seldom meet."

"He that goes softly goes safely."

"What raging rashly is begun
Challengeth shame before half done."

"To climb steep hills
Requires slow pace at first." SHAKS.

"A hand may first, and then a lip be kiss'd. BYRON.

"We may outrun,
By violent swiftness, that which we run at,
And lose by over-running." SHAKS.

See "*Da spatium.*" "*Qui nimis.*"

*Festināre nocet, nocet et cunctatio sæpe,
Tempŏre quæque suo qui facit, ille sapit.* OVID.

Haste is productive of injury, and so is too much hesitation. He is the wisest man who does everything at the proper time.

"The hasty angler loses the fish."

Festinātio tarda est.—Haste is slow.

"Most haste worst speed."

*Festo die si quid prodēgĕris
Profesto egēre līceat, nisi pepercĕris.* PLAUT.

If you squander on a holyday, you will want on a workday unless you have been sparing.

"He sups ill who eats up all at dinner."

"A fat kitchen makes a lean will."

"Waste not want not."

"For age and want save while you may,
No morning sun lasts a whole day."

"They who sing through the summer must dance in the winter."

"He that keeps nor crust nor crumb,
Weary of all shall want some." SHAKS.

See "*Cogitāto.*" "*Ne quære.*"

Festūcam ex oculo alterĭus dejĭcĕre.—To cast out the mote from the eye of another.

> "The hunchback does not see his own hump, but he sees his brother's."

> "The faults of our neighbours with freedom we blame,
> But tax not ourselves, though we practise the same."
> CUNNINGHAM.

Fiat experimentum in corpŏre vili.—Make your experiment on a worthless subject.

> "A barber learns to shave by shaving fools."

> "Her prentice han' she tried on man,
> And then she made the lasses O!" BURNS.

> See "*In capĭte orphăni.*"

Fiat justĭtia, ruat cœlum!—Let justice be done, though the heavens fall!

Ficta voluptātis causâ sint proxĭma veris. HOR.—Fiction intended to please, should resemble truth as much as possible.

Ficum cupit.*—He is looking out for a fig.

[He is planning for himself.]

> "He that is kinder than he was wont hath a design upon thee."

> "When the fox wants to catch geese, he wags his tail."

---

* In allusion to the unusual civility shown by the nobles at Athens to the peasants on the approach of the fig season.

Ficus ficus, ligōnem ligōnem vocat.—Figs he calls figs, a spade a spade.

[Said of a man who speaks with sincerity and means what he says.]

"The pen of the tongue should be dipped in the ink of the heart."

Fide abrogātā omnis humāna sociĕtas tollĭtur. Livy.—Once let good faith be abandoned, and all social existence would perish.

Fide, sed cui vide.—Have confidence, but beware in whom.

"Before you make a friend eat a peck of salt with him."

"It is an equal failing to trust everybody, and to trust nobody."

"Trust makes way for treachery."

"Sudden friendship, sure repentance."

See "*Ne cuivis.*" "*Nervi et.*" "*Qui in amōrem.*"

Fidem qui perdit, quo se servat in rĕlĭquum? Syr.—He who hath lost his good name how shall he in future gain his living.

"He that hath lost his credit, is dead to the world."

"Give a dog an ill name, and you may as well hang him."

"Credit lost is like a broken looking-glass."

"One may better steal a horse than another look over the hedge."

"Who steals my purse, steals trash: 'tis something, nothing;
'Twas mine, 'tis his, and has been slave to thousands:
But he that filches from me my good name,
Robs me of that which not enriches him,
And makes me poor indeed." Shaks.

Figŭlus figŭlo invĭdet; faber fabro.—Potter envies potter, and smith smith.

> "In every age and clime we see,
> Two of a trade can ne'er agree." Gay.

Filii ex senĭbus nati rarò sunt firmi temperamenti.—Old men's children are rarely of good constitution.

Finis corōnat opus.—The end crowns the work.

> "At the end of the work you may judge of the workmen."
>
> "All's well that ends well."
>
> "Good to begin well, better to end well."
>
> "Judge not of a ship as she lies on the stocks."
>
> "Praise a fair day at night."
>
> "'Tis not the fight that crowns us, but the end." Herrick.
>
> See "*Exĭtus acta.*"

Fit citò per multas præda petīta manus. Ovid.—Gain, acquired by many agents, soon accumulates.

> "Have two strings to your bow."

Flamma fumo est proxĭma. Plaut.—Fire is next akin to smoke.

> "Where there is smoke there is fire."

Flare simul et sorbēre haud făcĭle est. Plaut.—It is difficult to whistle and drink at the same time.

> "Blow first, and sip afterwards."
>
> "Nae man can baith sup an' blaw thegither."
>
> "No man can serve two masters."
>
> "A man cannot spin and reel at the same time."
>
> "He that doth most at once doth least."
>
> See "*Defĭcit.*" "*Duos qui.*"

Flectĕre si nequĕo supĕros Achĕronta movĕbo. Vir.—If I cannot move the powers above, Acheron itself shall be appealed to.

[If fair means cannot, foul shall.]

Flēre ad novercæ tŭmŭlum.—To weep at the tomb of a stepmother.

[Hypocrisy.]

See "*Hærēdis fletus.*"

Flet victor, victus interiit.—The conqueror weeps, the conquered is ruined.

[Both sides suffer in war or litigation.]

Fletumque labellis Exsorbes. Juv.

You kiss away her tears.

"Two other precious drops that ready stood,
Each, in their crystal sluice, he ere they fell
Kiss'd." Milton.

Fluvii cursus non detorquendus.—The course of a river is not to be altered.

[We cannot alter a natural bent.]

Fœcundi călices quem non fecêre disertum. Hor.—Whom has not the inspiring bowl made eloquent.

"The fool sucks wisdom, as he porter sups,
And cobblers grow fine speakers in their cups."

"Whom drink made wits, though nature made them fools."
Churchill.

Fœdum est et mansisse diu vacuumque redisse.—It is inexcusable to have remained long away, and return empty-handed.

Fœdum inceptu, fœdum exitu. Livy.—Bad beginnings, bad endings.

Fœmina ridendo, flendo, fallitque canendo.—The laughter, the tears, and the song of a woman are equally deceptive.

Fœnum habet in cornu.* Hor.—He has hay upon his horn.
 [He is a mischievous person.]

Fontes ipsi sitiunt.—Even the fountains thirst.
 [Avarice is never satisfied.]

Formosa facies muta commendatio est. Syr.—Handsome features are a silent recommendation.

Forsan et hæc olim meminisse juvabit. Vir.
Perhaps the day may come when we shall remember these sufferings with joy.

"So—now the danger dared at last,
Look back and smile at perils past!" Scott.
See "*Carius est.*" "*Jucunda est.*" "*Fortiter malum.*"

---

* Fœnum. "Hay." The ancients used to tie hay at the end of the horns of mischievous cows.

Forsan miséros meliōra sequentur. VIR. — Better times perhaps await us who are now wretched.

> "It is a long lane that has no turning."
>
> "Heaviness may endure for a night, but joy cometh in the morning."
>
> "The hindmost dog may catch the hare."
>
> "All's not lost that's in danger."
>
> "But sighs subside, and tears (even widows') shrink,
> Like Arno in the summer, to a shallow." BYRON.
>
> See "*Nondum incurvam.*" "*Nunc pluit.*"

Forsĭtan invenies Galathēam vel meliōrem Formâ aliam. Perhaps you will soon find another, and a fairer, lover.

> "Fresh feres will dry the bright blue eye
> We late saw streaming o'er." BYRON.

Fortes creantur fortĭbus et bonis. HOR.—The brave are born from the brave and good.

> "A chip of the old block."
>
> See "*Est in juvencis.*"

Fortes fortūna juvat.—Fortune helps the brave.

> "Faint heart never won fair lady."
>
> "He that handles a nettle tenderly is soonest stung."
>
> See "*Audentes fortūna.*" "*Timĭdi nunquam.*"

Fortis cadĕre, cedĕre non potest.—The brave man may die, but he will never say "die."

Fortis esto non ferox.—Be brave, not ferocious.

Fortĭter ferendo vincĭtur malum quod evitāri non potest.—By a brave endurance of unavoidable evils, we conquer them.

>See "*Feras non.*"

Fortĭter malum qui patĭtur, post potĭtur bonum. PLAUT.— He who bravely endures evils, in time reaps the reward.

>"He shall find the rugged thistle bursting
>Into glossy purples, that outredden
>All voluptuous garden roses." TENNYSON.

>"Life's cares are comforts; such by heaven design'd;
>He that has none, must make them or be wretched."
>>>>>>>>>>>>>>>>>>>>>>YOUNG.

>"The bitter past, more welcome is the sweet." SHAKS.

>See "*Forsan et hæc.*"

Fortius e multis mater desīdĕrat unum,
Quam quæ flens clamat, "Tu mihi solus eras!" OVID.

The mother endures with greater courage the loss of one out of many children, than she who, in her tears, exclaims, "Thou wast my only one!"

Fortūna favet fatuis.—Fortune favours fools.

>"Providence tempers the wind to the shorn lamb."

Fortūna magna magna dŏmĭno est servĭtus. SYR.—A great fortune enslaves its owner.

>"A great fortune is a great slavery."

Fortūna multis dat nĭmium, nulli satis. MART.—Fortune gives too much to many, to no one enough.

> "Will fortune never come with both hands full,
> But write her fair words still in foulest letters?
> She either gives a stomach and no food;
> Such are the poor in health: or else a feast
> And takes away the stomach; such are the rich,
> That have abundance, and enjoy it not." SHAKS.

Fortūna nimium quem fovet, stultum facit. SYR.—Fortune, by being too lavish of her favours on a man, only makes a fool of him.

> "Beggars mounted ride their horses to death."

> "How much a dunce that has been sent to roam
> Excels a dunce that has been kept at home." COWPER.

> See "*Asperius.*"

Fortūna nulli obesse contenta est semel. SYR.—Fortune is never satisfied with bringing one sorrow.

> "Thus woe succeeds a woe, as wave a wave." HERRICK.

> "One woe doth tread upon another's heel,
> So fast they follow." SHAKS.

> "When sorrows come, they come not single spies,
> But in battalions." SHAKS.

> See "*Malis mala.*"

Fortūna nunquam perpĕtuŏ est bona.—Good luck lasts not for ever.

> "The highest spoke in fortune's wheel may soon turn lowest."

> "Turn, Fortune, turn thy wheel, and lower the proud." TENNYSON.

> See "*Nescis quid.*"

Fortūna opes auferre, non anĭmum potest. SEN.—Fortune may rob us of our wealth, not of our courage.

Fortūna reddit insolentes.—Success leads to insolence.
>See "*Asperius nihil.*"

>*Fortūna sævo læta negotio, et*
>*Ludum insolentem ludĕre pertĭnax,*
>*Transmūtat incertos honōres.* HOR.

Fortune, delighting in her cruel task, and playing her wanton game untiringly, is ever shifting her uncertain favours.

>" Fortune to one is mother, to another step-mother."
>" Every may-be hath a may-be not."
>" He that falls to-day may be up again to-morrow."

Fortūna vĭtrĕa est; tum, cum splendet, frangĭtur. SYR.— Fortune is like glass; she breaks when she is brightest.

Fortūnam cĭtius reperĭas quam retĭneas.—It is easier to win good luck than to retain it.

>"A fool may meet with good fortune, but the wise only profits by it."

>*Fragĭli quærens illīdere dentem,*
>*Offendit solĭdum.* HOR.

Thinking to bite something soft, he found it hard.
>[Catching a Tartar.]

Frangĭtur ira gravis cum fit responsĭo suavis.—The force of anger is broken by a soft answer.

>" He that can reply to an angry man is too hard for him."
>" When one will not, two cannot quarrel."
>>See "*Favōre.*" "*Ignis non.*" "*Sermōnes blandi.*"

Fratrum inter se iræ sunt acerbissimæ.—Most bitter are the quarrels of brothers.

"A little more than kin, and less than kind." SHAKS.

See "*Acerrima.*"

Fraus est celāre fraudem.—It is a fraud to connive at a fraud.

"The receiver is as bad as the thief."

Fronte capillāta est, post est occasio calva.—Time has a forelock, but is bald behind.

"The mill cannot grind with the water that is past."

See "*Nosce tempus.*"

Fronte polītus,
Astūtam vapĭdo servas sub pectŏre vulpem. PERS.

Ostensibly polite, you nourish the cunning of the fox in the hollowness of your heart.

"Fair without, foul within."

"An open countenance often conceals close thoughts."

"The devil hath power
To assume a pleasing shape." SHAKS.

"O, what may man within him hide,
Though angel on the outward side!" SHAKS.

See "*Decipĭmur.*" "*Habent insidias.*" "*Nunquam te fallant.*" "*Mel in ore.*"

Fronti nulla fides. Juv.—There is no reliance to be placed on appearance.

> "All is not gold that glitters."
>
> "A white glove often conceals a dirty hand."
>
> "Fair hair may hae foul roots."
>
> "Yet gold all is not that doth golden seem." Shaks.

Fronti ocrĕam, tībĭæ gălĕam applĭcat. Luc.—He puts his boot on his head, and his foot in his helmet.

> "To put the cart before the horse."

Fructu, non foliis arbŏrem æstĭma. Phaed.—Judge of a tree by its fruit, not by its leaves.

> See "*Ne verba.*"

Fructus amōris amor.—Love is the fruit of love.

> "Love without return is like a question without an answer."
>
> "She loved me for the dangers I had passed,
> And I loved her for having pitied them." Shaks.

Fructus amicitiæ magnæ cibus.—Juv.—The only gain from the friendship of the great is a fine dinner.

Fruges consumĕre nati. Hor.—Men born only to eat.

> "All goes down gutter lane."
>
> See "*Quibus in.*" "*Nulli major.*"

Frustrà fit per plura, quod fĭĕri potest per pauciōra.—It is vain to do that by a multitude which a few can accomplish.

"Keep no more cats than will catch mice."
"Make not thy tail broader than thy wings."
[Keep not too many attendants.]
"Too many cooks spoil the broth."

Frustrà habet qui non utĭtur.—In vain does a man possess property if he makes no use of it.

"Wealth is not his who gets it, but his who enjoys it."
"Wine in the bottle does not quench thirst."
See "*Manifesta.*" "*Quo mihi.*"

Frustrà jacĭtur rete ante ocŭlos pennatōrum.

"Surely in vain the net is spread in the sight of any bird."

Frustrà labōrat qui omnibus placēre studet.—He labours in vain who attempts to please everybody."

"No man can like all, or be liked by all."
"He had need rise betimes who would please everybody."
See "*Laudātur.*"

Frustrà vitĭum vitavĕris illud,
Si te alio pravum detorsĕris. HOR.

In vain will you fly from one vice if in your wilfulness you embrace another.

"'Tis all in vain to keep a constant pother
About one vice and fall into another." POPE.
See "*Dum vitant.*"

Fugĕre nemĭne persequente.—To fly, when no one pursues us.

    [Great timidity.]

        See "*Lĕpŏris.*"

Fugiendo in media sæpe ruĭtur fata. Livy.—By flying, men often rush into the midst of calamities.

        See "*Dum vitant.*"

Fugit irrevocābĭle tempus. Vir.—Time flies never to be recalled.

    "Lost time is never found again."

    "No man can call again yesterday."

    "What greater crime than loss of time?"

    "He that neglects time, time will neglect."

    "Time stoops to no man's lure." Swinburne.

        See "*Labĭtur occultæ.*" "*Nec quæ.*" "*Trudĭtur dies.*"

Fuit Ilium.—Troy is a thing of the past.

Fulĭcam cygno compăras.—You compare the moorhen to the swan.

    "Fleas are not lobsters."

Fumum fugiens in ignem incĭdi.—While avoiding the smoke I have fallen into the flame.

        See "*De fumo.*" "*Dum vitant.*"

Fundum aliēnum arat, suum incultum dēsĕrit.—He ploughs the land of others, and leaves his own untilled.

Funem abrumpĕre nimium tenendo.—To break the rope by overstraining.

> See "*Jocandum.*"

Funĭcŭlis ligātum vel puer verberāret.—Even a boy can beat a man when bound.

> See "*Captīvum.*"

Funĭculus triplex non facĭlĕ rumpĭtur.—A triple rope is not easily broken.

> "Union is strength."
>
> See "*Mutua defensio.*"

Furem fur cognoscit, et lupum lupus.—Thief knows thief, and wolf knows wolf.

Fures clamōrem.—Thieves dread a commotion.

Fures in lite pandunt abscondĭta vitæ.—When rogues fall out, many a secret is revealed.

> "When rogues fall out, honest men come by their own."

Fures privāti in nervo, publĭci in auro.

> "Poor thieves in halters we behold;
> And great thieves in their chains of gold."   QUARLES.
>
> "We hang little thieves, and take off our hats to great ones."

Furis passu progrĕdi.—To tread softly like a thief.

> "Treading softly like a thief,
> Lest the harsh shingle should grate underfoot,
> And feeling all along the garden wall."   TENNYSON.

Furor arma ministrat. Vir.—Fury itself supplies arms.

Furor est post omnia perděre naulum. Juv.—It is sheer folly when all is gone to lose even one's passage money.

> "To throw the rope after the bucket."
>
> See "*Ad perdĭtam.*"

Furor fit læsa sæpius patientia.—Patience overtaxed turns to rage.

> "A man may cause his own dog to bite him."
>
> "Beware of vinegar made of sweet wine."
>
> "Though the mastiff be gentle, yet bite him not by the lip."
>
> "It's enough to make a parson swear, or a quaker kick his mother."
>
> "Beware the fury of a patient man." Dryden.

Furor iraque mentem Præcipitant. Vir.
Passion and strife bow down the mind.

> "Anger is more hurtful than the injury that caused it."

Furtīvus potus plenus dulcedĭne totus.

> "Stolen waters are sweetest."
>
> See "*Nitĭmur.*"

*GALEATUM sero duelli,
Pœnitet.* Juv.
When your armour is on, it is too late to retreat.
"Look before you leap."

Gallus in suo sterquilīnio plurĭmum potest. SEN.—Every cock fights best on his own dunghill.
"Every dog is valiant in his own kennel."

*Garrit anīles
Ex re fabellas.* HOR.
He tells old wives' tales much to the point.

Gaudendum cum gaudentĭbus.—Rejoice with those that do rejoice.

Gaudent scribentes, et se venĕrantur. HOR.—Scribblers are a self-conceited and self-worshipping race.

Gaudetque viam fecisse ruinâ. Luc.—He rejoices to have made his way by the ruin of others.

Gaudet tentamĭne virtus.—Virtue and valour rejoice in being put to the test.
>See " *Virtus, vel.*"

Gaudet patientia duris. Luc.—Patience revels in misfortunes.

Gaudia princĭpĭum nostri sunt sæpe dolōris. Ovid.—Pleasure is often the introduction to pain.
>" Amid the roses fierce Repentance rears
>Her snaky crest." Thomson.
>See " *Medio de fonte.*"

Genĭtrix virtūtum frugalĭtas. Justin.—Frugality is the mother of all virtues.

Gens humāna ruit per vĕtĭtum nefas. Hor.—The tendency of humanity is towards the forbidden.
>See " *Nitĭmur.*" " *Illĭcĭta.*"

Gladiātor in arēnâ consilĭum capit.—The gladiator seeks advice, when in the very lists.
>See " *Galeātum.*"

Glaucōma ob ocŭlos objicĕre.—To throw dust in one's eyes.

Glomerāre inglomerābilia.—To unite that which cannot be united. To attempt an impossibility.
>" To make two extremes meet."

Gracŭlus inter musas.—A jackdaw among the muses.

Grata brevĭtas.—Brevity is pleasing.
   " Brevity is the soul of wit."

Grata novĭtas.
   " Novelty always appears handsome."

Grata supervĕniet, quæ non sperābĭtur, hora. Hor.—The hour of happiness which comes unexpectedly is the happiest.

Gratĭa ab officio, quod mora tardat, abest. Ovid.—No thanks attach to a kindness long deferred.
   " A gift long waited for is sold, not given."
   " A courtesy much entreated is half recompensed."
   " Good, that comes too late, is good as nothing."
      See " *Bis dat.*" " *Tarde benefacĕre.*"

Gratĭa gratĭam parit.
   " One good turn deserves another."
   " The hand that gives gathers."
   " Kindnesses, like grain, increase by sowing."
   " Who gives, teaches a return."
   " One kindness is the price of another."
      See " *Altĕrius.*" " *Manus manum.*" " *Petĭmusque.*"

Gratis anhēlans ; multa agendo nihil agens. Phaed.—Out of breath to no possible purpose ; in attempting everything, doing nothing.

 See " *Operōse.*"

Grave nihil est quod fert necessĭtas.—Nothing is grievous which necessity enjoins.

 " Gnaw the bone which is fallen to thy lot."

 See " *Feras non.*"

Graviōra quædam sunt remedia perīculis. Syr. — Some remedies are worse than the disease itself.

Gravis ira regum semper. Sen.—The anger of those in authority is always weighty.

 " The ire of a despotic king
 Rides forth upon destruction's wing." Scott.

Gravissĭmum est imperĭum consuetudĭnis. Syr.—All powerful is the rule of fashion.

Gravius est peccātum dīlĭgĕre quam perpetrāre.—It is more wicked to love a sin than to commit one.

 See " *Cujusvis.*"

 Grex totus in agris
Unīus scabie cadit et porrigĭne porci. Juv.

From the disease of one the whole flock perishes.

 " The rotten apple injures its neighbour."

 See " *Corrumpunt bonos.*" " *Si juxta.*" " *Unĭca prava.*"

Gubernatōri somnolento ne benefacĭto.—Reward not a sleeping pilot.

Gutta cavat lapĭdem non vi sed sæpe cădendo.—Dropping water makes the rock hollow, not by its force, but by constant action.

>"A mouse in time may bite in two a cable."
>
>"Step after step the ladder is ascended."
>
>See "*Caudæ pilos.*" "*Multis ictĭbus.*"

Gutta fortūnæ præ dolĭo sapientiæ.—A drop of luck is worth a cask of wisdom.

>"A fortunate man may be anywhere."
>
>"Fling him into the Nile, and he will come up with a fish in his mouth."

HABENT *insidias homĭnis blanditiæ mali.* PHAED.
The soft speeches of the wicked are full of deceit.

"The cross on his breast, and the devil in his heart."

"All saint without, all devil within."

"Beads about the neck, and the devil in his heart."

"No villain like the conscientious villain."

"Behind the cross stands the devil."

"Slight are the outward signs of evil thought." BYRON.

"'Rogue that I am,' he whispers to himself,
'I lie, I cheat—do anything for pelf,
But who on earth can say I am not pious?'" HOOD.

"All was false and hollow, though his tongue
Dropt manna, and could make the worst appear
The better reason." MILTON.

"Ah, that deceit should steal such gentle shapes,
And with a virtuous vizor hide deep vice!" SHAKS.

See "*Decĭpĭmur.*" "*Fronte polītus.*" "*Mel in ore.*" "*Habet suum.*"

Habet Deus suas horas et moras.—Providence may delay, but punishment will come at length.

> "God cometh with leaden feet, but striketh with iron hands."
> See "*Rarò.*"

Habet et musca splenem.—Even a fly can show temper.

> See "*Inest et.*"

Habet suum venēnum blanda oratio. Syr.—The honied tongue hath its poison.

> "Honey is sweet, but the bee stings."

> "He is like a silver pin,
> Fair without, but foul within."

> "The devil can cite Scripture for his purpose." Shaks.

> "And thus I clothe my naked villany
> With old odd ends, stol'n out of holy writ,
> And seem a saint when most I play the devil." Shaks.

> See "*Habent insidias.*"

Hâc jacet in tumbâ Rosa mundi, non Rosa munda,
Non redŏlet, sed olet, quæ redolēre solet.

> "Here lies, not Rose the chaste, but Rose the fair!
> Her scents no more perfume, but taint the air."
>
> [Epitaph on Fair Rosamund.]

Hæc pro amicĭtiâ nostrâ non occultavi. Suet.—These things by reason of our friendship I have not hesitated to communicate.

Hæc te victoria perdet. Ovid.—This victory will be your ruin.

Hærēdis fletus sub persōnâ risus est. Syr.—The grief of an heir is only masked laughter.
> See "*Nulli jactantius.*"

Hærēre in iisdem scopŭlis.—To be aground on the same rock.
> [To be in the same dilemma.]

Hæres
Hærēdem alterĭus, vĕlut unda supervĕnit undam. Hor.
Heir follows heir, as wave succeeds to wave.

Hæsitantia cantōris tussis.—A cough assists a musician when he hesitates.
> "When a musician hath forgotten his note,
> He makes as though a crumb stuck in his throat."

Hanc technam in teipsum struxisti.—In the snare laid for others is your foot taken.
> See "*Captantes capti.*" "*Neque enim.*" "*Qui capit.*"

Has pœnas garrŭla lingua dedit. Ovid.—These are the evils which result from gossiping habits.

Haud canit paternas cantiōnes.—He does not sing his father's songs.

[He does not imitate the good example of his father.]

Haud est nocens, quicunque non sponte est nocens. SEN.—He sins not, who is not wilfully a sinner.

"As he thinketh in his heart, so is he."

See "*Injuriam qui.*" "*Nam scelus inter.*"

Haud facĭle emergunt, quorum virtūtibus obstat Res angusta domi. JUV.

Their rise is one of difficulty, whose merits are impeded by poverty.

"Fruit ripens not well in the shade."

"Without favour, art is like a windmill without wind."

"Flight towards preferment will be but slow without some golden feathers."

"Slow rises worth by poverty depressed." JOHNSON.

"His wit got wings and would have flown,
But poverty still kept him down."

"He that was born under a three-halfpenny planet shall never be worth twopence."

See "*Ab inopiâ.*"

Haud furto melior sed fortĭbus armis. VIR.—Not surpassing in crafty measures, but in the power of arms.

"The Fox's wiles will never enter the lion's head."

Haud semper errat fama. Tac.—Common report is not always wrong.

> "Common fame is seldom to blame."
> "If one, two and three say you are an ass, put on the ears."
> "That is true which all men say."
>
> See "*Non omnīno.*" "*Interdum vulgus.*"

Haud ullas portābit opes Acherontis ad undas. Prop.—He will not carry his wealth to the waters of Acheron.

Herè servus, hodie liber.—A slave yesterday, to-day a freedman.

Heu! patior telis vulnĕra facta meis!—Alas! I suffer from self-inflicted wounds!

Heu! Quam difficĭle est crimen non prodĕre vultu! Ovid.—Alas! How difficult it is to prevent the countenance from betraying our guilt!

> "An evil conscience breaks many a man's neck."
>
> See "*Qui capit, ille.*"

Heu! quam difficilis gloriæ custodia est! Syr.—Alas how difficult is it to preserve a high reputation!

Heu! quanto minus est cum relĭquis versāri quàm tui meminisse!—Alas! how much smaller a thing it is to be with others, than to remember thee!

> "To live with them is far less sweet,
> Than to remember thee." Moore.

Heus! proxĭmus sum egŏmet mihi. Ter.—Look you! I myself am nearest to myself.

>"Every man for himself and God for us all."
>
>"Close sits my shirt, but closer my skin."
>
>"Every one rakes the fire under his own pot."
>
>"Let every fox take care of his own tail."
>
>"No. 1 is the first house in the row."
>
>"A fly before his own eye is bigger than an elephant in the next field."
>
>"Near is my petticoat but nearer is my smock."
>See "*Suam quisque.*"

Hi sunt qui trepĭdant et ad omnĭa fulgŭra pallent. Juv.—The guilty are alarmed and turn pale at the slightest thunder.

>"A sinful heart makes feeble hand." Scott.
>
>"The wicked flee when no man pursueth."
>
>"Thus conscience does make cowards of us all." Shaks.
>See "*Tacitâ sudant.*"

Hic dictis, hastâ longe præstantior ille. Vir.—One man excels in eloquence, another in arms.

Hic est, aut nusquam, quod quærĭmus. Hor.—Here, or nowhere, is the thing we seek.

Hic murus ahēneus esto,
Nil conscīre sibi, nullâ pallescĕre culpâ. HOR.

Be this our wall of brass, to be conscious of having done no evil, and to grow pale at no accusation.

Hic patet ingĕniis campus. CLAUD.—Here is a fine field for talent.

Hic telam texuit, ille deduxit.—One has woven the thread, another has drawn it forth.

[One man invents, another developes the idea.]

Hĭlărisque tamen cum pondĕre virtus. STAT.—Virtue may be cheerful without forgetting its dignity.

Hinc illæ lachrymæ. HOR.—This is the real secret of all that indignation.

Hoc agit, ut doleas. JUV.—He only does it to annoy you.

Hoc est
Vivĕre bis, vitâ posse priōre frui. MART.

It is as good as second life to be able to look back upon our past life with pleasure.

"Memory is the treasurer of the mind."

Hoc retine verbum, frangit Deus omne superbum.—Providence crushes pride.

"Pride will have a fall."
"Pride goeth before destruction, and a haughty spirit before a fall."
"Pride that dined with vanity supped with poverty."

"My high-blown pride
At length broke under me, and now has left me
Weary and old with service." SHAKS.

Hoc scio pro certo, quod si cum stercŏre certo,
Vinco, seu vincor, semper ego macŭlor.
If I wrestle with a filthy thing, win or lose, I shall be defiled.

"If you wrestle with a collier you will get a blotch."
"He that toucheth pitch shall be defiled therewith."
"He that deals in dirt has ay foul fingers."
"A blow from a frying-pan, if it does not hurt, smuts."

Hoc volo, sic jubeo, sit pro ratione voluntas. JUV.—This is my wish, this is my command, my pleasure is my reason.

Hodie ille, cras ego.—He fell to-day, I may fall to-morrow.

"'Tis his turn to-day, it will be mine to-morrow."

Hodie nullus, cras maximus.—A nobody to-day, a prince to-morrow.

[The reverse of "To-day a man, to-morrow a mouse."]

Homĭnes ad deos nullâ re propius accēdunt quam salūtem homĭnĭbus dando. CIC.—In nothing do men so much resemble the gods as in giving help to their fellow creatures.

Homines nihil agendo discunt malè agĕre. CATO.—In doing nothing men learn to do evil.

    See "*Facĭto.*"

Homĭni diligenti semper alĭquid supĕrest.—A diligent man ever finds that something remains to be done.

> "Labour with what zeal we will,
> Something still remains undone,
> Something uncompleted still
> Waits the rising of the sun." LONGFELLOW.

    See "*Nil actum.*"

Homĭnis est errāre, insipientis perseverāre.—To err is human, to persevere in error is the act of a fool.

> "It is better to turn back than go astray."
> "A wilful fault has no excuse, and deserves no pardon."

Homo bombilius.—A noisy useless fellow.

Homo et mulier, ignis et palea.—Man and woman, fire and chaff.

> "When two agree in their desire,
> One sparke will set them both on fire." QUARLES.

Homo gĕnĭbus elephantĭnis.—A proud man who will not bend the knee.

Homo homini aut deus aut lupus. ERAS.—Man is to man a god or a wolf.

Homo homĭni lupus, homo homĭni dæmon.—Man is to man a wolf, man is to man a demon.

> " For without transformation
> Men become wolves on every slight occasion." BYRON.

> " Man's inhumanity to man
> Makes countless thousands mourn." BURNS.

Homo propōnit, sed Deus dispōnit.—Man proposeth, God disposeth.

Homo solus aut deus aut dæmon.—A man if he lives alone is either a god or a demon.

> " A solitary man is either a brute or an angel."

> " One would not be alone in Paradise."

> "Who could be happy and alone or good?" BYRON.

Homo sum; humāni nihil a me aliēnum puto. TER.— I am myself a man, and nothing relating to men is a matter of indifference to me.

> " Human blood is all of one colour."

> "Skins may differ, but affection
> Dwells in white and black the same." COWPER.

Homo toties mŏrĭtur, quotĭes amittit suos. SYR.—A man suffers death himself as often as he loses those dear to him.

Homo triŏbŏli.—A three-halfpenny fellow.

Homo trium literārum. PLAUT.—A man of three letters, "F U R."

Honestā paupērtas prior quam opes malæ.—Honesty with poverty is better than ill-gotten wealth.

> "Better go to heaven in rags than to hell in embroidery."

> "Thrive by honesty or remain poor."

> See "*Puras Deus.*"

Honesta quædam scĕlĕra successus facit. SEN.—Success gives the character of honesty to some classes of wickedness.

> "Success makes a fool seem wise."

> "It is success that colours all in life.
> Success makes fools admir'd, makes villains honest." THOMPSON.

> "Let them call it mischief;
> When it is past and prosper'd, 'twill be virtue." BEN JONSON.

> See "*Prospĕrum.*"

Honōres mutant mores.—Success alters our manners.

Honos alit artes, et virtus laudāta crescit. CIC.—Honourable mention encourages science, and merit is fostered by praise.

> "Where honour ceaseth, there knowledge decreaseth."

> "Praise is the hire of virtue."

> "Our praises are our wages." SHAKS.

> "Where none admire, 'tis useless to excel;
> Where none are beaux, 'tis vain to be a belle." E. MOORE.

> See "*Quis enim.*"

Hora ruit.—The hour is passing.

> "Life like an empty dream flits by." LONGFELLOW.

Horrĕa formīcæ tendunt ad inania nunquam,
Nullus ad amissas ibit amīcus opes. OVID.

Ants will not go to an empty granary, and friends will not visit us when our wealth is gone.

> "The poor is hated by his neighbour, but the rich hath many friends."

> "In times of prosperity friends will be plenty,
> In times of adversity, not one in twenty."

> "Ah! when the means are gone that buy this praise,
> The breath is gone whereof this praise is made." SHAKS.

> See "*Cum fortūna.*" "*Felicium.*" "*Fervet olla.*"

Horresco refĕrens. VIR.—I shudder when relating it.

Horret capillis, ut marīnus, aspĕris,
Echīnus, aut currens aper. HOR.

He bristles with hair, like a sea-urchin or a hunted boar.

> "What a beard hast thou got! thou hast got more hair on thy chin than Dobbin my thill-horse has on his tail." SHAKS.

Hos ego versĭcŭlos feci, tulit alter honōres. VIR.—I wrote these verses, but another claimed the merit of them.

> "Give every man his due."

> "Borrowed garments never sit well."

Hostes incurris, dum fugis hostem.—In flying from one enemy you encounter another.

> See "*Cucurrit quispiam.*"

Hostis est uxor invīta quæ ad virum nuptum datur. PLAUT. That wife is an enemy to her husband who is given in marriage against her will.

> "Married in haste we may repent at leisure." CONGREVE.

Hostium munĕra, non munĕra.—Presents from an enemy must be received with suspicion.

> "Gifts from enemies are dangerous."
> See "*Timeo Dănăos.*"

Huc anĭmus mihi versanti inclinābat et illuc.—My inclination first leads me in one direction, then in the opposite.

Hypsæâ cæcior.—Blinder than a beetle.

INUNC, *magnificos, victor, molīre triumphos.*—
VIR. Go forth a conqueror and win great victories.

> "So get the start of the majestic world
> And bear the palm alone." SHAKS.

Id facĕre laus est quod decet, non quod licet. SEN.—Do what you should, not what you may.

> "Do not all you can; spend not all you have; believe not all you hear; and tell not all you know."

Idem velle, et idem nolle, ea demum firma amicitia est. SALL. To have the same likes and dislikes, therein consists the firmest bond of friendship.

See "*Similes simili.*"

Ignāvis semper fēriæ sunt.—With the idle it is always holy day time.

Ignem igni ne addas.—Add not fire to fire.

Ignis cineribus alĭtur suis.—A fire is nourished by its own ashes.

[Difficulties embolden rather than impede the brave.]

Ignis, mare, mulier; tria mala.—Fire, the sea, and woman; these are three ills.

Ignis non extinguĭtur igni.—Fire will not put out fire. Anger is not appeased by anger.

"Soft words and hard arguments."

"Ill words are bellows to a slackening fire."

"The second blow makes the fray."

See "*Frangĭtur ira.*" "*Favōre.*" "*Sermōnes blandi.*"

Ignōti nulla cupīdo.—We covet not that of the existence of which we are ignorant.

Ignōtum per ignotius.—What is not understood [explained] by what is less understood.

[To make confusion still more confounded.]

See "*Cæcus.*"

Iliăcos intra muros peccātur et extra. Hor.—Faults are committed within the walls of Troy and also without.

[There is fault on both sides.]

"Six of one, and half a dozen of the other."

Illa dolet verè quæ sine teste dolet. MART.—Her grief is real who grieves when no one is by.

> "She never told her love,
> But let concealment, like a worm i' the bud,
> Feed on her damask cheek; she pined in thought." SHAKS.

Illa mihi patria est, ubi pascor, non ubi nascor.—That country will I call mine which supports me, not that which gave me birth.

> "A clever man's inheritance is found in every country."

> "All places that the eye of heaven visits,
> Are to a wise man ports and happy havens." SHAKS.

Ille crucem sceleris pretium tulit, hic diadema. JUV.—One gets a cross for his crime, the other a crown.

> "One murder made a villain,
> Millions a hero." B. PORTEUS.

> "One to destroy is murder by the law,
> And gibbets keep the lifted hand in awe;
> To murder thousands takes a specious name,
> War's glorious art, and gives immortal fame." YOUNG.

Ille regit dictis animos, et temperat iras. VIR.—He subdues their rising passion and soothes their anger by soft remonstrance.

> "More flies are taken with a drop of honey than a tun of vinegar."

> "Mildness governs more than anger."

> "Rebukes ought not to have a grain more salt than sugar."

> See "*Ignis non.*"

Ille velut pelăgi rupes immōta resistit. VIR.—He like a rock in the sea unshaken stands his ground.

Illi mors gravis incŭbat,
Qui, notus nimis omnĭbus,
Ignōtus morĭtur sui. SEN.

Death falls heavily on that man who, known too well to others, dies in ignorance of himself.

Illīberāle est mentīri, ingĕnuum verĭtas decet.—It is ungentlemanly to lie; truthfulness becomes the gentleman.

Illĭcĭta amantur: excĭdit, quidquid licet. SEN.—That which we are not permitted to have we delight in; that which we can have is disregarded.

"Nothing so good as forbidden fruit."

"Bliss itself is not worth having,
If we're by compulsion blest." MOORE.

See "*Nitĭmur.*" "*Quod licet.*"

Illo lacte fovētur,
Propter quod secum comĭtes edūcit asellas. JUV.

She is kept alive on the milk of asses which she takes with her wherever she goes.

"The doctors gave her over—to an ass." HOOD.

Ima summis mutāre.—To turn things upside down.

Imbrem in cribrum gĕrĕre.—To catch the shower in a sieve.

[To lose one's time and pains.]

See "*Cribro.*"

Immodĭcis brevis est ætas, et rara senectus.—The intemperate die young, and rarely enjoy old age.

"A man as he manages himself may die old at thirty, or young at eighty."
"Bacchus hath drowned more men than Neptune."
"Diet cures more than the lancet."
"Old young, and old long."
See "*Ense cadunt.*" "*Plures crapŭla.*"

Immorĭtur studiis, et amōre senescit habendi. Hor.—He wears himself out by his labours, and grows old through his love of possessing wealth.

Immortāle odĭum, et nunquam sanabĭle vulnus. Juv.—An undying hatred, and a wound never to be healed.

Impĕdit omne forum defectus denariōrum.—A want of pence stops all your marketing.

"No means, no market."

Impĕrāre sĭbi maxĭmum impĕrium est. Sen.—The greatest power of ruling consists in the exercise of self-control.

"He that is master of himself will soon be master of others."

Impĕrat aut servit collecta pecunia cuique. Hor.—Money, as it increases, becomes either the master or the slave of its owner.

"A great fortune in the hands of a fool is a great misfortune."
"Riches abuse them who know not how to use them."
"If money be not thy servant, it will be thy master."
"Command your wealth, else that will command you."
"Riches serve a wise man, but command a fool."

Imperātor bonus et idem robustus miles.—At once a good general and a stout soldier.

Imperītus subligāculo indūtus omnĭbus id ostentat.—Unaccustomed to wear them, he displays the breeches he has on to every one he meets.

Impĕrium flagĭtio acquisītum nemo unquam bonis artĭbus exercuit. Tac.—Power won by crime no one ever yet turned to a good purpose.

"Such a beginning, such an end."

Impĭa sub dulci melle venēna latent. Ovid.—Accursed poison lies hid beneath sweet honey.

"Bees that have honey in their mouths have stings in their tails."

"Joy and sorrow are next door neighbours."

"And he repents in thorns that sleeps in beds of roses."
Quarles.

"The rills of pleasure never run sincere,
(Earth has no unpolluted spring)
From the cursed soil some dang'rous taint they bear;
So roses grow on thorns, and honey wears a sting." Watts.

See "*Medio de fonte.*"

Implacābĭles plerumque læsæ muliĕres.—Women when injured are generally not easily appeased.

"Heaven has no rage like love to hatred turn'd,
"Nor hell a fury like a woman scorn'd." Congreve.

"As fierce as hell, or fiercer still,
A woman piqued who has her will." Byron.

See "*Vindicta nemo.*"

Implētus venter non vult studēre libenter.—We are not disposed to study much after heavy meals.

> "A bellyfull of gluttony will never study willingly."

Impōnit finem sapiens et rebus honestis. Juv.—The wise man sets bounds even to his innocent desires.

*Imprŏbæ
Crescunt divitiæ; tamen
Curtæ nescio quid semper abest rei.* Hor.

Riches with their wicked inducements increase; nevertheless, avarice is never satisfied.

> See "*Crescit amor.*" "*Quo plus.*"

Imprŏbĕ Neptūnum accūsat, qui naufragium itĕrum facit. Syr.—He blames Neptune unjustly who twice suffers shipwreck.

> "He who stumbles twice over one stone deserves to break his shins."
>
> "Even an ass will not fall twice in the same quicksand."
>
> "If a man deceive me once, shame on him; if he deceive me twice, shame on me."
>
> See "*Itĕrum eundem.*"

Imprŏbis aliēna virtus semper formidolōsa est. Sall.—By the wicked the good conduct of others is always dreaded.

Improbĭtas muscæ.—The provoking pertinacity of a fly.

Impulsu, et cæcâ magnâque cupīdĭne ducti. Juv.
Led on by impulse, and blind and ungovernable desires.

"A headstrong man and a fool may wear the same cap."

Impunĭtas semper ad deteriōra invītat. Coke.—Success in crime always invites to worse deeds.

" He invites future injuries who rewards past ones."

See " *Successus improbōrum.*"

In aĕre piscāri. Venāri in mari.—To fish in the air. To hunt in the sea.

In aliēno choro pedem ponĕre.—To interfere in the affairs of others.

"To put your finger into another man's pie."

" Mind your own business."

In angustis amīci boni appārent.—True friends are tested in adversity.

" Poverty trieth friends."
See " *Amicus certus.*"

In asĭni aures canĕre.—To sing to an ass.

" To throw pearls before swine."

In cadūcum parĭĕtem inclināre.—To lean against a tottering wall.

"A chair unsound
Soon finds the ground."

In calamitōso risus etiam injūria est. Syr.—Even to smile at the misfortunes of others is to do an injury.

In capĭte orphăni discit chirurgus.—A surgeon tries his experiments on the heads of orphans.

    See "*Fiat experimentum.*"

In Care perīcŭlum.*—Test the danger by the Carians.

    [Practise new experiments on things of little value.]

    "Try your skill in gilt first, and then in gold."

    See above.

In cælum jaculāris.—You war against heaven.

    "It is hard for thee to kick against the pricks."

    "None ever took a stone out of the temple but the dust did fly in his eyes."

    See "*Cede deo.*" "*Ludĕre cum.*"

In eâdem es navi.—You sail in the same boat.

    [You are in the same danger.]

In eburnâ vagīnâ plumbeus gladius.—A sword of lead in a scabbard of ivory.

    "An ass in a lion's hide."

In eodem luto hæsĭtas. TER.—You stick in the same mire.

In eōdem valetudinario jacēre.—To be in the same hospital.

    [To be in the same dilemma.]

---

* The Carians were employed as mercenary soldiers.

In flagranti delicto.—In the very act of committing an offence.

[Taken red handed.]

In foro conscientiæ.—At the bar of one's own conscience.

In frigĭdum furnum panes immittĕre.—To put bread into a cold oven.

In garrŭlo verbōrum flumen, mentis gutta.—In chatter a river, in understanding but a single drop.

"A fool's voice is known by a multitude of words."
See "*Audīto.*"

In lucem semper Acerra bibit. MART.—Acerra always drinks till dawn.

"The gallant Sir Robert fought hard to the end,
But who can with fate and quart bumpers contend?
Though Fate said, a hero should perish in light;
So up rose bright Phœbus, and down fell the knight." BURNS.

In mari aquam quærit.—He is hunting for water in the sea.

In mari magno pisces capiuntur.—In the great sea fish is always to be caught.

[There is a greater chance for enterprise in a large place.]

"No fishing like fishing in the sea."

In medio terræ sĭmul, et stellantis Olympi.—Midway between the earth and the starry Olympus.

[In a quandary. In a fix.]

In melius orsa reflectĕre. VIR.—To change the course we have begun for the better.

> "To turn over a new leaf."

> "To sow our wild oats."

In mĭnĭmis cauti, in maxĭmis negligentes.—Cautious in small matters, careless in great.

> "Penny wise, pound foolish."

> See "*Ad mensūram.*"

In modum gramĭnis.—As thick as hail.

In morbo recollĭgit se anĭmus. PLIN.—In time of sickness the soul collects itself anew.

> "The chamber of sickness is the chapel of devotion."

> See "*Ægrōtat dæmon.*" "*Quum infirmi.*"

In morte alterĭus spem tu tibi ponĕre noli. CATO.—Do not expect good from another's death.

> "Look not out for dead men's shoes."

In nihil sapiendo jucundissima vita.—He spends the happiest life who knows nothing.

> "The less wit a man has, the less he knows that he wants it."

> "Children and fools have merry lives."

> See "*Amissum quod.*" "*Certe ignorantia.*"

In nocte consilium.—Our pillow should be our counsellor.

> [Sleep upon an idea.]

> "Night is the mother of councils."

In occĭpĭtio ocŭlos gerit.—He has eyes in the back of his head.

In ore leōnis favus mellis!—A honey-comb in the mouth of a lion!

In pace leōnes, in prælio cervi.—Lions in time of peace; deer in war.

> "Of war all can tattle,
> Away from the battle."

> "Thou wear a lion's hide! doff it for shame,
> And hang a calf's skin on those recreant limbs." SHAKS.

> "How many cowards * * * * *
> * * * * * * wear yet upon their chins
> The beards of Hercules and frowning Mars! SHAKS.

In parvŭlis nulla culpa.—We pardon faults in youth.

In periculōso negotio non est dormītandum.—Sleep not in time of peril.

In pertūsum congĕrĕre dicta dolium. PLAUT.—To waste one's breath; to pump into a sieve.

In pulĭcis morsu Deum invŏcat.—He invokes heaven if a flea bites him.

In puris naturālĭbus.—Stark naked.

In re malâ, anĭmo si bono utāre, adjŭvat. PLAUT.—In misfortune if you cultivate a cheerful disposition you will reap the advantage of it.

"Misfortunes that can't be avoided must be sweetened."

"Patience is sorrow's salve." CHURCHILL.

"How poor are they that have not patience!
What wound did ever heal but by degrees?" SHAKS.

See "*Feras non.*" "*Levius fit.*"

In rebus dubĭĭs, plurĭmi est audācĭa. SYR.—In doubtful matters boldness is everything.

"Boldness in business is the first, second, and third thing."

"Who bravely dares must sometimes risk a fall." SMOLLET.

See "*Audentes.*"

In saltu uno duos apros capĕre.—To take two boars in one thicket.

"To kill two birds with one stone."

See "*Duos parĭĕtes.*"

In se magna ruunt. LUC.—Great things rush to the destruction of each other.

"Love and lordship like no fellowship."

"Two Sir Positives can scarce meet without a skirmish."

See "*Mons cum.*"

In secundis meditāre, quo pacto feras adversa.—In time of prosperity consider how you will bear adversity.

> "Who looks not before finds himself behind."

> "The bee, from her industry in the summer, eats honey all the winter."

> See "*Dum vires.*"

In sudōre vultûs tui comĕdes panem tuum.

> "In the sweat of thy face shalt thou eat thy bread."

> "No sweet without sweat."

> "There is no fishing for trout in dry breeches."

> See "*Dii laborĭbus.*" "*Neque mel.*" "*Nil sine.*"

In sylvam ligna ferre.—To carry wood to the forest.

> See "*Athenas.*"

In tempŏre cavenda poena mali.—The penalty attaching to evil deeds should be thought of in time.

In toga saltantis persōnam inducĕre.—To put on the mask of a dancer when wearing the toga.

> [To do that which is out of place and inconsistent.]

In trivio sum.—I am in a fix. [In a place where three ways meet.]

In tuum ipsius malum lunam dedūcis.—You bring your own evil deeds to light.

In vestimentis non stat sapientia mentis.—Wisdom does not consist in dress.
> " It's not the gay coat that makes the gentleman."
> " Worship and birth to me are known
> By look, by bearing, and by tone,
> Not by furred robe, or broidered zone." SCOTT.
> " As the sun breaks through the darkest clouds,
> So honour peereth in the meanest habit." SHAKS.
> See " *Licet superbus.*" " *Simia simia.*"

In vili veste nemo tractātur honeste.—No one in a shabby coat is treated with respect.
> See " *Vestis virum.*"

In vino vērĭtas.—Wine brings forth the truth.
> " Wine wears no breeches."
> " When wine sinks, words swim."
> See " *Quando tumet.*" " *Quod est in.*" " *Vinum anĭmi.*"

In vitium ducit culpæ fuga, si caret arte. HOR.—In avoiding one evil we fall into another, if we use not discretion.
> " Out of the frying-pan into the fire."
> " But what avail'd this temperance, not complete
> Against another object more enticing?" MILTON.
> See " *Dum vitant.*"

Ināni spe flagrat.—He is consumed by a vain hope.
> " Hope deferred maketh the heart sick."
> See " *Qui spe.*"

Inānĭum inānĭa consilia.—Worthless is the advice of fools.

    See "*Stultus stulta.*"

                         Incēdis per ignes
Supposĭtos cinĕri dolōso. Hor.
You walk over red-hot lava hidden beneath treacherous ashes.

    See "*Latet anguis.*" "*Sub omni.*"

Incendit omnem femĭnæ zelus domum.—A jealous woman will set a whole house on fire.

Incesto addĭdit intĕgrum. Hor.—God has joined the innocent with the guilty.

    "All are not thieves that dogs bark at."

    "Some innocents 'scape not the thunderbolt." Shaks.

Incĭdit in fovĕam quam fēcit.—He falls into the pit which he himself made.

    See "*Captantes capti.*" "*Qui capit.*"

    Incĭdit in Scyllam cupiens vitāre Charybdim.
In avoiding Charybdis, he falls into Scylla.

    See "*Dum vitant.*" "*Frustrà vitium.*" "*In vitium.*"

Incipĕre multo est, quam impetrāre, facilĭus. Plaut.—It is far easier to begin a task than to finish it.

Incĭta equum juxta nyssam.—Urge the horse close to the turning-post.

    [Don't let him run wide; keep to the point in question.]

Incitamentum enim amōris musĭca.—Music provokes love.
"If music be the food of love, play on." SHAKS.

Incitantur enim hominēs ad agnoscenda quæ differuntur. PLIN.—The desire to know a thing is heightened by its gratification being deferred.
"Desires are nourished by delays."

Incus maxĭma non metuit strepĭtum.—A great anvil fears not noise.

Indictum sit.—Let it be unsaid.
[Let the observation be withdrawn.]

Indocti discant et ament meminisse perīti.—Let the ignorant learn, and the learned delight in refreshing the memory.

Indoctum doctumque fugat recĭtātor ăcerbus. HOR.—A bad reader soon puts to flight both wise men and fools.

Indulge věnĭam pŭĕris. JUV.—Make all fair allowance for the mistakes of youth.
"Apelles was not a master painter the first day."

Indus elephantus non curat culĭcem.—The great elephant of India cares not for a gnat.
See "*Latrantem.*"

Inest et formīcæ et serpho bilis.*—Even the ant hath its anger.

> "Tread on a worm and it will turn."
>
> "No viper so little but hath its venom."
>
> See "*Nec asperandum.*"

Inest sua gratia parvis.—Small things have their own peculiar charm.

> "Little things are pretty."
>
> "Willows are weak, yet they bind other wood."
>
> "Small rain lays great dust."
>
> "The greatest things are done by the help of small ones."
>
> "Great weights may hang on small wires."
>
> "A lion may be beholden to a mouse."
>
> See "*Quod contemnĭtur.*"

Infinīta est velocĭtas tempŏris, quæ magis appāret respicientĭbus. SEN.—The swiftness of time is infinite, which is the more evident to those who look back on what has passed.

> "We take no note of time
> But from its loss." YOUNG.

---

* "*Serphus.*" A kind of insect like an ant.

Infirmi est animi exĭgŭique voluptas Ultio. Juv.

It is but the weak and little mind that rejoices in revenge.

"To forget a wrong is the best revenge."

"The revenge of an idiot is without mercy."

"Anger is shortlived in a good man."

"Revenge in cold blood is the devil's own act and deed."

"To err is human, to forgive divine." POPE.

"Think'st thou it honourable for a noble man
Still to remember wrongs?" SHAKS.

See "*Quo quisque.*"

Infrà tuam pellĭcŭlam te contĭne.—Live according to your means.

"Let your purse be your master."

"He, who more than he is worth doth spend,
E'en makes a rope, his life to end."

"Silks and satins put out the kitchen fire."

"Stretch your legs according to your coverlet."

"Who dainties love shall beggars prove." GAY.

See "*Inops potentem.*" "*Messe tenus.*" "*Sumptus censum.*" "*Tecum habĭta.*"

Ingenio stat sine morte děcus.—Immortal glory waits on talent.

> "For 'tis the mind that makes the body rich;
> And as the sun breaks through the darkest clouds,
> So honour peereth in the meanest habit." SHAKS.

Ingĕniōrum cos æmulātio.—Emulation is the whetstone of talent.

Ingens malōrum remĕdium ignorantia.—A strong remedy for evils is ignorance of them.

> "He that is not sensible of his loss has lost nothing."

> "Oh Ignorance
> Thou art fall'n man's best friend!" KIRKE WHITE.

See "*Amissum quod.*" "*Certe ignoratio.*"

Ingens telum necessĭtas.—Necessity is a strong weapon.

> "Necessity and opportunity may make a coward valiant."
> "Despair gives courage to a coward."
> "Put a coward to his metal an' he'll fight the de'il."
> "A coward's fear may make a coward valiant."
> "Drive a rat into a corner, and he'll jump at you."

> "The strongest and the fiercest spirit
> That fought in heaven, now fiercer by despair." MILTON.

*Ingĕnŭas dĭdĭcisse fĭdēliter artes
Emollit mores, nec sinit esse feros.* OVID.

To have properly studied the liberal sciences gives a polish to our manners, and removes all awkwardness.

Ingrātum si dixĕris, omnia dīcis.—If you say that he is guilty of ingratitude, you need say no more.

"Gratitude is the least of virtues, but ingratitude the worst of vices."
"Hell is crowded with ungrateful wretches."
"I hate ingratitude more in man
Than lying, vainness, babbling, drunkenness,
Or any taint of vice." SHAKS.

Ingrātus est qui, remōtis testĭbus, agit gratiam. SEN.—He may as well not thank at all, who thanks when none are by.

Ingrātus unus misĕris omnĭbus nocet. SYR.—One ungrateful man injures all who need assistance.

Ingrātus vir dolium est perforātum.—An ungrateful man is a tub full of holes.

"All's lost that's put in a riven dish."
See "*Perit quod.*"

Initio confīdens, in facto timĭdus.—Bold in design, but timid in execution.

Injuriă solvit amōrem.—Injuries destroy affection.

Injuriæ spretæ exolescunt; si irascāris agnĭtæ videntur.—Injuries, when treated with contempt, vanish and have no effect. If you show anger their effect would appear to be acknowledged.

"Neglect will sooner kill an injury than revenge."
"He that shows his passion, tells his enemy where he may hit him."
"Where it concerns himself,
Who's angry at a slander, makes it true." SHAKS.

Injuriam qui factūrus est, jam facit. SEN.—To meditate an injury is to commit one.

> "Injury is to be measured by malice."
>
> See "*Haud est.*" "*Nam scelus inter.*"

Injusta ab justis impetrāri non decet;
Justa autem ab injustis petĕre, insipientia est. PLAUT. To ask that which is unjust at the hands of the just, is an injustice in itself; to expect that which is just from the unjust, is simple folly.

Inops, potentem dum vult imitāri, perit. PHAED.—The poor man, while he apes the wealthy, effects his own ruin.

> [The fable of frog and the cow.]
>
> "Dress drains our cellar dry,
> And keeps our larder lean." COWPER.
>
> "A princely mind will undo a private family."
>
> See "*Infrà tuam.*"

Inquĭnat egrĕgios adjuncta superbia mores. CLAUD.—The best manners are stained by haughtiness.

> "Affectation is a greater injury to the face than small-pox."
>
> "Pride joined with many virtues chokes them all."

Insania non omnĭbus eădem.—The same failings attach not to all.

> "Compound for sins they are inclined to,
> By damning those they have no mind to." BUTLER.
>
> "Who backs his rigid Sabbath, so to speak,
> Against the wicked remnant of the week." HOOD.

Insanīre facit sanos quoque copia vini.—Too much wine will make a sane man mad.

Insānus omnis furĕre crēdit cætĕros. SYR.—Every madman considers every one else a madman.

Insĭta homĭnĭbus natūra violentiæ resistĕre. TAC.—It is a part of the nature of man to resist compulsion.

> "Oppression causeth rebellion."

> "You may take a horse to the water, but you can't make him drink."

> "If reasons were as plentiful as blackberries,
> I would give no man a reason upon compulsion." SHAKS.

Insperāta accĭdunt magis sæpe quam quæ speres. PLAUT.—Unexpected results are the rule rather than the exception.

Intellĭgunt se mutuò, ut fures in nundĭnis.—They understand each other, like thieves at a fair.

> "A thief knows a thief, as a wolf knows a wolf."

Intempestīva benevolentia nihil a simultāte differt.—Assistance given when it is not required, is as bad as an injury.

> "Heaven preserve me from my friends!"

> "Proffered service stinks."

> See "*Nemo cogendus.*" "*Officium ne.*"

Inter arma silent leges. Cic.—When war is raging the laws are dumb.

Inter cæcos regnat luscus.—Among the blind a one-eyed man is a king.

Inter delicias semper aliquid sævi nos strangulat.—In the midst of our mirth some annoyance always arises to vex us.

    " No joy without alloy."

    " Full from the fount of joy's delicious springs
    Some bitter o'er the flowers its bubbling venom flings." Byron.

    " There rose no day, there roll'd no hour
      Of pleasure unembitter'd;
    And not a trapping deck'd my power,
      That gall'd not while it glitter'd." Byron.

        See " *Medio de fonte.*" " *Nihil est ab.*" " *Omnis commoditas.*"

Inter lugentes jocari.—To indulge in a joke when surrounded by mourners.

    [To jest out of season.]

    " Bring not a bagpipe to a man in trouble."

    " Music helps not the toothache."

Inter malleum et incudem.—Between the hammer and the anvil.

    [Between two difficulties.]

Inter manum et mentum.—Between the hand and the chin.

        See " *Multa cadunt.*" " *Non omnia eveniunt.*"

Inter spem curamque, timōres inter et iras. HOR.—'Twixt hope and fear, anxiety and anger.

Interdum lăchrymæ pondĕra vocis habent. OVID.—Tears are at times as eloquent as words.
>[Weeping hath a voice.]
>"Her tears will pierce into a marble heart." SHAKS.
>
>"Oh! too convincing—dangerously dear—
>In woman's eye the unanswerable tear!" BYRON.
>
>"The rose is sweetest wash'd with morning dew,
>And love is loveliest when embalm'd in tears." SCOTT.
>
>"Give me the soft sigh, whilst the soul-telling eye
>Is dimm'd for a time with a tear." BYRON.
>
>"What, lost a world, and bade a hero fly?
>The timid tear in Cleopatra's eye." BYRON.

Interdum stultus bene loquĭtur.—Even a fool sometimes speaks to the purpose.
>"A fool may give a wise man counsel."
>"A fool may chance to put something into a wise man's head."
>"Nothing so bad as not to be good for something."
>"A fool's wild speech confounds the wise." SCOTT.
>"A fool must now and then be right by chance." COWPER.
>See "*Quis est enim.*"

Interdum vulgus rectum videt. HOR.—The mob will now and then see things in a right light.
>"A thing is never much talked of but there is some truth in it."
>See "*Haud semper.*" "*Non omnīno.*"

Intŏlĕrābĭlius nihil est quàm fœmĭna dives. Juv.—Nothing is so intolerable as a woman with a long purse.

Intus Nero, foris Cato.—A Nero at home, a Cato abroad.

Invēni portum, Spes et Fortūna valēte,
Sat me lusistis, ludĭte nunc alios.
"I've reach'd the harbour, Hope and Chance adieu!
You've play'd with me, now play with others too."

Invĕnĭes alium, si te hic fastīdit Alexis. Vir.—If one swain scorns you, you will soon find another.
"There are as good fish in the sea as ever came out of it."
"There's seldom a cake but there's more of the make."

Inverte, et averte.—Turn it inside and out.

Invĭcem cedunt dolor et voluptas.—Pleasure and pain succeed each other.
"The holydays of joy are the vigils of sorrow."
"Every medal has its reverse."
"Every day hath its night, every weal its woe."
"Each must drain
His share of pleasure, share of pain." Scott.
"O, how this spring of love resembleth
The uncertain glory of an April day;
Which now shows all the beauty of the sun,
And by-and-by a cloud takes all away." Shaks.
See "*Voluptāti.*"

Invĭdia festos dies non habet.—Envy never has a holiday.

Invĭdiam ferre aut fortis aut felix potest. Syr.—The brave or the fortunate can afford to laugh at envy.

Invĭdus altĕrius macrescit rebus opīmis. Hor.—An envious man grows lean at another's fatness.

> "Base envy withers at another's joy,
> And hates that excellence it cannot reach." · Thompson.

Invīso semel princĭpe, seu benĕ, seu malĕ, facta premunt. Tac.—A man in power, once becoming obnoxious, his acts, good or bad, will work out his ruin.

> "When a man is not liked, whatever he doth is amiss."

> See "*Ad calamitātem.*" "*Semel malus.*" "*Quicunque turpi.*"

Invītat culpam qui peccātum prætĕrit. Syr.—He who leaves a fault unpunished invites crime.

> "Spare the rod, spoil the child."

> See "*Melior est justitia.*"

Invītis canĭbus venāri.—To hunt with unwilling hounds.

> "To go rabbit hunting with a dead ferret."
> "Drive the nail that will go."

Invītos boves plaustro inducĕre.—To harness unwilling oxen.

> See "*Invītis.*"

Invītum qui servat ĭdem facit occīdenti. Hor.—He who preserves a man's life against his will does the same thing as if he slew him.

> See "*Intempestīva.*" "*Nemo cogendus.*" "*Officium.*"

Ipsa dies quandōque parens, quandōque noverca est.—The passing hour is sometimes a mother, sometimes a stepmother.

"Fortune wearies with carrying one and the same man always."

Ipsa scientia potestas est.

"Knowledge is power."

Ipsa se fraus, etiamsi initio cautĭor fuĕrit, dētĕgit.—Treachery will eventually betray itself, though wary enough at first.

"Crimes may be secret, yet not secure."

"Murder will out."

"For murder though it have no tongue, will speak
With most miraculous organ." SHAKS.

Ipsa senectus morbus est.—Old age is in itself a disease.

Ipse mihi asciam in crus impēgi. PET.—I have cut my leg with my own adze.

Ipse semet canit.—He sings his own praises.

"He is his own trumpeter."

Ipsum ostii limen, tetĭgisti.—You have hit the point exactly.

"You have hit the nail on the head."

Ira furor brevis est.—Anger is a transient madness.

"Choleric men are blind and mad."

*Ira, quæ tĕgĭtur, nocet;
Professa perdunt odĭa vindictæ locum.* SEN.

Concealed anger is to be feared; but hatred openly manifested destroys its chance of revenge.

"Fire that's closest kept burns most of all." SHAKS.

"More mild, but yet more harmful; kind in hatred." SHAKS.

Iræ senectus mors.—Hate knows no age but death.

"Revenge of an hundred years old hath still its sucking teeth."

Iram
Collĭgit ac ponit tĕmĕrè, et mutātur in horas. HOR.

His anger is easily excited and appeased, and he changes from hour to hour.

Iras et verba locant. MART.—They let out on hire their passions and eloquence.

[Referring to lawyers.]

Iracundĭam qui vincit, hostem supĕrat maxĭmum. SYR.—He who gets the better of an irascible temperament conquers his worst enemy.

"He's a wise man that leads passion by the bridle."

Irascĕre interfectōri, sed miserēre interfecti.—Be angry with a murderer, but keep your compassion for his victim.

Irātus cum ad se redit, sibi tum irascĭtur. SYR.—An angry man, when he returns to reason, will be again angry with himself.

"The end of passion is the beginning of repentance."

"Malice drinketh its own poison."

"Anger is like
A full hot horse; who being allowed his way,
Self-mettle tires him." SHAKS.

See "*Malè cuncta.*" "*Non est ratio.*"

Irritāre crabrōnes.—To worry hornets.

"To wake a sleeping lion."

Is cadet ante senem, qui sapit ante diem.—He will die before he's old who's wise before his time.

"Early ripe, early rotten."

"So wise, so young, they say, do ne'er live long." SHAKS.

See "*Citò matūrum.*"

Is minĭmo eget mortālis, qui mĭnĭmum cupit. SYR.—He is the least in want who is the least covetous.

"Content is more than a kingdom."

"A contented mind is a continual feast."

"He is rich who is satisfied."

See "*Benè est.*" "*Lætus sorte.*"

Is sapiens qui se ad casūs accommŏdet omnes.—He is a wise man who accommodates himself to all circumstances.

"A wise man will make tools of what comes to hand."

See "*Si stimŭlos.*" "*Nunquam direxit.*"

Ista decens făcĭes longis vĭtĭābĭtur annis,
Rugaque in antīquâ fronte senīlis erit. OVID.

That fair face will as years roll on lose its beauty, and old age will bring its wrinkles to the brow.

"Beauty is but a flower,
Which wrinkles will devour." T. NASH.

"His golden locks time hath to silver turned." PEELE.

Iter pigrōrum quasi sepes spinārum.
> "The way of a slothful man is as a hedge of thorns."
> "Sloth is the mother of poverty."

Itĕrum eundem ad lapĭdem offendĕre.—To stumble twice over the same stone.
> "What! would'st thou have a serpent sting thee twice?" SHAKS.
> See "*Improbe Neptūnum.*"

Itĕrum precor et obtestor, vīvĭte læti; illud, quod cor urit, neglĭgĭte.—Again and again I beg and pray of you to live merrily: should aught distress you, dismiss it from your minds.
> "A pennyworth of mirth is worth a pound of sorrow."
> See "*Ride si.*"

JACTA est alĕa.—The die is cast.
> [The Rubicon is crossed.]

Jactantiæ comes invidia.—Envy waits on boasting.
> "You can't fare well, but you must cry roast meat."
> See "*Tacitus.*"

Jam fuĕrit, nec post unquam revocāre licēbit. Lucr.—Yet a little while, and (the happy hour) will be over, nor ever more shall we be able to recall it.

> "'Tis gone: a thousand such have slipt
>   Away from my embraces:
> And fallen into the dusty crypt
>   Of darken'd forms and faces." Tennyson.

> " Swiftly our pleasures glide away,
> Our hearts recall the distant day
> With many sighs." Longfellow.

> " But pleasures are like poppies spread:
> You seize the flower,—its bloom is shed." Burns.

Jejūnus raro stomăchus vulgāria temnit. HOR.—A hungry stomach rarely despises rough food.

"Hunger finds no fault with the cookery."

"A hungry dog will eat dirty pudding."

"A hungry horse maketh a clear manger."

See "*Fabas.*"

Jejūnus venter non audit verba libenter.—A hungry man will listen to nothing.

"Hungry bellies have no ears."

Jocandum, ut seria agas.—Mirth must be indulged in to prepare the mind for more serious matters.

"All work and no play
Makes Jack a dull boy."

"A bow long bent at length waxeth weak."

"A little nonsense now and then
Is relish'd by the best of men."

See "*Stare diu.*" "*Otia corpus.*"

Jucunda est memoria præterĭtōrum malōrum. CIC.—Pleasant is the recollection of dangers past.

"That which was bitter to endure may be sweet to remember."

"Wept o'er his wounds, or tales of sorrow done,
Shoulder'd his crutch, and show'd how fields were won."
GOLDSMITH.

See "*Carius est.*" "*Forsan.*" "*Fortĭter.*"

Jucundi acti labōres. CIC.—Sweet is the recollection of difficulties overcome.

> See "*Carius est.*" "*Forsan et.*" "*Jucunda.*"

Jucundiōres amōrum post injūrias delĭciæ.—The pleasures of love are enhanced by injuries.

> See "*Amantium iræ.*"

Jucundissĭma navĭgātio juxta terram; ambulatio juxta mare.—The most pleasant cruise is near the land; the most inviting walk near the sea.

> See "*Sub tecto.*"

Jucundum nihil est nisi quod rĕfĭcit varietas. SYR.—Nothing pleases which is not freshened by variety.

> "A duck will not always dabble in the same gutter."
>
> "How the devil is it that fresh features
> Have such a charm for us poor human creatures?" BYRON.
>
> See "*Est natūra.*" "*Est quoque.*" "*Rarum carum.*"

Judex damnātur cum nocens absolvĭtur. SYR.—The judge is condemned when the guilty are acquitted.

Jugulāre aliquem plumbĕo glādĭo.—To cut a man with a sword of lead.

> "To cut his throat with a feather."

Jugulāre mortŭos.—To stab the dead.

Justum ab injustis petĕre insipientia est.—It is sheer folly to expect justice from the unprincipled.

> "What can you expect from a pig but a grunt?"

Juvenīle vitĭum regĕre non posse impĕtum. SEN.—It is the fault of youth that it cannot restrain its own impetuosity.

"You can't put an old head on young shoulders."

See "*Temerĭtas est.*"

*Juvenilibus annis
Luxuriant animi.* OVID.

The spirits run riot in youth.

Juxta fluvĭum pŭteum fodit.—Hard by a river he digs a well.

"To swim a river with a bridge close by."

See "*Quum adsit.*"

LABITUR et labētur in omne volūbĭlis ævum.
HOR.—Still rolls and to all time shall roll the tumbling flood.

"A thousand years hence the river will run as it did."

" No check, no stay this streamlet fears :
   How merrily it goes!
'Twill murmur on a thousand years,
   And flow as now it flows." WORDSWORTH.

See "*Fugit irrevocabĭle.*" "*Nec quæ.*"

Labĭtur occultè, fallitque volūbilis ætas. OVID.—Imperceptibly the hours glide on, and beguile us as they pass.

"Old age creeps on us ere we think it nigh." DRYDEN.

" Oh, sweet youth, how soon it fades!
Sweet joys of youth, how fleeting!" MOORE.

See "*Dum bĭbĭmus.*" "*Fugit irrevocabĭle.*"

Labor ipse voluptas.—The labour is in itself a pleasure.

> " No endeavour is in vain;
> Its reward is in the doing." LONGFELLOW.

Labor omnia vincit.—Labour conquers all things.

> " Perseverance kills the game."

Labra, non palātum, rigat.—He moistens the lips, but leaves the palate dry.

> [Trifling assistance, of little or no use.]

Labris primorĭbus degustāre. CIC.—To have a smattering knowledge of anything.

Lābuntur anni.—Years roll on.

> See " *Fugit irrevocabĭle.*"

Lacrymâ nihil cĭtius arescit.—Nothing dries up more quickly than a tear.

> " Heaviness may endure for a night, but joy cometh in the morning."
>
> " Beware of desperate steps; the darkest day,
> Live till to-morrow, will have passed away." COWPER.
>
> " Behind the clouds is the sun still shining." LONGFELLOW.

Læsus timet.—He that has been hurt, fears.

> " Once bit, twice shy."
>
> " The bird that hath been limed in a bush
> With trembling wing misdoubteth every bush." SHAKS.
>
> See " *Piscātor.*"

*Lætus in præsens animus, quod ultra est,
Oděrit curāre.* Hor.

Let your mind, happily contented with the present, care not what the morrow will bring with it.

"Wouldst thou, or thou,
Forego what's *now*,
For all that hope may say?
No—joy's reply,
From every eye,
Is, 'Live we while we may.'" Moore.

See "*Carpe diem.*" *Nosce tempus.*"

Lætus sorte tuâ vīves sapienter.—If you are contented with your lot, you will live wisely.

"He who wants content can't find an easy chair."

"Content is the philosopher's stone, that turns all it touches into gold."

"Enjoy your little, while the fool seeks for more."

See "*Benè est.*" "*Is minimo.*"

Lanārum nigræ nullum colōrem bibunt. Plin.

"Black will take no other hue."

"Sour grapes will ne'er make sweet wine."

"Barren corn makes bitter bread." Swinburne.

See "*Lignum tortum.*"

Lapĭdi loquĕris!—You are talking to a stone.

Lapsănâ vīvĕre.*—To fare hard.

---

* *Lapsăna.*—Wild coleworts, or dock-cress.

*Laqueo tenet ambitiōsi
Consuetūdo mali.* Juv.
The love of popularity holds you in a vice.

Lateat scintillŭla forsan.—Some small spark may yet by chance lie hidden.

Latet anguis in herbâ.—A snake lies concealed in the grass.
" Look before you leap,
For snakes among sweet flowers do creep."
See " *Incēdis per.*" " *Sub omni.*"

Latrans stŏmăchus.—A barking stomach.
" A wolf in his belly."

Latrante uno, latrat statim et alter canis.—When one dog barks, another will follow suit.
" One fool makes many."

Latrantem curatne alta Diana canem?—Doth the moon on high care for the barking of a dog?
" Is the sun dimmed, that gnats do fly in it?" Shaks.

Laudando præcipĕre.—To give instruction in the form of praise.
" He would stroke
The head of modest and ingenuous youth,
That blushed at its own praise." Cowper.

Laudāri a viro laudāto. Cic.—To be praised by a man who has won his laurels.

*Laudātaque virtus
Crescit, et immensum gloria calcar habet.* Ovid.
Virtue is increased by the smile of approval; and the love of renown is the greatest incentive to honourable acts.

> "Virtue would not go far, if a little vanity walked not with it."

> "Fame is the spur that the clear spirit doth raise,
> To scorn delights, and live laborious days." Milton.

*Laudātor tempŏris acti
Se puero.* Hor.
He who sings the praises of his boyhood's days.

> "Ah, happy years, once more who would not be a boy!"
> Byron.

Laudātur ab his, culpātur ab illis. Hor.—He is praised by some, blamed by others.

> "He that would please all, and himself too,
> Undertakes what he cannot do."
> See "*Frustrà labōrat.*"

Laudĭbus arguĭtur vini vinōsus. Hor.—The drunkard is convicted by his praises of wine.

> "Out of the abundance of the heart the mouth speaketh."
> "Such as the man is, such will be his discourse."

Laureŏlam in mustāceo quærĕre. Cic.—To seek a laurel wreath from a bride-cake.

> [To seek glory by some trifling performance. A carpet knight.]

Laureum baculum gesto.*—I bear the laurel-branch.

Laurum momordit. Juv.—He has nibbled at the bay.
> [A poetaster.]

Lavant lacrymæ delictum. Aug.—Repentant tears wash out the stain of guilt.
> "If ye do wrang, mak amends."
>
> "While tears that from repentance flow,
> In bright exhalement reach the skies." Moore.
>
> See "*Quem pœnitet.*"

Lavi manus.—I have washed my hands of it.

Leberide cæcior.†—More blind than the cast-off skin of a serpent.
> "His eyes are like two burnt holes in a blanket."
> Irish Proverb.

Legatus sine mandatis.—An ambassador without authority.

Leniter volat, sed graviter vulnerat.—It flies gently, but wounds deeply.
> [Slander.]

Leonem larvâ terres!—You would frighten a lion with a mask!

Leonem stimulas.—You rouse the fury of the lion.

---

* The laurel was considered an antidote against poison.

† *Leberis*, the old dry cast-off skin of a serpent. The proverb refers to the holes left in the skin where the eyes had been.

Leonīna societas.—A partnership with a lion.

    [The lion takes all.]

    " He, who shareth honey with the bear, hath the least part of it."

Leōnis catŭlum ne alas.—Nourish not a lion's whelp.

    See "*Ale lupōrum.*" "*Tigrĭdis.*"

Leōnis exuvium super crŏcūtam.*—The skin of a lion covering some mongrel beast.

Lĕpŏrem frondium crepĭtus terret.—Even the rustling of leaves will alarm the hare.

Lĕpŏris vitam vivit.—He lives the life of a hare.

    [Ever in fear.]

Leve fit quod benè fertur onus. OVID.—A burthen cheerfully borne becomes light.

    " All things are easy that are done willingly."

    " He never did a good day's work who went grumblingly about it."

    " Not a long day, but a good heart, rids work."

    " No profit grows where is no pleasure ta'en." SHAKS.

Levis est dolor, qui capĕre consilĭum potest. SEN.—Light is that grief, which counsel can allay.

    See "*Strangŭlat.*"

---

    * *Crocūta.* A kind of mongrel beast of Ethiopia.

Levius fit patientiâ,
Quicquid corrigĕre est nefas. Hor.
Patience lightens the burthen we cannot avert.

"What can't be alter'd must be borne, not blamed."

"One must needs like what he cannot hinder."

See "*Feras non.*" "*In re malâ.*" "*Stultum est.*"

Levius solet timēre, qui propĭus timet. Sen.—Our fears vanish as the danger approaches.

"The sense of death is most in apprehension." Shaks.

"Just as the felon condemn'd to die—
With a very natural loathing—
Leaving the sheriff to dream of ropes,
From his gloomy cell in a vision elopes,
To caper on sunny greens and slopes,
Instead of the dance upon nothing." Hood.

Lex taliōnis.—The law of requital of injury by injury.

"If strokes are good to give, they are good to receive."

"What's sauce for the goose is sauce for the gander."

See "*Par pari.*" "*Quid pro.*" "*Ut salutāris.*"

Libĕra me ab homĭne malo, a meipso.—Liberate me from that bad fellow, myself.

"No man has a worse friend than he brings with him from home."

Lībero lecto nihil jucundius. Cic.—A bachelor's bed is the most pleasant.

"Honest men marry soon, wise men never."

"He who marrieth does well, but he who marrieth not, better."

See "*Stulta maritāli.*"

Licet superbus ambŭles pecuniâ,
Fortūna non mutat genus. Hor.

Although you may strut about, proud of your purse, fortune changes not birth.

"No fine clothes can hide the clown."

See "*Asperius.*" "*In vestimentis.*"

Lignum tortum haud unquam rectum.—A crooked log is not to be straightened.

"A depraved mind never comes to good."

"Crooked by nature is never made straight by education."

"Ill beef ne'er made gude broo."

See "*Lanārum nigræ.*"

Ligōnibus aurĕis terram fodĕre.—To dig with golden spades.

[To waste means.]

"To put a racehorse to the plough."

Limis ocŭlis in res aliēnas inquirens.—Prying with sidelong glance into other people's business.

[A busy-body.]

Lingua lapsa verum dicit.—An unguarded speech reveals the truth.

> "A fool's heart dances on his lips."

Lingua mali loquax malæ mentis est indĭcĭum. SYR.—A tongue prone to slander is the proof of a depraved mind.

> "Slanderers are the devil's bellows, to blow up contention."

Lingua mali pars passĭma servi. JUV.—The tongue is the worst part of a bad servant.

Lingua quidem segnis, sed dextĕra viget.—His tongue says little, but powerful is his right arm.

> "Words are for women, actions for men."

> "Strong of his hands, and strong on his legs, but still of his tongue." TENNYSON.

> See "*Destināta.*"

Lingua susurrōnis est pejor felle dracōnis.—The whisperer's tongue is worse than serpent's venom.

> "The poison of asps is under their lips."

> "But scandal's my aversion—I protest
> Against all evil speaking, even in jest." BYRON.

Linguam frænāre plus est quam castra domāre.—It is more difficult to bridle the tongue than to conquer an army.

Linum incīdĕre.—To cut the thread.

[To open a letter; to break a seal.]

Lis litem gĕnĕrat.—One lawsuit begets another.

Litem movēbit, si vel asĭnus canem momordĕrit.—He will embark in litigation, even if a donkey has bitten his dog.

"Some go to law, for the wagging of a straw."

Litĕra scripta manet.—A letter once written cannot be recalled.

Literārum radīces amārœ, fructūs dulces.—Learning has sour roots, but pleasant fruits.

See "*Nil sine.*"

Littŏri loquĕris.—You may as well talk to the sea-shore.

Littus ama;
Altum alii teneant. VIR.
Hug the shore; let others try the deep.

"Wherries must not put out to sea."

"Vessels large may venture more,
But little boats must keep near shore."

Littus sterĭli versāmus arātro. JUV.—We plough the sand on the sea shore.

"We sow the wind, and reap the whirlwind."

Locus est et pluribus umbris.* Hor.—There is room left also for several to bring their friends.

Longo in itinere etiam palea oneri est.—Even a straw becomes heavy, if you carry it far enough.
> "Light burdens, long borne, grow heavy."

Longum est iter per præcepta, breve et efficax per exempla. Sen.—Long is the road to learning by precepts, but short and successful by examples.
> "Precepts may lead, but examples draw."
> See "*Præcepta.*" "*Segnius.*"

Loripedem rectus derideat, æthiopem albus. Juv.—Let the straight-limbed laugh at the club-footed, the white-skinned at the blackamoor.

Lotum gustavit.†—He has tasted of the lotus.

Lucerna sub modio.—A candle under a bushel.
> [Unrevealed merit or skill.]

Lucernam adhibes in meridie.—You use a lantern at noonday.
> "How commentators each dark passage shun,
> And hold their farthing candle to the sun. Young."
> See "*Solem adjuvare.*"

---

* *Umbra,* "a shadow," literally, but used also in the sense of "a guest's friend."
† The fruit of the Lotus was supposed to induce forgetfulness of home.

Lucernam olet. Hor.—It smells of midnight oil.
> [An elaborate piece.]

> *Lucri bonus est odor ex re
> Qualibet.* Juv.

The smell of money is good, come whence it may.
> [Alluding to Vespasian's tax on ordure.]

Lucrum malum æquale dispendio.—An evil gain is equal to a loss.
> "Gaming gains a loss." Byron.

Lucus a non lucendo.*—A grove [so called because you cannot see into it.]

Ludĕre cum sacris.—To indulge in jest on sacred matters.
> "Jest not with the eye, or religion."
> See "*Cede deo.*" "*In cælum.*"

Ludĭte, sed castè.—Observe decorum even in your sport.
> See "*Sint sales.*"

> *Ludus anĭmo debet alĭquando dari,
> Ad cōgĭtandum melior ut redeat tibi.* Phaed.

Relaxation should at times be given to the mind, the better to fit it for toil when resumed.
> See "*Jocāndum.*" "*Stare diu.*" "*Misce.*"

---

* A ridiculous derivation by which a thing is supposed to obtain its name from a quality which it does not possess.

Ludus enim genuit trepĭdum certāmen et iram. HOR.—Even play has ended in fierce strife and anger.

> "Leave jesting whiles it pleaseth, lest it turns to earnest."
> "Play's gude, while it is play."
> "They play till they quarrel."
> See "*Adhibenda.*" "*Cum jocus.*" "*Temperātæ.*"

Lunæ radiis non maturescit botrus.—The grape is not ripened by the rays of the moon.

Lupi alas quæris.—You are looking for wings in a wolf.

> [You hunt for impossibilities.]

> *Lupis et agnis quanta sortīto obtĭgit,*
> *Tecum mihi discordia est.* HOR.

There is as much love between you and me as between the wolf and the lamb.

> "To love as the cat loves mustard."
> "He loves me as the devil loves holy water."
> "Can a mouse fall in love with a cat?"

Lupum aurĭbus tenēre.—To hold a wolf by the ears.

> [To be between two difficulties.]
> See "*A fronte.*"

Lupus circum puteum chorum agit.—The wolf dances round the well.

> [Longing for the water he cannot reach.]

Lupus pilum mutat, non mentem.—The wolf changes his hair, but not his nature.

"The fox may grow gray, but never good."

See "*Natūram expellas.*" "*Pardus macŭlas.*"

Lux affulsit.—There is a good time coming.

"Come what come may,
Time and the hour runs through the roughest day." SHAKS.

Luxurĭant anĭmi rebus plerumque secundis. OVID.—Our hearts run riot in prosperity.

See "*Asperius nihil.*"

MACHINAS post bellum adferre.—To bring out the implements of war, when the battle is over.

"After meat comes mustard."
See "*Mortuum unguento.*" "*Post bellum.*"

Magis exūrunt, quos secrētæ lacĕrant curæ. SEN.—Those griefs burn most which gall in secret.

"Sorrow concealed, like an oven stopp'd,
Doth burn the heart to cinders, where it is." SHAKS.
See "*Curæ leves.*" "*Levis est.*" "*Strangŭlat.*"

Magis illa juvant, quæ pluris emuntur. JUV.—Those things please more, which are more expensive.

"Things hardly attained are the longer retained."
See "*Quod datur.*" "*Quod rarum.*"

Magistrātus indĭcat virum.—Office tests the man.

"But man, proud man,
Drest in a little brief authority,—
Plays such fantastic tricks before high heaven
As make the angels weep." SHAKS.

Magna cīvĭtas, magna solitūdo.—A great city, a great desert.
> "A crowd is not company."

Magna est verĭtas et prævalēbit.—Truth is great and will prevail.
> "Oil and truth will get uppermost at last."
> "The credit got by a lie lasts only till the truth comes out."
> "O, while you live, tell truth, and shame the devil." SHAKS.
> "An honest tale speeds best." SHAKS.
> "Falsehood is often rocked by truth, but she soon outgrows her cradle, and discards her nurse." COLTON.
>> See "*Verĭtas premĭtur.*" "*Vincit omnia.*"

Magna servĭtus est magna fortūna. SEN.—A great fortune is a great slavery.

Magnas inter opes inops.—Poor though in the midst of wealth.

Magni animi est injurias despĭcĕre. SEN.—It is a proof of nobility of mind to despise injuries.
> "Write injuries in dust, but kindnesses in marble."
> "For ill do well,
> Then fear not hell."
>> See "*Infirmi est.*" "*Quo quisque est.*"

Magni nomĭnis umbra. LUC.—The shadow of a mighty name.

Magnum est vectīgal parsimonia.—Frugality is a great revenue.

"Frugality is an estate alone."
"A fool and his money are soon parted."
"Penny and penny laid up will be many."
"Thrift is better than an annuity."
See "*Cogitāto.*" "*Festo die.*"

Magnus Alexander corpŏre parvus erat.—Alexander the Great was but of small stature.

"A little body doth often harbour a great soul."

Magnus sine virĭbus ignis Incassum furit. VIR.
Impotent fury rages powerless and to no purpose.

"And quick his colour went and came,
As fear and rage alternate rose." SCOTT.
"Anger can't stand, without a strong hand."
"Anger without power is folly."

Majōra perdes, parva ni servavĕris.—He, who neglects the little, loses the greater.

"Take care of the halfpence and pence, and the shillings and pounds will take care of themselves." FRANKLIN.
See "*Magnum est.*"

Malâ ducis avi domum. HOR.—In an evil hour thou bring'st her home.

[You are marrying a shrew.]

Mala gallīna, malum ovum.—Bad fowl, bad egg.

"Muddy springs will have muddy streams."

See "*Mali corvi.*"

Mala mens, malus anĭmus.—Bad head, bad heart.

Mala sĕnium accelĕrant.—Sorrow brings on premature old age.

"Stained
With grief, that's beauty's canker." SHAKS.

"My hair is grey, but not with years." BYRON.

Mala ultro adsunt.—Sorrows come uninvited.

"Sorrow and ill weather come unsent for."

Malè conjugāti.—An ill-assorted couple.

"Ill-yoked."

"Tied to the sowre apple-tree."

Malè cuncta mĭnistrat Impĕtus. STAT.
Anger manages everything badly.

"A headstrong man and a fool may wear the same cap."

See "*Irātus cum.*" "*Non est ratio.*"

Malè narrando fabŭla depravātur.—The tale is marred in the telling.

"Tell it well, or say nothing."

Malè parta, malè dīlābuntur.

"Evil gotten, evil spent."

"Ill gotten goods seldom prosper."

"What comes from the fife goes back to the drum."

"As won, so spent."

"Lightly come, lightly go."

"Didst thou never hear,
That things ill got had ever bad success?" SHAKS.

See "*De malè.*"

Malè sapit, qui sibi non sapit.—He is wise to no purpose, who is not wise for himself.

Malè secum agit æger, medĭcum qui hærēdem facit. SYR.—Little does the sick man consult his own interests, who makes his physician his heir.

Malĕdĭcus a malĕfĭco non distat nisi occāsiōne. QUINT.—He who speaks evil only differs from him who does evil in that he lacks opportunity.

Malĕfacĕre qui vult, nusquam non causam invĕniet. SYR.—He who wishes to injure another, will soon find a pretext.

"Faults are thick where love is thin."

"'Tis an easy thing to find a staff to beat a dog."

"The wolf never wants a pretext against the lamb."

"He that would hang his dog, gives out first, that he is mad."

"But when to mischief mortals bend their will,
How soon they find fit instruments of ill." POPE.

Mali corvi malum ovum.

>"Bad the crow, bad the egg."
>
>"If better were within, better would come out."
>
>"When the root is worthless so is the tree."
>
>See "*Mala gallīna.*"   "*Nunquam ex.*"

Mali prīncĭpii malus finis.—Bad beginnings lead to bad results.

>"Who begins amiss ends amiss."
>
>"A crooked stick will have a crooked shadow."
>
>"A bad day never hath a good night."
>
>"Bad grass does not make good hay."
>
>See "*Lignum.*"

Mali viri inutĭlia munĕra.—We never profit by the gifts of the wicked.

>"A wicked man's gift hath a touch of his master."

Malis avibus.—With bad luck.

Malis mala succēdunt.—Evils follow each other.

>"It never rains but it pours."
>
>"Fortune rarely brings good or evil singly."
>
>"Woes cluster; rare are solitary woes;
>They love a train, they tread each other's heel."   YOUNG.
>
>"One sorrow never comes but brings an heir,
>That may succeed as his inheritor."   SHAKS.
>
>See "*Fortūna nulli.*"

Malo malo malo malo.—I would rather be in an apple-tree, than a bad man in distress.

Malo mori quàm fœdāri.—I prefer death to disgrace.

Malo nodo malus quærendus cuneus.—A hard knot requires a hard wedge.
> "One heat another heat expels." SHAKS.
>> See "*Amāra bilis.*" "*Extremis.*" "*Non opus est.*"

Malum benè condĭtum ne mōvĕris.—Re-open not a wound once healed.
> "When ill-luck falls asleep let nobody wake her."
> "Do not rake up old grievances."
>> "You rub the sore
> When you should bring the plaster!" SHAKS.
>> See "*Parcendum.*" "*Quæ dolent.*" "*Quiēta non.*"

Malum consilium consultōri pessĭmum.—He that gives bad counsel suffers most by it.
> "Who sows thorns let him not walk bare-foot."

Malum malo medicāri.—To cure evil by evil.
> "Poison quells poison."
>> See "*Dæmŏna dæmŏne.*" "*Extrēmis.*"

Malum vas non frangĭtur.—A useless pitcher does not get broken.
> "Nought is never in danger."
> "Ill vessels seldom miscarry."
> "A bad thing never dies."
> "A creaking door hangs long on its hinges."

Malus, ubi bonum se simŭlat, tunc est pessĭmus. SYR.—A bad man becomes worse when he apes a saint.

> "No rogue like the godly rogue."
>
> "No villain like the conscientious villain."
>
> "Hypocritical piety is double iniquity."
>
> "The more honesty a man has the less he affects the air of a saint." LAVATER.
>
> "With devotion's visage,
> And pious action, we do sugar o'er
> The devil himself." SHAKS.
>
> "A man may cry, Church! Church! at ev'ry word,
>   With no more piety than other people—
> A daw's not reckoned a religious bird
>   Because it keeps a-cawing from a steeple." HOOD.
>
> See "*Fronte polītus.*" "*Habent insidias.*"

Mandrabūli in morem.—After the manner of Mandrabulus [*i. e.*, going from worse to worse].

Manĭbus pedĭbusque.—Hand and foot [with all our strength and resolution.]

> "Tooth and nail."

*Manifesta phrenēsis,
Ut lŏcŭples moriāris, egenti vivĕre fato?* JUV.

Is it not sheer madness to live poor to die rich?

> "It would make a man scratch where it doth not itch,
> To see a man live poor to die rich.
>
> See "*Frustrà habet.*" "*Quo mihi.*"

Manum ad os apponĕre.—To put his finger on his lips.
> [To refuse to reveal what he knows.]

Manus manum lavat.—One hand washes the other.
> "Do good if you expect to receive it."
> "Trim my beard, and I will trim your top-knot."
> See "*Gratia gratiam.*" "*Petimusque.*"

Mari aquam addĕre.—To add water to the ocean.
> See "*Athenas noctuas.*"

Mărĭtĭmus quum sis, ne velis fĭĕri terrestris.—When once at sea, do not long to be on shore.
> [Be satisfied with your calling in life.]
> "Being on sea, sail; being on land, settle."

Mars gravĭor sub pace latet. CLAUD.—A far greater warfare lies hidden under this assumed peace.
> See "*Ira, quæ.*"

Mater artĭum necessĭtas.
> "Necessity is the mother of invention."

Matĕriem superābat opus.—The workmanship surpassed the material.

Maturè fias senex, si diu velis esse senex.—Be old betimes, if you wish your old age to last.
> "Be old when young, if you would be young when old."
> "Old young, and old long."
> "He that corrects not youth, controls not age."
> "Diseases are the interest of pleasures."
> See "*Bonum servat.*" "*Quæ peccāmus.*"

Maxĭma debētur puĕro reverentia. Juv.—The greatest consideration is due to the innocence of youth.

> "Little pitchers have long ears."
> "Children have wide ears and long tongues."
> "Where old age is evil youth can learn no good."
> "Children pick up words, as pigeons peas,
> And utter them again as God shall please."
> "The child saith nothing but what he heard at the fireside."
> "For 'tis not good that children should know any wickedness."
> Shaks.
> See "*Nil dictu fœdum.*"

Maxĭma illĕcĕbra est peccandi impūnitātis spes. Cic.—The hope of escaping with impunity is the greatest incentive to vice.

> "Nothing emboldens sin so much as mercy." Shaks.

Maxĭma quæque domus servis est plena superbis. Juv.—Every great house is full of saucy servants.

> "Like master, like man."

Maxĭmus in minĭmis.—Unequalled in the smallest matters.

Meâ virtūte me involvo. Hor.—In my integrity I'll wrap me up.

Medĭo de fonte lepōrum
Surgit amāri alĭquid, quod in ipsis florĭbus angit. Lucr.

From the midst of the very fountain of pleasure, something of bitterness arises to vex us in the flower of enjoyment.

> "There's not a string attuned to mirth,
> But has its chord in melancholy." Hood.

"So comes a reck'ning when the banquet's oer,
The dreadful reckoning, and men smile no more." **Gay.**

"Our sincerest laughter
With some pain is fraught:
Our sweetest songs are those which tell of saddest thought."
Shelley.

See "*Inter delicias.*" "*Nihil est ab.*" "*Omni malo.*"

Medio tutissĭmus ibis.—A middle course is the safest.

*Mel in ore, verba lactis,
Fel in corde, fraus in factis.*

Honey-tongued, soft spoken, malicious, and unprincipled in conduct.

"A honey tongue, a heart of gall."

"He was a man
Who stole the livery of the court of Heaven
To serve the devil in." **Pollok.**

"Demons in act, but gods at least in face." **Byron.**

"There is no vice so simple, but assumes
Some mark of virtue on his outward parts." **Shaks.**

See "*Decipĭmur.*" "*Fronte polītus.*" "*Habent insidias.*"

Mel satietātem gignit.—Honey cloys.

"Even sugar itself may spoil a good dish."

"The sweetest honey
Is loathsome in its own deliciousness." **Shaks.**

"Poor Peggy hawks nosegays from street to street
Till—think of that who find life so sweet!—
She hates the smell of roses!" **Hood.**

Melior est justĭtia verè præveniens, quam sevērè puniens.—
Justice is exercised in the proper prevention, rather than in the severe punishment, of crime.
> "Prevention is better than cure."

> "Criminals are punished, that others may be amended."

Meliorem præsto magistro Dīscipŭlum. Juv.
The pupil will eclipse his tutor, I warrant.

Melius est cavēre semper, quam pati semel.—It is better to be always prepared than to suffer once.
> [Keep oil in your lamps.]

> "He that fears danger in time seldom feels it."

> See "*Prævīsus.*" "*Monĭti.*" "*Tempŏre pacis.*"

Melius est habēre malōrum odium, quam consortium.—The hatred of knaves is to be preferred to their company.

Melle litus gladius.—A sword anointed with honey.
> "I kissed thee, ere I killed thee." Shaks.

> See "*Nullæ sunt.*" "*Ira, quæ.*"

Mellītum venēnum blanda oratio.—A soft-spoken compliment is honied poison.
> "For over-warmth, if false, is worse than truth." Byron.

Memento quod es homo.—Forget not that you are a man.
> See "*Homo sum.*"

Mĕmŏrem immĕmŏrem facit, qui monet quod memor memĭnit.
PLAUT.—Remind a man of what he remembers, and you will make him forget it.

Memŏrem mones.   PLAUT.—You needn't remind me of that.

Mendācem memŏrem esse oportet.   QUINT.
"A liar should have a good memory."

Mendāci hŏmĭni, ne verum quidem dīcenti, crēdĕre solēmus.
CIC.—We believe not a liar, even when he is speaking the truth.

Mendīco ne parentes quidem amīci sunt.—A beggar is not favoured even by his relations.

Mens immōta manet; lachrymæ volvuntur inānes.   VIR.—His resolution is unshaken; tears, though shed, avail not.

"But neither bended knees, pure hands held up,
Sad sighs, deep groans, nor silver-shedding tears,
Could penetrate her uncompassionate sire."   SHAKS.

Mens sibi conscia recti.—A mind conscious of its own rectitude.

"What stronger breast-plate than a heart untainted."   SHAKS.

Mensque pati durum sustĭnet ægra nihil.   OVID.—When the heart is sick it cannot bear the slightest annoyance.

"The tear that is wiped with a little address,
May be follow'd perhaps by a smile."   COWPER.

Mense Maio nubunt malè.*—They marry under bad auspices who marry in the month of May.

---

* It was considered by the ancients unlucky to marry in the month of May."

Mentis gratissimus error.—A delightful hallucination.

"I found not Cassio's kisses on her lips." SHAKS.

Merx ultrōnea putet.—Puffed goods are putrid.

"Good wine needs no bush."

"Self-praise is no recommendation."

"He that laughs at his ain joke spoils the sport o't."

Messe tenus propriâ vive. PERS.—Live according to your income.

"Cut your coat according to your cloth."

"The goat must browse where she is tied."

See "*Infra tuam.*"

Metīri se quemque suo mŏdŭlo ac pede verum est. HOR.—It is proper that every man should measure himself by his own proportion and standard.

"Stretch your arm no further than your sleeve will reach."

See "*Infra tuam.*"

Metŭe senectam, non enim sola advĕnit.—Fear increasing age, for it does not come without companions.

"They kindly leave us, but not quite alone,
But in good company, the gout or stone." BYRON.

Metum inānem metuisti.—You are needlessly alarmed.

"Frightened at bugbears."

Metus enim mortis musĭcâ depellĭtur.—Even the fear of death is dispelled by music.

"The shrill trump,
The spirit-stirring drum, the ear-piercing fife." SHAKS.

Minĭma possunt, qui plurĭma jactant.—They can do least who boast loudest.

"A long tongue is a sign of a short hand."

"His bark is worse than his bite."

"Threatened folk live long."

"Empty pitchers ring loudest."

See "*Canes timĭdi.*" "*Vacuum vas.*"

Minor est quàm servus, dŏmĭnus qui servos timet. Syr.—He who fears his servants is less than a servant.

Minùs de istis labōro quàm de ranis palustrĭbus.—I am less concerned about them than about the croaking frogs in the marsh.

Minus placet, magis quod suadētur. Plaut.—That least pleases us which is most urged on us.

Minūtŭla pluvia imbrem parit.—Little drops produce the shower.

"Grain by grain the hen fills her crop."

"The whole ocean is made up of single drops."

"Mony sma's mak a great."

"Link by link the coat of mail is made."

"Word by word the big books are made."

See "*De parvis.*" "*Nihil est aliud.*"

Mĭnuunt præsentia famam.—Things rumoured lessen in importance as they assume reality.

> "The lion's not half so fierce as he's painted."
>
> "The fear of war is worse than war itself."
>
> "The wolf is always said to be more terrible than he is."
>
> "Present fears
> Are less than horrible imaginings." SHAKS.
>
> See "*Omne ignōtum.*"

Misce stultitiam consiliis brevem. HOR.—Add a sprinkling of folly to your long deliberations.

> "Mix with your grave designs a little pleasure;
> Each day of business has its hour of leisure." WEST.
>
> See "*Dulce est.*"

Miscēbis sacra profānis.—You will mix what is sacred with what is profane.

Miscentur tristia lætis.—Pain mingles with pleasure.

> "No sunshine but hath some shadow."
>
> "From the cradle to the tomb,
> Not all gladness, not all gloom."
>
> See "*Inter delicias.*"

Miserrĭma est fortūna quæ caret inimīco. SYR.—It is a most miserable lot to be without an enemy.

> [No man can be successful without being envied and hated.]
>
> "Towers are measured by their shadows, and great men by their calumniators."
>
> "By many indignities we come to dignities."
>
> "The fox thrives best when he is most cursed."

"If you have no enemies it is a sign fortune has forgot you."

"He who surpasses or subdues mankind,
Must look down on the hate of those below." BYRON.

Misĕrum est ab eo lædi de quo non possis queri. SYR.—It is a wretched thing to suffer at the hand of one of whom we cannot complain.

Misĕrum est alienâ vivĕre quadrâ.—It is a wretched position to be dependent on others for support.

*Misĕrum est aliōrum incumbĕre famæ,
Ne collapsa ruant subductis tecta columnis.* JUV.

It is a wretched thing to rest upon the fame of others, lest, the supporting pillar being removed, the superstructure should collapse in ruin.

Misĕrum est fuisse.—The remembrance of past pleasures adds to present sorrows.

"The memory of happiness makes misery woful."

"Of joys departed
Not to return, how painful the remembrance." R. BLAIR.

"No greater grief than to remember days
Of joy when misery is at hand." CAREY'S DANTE.

"This is truth the poet sings,
That a sorrow's crown of sorrows is remembering happier things."
TENNYSON.

Moderāta durant.—Moderate measures succeed best.

"Too hot to last."

Modŏ idiōta, mox clērĭcus.—Now a layman, to-morrow a clerk.

Modŏ togātus, modŏ palliātus. Cic.—Now clothed like a Roman, now like a Greek.

[An inconstant, perfidious man.]

See "*Quo teneam.*"

Mœrent omnes, et si roges eos reddĕre causam, non possunt.—All men grieve, and if you ask them the reason why, they cannot tell it.

"A tear bedews my Delia's eye,
From morn till dewy eve;
But if you ask the reason why,
She can't tell, I believe."

See "*Uberĭbus.*"

Mollia tempŏra fandi. Hor. — Opportune times for speaking.

"When his heart is glad
Of the full harvest, I will speak to him." Tennyson.

Monĭti meliōra sequāmur.—Being warned, let us pursue a better course.

"If you will not hear reason, she will surely rap your knuckles."

"They that will not be counselled cannot be helped."

"He was slain that had warning, not he that took it."

See "*Turbĭnem felix.*"

Mons cum monte non miscebĭtur.—Mountains never unite.

    [Haughty people rarely fraternize.]

    "Friends may meet, but mountains never greet."

        See "*In se magna.*"

        Monstrum nullâ virtūte redemptum
A vitiis. Juv.

A brute without a single redeeming point.

Mora omnis ingrāta est, sed facit sapientiam. Syr.—All delay is irksome, but it teaches us wisdom.

    "There is no royal road to learning."

        See "*Romanus.*"

Morbum morbo addĕre—To add malady to malady.

Mordēre labrum.—To bite the lip.

    [To manifest indignation.]

Mores dispăres dispăria studia sequuntur. Cic.—Men of different tastes have different pursuits.

    "No dish pleases all palates alike."

    "Many men, many minds."

        See "*Alia aliis.*" "*Non omnes eadem.*"

Moriendum priusquam!—Death is preferable.

Mors in ollâ.—There's death in the pot.

    "A rich mouthful, a heavy groan."

Mors lupi, agnis vita.—Death to the wolf is life to the lambs.

Mors omnĭbus commūnis.—Death is common to all.

> "Death is a black camel which kneels at every man's gate."
>
> "Death rides on every passing breeze:
> He lurks in every flower." HEBER.

Mors optĭma rapit, deterrĭma relinquit.—Death snatches away the most deserving, and leaves the wicked.

> "The good die first:
> And those, whose hearts are dry as summer dust,
> Burn to the socket."
>
> See " *Optĭma citissimè.*" " *Quem dî.*"

Mors sceptra ligōnĭbus æquat.—Death brings to a level spades and sceptres.

> "A thousand pounds and a bottle of hay are all one at domesday."
>
> "The greatest king must at last go to bed with a shovel."
>
> "Sceptre and crown must tumble down
> And in the dust be equal made
> With the poor crooked scythe and spade." SHIRLEY.
>
> "We start from the Mother's Arms and we run to the Dust-shovel." DICKENS.

Mortui non mordent.—Dead men do not bite.

Mortŭo leōni et lĕpōres insultant.—Even hares insult a dead lion.

> "A ploughman on his legs is higher than a gentleman on his knees."
>
> See " *Captīvum impūne.*"

Mortuo verba facit.—He talks to a dead man.

"He talks to the wind."

Mortuum unguento perungis.—You anoint the dead man with salve.

"After death the doctor."

See "*Machĭnas post.*" "*Post bellum.*"

Moveat cornīcŭla risum
Furtīvis nudāta colōribus. HOR.

The jackdaw, stript of her stolen colours, provokes our laughter.

Mox
Bruma recurrit iners. HOR.

Dull winter will re-appear.

"Winter is summer's heir."

Muliĕbrem tollĭte luctum!—Away with grieving, only fit for women.

"For gnarling sorrow hath less power to bite
The man, that mocks at it, and sets it light." SHAKS.

"O let not women's weapons, water-drops,
Stain my man's cheeks!" SHAKS.

Mulier imperātor et mulier miles.—A woman for a general, and the soldiers will be women.

"A woman's general: what should we fear?" SHAKS.

Mulier sævissima tunc est,
Quum stimŭlos odio pudor admŏvet. JUV.

A woman is most merciless when shame goads on her hate.

>"A woman scorn'd is pitiless as fate,
>For then the dread of shame adds stings to hate." GIFFORD.

>" A tigress, robb'd of young, a lioness,
> Or other interesting beast of prey,
>Are similes at hand for the distress
> Of ladies who cannot have their own way." BYRON.

>See "*Implacābĭles.*"

Mŭlĭĕrem ornat silentium.—Silence is the greatest ornament in a woman.

>"Silence is a fine jewel for a woman, but it is little worn."

Mŭlĭĕri nè credas, nè mortuæ quidem.—Trust not a woman, even when dead.

>[She may feign death.]

Multa cadunt inter călĭcem suprēmaque labra. LABER.

>"There's many a slip,
>'Twixt the cup and the lip."

>" Though the bird's in the net
>It may get away yet."

>See "*Inter manum.*" "*Non omnia eveniunt.*"

Multa docet fames.—Hunger teaches us many a lesson.

>"Only by the candle, held in the skeleton hand of Poverty, can man read his own dark heart." BULWER.

*Multa petentĭbus
Desunt multa.* Hor.

The covetous are always in want.

"When all sins grow old covetousness is young."

"Poor and content, is rich, and rich enough,
But riches, fineless, is as poor as winter
To him that ever fears he shall be poor." Shaks.

See "*Crescit amor.*"

Multa senem circumvĕniunt incommŏda.—Many annoyances surround an aged man.

"Care keeps his watch in every old man's eye." Shaks.

Multa verba, modĭca fides.—Many words, little credit.

"Great boast, small roast."

"Great talkers, little doers."

"Friend, for your epitaph I'm grieved,
  Where still so much is said;
One half will never be believed,
  The other never read." Pope.

Multæ manus onus levĭus facĭunt.

"Many hands make light work."

"Three, helping one another, bear the burden of six."

See "*Divīsum sic.*"

Multæ regum aures atque ocŭli.—Kings have many ears and many eyes too.

Multæ terricŏlis linguæ, cœlestĭbus una.—There are many languages on earth, but one in heaven.

Multas amicitias silentium dirēmit.—The silence resulting from absence has destroyed many a friendship.

"Long absent, soon forgotten."

"Out of mind, when out of view." GAY.

"The remedy for love is—land between."

See "*Absens hæres.*" "*Non sunt amīci.*"

Multi morbi curantur abstinentiâ. CELS.—Many diseases may be cured by abstinence.

"Diet cures more than the lancet."

"By suppers more have been killed than Galen ever cured."

See "*Plures crapŭla.*"

Multi qui boves stimŭlent, pauci aratōres.—Many can drive an ox; few can plough.

"All are not hunters that blow the horn."

"More belongs to riding than a pair of boots."

See "*Non est venātor.*" "*Non ōmnes qui.*" "*Qui tauros.*"

Multi te odĕrint si teipsum ames.—Many will hate you if you love yourself.

"A man gains nothing by vain glory but contempt and hatred."

"He that boasteth of himself affronteth his company."

See "*Proprio laus.*"

Multis ictĭbus dejicitur quercus.—By repeated blows even the oak is felled.

"Little strokes fell great oaks."

See "*Gutta cavat.*"

Multis minātur, qui uni facit injuriam. SYR.—He who injures one man threatens many.

"He threatens many that hath injured one." BEN JONSON.

Multis parâsse divĭtias non finis misĕriārum fuit sed mutātio. SEN.—To have acquired wealth is with many not to end but to change the nature of their troubles.

"Little wealth, little care."

"Who would not wish to be from wealth exempt,
"Since riches point to misery and contempt?" SHAKS.

See "*Crescentem.*"

Multis terrĭbĭlis, cavēto multos. AUSON.—If you are dreaded by many then beware of many.

Multitūdo non ratīone ducĭtur, sed impĕtu.—The rabble is not influenced by reason, but blind impulse.

Multò plures satiĕtas quam fames perdĭdit viros.—Satiety has killed more men than hunger.

"More die by food than famine."

See "*Plures occĭdit.*" "*Multi morbi.*"

Multōrum manĭbus grande levātur onus.—By the hands of many a great work is made light.

See "*Multæ manus.*"

Multos in summâ periculâ misit,
Venturi timor ipse mali. Luc.

The apprehension of approaching evil has hurried many into the utmost danger.

Multos ingrātos invĕnīmus, plures făcĭmus.—We find much ingratitude, and create more.

Munerĭbus vel Dii capiuntur.—Even the gods are conciliated by offerings.

Munĕrum anĭmus optĭmus est.—The goodwill accompanying the gift is the best portion of it.

"A cheerful look makes a dish a feast."

"Welcome is the best cheer."

See "*Dat benè.*"

Munus exĭguum sed opportūnum.—A small gift, but well-timed.

Murem pro leōne ostendit.—He makes a lion of a mouse.

"All his geese are swans."

"He cries wine, and sells vinegar."

See "*Arcem ex.*" "*Parturiunt.*"

Mures migravĕrunt.—The mice have taken themselves off.

"Wise rats run from a falling house."

"The very rats
Instinctively had quit it." SHAKS.

Muris in morem.—After the fashion of a mouse. [*i. e.* living off others.]

Murus æreus conscientia sana.—A clear conscience is a wall of brass.

> "A peace above all earthly dignities,
> A still and quiet conscience." SHAKS.

Mus in pice.—A mouse in pitch.

> [A man engaged in useless and perplexing inquiries.]

Mus non uni fidit antro. PLAUT.—A mouse relies not solely on one hole.

> "The rat which has but one hole is soon caught."

> "The mouse that only trusts to one poor hole,
> Can never be a mouse of any soul."

Mus salit in stratum, cum scit non adfŏre catum.

> "When the cat's away,
> The mouse will play."

Musca, canes, mimi, veniunt ad fercŭla primi.—Flies, dogs, and mimics are the first to rush to the dish.

Musĭca est mentis medicīna mœstæ.—Music is the best cure for a sorrowing mind.

> "My soul is dark! oh quickly string
> The harp I yet can brook to hear." BYRON.

Musĭca multos magis dementat, quam vinum.—Music induces more madness in many than wine.

Musĭca serva dei.—Music is the handmaid of divinity.

*Mutāto nōmĭne, de te
Fabŭla narrātur.* Hor.

Change but the name, and you are the subject of the story.

"And Nathan said unto David: 'Thou art the man.'"

Mutua defensio tutissĭma.—A combined defence is the safest.

"The lone sheep is in danger of the wolf."
See "*Vis unīta.*"

Mutum est pictūra poēmă.—A picture is a poem wanting words.

Mutuum muli scabunt.—Mules help to scratch each other.

[The bad commend each other.]

Myrīcæ citius poma ferent.—Sooner will the tamarisk bear apples.

*Nam dives qui fĭĕri vult,
Et cito vult fĭĕri.* Juv.

He who desires to become rich, wishes to become so as quickly as possible.

*Nam gĕnus et prŏăvos et quæ non fēcĭmus ipsi,
Vix ea nostra voco.* Ovid.

Pedigree and ancestry and what we ourselves have not achieved, I scarcely recognize as our own.

"Nobility is nothing but ancient riches, and money is the world's idol."

"He is the best gentleman, who is the son of his own deserts."

"What boots it on the lineal tree to trace
Through many a branch the founders of our race." Gifford.

"Fall back upon a name? rest, rot in that?
Not keep it noble, make it nobler? Fools!" Tennyson.

See "*Nobilĭtas morum.*" "*Nobilitas sine.*" "*Qui genus.*" "*Stemmăta.*"

Nam neque divitibus contingunt gaudia solis. Hor.—God made not pleasures for the rich alone.

Nam quod uni profŭit, hoc aliĭs erat exitio.—What has benefited one has destroyed others.

> "One man's breath 's another man's death."
>
> "Where the bee sucks honey the spider sucks poison."
>
> "But that old man, who is lord of the broad estate and the hall, Dropped off gorged from a scheme which left us flaccid and drained." TENNYSON.
>
> See "*Quod cibus.*" "*Quod suave.*"

Nam scĕlus intra se tacĭtum qui cogĭtat ullum,
Facti crīmĕn habet. JUV.

He who meditates a crime secretly within himself has all the guilt of the act.

> "He that looketh on a woman to lust after her, hath committed adultery already with her in his heart."
>
> "Man punishes the action, but God the intention."
>
> "What is the sin which is not
> Sin in itself? Can circumstance make sin
> Or virtue?" BYRON.
>
> See "*Injuriam.*"

Nam ut quisque est vir optĭmus, ita difficillĭme esse alios imprŏbos suspĭcātur. CIC.—The more virtuous a man himself is, the less does he suspect baseness in others.

> "Suspicion always haunts the guilty mind." SHAKS.

Narrat quod nec ad cœlum, nec ad terram, pertĭnet.—He says what is wholly irrelevant.

> "He tells a tale of a tub."

*Narrātur et prisci Catōnis
Sæpe mero căluisse virtus.* Hor.

It is said that the propriety even of old Cato often yielded to the exciting influence of the grape.

Nasci misĕrum, vivĕre pœna, angusta mori.—It is a misery to be born, a punishment to live, and a trouble to die.

"I wept when I was born, and every day shows why."

"He that will have no trouble in this world must not be born in it."

Nascĭmur poetæ, fĭmus oratōres. Cic.—We are born poets, we become orators.

*Nascĭtur in vento, vento restinguitur ignis;
Lenis alit flammam, grandior aura necat.* Ovid.

A light breath fans the flame, a violent gust extinguishes it.

"Little sticks kindle a fire, great ones put it out."

"Though little fire grows great with little wind,
Yet extreme gusts will blow out fire and all." Shaks.

Natio comæda est. Juv.—Acting is the forte of all their race.

*Natūra beātis
Omnibŭs esse dedit, si quis cognōvĕrit uti.* Claud.

Nature has placed his own happiness in each man's hands, if he only knew how to use it.

"Ourselves are to ourselves the cause of ill." Churchill.

Natūra dedit agros, ars humāna ædificāvit urbes. Varro.—Nature made the fields and man the cities.

> "God the first garden made, and the first city Cain." Cowley.
> "God made the country and man made the town." Cowper.

Natūra tu illi pater es, consiliis ego. Ter.—You are his father by nature, I by counsel.

Natūram expellas furcâ, tamen usque recurret. Hor.—You may suppress natural propensities by force, but they will be certain to re-appear.

> "What's bred in the bone will never out of the flesh."
> "Plant the crab-tree where you will it will never bear pippins."
> "Whether you boil snow or pound it you can have but water of it."
>> See "*Lupus pilum.*" "*Pardus macŭlas.*"

Naufrăgium rerum est mulĭer malefĭda marīto.—A faithless wife is shipwreck to a house.

Ne ad aures quidem scalpendas otium est.—He has not leisure even to scratch his ears.

Ne Apollo quidem intellĭgat.—It would puzzle even Apollo to understand it.

Ne, cinĕrem vitans, in prunas incĭdas.—See that in avoiding cinders you step not on burning coals.

Ne cortĭcem quidem dedĕrit.—He won't give us so much as the skin.

Ne credas undam placidam non esse profundam.—Believe not that the stream is shallow because its surface is smooth.

> "In the coldest flint there is hot fire."
> "Deep rivers move with silent majesty, shallow brooks are noisy."
> See "*Altissima.*" "*Cave tibi.*"

Ne cui de te plus quam tibi credas.—Believe no man more than yourself when you are spoken of. [Let your own conscience be a check against the effect of the flattery of others.]

Ne cuivis dextram injeceris.—Offer not the right hand of friendship to every one.

> "He who makes friends of all keeps none."
> "Sudden trust brings sudden repentance."
> See "*Fide sed cui.*" "*Nervi et.*" "*Qui in amōrem.*"

Ne cuivis invideas.—Envy no man.

Ne cuivis serviat ensis.—Let not your sword be drawn at any man's bidding.

Ne depugnes in alieno negotio.—Interfere not in the quarrels of others.

> "He that passeth by, and meddleth with strife belonging not to him, is like one that taketh a dog by the ears."
>
> "Those, who in quarrels interpose,
> Must often wipe a bloody nose." GAY.

Ne despicias debĭlem; nam culex fodit ocŭlum leōnis.—Despise not the weak: the gnat stings the eyes of the lion.

> "Despise your enemy and you will soon be beaten."
>> See "*Inest et.*" "*Nihil tam firmum.*"

Ne festīna loqui.—Never speak in a hurry.

Ne gladium tollas, mulier.—Being but a woman, raise not the sword.

> [Offer not assistance when you can be of no service.]

Ne gleba agri illi relicta ad locum sepultūræ.—He has not even a clod of earth left to cover his remains.

> [A man reduced to extreme poverty.]

Ne Hercules quidem adversus duos.—Hercules himself could not cope with two assailants.

> "Two to one is odds."
>> See "*Uni cum.*"

Ne Jupiter quidem omnĭbus placet.—Jupiter himself cannot please everybody.

> "He that would please all and himself too
> Undertakes what he cannot do."

Ne major benignĭtas sit, quam facultates. Cic.—Our liberality should not exceed our ability.

Ne malōrum memineris.—Bear no malice.

> "Let not the sun go down upon your wrath."
> "Sweet mercy is nobility's true badge." Shaks.
>> See "*Infirmi est.*" "*Magni animi.*"

Ne prius antĭdŏtum quam venēnum.—Take not the antidote before the poison.

> "Cry not out before you are hurt."
> "Call not a surgeon before you are wounded."
> "Never ask pardon before you are accused."

Ne pŭero glădium.—Trust not a sword in the hands of a boy.

Ne quære mollia, ne tibi contingant dura.—Seek not the luxuries of life lest you reap sorrow.

> "Life ain't all beer and skittles." SAM SLICK.
>> See "*Festo die.*"

Ne quid expectes amīcos facĕre, quod per te queas.—Never expect your friends to do for you that which you can yourself accomplish.

Ne quid moveāre verbōrum strepĭtu.—Don't be frightened at high-sounding words.

> "Must I give way and room to your rash choler?" SHAKS.
>> See "*Canes timĭdi.*"

Ne quid nimis. TER.—Too much of anything is bad.

> "More than enough is too much."
> "Too much of one thing is good for nothing."
> "Enough's as good as a feast."
>> See "*Omne nimium.*"

Ne sis unquam elātus.—Never be too much elated.

Ne stilla quidem.—Not even a drop is left.

> "O churl! drink all; and leave no friendly drop!" SHAKS.

Ne supra pedem calceus.—Wear not boots too big for your feet.
> See "*Ne sutor.*"

Ne sutor ultra crĕpĭdam.—The cobbler should not go beyond his last.

> [Meddle not in things which you do not understand.]
> "Blind men should not judge of colours."

Ne te semper inops agĭtet vexetque cupīdo. HOR.—Be not for ever harassed by impotent desire.

> "Our content
> Is our best having." SHAKS.
> "A man's discontent is his worst evil."
> "He is well constituted who grieves not for what he has not, and rejoices for what he has."
> "The pleasures we enjoy are lost by coveting more."
> See "*Is minĭmo.*" "*Præstat possidēre.*"

Ne tentes aut perfĭcē.—Either never attempt a thing or carry it out.

> "Leave no nail unclenched."
> "If thy heart fail thee, do not climb at all."
> See "*Non intrandum.*"

Ne utĭle quidem est scire quid futūrum sit; misĕrum est enim nihil prōficientem angi. CIC.—It is of no avail to know what is about to happen; for it is a sad thing to be grieved when grief can do no good.

> See "*Ingens malōrum.*"

Ne verba pro farīnâ.—Promises must not fill the place of gifts.

"Fair words won't feed a cat."

"Less of your courtesy, and more of your purse."

"Saying and doing are two things."

"Praise is not pudding."

See "*Destināta.*" "*Ex factis.*" "*Non verbis.*"

Ne vestigium quidem.—Not even a trace is left.

"Leave not a rack behind." SHAKS.

Ne vile velis.—Desire nothing that would bring disgrace.

Nebŭlas diverbĕrāre.—To whip the air.

"To saw the air." SHAKS.

Nec amet quenquam nec amētur ab ullo! JUV.—Let him love none and be by none beloved!

Nec asperandum quamvis exiguum nullum.—Nothing, however small, is to be irritated.

"It is possible for a ram to kill a butcher."

"The smallest worm will turn being trodden on." SHAKS.

See "*Inest et.*" "*Nihil tam.*" "*Quamvis.*"

Nec bella, nec puella.—Neither beautiful, nor young.

Nec caput, nec pedes. CIC.—Neither head, nor feet.

[Referring to anything very intricate.]

"One can't make head or tail of it."

Nec crepĭtu quidem dĭgĭti dignum.—Not worthy the snap of a finger.

Nec deus intersit, nisi dignus vindĭce nodus.* Hor.—Let not a god interfere unless where a god's assistance is necessary.

[Adopt extreme measures only in extreme cases.]

Nec domo dŏmĭnus sed dŏmĭno domus honestanda est. Cic.—The house should derive dignity from the master, not the master from the house.

"It is thou must honour the place, not the place thee."

*Nec dulces amōres
Sperne, puer, neque tu chorĕas.* Hor.

Despise not sweet inviting love-making nor the merry dance.

"On with the dance, let joy be unconfined." Byron.

See "*Nunc est.*"

*Nec imbellum ferōces
Progĕnĕrant ăqŭilæ columbam.* Hor.

Fierce eagles breed not the tender dove.

"Do men gather grapes of thorns, or figs of thistles?"

See "*Mali corvi.*" "*Nunquam ex.*"

Nec lusisse pudet, sed non incidĕre ludum. Hor.—Be not ashamed to have had wild days, but not to have sown your wild oats.

---

* Alluding to the custom of introducing gods upon the stage.

Nec me pudet, ut istos, fatēri nescīre quod nescĭam. Cic.—
Nor am I ashamed, as some are, to confess my ignorance of those matters with which I am unacquainted.

Nec obŏlum habet unde restim emat.—He hath not a farthing left wherewith to buy a rope to hang himself.

Nec omnĭa, nec passim, nec ab omnĭbus.—We must not expect everything, everywhere, and from everybody.

*Nec
Otia divitiis Arăbum liberrima muto.* Hor.

I would not exchange my life of ease and quiet for the riches of Arabia.

"Far from court, far from care."

"Who that has reason, and his smell,
Would not among roses and jasmin dwell?" Cowley.

See "*Beatus ille.*" "*Si curam.*"

*Nec pietas moram
Rugis, et instanti senectæ
Afferet, indomitæque morti.* Hor.

Not even piety will stay wrinkles, nor the encroachments of age, nor the advance of death, which cannot be resisted.

"Death will have his day." Shaks.

Nec placĭdam membris dat cura quiētem. VIR.
Cares deny all rest to weary limbs.

> "At night, to his own sharp fancies a prey;
> He lies like a hedgehog rolled up the wrong way,
> Tormenting himself with his prickles." HOOD.

*Nec, quæ præterĭit, itĕrum revocābĭtur unda;
   Nec, quæ præterĭit, hora redīre potest.* OVID.
Neither shall the wave, which has passed on, ever be recalled; nor can the hour, which has once fled by, return again.

> "Time and tide wait for no man."
> "Nae man can tether time nor tide." BURNS.
>
> See "*Fugit irrevocābĭle.*"   "*Labĭtur occultæ.*"

Nec quicquam acrĭus, quam pecuniæ damnum, stimŭlat.
LIVY.—Nothing stings us so bitterly as the loss of money.

Nec retĭnent pătŭlæ commissa fidēliter aures. HOR.—The ears that gape after secrets retain not faithfully what is entrusted to them.

Nec scīre fas est omnĭa. . . HOR.—It is not permitted that we should know everything.

> "One science only can one genius fit,
> So vast is art, so narrow human wit."
>
> See "*Nihil inănius.*" "*Noli altum.*"

Nec semper fĕriet quodcunque minābĭtur arcus. Hor.—The arrow will not always find the mark intended.

"Threatened folk live long." Scott.

"He struck at Tib, but down fell Tim."

Nec, si non obstātur, proptĕrea etiam permittĭtur. Cic.—That which is not forbidden, is not on that account permitted.

Nec sĭbĭ, nec aliis utĭlis. Of no sort of good to himself, or to anybody else.

Nec tecum possum vivĕre, nec sine te.—I cannot get on with you, or without you.

Nec tibi quid licĕat, sed quid fecisse decēbit, Occurrat. Claud.

Consider not what you may do, but what it will become you to do.

Nec vixit malè, qui natus moriensque fefellit. Hor.—Nor has he lived in vain, who from his cradle to his grave has passed his life in seclusion.

"A life of leisure, and a life of laziness, are two things."

"Solitude is the nurse of wisdom."

Necessarium malum.—A necessary evil. [*e. g.*, a wife.]

"He that would have eggs must endure the cackling of hens."

Necesse est cum insanientĭbus furĕre, nisi solus relinquĕrĕris.
—You must rave with the insane, unless you would be left alone.

"He, who kennels with wolves, must howl."

"But he, whose humours spurn law's awful yoke,
Must herd with those, by whom law's bonds are broke." Scott.

See "*Consŏnus.*"

Necesse est făcĕre sumptum, qui quærit lucrum. Plaut.—To make any gain some outlay is necessary.

"You must lose a fly, to catch a trout."

"Nothing stake, nothing draw."

"Set a sprat to catch a mackerel."

"Lay on more wood; ashes give money."

"Out of this nettle, danger, we pluck this flower, safety." Shaks.

"Our doubts are traitors,
And make us lose the good we oft might win,
By fearing to attempt." Shaks.

See "*Audentes fortunæ.*" "*Quid enim.*"

Necesse est ut multos tĭmeat, quem multi timent. Syr.—He must of necessity fear many whom many fear.

Necessĭtas cogit ad turpĭa.—Poverty makes a man mean.

"He must stoop that hath a low door."

"What an alteration of honour has
Desperate want made!" Shaks.

See "*Venia necessitāti.*"

Necessĭtas non habet legem.—Necessity recognizes no law.

"Need teaches things unlawful."

"And with necessity,
"The tyrant's plea, excused his devilish deeds." MILTON.

Necessĭtas ratiōnum inventrix.

"Necessity is the mother of invention."

Necessitāti ne quidem Dii resistunt. ERAS.—Not even the gods can withstand necessity.

Necessitāti qui se accŏmmŏdat, sapit.—He is wise, who suits himself to the occasion.

"A wise man will make more opportunities than he finds."

See "*Qui tempus.*"

Nefas nocēre vel malo fratri puta. SEN.—Bear in mind that you commit a crime by injuring even a wicked brother.

Negatio nihil implĭcat.—Negation proves nothing.

[Mere opposition to a theory does not commit you to anything.]

Neglecta solent incendĭa sumĕre vires. HOR.
Fire, if neglected, will soon gain strength.

"Nip the briar in the bud."

"Destroy the lion while he is but a whelp."

"To pluck the vicious quitch
Of blood and custom wholly out of him,
And make all clean and plant himself afresh." TENNYSON.

See "*Principiis obsta.*"

Neglectis urenda filix innascĭtur agris. Hor.—In neglected fields the fern grows, which must be cleared out by fire.

> "Weeds want no sowing."
> "The used plough shines, standing water stinks."
> "Ill weeds grow apace."
> "The brain, that sows not corn, plants thistles."
>
> > "Weeds are shallow-rooted,
> > Suffer them now, and they'll o'ergrow the garden,
> > And choke the herbs for want of husbandry." Shaks.
> >
> > See "*Ærūgo.*"

Nemĭni dixĕris, quæ nolis efferri.—Don't tell a secret to anybody, unless you want the whole world to know it.

> "A wise head hath a close mouth to it."
> "He who revealeth his secret maketh himself a slave."
> "He that tells his wife news is but lately married."

Nemĭni fidas, nisi cum quo prius mŏdium salis absumpsĕris. Trust no one, until you have eaten a peck of salt with him.

> "Trusting too much to others has been the ruin of many."
> "Trust was a good man; Trust-not was a better."
>
> > See "*Ne cuivis.*" "*Nervi et artus.*"

Nemo benè impĕrat, nisi qui paruĕrit impĕrio.—No man commands ably unless he has himself obeyed discipline.

> "A good servant makes a good master."

Nemo bis vexāri debet pro eādem causâ. Law Max.—No man ought to be twice tried for the same offence.

Nemo cogendus officii causâ.—Favours should never be forced upon others against their will.
> "Give neither counsel nor salt till you are asked for it."
> "Courtesie is cumbersome to them that ken it not."
>> See "*Intempestīva.*" "*Invītum.*" "*Officium.*"

Nemo doctus mutatiōnem consĭlii inconstantiam dixit esse. Cic.—No wise man has called a change of opinion inconstancy.
> "Wise men change their minds, fools never."

Nemo lædĭtur nisi a seipso.—Man is himself the author of every sorrow he endures.
> "Where shall a man have a worse friend than he brings from home."
>> See "*Faber quisque.*" "*Nostris ipsōrum.*" "*Sæpe in.*"

Nemo malus felix; minĭmè corruptor. Juv.—No wicked man knows happiness, and least of all the seducer of others.
> "Virtue alone is happiness below." Pope.

Nemo mortālium omnĭbus horis sapit. Plin.—No mortal man is wise at all times.
> "To err is human."
> "No one is a fool always, every one sometimes."
> "Every man hath a fool in his sleeve."
>> "But we are all men
> In our own natures frail." Shaks.
>> See "*Quandōque bonus.*"

Nemo nisi suâ culpâ diù dolet.—No man grieves long unless by his own fault.

> "O well for him whose will is strong,
> He suffers, but he will not suffer long." TENNYSON.

Nemo potest nudo vestimenta detrahĕre.

> "You cannot take a shirt from a naked man."
>
> "It is ill takin' the breeks off a highlandman."

Nemo potest persōnam fictam diu ferre. SEN.—No one can keep a mask on long.

> "Though a lie be well drest, it is ever overcome."

Nemo potest Thetĭdem simul et Galatean amāre.—You can't love Thetis and Galatea at the same time.

> "He who serves two masters must lie to one of them."
>
> "Betwixt two stools the doup fas down."
>
> "It's good to be off wi' the old love,
> Before ye be on wi' the new."

Nemo prudens punit quia peccātum est, sed ne peccētur. SEN.—Prudence will punish to prevent crime, not to avenge it.

> See "*Melior est justitia.*"

Nemo repentè fit optĭmus.—No man acquires perfection all at once.

> "Rome was not built in a day."

Nemo repentè fuit turpissĭmus.—No one ever suddenly reached the height of vice.

> "There is a method in man's wickedness:
> It grows up by degrees." BEAUMONT AND FLETCHER.

Nemo seipso diligit quenquam magis.—No one loves another better than himself.

    "Self-love is a mote in every man's eye."

    See "*Heus! proximus.*" "*Omne animal.*"

Nemo suâ sorte contentus.—No man is contented with his lot in this life.

    "Your pot broken seems better than my whole one."

Neque defraudat neque marginem excedit.—He gives neither too little, nor too much.

Neque dignus est veniâ, qui nemini dat veniam. SEN.—He, who will not pardon others, must not himself expect pardon.

    "Mercy to him that shows it, is the rule." COWPER.

    "We do pray for mercy;
And that same prayer doth teach us all to render
The deeds of mercy." SHAKS.

    Neque enim lex æquior ullâ,
Quam necis artifices arte perire suâ. OVID.

There is no law more just, than that he, who plots death, should perish by his own craft.

    "He made a pit and digged it, and has fallen into the ditch which he made."

    "Every one is glad to see a knave caught in his own trap."

    "Rats and conquerors must expect no mercy in misfortune."

    See "*Captantes capti.*" "*Incidit in.*" "*Qui capit.*"

Neque fēmĭna, amissâ pudicĭtiâ, alia abnuĕrit. Tac.—A woman once fallen will shrink from no impropriety.

"Where the heart is past hope, the face is past shame."

"We hold our greyhound in our hand,
  Our falcon on our glove;
But where shall we find leash, or band,
  For dame that loves to rove?" Scott.

Neque mel, neque apes.—No bees, no honey.

"No song, no supper."

"A horse that will not carry a saddle must have no oats."
See "*Dii laborĭbus.*" "*In sudōre.*" "*Nil sine.*"

Neque nulli sis amīcus, neque multis.—It is as bad to have too many friends as no friend at all.

See "*Fide sed cui.*"

*Neque semper arcum,
Tendit Apollo.* Hor.
Apollo does not always bend his bow.

See "*Dulce est.*"

Neque terræ motus timet, neque fluctus.—He fears neither the earthquake nor the fury of the waves.

Nequicquam sapit, qui sibi non sapit.—He is wise in vain who does not use his wisdom for his own advantage.

"'Tis altogether vain to learn wisdom, and yet live foolishly."

"Is there a man whose judgment clear
Can others teach the course to steer,
Yet runs himself life's mad career,
  Wild as the wave?" Burns.

See "*Sibi non.*"

Nequidquam pătrĭas tentâsti lubrĭcus artes. Vir.—In vain have you tried your father's arts, you slippery one.

Nervi et artus sapientiæ sunt, non temerè crēdĕre.—It is the very backbone of wisdom not to trust too hastily.

>"Quick believers need broad shoulders."

>"If you trust before you try,
>You will repent before you die."

>See "*Ne cuivis.*" "*Nemĭni fidas.*"

Nescĭat manus dextra, quid facĭat sinistra.—Let not your right hand know what your left hand doeth.

>"A fool carveth a piece of his heart to every one that sits near him."

>"If my shirt knew my design, I'd burn it."

>"Keep counsel, thyself first."

>"'Tis not long after
>But I will wear my heart upon my sleeve,
>For daws to peck at." Shaks.

>"Give thy thoughts no tongue." Shaks.

Nescio quâ natāle solum dulcēdĭne mentem,
Tangit, et immemŏrem non sinit esse sui. Ovid.

Our native land attracts us with some mysterious charm, never to be forgotten.

>"Breathes there the man, with soul so dead,
>Who never to himself hath said,
>'This is my own, my native land?'" Scott.

>See "*Bos alienus.*" "*Patriæ fumus.*"

Nescis quid serus vesper vehat.—You know not what the evening may bring with it.

"No one knows what will happen to him before sunset."

"No one knows what a day may bring forth."

See "*Fortūna nunquam.*"

Nescis tu quam meticulōsa res sit, ire ad judĭcem. PLAUT.—Little do you know what a gloriously uncertain thing law is.

"Lawyers' houses are built on the heads of fools."

"Fools and the perverse
Fill the lawyer's purse."

See "*Felix qui.*" "*Quum licet.*"

Nescit seipsum.—He forgets himself.

Nescit vox missa reverti. HOR.—A word once spoken cannot be recalled.

"What you keep by you, you may change and mend;
But words once spoke can never be recall'd." ROSCOMMON.

Neve hæc nostris spectentur ab annis. VIR.—Let not our proposal be disregarded on the score of our youth.

"Young in limbs, in judgment old." SHAKS.

Nigrum in candĭda vertunt. JUV.—They will swear black is white.

Nihil ad rem.—Nothing to the point.

Nihil ægrius quam disciplīnam accĭpĭmus.—We receive nothing with so much reluctance as advice.

Nihil agendo homĭnes malĕ agĕre discunt.—By doing nothing men learn to do evil.
> " If the devil catch a man idle he'll set him at work."
>
> " Idleness is the root of all evil."
>
> " Doing nothing is doing ill."
>
> " He that is busy is tempted but by one devil, he that is idle by a legion."
>
> "Without business, debauchery."
>
> See "*Dæmon te.*" "*Facĭto alĭquid.*" "*Res age.*"

Nihil cunctandum.—Let there be no delay.
> " Delays are dangerous."
>
> " Dull not device by coldness and delay." SHAKS.

Nihil diffĭcĭle amanti. CIC.—Nothing is difficult in the eyes of a lover.
> " Love laughs at locksmiths."
>
> " Love is incompatible with fear."
>
> " A fence between makes love more keen."
>
> " And what love can do, that does love attempt." SHAKS.
>
> See "*Quid non possit.*"

Nihil enim refert, rerum sis servus, an homĭnum.—It matters little whether we are the slaves of circumstance, or of man.

*Nihil est ab omni,
Parte beatum.* Hor.

There is no such thing as perfect happiness.

"The brightest of all things, the sun, hath its spots."

"Wherever a man dwells, he shall be sure to have a thorn-bush near his door."

"Every path hath a puddle."

"There is a skeleton in every house."

"Into each life some rain must fall,
Some days must be dark and dreary." Longfellow.

"Some flowers of Eden ye yet inherit,
But the trail of the serpent is over them all." Moore.

See "*Inter Delicias.*" "*Medio de.*" "*Omni malo.*"

Nihil est aliud magnum quam multa minūta.—Every great thing only consists of many small particles united.

"Think nought a trifle, though it small appear;
Small sands the mountain, moments make the year,
And trifles life." Young.

See "*De parvo.*" "*Minutūla.*"

*Nihil est audacius illis
Deprensis: iram atque animos a crimine sumunt.*

Juv.

Nothing is more audacious than these women when detected; they assume anger, and take courage from the very crime itself.*

---

* For illustration of this sentence, see "Don Juan," I.145 and following cantos.

Nihil est, nihil deest.—Where there is content there is abundance.

    "He that desires but little has no need of much."

    "He is not poor that hath not much, but he that craves much."

        See "*Is minimo.*" "*Lætus sorte.*" "*Non habēre.*"

Nihil est tam utĭle quod in transĭtu prosit. SEN.—No work is of such merit as to instruct from a mere cursory perusal.

Nihil est tam vŏlŭcre quam maledictum, nihil facĭlius emittĭtur, nihil cĭtius excĭpĭtur, nihil latius dissipātur. CIC.—Nothing is so swift as calumny, nothing is more easily propagated, nothing more readily credited, nothing more widely circulated.

    "The nimblest footman is a false tale."

        "What king so strong,
Can tie the gall up in a slanderer's tongue?" SHAKS.

        See "*Famâ nihil.*" "*Non est remedium.*"

Nihil eum commendat præter simulātam versutamque tristitiam. CIC.—He has no other recommendation, save an assumed and crafty solemnity of demeanour.

    "'Tis too much proved,—that with devotion's visage,
And pious action, we do sugar o'er
The devil himself." SHAKS."

    "When devils will the blackest sins put on,
They do suggest at first with heavenly shows!" SHAKS.

        See "*Fronte polĭtus.*" "*Malus ubi.*"

Nihil fortunāto insĭpiente intŏlerabĭlius.—There is nothing so intolerable as a fortunate fool.

    See "*Asperius.*" "*Licet superbus.*"

Nihil hŏmĭni amīco est oportūno amīcius. PLAUT.—Nothing is more acceptable to a man, than a friend in time of need.

    See "*Amīcus certus.*" "*Plus dat.*"

Nihil inānius quàm multa scirè.—Nothing is more foolish than to dabble in too many things.

    "He that hath many irons in the fire, some of them will cool."

    "Drive not too many ploughs at once, some will make foul work."

    "Jack of all trades and master of none."

    "Drive not a second nail till the first be clinched."

    "A lass that has many wooers often fares the worst."

    "The more the eggs, the worse the hatch,
    The more the fish, the worse the catch." HOOD.

Nihil minus expĕdit quam agrum optĭmè colĕre.—Nothing answers worse than too high farming.

Nihil, nisi quod ipse facit, rectum putat. He thinks nothing right, but what he does himself.

Nihil prodest imprŏbam mercem ĕmĕre.—There is nothing to be gained by buying inferior goods.

    "Cheat me in the price, but not in the goods."

Nihil recusandum quod donātur.—Never refuse a good offer.

"Fools refuse favours."

Nihil scire est vita jucundissĭma.—To know nothing is the happiest life.

"If the eye do not admire, the heart will not desire."

"No creature smarts so little as a fool."

See "*Amissum quod.*" "*In nihil.*"

Nihil semper floret; ætas succĕdit ætāti. Cic.—Summer lasts not for ever; seasons succeed each other.

"The fall of the leaf, is a whisper to the living."

See "*Nescis quid.*"

Nihil sub sole novi.—There is nothing new under the sun.

"And on her lover's arm she leant,
And round her waist she felt it fold,
And far across the hills they went,
In that new world that is the old." Tennyson.

Nihil tam firmum est, cui pericŭlum non sit, etiam ab invă-lĭdo. Quin. Curt.—Nothing is so secure in its position as not to be in danger from the attack even of the weak.

"Even the lion must defend himself against the flies."

"A fly, a grape-stone, or a hair can kill." Pope.

See "*Nec asperandum.*" "*Quamvis sublĭmis.*"

Nihil tam firmum est, quod non expugnari pecunia possit. Cic.—Nothing is so secure as that money will not defeat it.

> "Fight thou with shafts of silver, and o'ercome
> When no force else can get the masterdom." Herrick.
>
> "'Tis gold
> Which makes the true man killed, and saves the thief;
> Nay, sometimes hangs both thief and true man; what
> Can it not do, and undo?" Shaks.

See "*Contrà lucrum.*"

Nihil turpius est convitio, quod in auctōrem rĕcĭdit.—Nothing is more humiliating than when a reproach recoils on the head of him who utters it.

> "A second Daniel!
> I thank thee, Jew, for teaching me that word." Shaks.

Nil actum rĕpŭtans, dum quid superesset agendum. Luc.—Regarding nothing as done, while ought remained to be done.

See "*Homini.*"

Nil agit exemplum, litem quod lite resolvit. Hor.—The explanation avails nothing, which in leading us from one difficulty involves us in another.

> "To make one hole by way of stopping another."

See "*Cæcus iter.*" "*Obscūrum.*"

Nil desperandum.—Never say, "die!"

> "If to-day will not, to-morrow may."

*Nil dictu fœdum visūque hæc līmĭna tangat
Intra quæ puer est.* JUV.

Let nothing offensive to the ear or the eye enter these thresholds, within which youth dwells.

"Youth and white paper take any impression."

"And in the morn and liquid dew of youth,
Contagious blastments are most imminent." SHAKS.

See "*Maxĭma debētur.*"

Nil dictum, quod non dictum prius.—Nothing can be said which has not been said already.

"There is nothing new under the sun."

Nil fictum est diuturnum.—Nothing counterfeit will last long.

*Nil fuit unquam
Sic dispar sibi.* HOR.

Never was anything so inconsistent.

Nil intentātum relīquit.—He has left no means untried.

"He has left no stone unturned."

Nil intra est ŏlĕam, nil extra est in nuce duri.* HOR.—There is nothing hard inside the olive; nothing hard outside the nut.

"He'll swear through an inch board."

---

* Ironical. The meaning is, that a man who will make a statement so palpably untrue will swear to anything.

Nil mortalĭbus arduum est. Hor.—Nothing is so difficult but that man will accomplish it.

> "The word 'impossible' is not in my dictionary." (A saying of Napoleon the First.)

Nil prodest, quod non lædĕre possit idem. Ovid.—There is no useful thing which may not be turned to an injurious purpose.

Nil simĭlius insāno quam ebrius.—Nothing bears a stronger resemblance to a madman than a man when drunk.

> "Drunkenness is nothing but voluntary madness."

> "Drunkenness makes some men fools, some beasts, and some devils."

> See "*Nox et amor.*"

Nil sine labōre. Hor.—Nothing is achieved without toil.

> "The mill gets by going."

> "It is not with saying, 'Honey,' 'Honey,' that sweetness will come into the mouth."

> "He that will conquer must fight."

> "Whither shall the ox go, where he will not have to plough?"

> "Who moves, picks up, who stands still, dries up."

> "O how full of briars is this working-day world." Shaks.

> See "*Dii laborĭbus.*" "*In sudōre.*"

Nimia cura detĕrit magis quam emendat.—Too much care does more harm than good.

> "Too much care may be as bad as downright negligence."
> "Too much consulting confounds."
> "Who does too much, often does little."
> "To kill with kindness."
>> See "*Actum ne.*"

Nĭmia familiārĭtas parit contemptum.

> "Too much familiarity breeds contempt."

> "The man that hails you Tom or Jack,
> And proves by thumps upon your back,
>   How he esteems your merit,
> Is such a friend, that one had need,
> Be very much a friend indeed,
>   To pardon, or to bear it." COWPER.

>> See "*Nulli te facias.*"

Nĭmio id quod pudet făcĭlius fertur, quam illud quod piget. PLAUT.—We can more easily endure that which shames than that which vexes us.

> *Nīmīrum sapĕre est abjectis utĭle nugis,*
> *Et tempestīvum puĕris concēdere ludum.* HOR.

In truth it is best to learn wisdom, and abandoning all nonsense, to leave it to boys to enjoy their season of play and mirth.

*Nimis uncis
Narĭbus indulges.* Pers.

You are too sarcastic.

Nĭmium altercando verĭtas amittĭtur.—Truth becomes lost in the turmoil of arguments.

> "Great disputing repels truth."

Nimium propĕrans serius absolvit.—Make too much haste and pay the penalty.

> "He that walks too hastily, often stumbles in plain way."
>
> See "*Festīna.*"

Nimium risûs pretium est, si probitātis impendio constat. Quint. A laugh, if purchased at the expense of propriety, costs too much.

> See "*Ludīte sed.*" "*Sint sales.*"

Nisi Dŏmĭnus, frustrà.—All is in vain unless Providence is with us.

Nisi utĭle est quod facĭas, stulta est gloria. Phaed.—Unless your works lead to profit, vain is your glory in them.

Nitĭdè, non delĭcātè.

> "Rich not gaudy." Shaks.

Nĭtĭdæ vestes ornatĭōnem reddunt.—Showy clothes attract most.

"Fair feathers make fair fowls."

"Fine dressing is a foul house, swept before the windows."

"So may the outward shows be least themselves;
The world is still deceived with ornament." SHAKS.

See "*Vestis virum.*"

Nītĭmur in vĕtĭtum semper, cupĭmusque negāta. OVID.—We always strive for that which is forbidden, and desire that which is denied us.

"Stolen waters are sweet."

"For no one cares for matrimonial cooings,
There's nothing wrong in a connubial kiss." BYRON.

See "*Illĭcĭta.*" "*Quæ venit ex.*" "*Quicquid licet.*"

Nive candĭdius.—Whiter than snow.

Nobĭlĭtas morum plus ornat quam gĕnĭtōrum.—Nobility of conduct is a greater recommendation than nobility of birth.

"From our ancestors come our names, but from our virtues our honours."

See "*Nam genus.*" "*Qui genus.*" "*Stemmăta.*"

Nobĭlĭtas, sine re projectâ, vīlĭor algâ.—Nobility without wealth is more worthless than the seaweed which the tide has left.

"Gentility, sent to market, will not buy a peck of meal."

See "*Stemmăta.*"

Nocet empta dolōre voluptas. Hor.—Pleasure bought with pain does harm.

Nocte lucĭdus, interdiu inutĭlis.—Bright enough in the dark, dull in time of day.

> [Learned in what is of no use, ignorant of everything at all available.]

Noctu urgenda consilia.—Take counsel of your pillow.

> See "*Per noctem.*"

Nocturnâ versāte manu, versāte diurnâ. Hor.—Work at it night and day.

Nocuit, et nocēbit.—It has caused injury and will do so again.

> "She has deceived her brother, and may thee." Shaks.

Nŏcumenta dŏcumenta.—Injuries put us on our guard.

> "Bought wit is best."
>
> "A scalded cat fears cold water."

Nodum in scirpo quærĕre.*—To hunt for a knot in a rush which has no knots.

> [To raise unnecessary scruples.]

Nodum solvĕre.—To untie the knot.

> [To solve a difficulty.]

---

* "Scirpus," a rush without a knot, used for making mats.

Nolens volens.—Whether he will or no.

"Willy nilly."

Noli altum sapĕre.—Limit your inquiry after knowledge.

"Hew not too high, lest a chip fall in thine eye."

"He that pryeth into the clouds, may be struck with a thunderbolt."

See "*Nec scire.*"

Noli irritāre crabrōnes.—Have a care how you irritate the wasps.

[Meddle not with waspish people. Attack not a combined force.]

Nolunt ubi velis; ubi nolis cupiunt ultrò. Ter.—When you will, they wont, when you wont, they will.

"He is a fool who thinks by force or skill,
To turn the current of a woman's will." Sir S. Tuke.

Nomen bonum instar unguenti fragrantis.—A good name is like sweet smelling ointment.

"Take away my good name, take away my life."

"O I have lost my reputation! I have lost the immortal part, sir, of myself, and what remains is bestial." Shaks.

"He that filches from me my good name
Robs me of that, which not enriches him,
And makes me poor indeed." Shaks.

Nomĭna stultōrum semper pariĕtibus hærent.—The names of fools are always written on walls.

> "He is a fool and ever shall,
> Who writes his name upon a wall."

> "A white wall is the fool's paper."

Non benè conveniunt, nec in unâ sede morantur Majestas et amor. OVID.
Love and dignity do not dwell together.

> "In robe and crown the king stepped down,
> To meet and greet her on her way." TENNYSON.

Non certātur de oleastro.*—It is bad to contend about trifles.

Non colit arva benè, qui semen mandat arēnæ.—He is but a poor husbandman, who sows in sand.

Non cuivis hŏmĭni contingit adīre Corinthum. HOR.—It is not every man that can afford to go to Corinth.

> "'Tis not for every one to catch a salmon."
> "Garlands are not for every brow."

Non decet defunctum ignāvo questu prosĕqui. TAC.—It is not becoming to grieve immoderately for the dead.

> "It is as much intemperance to weep too much, as to laugh too much."

> "To persevere
> In obstinate condolement is a course
> Of impious stubbornness: 'tis unmanly grief." SHAKS.

---

* "Oleaster," a wild olive-tree.

Non dēĕrat voluntas, sed facultas.—The means were wanting, not the will.

"Take the will for the deed."

Non deficiente crumēnâ. HOR.—Never without a shilling in my purse.

"There's always a shot in the locker."

Non e quovis ligno fit Mercurĭus.—The bust of Mercury cannot be cut from every wood.

"You cannot make a silk purse of a sow's ear."
"Every reed will not make a pipe."
"Jack will never make a gentleman."
"You can't make horn of a pig's tail."

Non eădem est ætas, non mens. HOR.—My age, my inclinations, are no longer what they were.

"My days of love are over: me no more
　The charms of maid, wife, and still less of widow,
Can make the fool of, that they made before:
　In fact I must not lead the life I did do." BYRON.

"Now, my sere fancy 'falls into the yellow
Leaf,' and imagination droops her pinion;
And the sad truth, which hovers o'er my desk,
Turns what was once romantic to burlesque." BYRON.

Non enim gazæ, neque consulāris
Summŏvet lictor misĕros tumultus
Mentis, et curas lăqueātā circum
Tecta volantes. Hor.

Not treasured wealth, nor the consul's lictor, can dispel the mind's bitter conflicts and the cares that flit, like bats, about your fretted roofs.

"Ease and honour are seldom bed-fellows."

See "*Beatus ille.*" "*Si curam.*" "*Nec otia.*"

Non enim paranda nobis solum, sed fruenda sapientia est. Cic.—Wisdom is not only to be acquired, but enjoyed.

See "*Frustrà habet.*"

Non esse cŭpĭdum, pecunia est.—To have no wants, is money.

"Golden dreams make men wake hungry."

See "*Is minĭmo.*"

Non est beātus, esse qui se nescĭat.—He is not happy who does not realize his happiness.

See "*Frustrà habet.*"

Non est bonum, quod non sit malum; ne malum, quod non sit bonum.—There is no good but contains some evil; no evil but contains some good.

"There is some soul of goodness in things evil." Shaks.

Non est curiōsus quin idem sit mălĕvŏlus.—An inquisitive man is always ill-natured.

Non est de sacco tanta farīna tuo.—All that meal comes not from your own sack.

Non est in mundo dives, qui dicit, "Abundo!"—No man is so rich as to say, "I have enough!"
>See " *Crescit amor.*" " *Multa petentibus.*"

Non est laudandus, ne in cœnâ quidem. He does not show a decent quality even over a good dinner.

Non est loquendum, sed gubernandum. SEN.—We have not to talk, but to steer the vessel.
>" Don't speak to the man at the helm."

Non est meum negotium; multum valeat!—It is no business of mine; may it go to the devil!
>" Farewell and be hanged; friends must part!"
>" He assigned it to regions more than tropical." DICKENS.

Non est ratio, ubi vis impĕrat.—Reason is absent, when impulse rules.
>" A man in a passion rides a horse that runs away with him."
>" When passion entereth at the fore-gate wisdom goes out at the postern."
>>See " *Irātus cum.*" " *Malè cuncta.*"

Non est remedium adversus sycophantæ morsum.—There is no remedy against the bite of a secret slanderer.
> "The evil wound is cured, but not the evil name."
> "A customary railer is the devil's bagpipe, which the world danceth after."
> "A tattler is war than a thief."
> "Slander leaves a score behind it."
> "No might nor greatness in mortality
> Can censure 'scape; back-wounding calumny
> The whitest virtue strikes." SHAKS.
> "Be thou as chaste as ice, as pure as snow, thou shalt not escape calumny." SHAKS.

Non est tam bonus, qui non cæspĭtet equus.—No horse is so good, but that he will at times stumble.
> "It is a good horse that never stumbles,
> And a good wife that never grumbles."
> See "*Quandoque bonus.*"

Non est tritĭcum sine palĕis.—There is no wheat without chaff.
> "You must take the fat with the lean."

Non est venātor quivis per cornua flator.—Every man who can blow a horn is not a huntsman.
> "There belongs more than whistling to going to plough."
> See "*Multi qui.*" "*Non omnes qui.*"

Non est vivĕre, sed valēre vita. MART.—Life consists not merely in existing, but in enjoying health.
> "He who has not health has nothing."

Non facĭle est æquâ commŏda mente pati. Ovid.—It is not easy to bear prosperity unruffled.
> "A full cup must be carried steadily."

Non fumum ex fulgōre, sed ex fumo dăre lucem. Hor.—Not to create confusion in what is clear, but to throw light on what is obscure.

Non habēre, sed non indĭgēre, vera abundantia.—Real wealth consists not in having, but in not wanting.
> "He is rich, that is satisfied."
> "Poor and content is rich, and rich enough." Shaks.
>> See "*Bene est.*" "*Is minĭmo.*" "*Lætus sorte.*"

Non habet anguillam, per caudam qui tenet illam.—An eel, held by the tail, is not yet caught.

Non hoc ista sibi tempus spectăcŭla poscit.—Vir. This is no time for staring about.

Non hodiè, aut herè institūtum.—An ancient custom, not of to-day or yesterday.

Non ignāra mali misĕris succurrĕre disco. Vir.—Myself acquainted with misfortune, I learn to help the unfortunate.
> "What sorrow was, thou bad'st her know,
> And from her own she learnt to melt at others' woe." Gray.

Non intrandum, aut penetrandum.—Enter not at all, or else pass through.
> "Who knows not the game, let him not play."
>> See "*Ne tentes.*"

Non licet in bello bis peccāre.—It is not allowed in war to blunder twice.

Non luctu, sed remĕdio, opus in malis.—In misfortune we need help, not lamentation.

"Grieving for misfortunes is adding gall to wormwood."

"Sorrow will pay no debt."

See "*De re amissâ.*" "*Rosam quæ.*"

Non missūra cutem nisi plena cruōris hirūdo. Hor.—A leech that will not quit the skin until sated with blood.

Non nobis solum nati sumus. Cic.—We are not born for ourselves alone.

Non omne, quod nitet, aurum est.

"All is not gold that glitters."

"All flesh is not venison."

Non omnem molĭtor, quæ fluit unda, videt.—The miller sees not every wave that flows.

Non omnes eădem mirantur, amantque. Hor.—All men do not admire and delight in the same objects.

"So many men, so many minds."

"Different men have different opinions;
Some like apples, some onions."

"As mony heads, as mony wits."

See "*Alius aliis.*" "*Mores dispăres.*" "*Quot homines.*"

Non omnes, qui cithăram tenent, citharœdi.—All are not harpers, who hold the harp.

> "Many talk of Robin Hood that never shot his bow,
> And many talk of Little John that never did him know."

> "All are not saints that go to church."

>> See "*Multi qui boves.*" "*Non est venātor.*" "*Qui tauros.*"

Non omnĭa eveniunt, quæ in anĭmo statuĕris.—All things come not to pass which the mind has conceived.

> "Between the hand and the mouth the soup is spilt."

> "Oft expectation fails, and most oft there,
> Where most it promises." SHAKS.

>> See "*Multa cadunt.*"

Non omnia per bovem obtinēbis.—The sacrifice of an ox will not bring us all we want.

Non omnia possŭmus omnes.—We cannot all of us do everything.

> "No living man all things can."

> "All keys hang not on one girdle."

> "An emmet may work its heart out, but can never make honey."

Non omnĭbus omnia.—All things are not good for all.

Non omnīno temĕrè est, quod vulgò dictĭtant.—All is not false which is publicly reported.

> "When all men say you are an ass, it is high time to bray."

>> See "*Haud semper.*" "*Interdum vulgus.*"

Non omnis calceus convĕnit cuilibet pedi.—The same shoe does not fit every foot.

> See "*Alius aliis.*" "*Non omnes eădem.*"

Non omnis fert omnia tellus.—Every soil does not bear the same fruit.

Non omnium est olēre moschum.—It does not fall to the lot of all to smell of musk.

> "He made me mad
> To see him shine so brisk and smell so sweet." SHAKS.

> "His essences turn the live air sick." TENNYSON.

> "This oiled and curled Assyrian bull,
> Smelling of musk and of insolence." TENNYSON.

Non oportet hospĭtem semper hospĭtem esse.—A guest should not remain for ever a guest.

> "A constant guest is never welcome."
> See "*Nullīus hospĭtis.*"

Non opus admisso subdĕre calcar equo.—Spur not a willing horse.

> "Spur not a free horse to death."

Non opus est verbis, sed fustĭbus.—Not words but knocks.

> "If he won't carry the sack, give him a whack."
> "I'ld charm her with the magic of a switch." BURNS.
> See "*Malo nodo.*"

Non progrĕdi est regrĕdi.—Not to advance is to recede.

> "The merchant who gains not, loseth."

Non purgat peccāta, qui negat.—He, who denies his faults, makes no atonement for them.

> "A fault once denied, is twice committed."

> "A fault confessed, is half redressed."

> "And, oftentimes, excusing of a fault,
> Doth make the fault the worse by the excuse." SHAKS.

Non quam latè, sed quam lætè habĭtes, refert.—How to live happily, not luxuriously, is the question.

> "Better a dinner of herbs where love is, than a stalled ox and hatred therewith."

> "Better an egg in peace, than an ox in war."

> "A cake eaten in peace, is worth two in trouble."

> "A happy heart is better than a full purse."

Non quidvis contingit quod optāris.—You cannot have all you wish for.

Non satis felīcĭter solēre procedĕre quæ ŏcŭlis agas aliēnis. LIV.—That business does not prosper which you transact with the eyes of others.

> "The foot of the owner is the best manure for his land."

> "One eye of the master sees more than four of the servants."

> "If you wish a thing done, go; if not, send."

> "Not to oversee workmen, is to leave your purse open."

> "He that by the plough would thrive,
> Himself must either hold or drive."

>> See "*Ocŭlus domĭni.*"

Non semper erit æstas.—Summer will not last for ever.
> "The morning sun never lasts a day."
>> See "*Fortūna nunquam.*" "*Nescis quid.*" "*Nihil semper.*"

Non semper erunt Saturnālia.—Holyday time will not last for ever.
> "Sadness and gladness succeed each other."
> "We shall never be younger."

> *Non semper imbres nubĭbus hispĭdos*
> *Manant in agros, aut mare Caspium*
> *Vexant inæquales procellæ.*   HOR.

Rains driven by storms fall not perpetually on the land already sodden, neither do varying gales for ever disturb the Caspian sea.
> "After rain comes fair weather."
> "After a storm comes a calm."
> "The wind keeps not always in one quarter."

> *Non, si malè nunc, et olim*
> *Sic erit.*   HOR.

If things look badly to-day they may look better to-morrow.
> "A rainy morn oft brings a pleasant day."
> "In the end things will mend."
> "A joyful evening may follow a sorrowful morning."
> "Things at the worst will cease, or e'en climb upward
> To what they were before."   SHAKS.
>> See "*Forsan misĕros.*"

Non si te rūpĕris inquit,
　Par eris. Hor.
Not if you burst yourself will you equal him.

Non soles respĭcere te, cum dicas injustè altĕri? Plaut. Are you not accustomed to look at home, when you abuse others?

"The fox thinks everybody eats poultry like himself."

"If the mother had never been in the oven, she would not have looked for her daughter there."

See "*Qualis quisque.*" "*Qui sibi.*"

Non stillant omnes, quas cernis in aëre nubes.—All clouds are not rain clouds.

Non sum qualis eram. Hor.—I am not what I once was.

See "*Tempŏra mutantur.*"

Non sunt amīci, qui degunt procul.—They cease to be friends who dwell afar off.

"Far from the eyes, far from the heart."

See "*Absens hæres.*" "*Multas amicitias.*"

Non tam ovum ovo simĭle.—More like than egg to egg.

"As like as two peas." "As like as eggs." Shaks.

Non temerārium est, ubi dives blandè appellat paupĕrem. Plaut.—It is not without a purpose when a rich man greets a poor one with kindness.

"He who caresses thee more than the occasion justifies, has either deceived thee or intends it."

See "*Ficum cupit.*"

Non terret princeps, magister, parens, judex; at ægritūdo superveniens omnia correxit.—A king, a master, a parent, a judge, may fail to frighten us; but sickness coming brings with it successful reproof.

 See "*Ægrōtat dæmon.*" "*In morbo.*"

Non unquam tăcuisse nocet, nocet esse locūtum.—To have been silent never does harm, but to have spoken does.

 "Who says little has little to answer for."

 "A wise head makes a close mouth."

 "Few words are best."

 "Silence is wisdom and gets a man friends."

 "A fool's heart dances on his lips."

 "A quiet tongue shows a wise head."

 "More have repented of speech than of silence."

 "If a word be worth one shekel, silence is worth two."

 "Speech is silvern, silence is golden." CARLYLE.

  See "*Audīto multa.*" "*Est tempus.*" "*Quid de quoque.*"

Non venit ad silvam qui cuncta rubēta verētur.—He who fears every bramble should not go to the woods.

Non uti libet, sed uti licet, sic vivĭmus.—We must live as we can, not as we would wish.

 "Make a virtue of necessity."

  See "*Præstat possidēre.*" "*Ut quimus.*"

Non verbis, at facto opus est.—Deeds not words are required.

"Words show the wit of a man, but actions his meaning."

"A man of words and not of deeds
Is like a garden full of weeds."

"One take-this, is better than two thou-shalt-haves."

See "*Destināta tantum.*" "*Ne verba.*" "*Pleno modio.*"

Non vidēmus mantīcæ quod a tergo est. CATULL.—We see not our own backs.

"O wad some power the giftie gie us
To see oursels as ithers see us." BURNS.

Non vis esse iracundus? ne sis curiosus. Qui inquirit, quid in se dictum sit, se ipse inquiētat. SEN.—Do you desire not to be angry? Be not inquisitive. He who inquires what is said of him only works out his own misery.

"Listeners hear no good of themselves."

Non volat in buccas assa columba tuas.—Birds fly not into our mouths ready roasted.

"No gains without pains."

"Would you have potatoes grow by the pot-side?"

"Better do it than wish it done."

"Wishing of all employments is the worst." YOUNG.

"If wishes were horses, beggars would ride."

"The sleeping fox catches no poultry."

"He that gapeth until he be fed,
Well may he gape until he is dead."

"The ripest fruit will not fall into your mouth."

"The scraping hen will get something; the crouching hen nothing."

"In idle wishes fools supinely stay;
Be there a will,—and wisdom finds a way." CRABBE.

Nondum incurvam cervīcem Jupiter habet.—Providence has not entirely deserted us.

"Blaw the wind ne'er so fast, it will lower at last."

"If to-day will not, to-morrow may."

"Light may come where all looks darkest,
Hope hath life, when life seems o'er." MOORE.

See "*Forsan misĕros.*"

Nondum omnĭum diērum sol occĭdit. LIVY.—My sun has not yet set for ever.

"There's a gude time coming." SCOTT.

"'Tis day still, while the sun shines."

"The hindmost dog may catch the hare."

"Where one door shuts another opens."

See "*Forsan misĕros.*" "*Nunc pluit.*"

Nos hæc novĭmus esse nihil. MART.—We know this to be all nonsense.

Nos viles pulli nati infelīcibus ovis. JUV.—We are worthless fowl, hatched from unlucky eggs.

"Look here, he cries (to give him words):
Thou feathered clay, thou scum of birds!
Look here, thou vile, predestined sinner,
Doomed to be roasted for a dinner." HOOD.

Nosce tempus.—Catch the opportunity.
> "Grind with every wind."
> "Take hold of a good minute."
> "A wise man turns chance into good fortune."
> "He that will not when he may,
> When he will he shall have nay."
>> See "*Collĭge.*" "*Dum Aurora.*" "*Dona præsentis.*"

Noscĭtur ex sociis.—A man is judged of by his companions.
> "Tell me the company you keep and I'll tell you what you are."
> "Tell me with whom thou goest
> I'll tell thee what thou doest."
> "Who friendship with a knave hath made,
> Is judg'd a partner in the trade." GAY.

Nôsse velint omnes, mercēdem solvĕre nemo. JUV.—All wish for knowledge, but no one wishes to pay the price of it.

Nostra intelligĭmus bona,
Cum, quæ in potestāte habuĭmus, ea amisĭmus. PLAUT.
We only appreciate the comforts of life in their loss.
> "How blessings brighten as they take their flight." YOUNG.
>> See "*Bonum magis.*" "*Rem carendo.*"

Nostris ipsōrum alis capĭmur.—We are the authors of our own disasters.
> "Who has deceived thee so oft as thyself?"
> "Let ilka herring hing by its ain head."
> "Like a young eagle, who has lent his plume
> To fledge the shaft by which he meets his doom." MOORE.
>> See "*Bis interĭmitur.*" "*Sibi quisque.*" "*Sæpe in.*"

Nota res mala optĭma. PLAUT.—It is best to know the worst at once.

Notum, qui pŭĕri, qualisque futūra sit uxor. JUV.—The gods alone know, what kind of wife a man will have.
   "Hanging and wiving go by destiny."

Nova peccāta, nova supplicia.—Strange sins, strange punishments.

Novacŭla in cotem.—The razor against the grindstone.
   "Diamond cut diamond."

Novi Simōnem, et Simon me.—I know Simon, and Simon knows me.
   [A couple of rogues.]
   "Ask my companion if I be a thief."
   "A fellow feeling makes us wondrous kind." POPE.
   "Tam lo'ed him like a vera brither;
   They had been fou for weeks thegither." BURNS.
     See "*Arcădes ambo.*"

Novos parans amīcos, vĕtĕres cole.—In forming new friendships, forget not old friends.
   "Old friends and old wine are best."
   "The friends thou hast, and their adoption tried,
   Grapple them to thy soul with hooks of steel." SHAKS.

Nox et amor vinumque nihil moderābĭle suadent.—Late hours and love and wine lead not to moderation in anything.
   "There is a devil in every berry of the grape."
     See "*Dives eram.*" "*Vina Venusque.*" "*Vino forma.*"

Nube pari.—Marry a person in your own rank in life.

    " Like blood, like good, and like age, make the happiest marriage."

    See " *Æqualem uxōrem.*"

Nuces relinquĕre.—To leave the nuts.

    [To put away childish things.]

Nudĭor lebĕrĭde.—More naked than the cast-off skin of a serpent.

Nudĭor paxillo.—More naked than a post.

Nudo mandas excubias.—You trust the guard to a naked or unarmed man.

Nudo vestimenta detrahĕre.—To take a shirt from a naked man.

    " To take blood from a stone."

Nugæ seria ducunt. [*In mala. Hor:*]—Trifles often lead to serious results.

    "Small faults indulged in are little thieves that let in greater."

    "Small habits well pursued betimes
May reach the dignity of crimes." HANNAH MORE.

    "Win us with honest trifles, to betray us
In deepest consequence." SHAKS.

    "Where lives the man that has not tried,
How mirth can into folly glide
And folly into sin!" SCOTT.

> "It is easier to suppress the first desire than to satisfy all that follow it."
>
> "For glances beget ogles, ogles sighs,
> Sighs wishes, wishes words, and words a letter." BYRON.
>
> "Do not make me kiss, and you will not make me sin."
>
> "Or wherefore trace, from what slight cause
> Its source one tyrant passion draws,
> Till mastering all within." SCOTT.

Nugis addĕre pondus. HOR.—To give importance to trifling matters.

Nulla ætas ad perdiscendam sera est.

> "It is never too late to learn."

Nulla certĭor custōdia innocentiâ.—No protection is so sure as that of innocence.

> "Thrice is he armed, that hath his quarrel just." SHAKS.
>
> "'Tis said the lion will turn and flee
> From a maid in the pride of her purity." BYRON.
>
> "A heart unspotted is not easily daunted." SHAKS.

Nulla dies sine lineâ.—No day should pass without something being done.

> "Every day in thy life is a leaf in thy history."
>
> "Catch, then, O catch the transient hour;
> Improve each moment as it flies!" JOHNSON.

Nulla est sincēra voluptas.　Ovid.—There is no such thing as perfect happiness.

> "No rose without a thorn."
>
> "But ask not thou if happiness be there,
> If the loud laugh disguise convulsive throe,
> Or if the brow the heart's true livery wear." Scott.
>
> "The web of life is of mingled yarn, good and ill together."
> 　　　　　　　　　　　　　　　　　　　Shaks.
>
> 　　See "*Inter delicias.*" "*Medio de fonte.*"

Nulla fere causa est, in quâ non fæmĭna litem Movĕrit.　Juv.

There is never a lawsuit but a woman is at the bottom of it.

> "Women's jars breed men's wars."
>
> 　　　"For there's no motion
> That tends to vice in man, but I affirm
> It is the woman's part." Shaks.

Nulla tam bona est fortūna, de quâ nil possis queri.　Syr.
No fortune is so good but that you may find something to grumble about.

Nullæ sunt occultiōres insidĭæ quam ea quæ, latent in simultatīone officii.　Cic.—No deceit is so veiled as that which lies concealed behind the semblance of courtesy.

> "Full of courtesy, full of craft."

Nulli jactantius mærent, quam qui maximè lætantur. TAC.
None make a greater show of sorrow than those who are most delighted.

See "*Hærēdis fletus.*"

Nulli major fuit usus edendi. JUV.—There was not a greater gourmand living.

See "*Fruges consumĕre.*"

Nulli te facias nimis sodālem;
Gaudēbis minus; et minus dolēbis. MART.
Be not too thick with anybody; your joys will be fewer, and so will your pains.

See "*Nimia.*"

Nullis amor est medicābilis herbis. OVID.—No herb can remedy the anguish of love.

Nullīus boni jucunda possessio sine socio.—We can enjoy nothing without some one to share the pleasure.

"All who joy would win
Must share it. Happiness was born a twin." BYRON.

Nullīus hospĭtis grata est mora longa.—The prolonged visit of no guest is pleasant.

"A guest and a fish after three days are poison."

"Wear not out your welcome."

See "*Non oportet.*"

Nullo scopo jaculāri.—To cast a dart without any fixed mark or aim.

[To have no settled purpose.]

"I sit within a helmless bark." TENNYSON.

Nullum cum victis certāmen et æthĕre cassis. VIR.—There should be no strife with the vanquished or the dead.

"Pour not water on a drowned mouse."

See "*Cum larvis.*" "*De mortuis.*" "*Pugna suum.*"

Nullum magnum ingenium sine mixtūra dementiæ. SEN. Great talent has always a little madness mixed up with it.

"Great wit to madness sure is near allied,
And thin partitions do their bounds divide." DRYDEN.

Nullum quod tetĭgit non ornāvit.*

"He touches nothing but he adds a charm." FENELON.

Nullum sine auctoramento malum est. SEN.—There is no evil without its compensation.

"By falling we learn to go safely."

"Some falls the means are happier to rise." SHAKS.

See "*Deus quos.*" "*Tribulatio.*"

Nullus dies omnīno malus. HES.—No day is wholly unproductive of good.

---

* From Johnson's epitaph on Goldsmith.

Nullus tantus quæstus, quam quod habes parcĕre.—There is no way to make money so certain as to save what you have.

> "A penny saved is a penny got."
>
> "A stitch in time saves nine."
>
> "Providence is better than a rent."
>
> "Good management is better than good income."
>
> See "*Magnum est.*"

Num, tibi cum fauces urit sitis, aurĕa quæris Pocŭla? Hor.

When your throat is parched with thirst, do you desire a cup of gold?

> *Nunc est bibendum, nunc pede libĕro Pulsanda tellus.* Hor.

Now to drink and trip it on the light fantastic toe.

> "It's a poor heart that never rejoices."
>
> "Who loves not women, wine and song,
> Remains a fool his whole life long."
>
> "Fill the bright goblet, spread the festive board!" Scott.
>
> "Strike up the dance, the cava bowl fill high." Byron.
>
> "They dance, they revel, and they sing,
> Till the rude turrets shake and ring. Scott.
>
> "Then let me quaff the foamy tide,
> And through the dance meandering glide." Moore.

Nunc meæ in arctum coguntur copiæ.—Now my resources are reduced to a narrow compass.

Nunc non e tumŭlo fortūnatâque favillâ
Nascentur viŏlæ? Pers.

Now o'er his tomb and happy ashes will not violets spring?

"Lay her in the earth,
And from her fair and unpolluted flesh
May violets spring." Shaks.

"And from his ashes may be made
"The violet of his native land." Tennyson.

Nunc pluit, et claro nunc Jupiter æthĕre fulget.—Now it rains, and again the sun shines forth brightly in the heavens.

"In the end, things will mend."

"So closely our whims on our miseries tread,
That the laugh is awak'd ere the tear can be dried." Moore.

See "*Forsan misĕros.*" "*Nondum incurvam.*"

Nunquam ălĭud Natūra, aliud Săpientĭa dicit. Juv.—Nature never says one thing, and science another.

Nunquam anĭmo pretiis obstantibus. Juv.—The price never stood in the way of her inclination.

Nunquam direxit brachia contra
Torrentem. Juv.

He never sought to stem the current.

[Of a statesman who accommodates his views to public opinion.]

Nunquam ex malo patre bonus filius.—A bad father has never a good son.

"Of evil grain no good seed can come."
See "*Mali corvi.*" "*Nec imbellem.*"

Nunquam hinc hodie ramentâ fies fortunatior. PLAUT. You will not be a chip the richer.

Nunquam minus solus, quam cum solus. CIC.—Never less alone, than when alone.

Nunquam nimis dicĭtur, quod nunquam satis discĭtur. SEN. That is never too often repeated which is never sufficiently learnt.

Nunquam non parātus.—Always ready.

Nunquam oportet virum sapientem mulĭeri remittĕre frenum. A wise man should never give his wife too much rein.

"If the husband once give way
To his wife's capricious sway,
For his breeches he next day
May go to whoop and holloa." TOM THUMB.

Nunquam partītur amīcum. JUV.—He claims a monopoly in friendship.

Nunquam sunt grati, quæ nŏcuēre, sales.—Jokes, which carry injury with them, are never agreeable.

See "*Adhibenda.*" "*Cum jocus est.*"

Nunquam te fallant animi sub vulpe latentes. HOR.—Be not caught by the cunning of those who appear in a disguise.

"Modred's narrow foxy face,
Heart hiding smile, and gray persistent eye." TENNYSON.

"A fair face may make a foul bargain."

"But in the glances of his eye
A penetrating keen and sly
Expression found its home." SCOTT.

"One may smile, and smile, and be a villain." SHAKS.

See "*Decipimur.*" "*Fronte politus.*" "*Habent insidias.*"

Nusquam tuta fides. VIR.—Confidence cannot find a place wherein to rest in safety.

Nux, asinus, mulier verbere opus habent.

"A spaniel, a wife, and a walnut tree,
The more you beat 'em the better they be."

"If you beat spice it will smell the sweeter."

"'Tis the same with common natures,
Use 'em kindly they rebel,
But be as rough as nutmeg graters,
And the rogues obey you well." A. HILL.

DOMUS antīqua quam dispări domĭno domināris!—O ancient house, by what a different master are you presided over!

O fortunātos nimĭum, sua si bona norint, Agricolas! Vir. Happy, twice happy, you who dwell in the country, if you only knew the pleasures which surround you!

See "*Beātus ille.*" "*Nec otia.*"

O mihi prætĕrĭtos rĕfĕrat si Jupĭter annos! Vir.—O that Jupiter would but bring back to me the years that have passed!

O præclarum custōdem ovium, lupum! Cic.—O rare protector of the sheep, a wolf!

"You give the wolf the wether to keep."

"What! give the lettuce in charge to the geese!"

"Pheasants are fools if they invite the hawk to dinner."

"And wer't not madness then
To make the fox surveyor of the fold." Shaks.

O tempŏra! O mores! Cic.—O these degenerate days!

Obedientia felicitātis mater.—Obedience is the mother of happiness.

>"I will be correspondent to command." Shaks.

Obĭter dictum.—A passing remark.

Obscæna pecunia. Juv.—Filthy lucre.

Obscūris vera involvens. Vir.—Veiling truth in mystery.

Obscūrum per obscurĭus.—Explaining what is obscure by what is still more obscure.

>[Making confusion worse confounded.]
>See "*Cæcus.*" "*Nil agit.*"

Obsequium amīcos, verĭtas odium parit. Ter.—Flattery brings friends, but the truth begets enmity.

>"Flattery sits in the parlour when plain dealing is kicked out of doors."

>"A friend's frown is better than a fool's smile."

>"Truth is a dog that must to kennel. He must be whipped, when Lady, the brach, may stand by the fire and stink."
>Shaks.

>"O, that men's ears should be
>To counsel deaf, but not to flattery!" Shaks.

Obtorto collo trahi.—To be dragged by the scruff of the neck.

>"Nothing is easy to the unwilling."

Occasĭo ægrè offertur, facĭlè amittĭtur.—An opportunity is found with difficulty and easily lost.

> See "*Nosce tempus.*"

Occasio facit furem.—Opportunity makes the thief.

> "The open door tempts a saint."
>
> "Where a chest lieth open, a righteous man may sin."
>
> "The hole invites the thief."
>
> "How oft the sight of means to do ill deeds
> Makes ill deeds done." SHAKS.

Occasione duntaxat opus improbitāti vel malitiæ.—Wickedness and malice only require an opportunity.

Occīdit mĭsĕros crambe repetīta magīstros. JUV.—The same dish cooked over and over again wears out the irksome life of the teacher.

Occultāre morbum funestum.—To conceal disease is fatal.

> "A disease known is half cured."
>
> "Counsel is irksome when the matter is past remedy."

Occultum quatiente anĭmo tortōre flagellum. JUV.—Conscience, the executioner, shaking her secret scourge.

> "The gods are just, and of our pleasant vices
> Make whips to scourge us." SHAKS.
>
> See "*Hi sunt.*" "*Tacitâ sudant.*"

Occupet extremum scabies!—Plague seize the hindmost!

"The devil take the hindmost."

Ocŭlis clausis agĕre.—To act with closed eyes.

Ocŭlis magis habenda fides quam aurĭbus.—We should trust more to our eyesight than to our ears.

"The eyes believe themselves, the ears other people."

"Let every eye negotiate for itself,
And trust no agent." SHAKS.

See "*Pluris est.*"

Ocŭlus domĭni sagīnat equum.—The master's eye makes the horse fat.

"The eye of the master will do more than both his hands."

"Woe to the mule that sees not her master."

See "*Non satis.*"

Ocyor accipĭtre.—Swifter than a hawk.

Odĕrint, dum mĕtuant.—Let them hate, so that they fear me.

Odērunt hilărem tristes tristemque jocōsi. HOR.—The sad dislike those who are cheerful, and the cheerful dislike the melancholy.

Odērunt peccāre boni virtutis amōre. HOR.—The good refrain from sin from the pure love of virtue.

Odērunt peccāre mali formīdine pœnæ.—The bad refrain from sin from fear of punishment.

Odi profānum vulgus et arceo. Hor.—I abhor the profane rabble and keep them at a distance.

>"Hence, ye profane; I hate ye all;
>Both the great vulgar, and the small." Cowley.

>"The applause of the people is a blast of air."

>"A puff of wind and popular praise weigh alike."

>"If the tag-rag people did not clap him and hiss him, according as he pleased and displeased them . . . . . I am no true man." Shaks.

Odi puĕrŭlos præcōci sapientiâ. Cic.—I hate all children of precocious talent.

>"To be precocious
>Was in her eyes a thing the most atrocious." Byron.

Odĭa in longum cocta.—Well-digested hatred.

Odĭa in longum jacĭens, quæ recondĕret auctăque promĕret. Tac.—Bottling up his malice to be suppressed and brought out with increased violence.

>See "*Ira, quæ.*"

Odĭmus accĭpĭtrem, quia semper vivit in armis. Ovid.—We hate the hawk because he ever lives in battle.

Odĭmus quem læsĭmus.—We hate the man whom we have wronged.

"The offender never pardons."

"He that does you a very ill turn will never forgive you."

"The more my wrong, the more his spite appears." SHAKS.

See "*Proprium humāni.*"

Offĭcĭum ne collocâris in invītum.—Force not favours on the unwilling.

"She had a good opinion of advice,
Like all who give and eke receive it gratis,
For which small thanks are still the market price." BYRON.

See "*Intempestīva.*" "*Nemo cogendus.*"

Oleo incendium restinguĕre.—To quench fire with oil.

Olĕo tranquillior.—Smoother than oil.

Olĕra spectant, lardum tollunt.—They look at the greens, but steal the bacon.

Oleum addĕre cămīno.—To throw oil on flames.

"To add fuel to fire."

Oleum et salem oportet emĕre.—It is well to buy oil as well as salt.

[Different remedies should be at hand when required.]

Olla malè fervet. PETRON.—The pot boils badly.

Omissis nugis, rem experiāmur.—Trifling at an end, now let us go to the point.

> "Turning these jests out of service, let us talk in good earnest."
> SHAKS.

Omne animal seipsum diligit. CIC.—Every animal loves itself.

> "Self-preservation is the first law of nature."
> See "*Heus ! proximus.*" "*Nemo seipso.*"

Omne epigramma sit instar apis, sit acūleus illi,
Sint sua mella, sit et corpŏris exigui. MART.

Every epigram should resemble a bee; it should have sting, honey, and brevity.

> "Three things must epigrams, like bees, have all,
> A sting, and honey, and a body small."

Omne ignōtum pro magnifico.—That which is not understood is always marvellous.

> "The lion's not half so fierce as he's painted."

> "The mighty pyramids of stone
> That wedge-like cleave the desert airs,
> When nearer seen, and better known,
> Are but gigantic flights of stairs." LONGFELLOW.

> See "*Quod tegitur.*"

Omne nimium non bonum.—Too much of a thing nauseates.

> See "*Ne quid nimis.*"

Omne nimĭum vertĭtur in vitĭum.—Excess in anything becomes a vice.

> "Joy surfeited turns to sorrow."
> See "*Ne quid nimis.*"

Omne pulchrum amābile.—Everything beautiful is loveable.

> "A thing of beauty is a joy for ever." KEATS.

Omne solum forti patria. OVID.—To a brave man every soil is his country.

> "All places that the eye of heaven visits
> Are to the wise man ports and happy havens." SHAKS.
> See "*Illa mihi.*"

Omne tulit punctum, qui miscŭit utĭle dulci. HOR.—He has carried every point, who has combined that which is useful with that which is agreeable.

Omnem movēre lapĭdem.—To leave no stone unturned.

Omnem rudentem movēre.—To move every rope: to cram on all sail.

Omnes sibi melĭus esse malunt quàm altĕri. TER.—All men have more consideration for themselves than for others.

> See "*Heus! proxĭmus.*"

Omnes tibīcĭnes insanĭunt; ubi semel efflant, avŏlat illĭco mens.—All flute-players are mad; when once they begin to blow, away goes reason.

Omni ex parte dies malus haud obvĕnĕrit unquam.—No day is wholly productive of evil.

    "It is a long lane that has no turning."

Omni malo punĭco inest granum putre.—In every pomegranate a decayed pip is to be found.

    "Every bean hath its black."
    "No house without a mouse."
    "Are there not spots on the sun?"
    "Loathsome canker lives in sweetest bud." SHAKS.

        See "*Inter delicias.*" "*Medio de fonte.*" "*Nihil est ab.*"

Omni pedi eundem calceum inducĕre.—To put the same shoe on every foot.

Omni petenti, non omnĭa pĕtenti.—To every one who doth ask, but not everything he doth ask.

Omni telōrum gĕnĕre oppugnāre.—To fight with every kind of weapon.

        Omnia ferre
    Si potes, et debes. JUV.

If you are capable of submitting to insult you ought to be insulted.

    "A man may bear till his back breaks."
    "He who makes himself honey will be eaten by flies."
    "There is a limit at which forbearance ceases to be a virtue."
                                           BURKE.
    "All lay load on the willing horse."

        See "*Vetĕrem ferendo.*"

Omnia mundāna nugas æstĭma.—Treat everything of this world as mere vanity.

> " Behold of what delusive worth
> The bubbles we pursue on earth,
> The shapes we chase." LONGFELLOW.

Omnia tempus habent.—Everything has its season.

> " There is a time for all things."

Omnia tuta timens.—Needlessly alarmed.

> " Afraid of his own shadow."

Omnĭa vincit amor : nos et cedāmus amōri. OVID.—Love conquers all things; let us own her dominion.

> " But he who stems a stream with sand,
> And fetters flame with flaxen band,
> Has yet a harder task to prove—
> By firm resolve to conquer love!" SCOTT.

> " Love rules the court, the camp, the grove,
> And men below and saints above,
> For love is heaven and heaven is love." SCOTT.

Omnĭbus est nomen, sed idem non omnibus omen.—Everybody has a name, but not always the same luck with it.

> " What's in a name ? " SHAKS.

> " A name, it has more than nominal worth,
> And belongs to good or bad luck at birth." HOOD.

Omnĭbus invideas ; nemo tibi. MART.—You may envy every one, but no one envies you.

Omnĭbus nervis.—With all his strength.

Omnis ars imitatio est natūræ. SEN.—Everything in art is but a copy of nature.

Omnis commodĭtas sua fert incommŏda secum.—Every advantage has its disadvantage.
> "That which is good for the back is bad for the head."
> "Every light hath its shadow."
> "No scene of mortal life but teems with mortal woe." SCOTT.
>> See "*Inter delicias.*" "*Medio de fonte.*" "*Nihil est ab.*"

Omnis innovatio plus novitāte perturbat, quàm utilitāte prodest.—Every innovation startles us more by its novelty than it benefits us by its utility.

Omnis potestas impatiens consortis est.—All power is impatient of a partner.
> "Love and lordship like no fellowship."
> "Love, well thou know'st no partnership allows,
> Cupid averse rejects divided vows." PRIOR.

Omnis virtus est mediocrĭtas.—Every virtue is but halfway between two vices.
>> See "*Virtus est.*"

Omnĭum quæ dixĕrat fecĕratque arte quâdam ostentātor. TAC.—One who sets off to the best advantage his every act and speech.
> "His tact, too, temper'd him from grave to gay,
> And taught him when to be reserved or free." BYRON.

Onos, onus.—Honour's onerous.

    See "*Si curam.*"

Opĕram et oleum perdĭdi.—I have lost my labour and my cost.

Opĕre in longo fas est obrēpĕre somnum. Hor.—In a long work sleep may be naturally expected.

Operosè nihil agentes. Sen.—Busily engaged in doing nothing.

    [A squirrel in a cage.]

    "Who more busy than they who have least to do?"

Opes, ut index, homĭnis ingenium arguunt.—Wealth, like an index, reveals the character of men.

Opiniōnum commenta delet dies, natūræ judĭcia confīrmat. Cic.—Time puts an end to speculation in opinions, and confirms the laws of nature.

    "Time tries a'."

    "But time strips our illusions of their hue,
    And one by one in turn some grand mistake
    Casts off its bright skin yearly like a snake." Byron.

    See "*Tempus omnia.*"

Oportet agrum imbecilliorem esse quàm agrĭcŏlam.—The field should be poorer than the farmer.

    [It is useless for a man to attempt farming without capital.]

Oportet iniquum petas ut æquum feras.—To obtain that which is just we must ask that which is unjust.

> "Ask but enough, and you may lower the price as you list."

Oportet remum ducĕre qui dĭdĭcit.—Let him take the oars who has learned to row.

Oportet testūdĭnis carnes aut edĕre, aut non edĕre.—You should eat plentifully of the flesh of the turtle or not at all.

> "The whole hog or none."
>
> "In for a penny in for a pound."
>
> "You may as well be hung for a sheep as a lamb."

Opportūnus crimĭnĭbus.—One against whom accusations when made are easily believed.

Opprobrium medicōrum.—A reproach to the doctors.

> [An incurable malady.]

Optat ephippĭa bos; piger optat arāre caballus. Hor.—The ox longs for the gaudy trappings of the horse; the lazy pack-horse would fain plough.

> [We envy the position of others, dissatisfied with our own.]
>
> See "*Cui placet.*" "*Fertilior.*" "*Nemo.*"

Optĭma citissimè perĕunt.—The best things are the first to perish.

> "The roses fall, the thorns remain."
>
> See "*Mors optĭma.*"

Optĭma medicīna temperantia est.

"Temperance is the best medicine."

"Feed sparingly and defy the physician."

See "*Plures crāpŭla.*" "*Immodicis.*"

Optĭma nomĭna non appellando fiunt mala.—A man may lose what are his clearest rights by not demanding them.

Optĭma quæque dies mĭsĕris mortalibus ævi Prima fugit. VIR.

All our sweetest hours fly fastest.

"They found no fault with Time, save that he fled." BYRON.

Optĭmi consiliarii mortui.—The dead are the best counsellors.

Optĭmum elĭge, suave et facile illud faciet consuetūdo.—Pursue that course which offers most advantages, habit will soon make it agreeable and easy.

Optĭmum est aliĕnâ frui experientiâ.—It is best to learn wisdom by the experience of others.

"Let another's shipwreck be your sea-mark."

"One man's fault is another man's lesson."

See "*Alienâ optĭmum.*" "*Feliciter.*"

Optimum est pati quod emendāre non possis. SEN.

"What can't be cured must be endured."

See "*Feras non.*" "*Levius fit.*"

Optĭmum opsonium labor senectūti.—An industrious life is the best security for food in old age.

See "*Festo die.*"

Opus opĭfĭcem probat.—The work tests the workman.

Orbâ tigrĭde pejor. Juv.—[A woman] fiercer than a cubless tigress.

See "*Implacabiles.*" "*Mulier.*"

Orĭmur, mŏrĭmur.—We are born; we die.

"Fill the cup and fill the can,
Have a rouse before the morn;
Every minute dies a man,
Every minute one is born." Tennyson.
See "*Carpe diem.*"

Ornat spina rosas, mella tegunt apes.

"Roses grow on thorns and honey wears a sting." Watts.

"Hath not thy rose a canker, Somerset?
Hath not thy rose a thorn, Plantagenet?" Shaks.
See "*Medio de fonte.*"

Oscĭtante uno deinde oscĭtat et alter.—One man yawning makes another yawn too.

See "*Unius dementia.*" "*Latrante.*"

Ossa ab ore rapta jējūnæ canis.—Bones snatched from the mouth of a hungry dog.

"I from the jaws of a gardener's bitch
Snatched this bone and then leapt the ditch." Ben Jonson.

*Otia corpus alunt, animus quoque pascitur illis;
Immodicus contrà carpit utrumque labor.* OVID.

Rest strengthens the body, the mind too is thus supported; but unremitting toil destroys both.

> See "*Jocandum.*" "*Stare diu.*" "*Quod caret.*"

*Otia si tollas, periēre Cupīdĭnis arcus,
Contemptæque jăcent, et sine luce faces.* OVID.

Let but the hours of idleness cease, and the bow of Cupid will become broken and his torch extinguished.

> "And maidens call it—Love in idleness." SHAKS.

Otio qui nescit uti, plus habet negotii quàm qui negotium in negotio.—He who knows not how to employ his leisure hath more cares on his mind than the most busy of busily-engaged men.

> "Idle folks have the most labour."
> "It is more painful to do nothing than something."

Otiōsis nullus adsistet Deus.—Providence assists not the idle.

> "Get thy spindle and thy distaff ready, and God will send the flax."
> See "*Dii facientes.*" "*Tollenti.*"

Otiōsus animus nescit quid velit.—The mind when unoccupied knows not what it wants.

Otium cum dignitāte.—Dignity in retirement.

> [Ease and dignity combined.]

Otium sine litĕris mors est, et homĭnis vivi sepultūra. SEN.— Retirement without literary amusements is death itself, and a living tomb.

Ovem lupo commisisti.—You have left the sheep with the wolf for safe custody.

See "*O præclārum!*"

Ovo nudĭor.—More naked than an egg.

Ovo prognātus eodem. HOR.—Hatched in the same nest.

PABULUM *Acherontis.* PLAUT.—Food for Acheron.

"With one foot in the grave."

Pacem orāre manu, præfigĕre puppĭbus arma. VIR.—To prate of peace, and arm your ironsides.

"Put your trust in God, and keep your powder dry."
"Love thy neighbour, but pull not down thy hedge."
See "*Tempŏre.*"

Pœnitentia sera rarò vera.—Late repentance is rarely sincere.

"When men grow virtuous in their old age they are merely making a sacrifice to God of the devil's leavings." SWIFT.

Palmam, qui meruit, ferat.—Let him bear the prize, who has deserved it.

"Do well and have well."
"A good dog deserves a good bone."
See "*Detur digniōri.*"

Panis filiōrum non objiciendus canĭbus.—That which should feed our children ought not to be given to dogs.
>See "*Prima carĭtas.*"

Par nōbĭle fratrum. Hor.—A precious pair of brothers [*i. e.* rascals].
>See "*Arcădes.*"

Par pari rĕfĕro.—That which I receive, that I return.
>"An eye for an eye, and a tooth for a tooth."
>"A Roland for an Oliver."
>"When a man makes up his mind to thrash another, he must also make up his mind to be a little thrashed himself." James.
>"Be stirring as the time, be fire with fire;
>Threaten the threat'ner, and outface the brow
>Of bragging horror." Shaks.
>>See "*Lex.*" "*Quid pro.*" "*Ut salutāris.*"

Parasitĭcam cœnam quærit.—He seeks to live like a parasite.
>[He wants to sponge upon somebody.]

Parcendum est anĭmo miserābĭle vulnus habenti. Ovid.—Have consideration for wounded feelings.
>"Misfortunes, when asleep, are not to be awakened."
>"The pain
>Remembrance gives, when the fix'd dart
>Is stirred thus in the wound again." Moore.
>>See "*Malum benè.*" "*Quiēta non.*"

Parcĕre persōnis, dicĕre de vitiis.—To condemn the error, but not to descend to personalities.

> See "*Bellum cum.*"

Parcĕre subjectis, et debellāre superbos. VIR.—To spare the vanquished, and subdue the proud.

> "A great man will not trample on a worm, nor sneak to an emperor."
>
> "'Tis godlike to have power, but not to kill." BEAUMONT AND FLETCHER.
>
> "To tame the proud, the fetter'd slave to free,
> These are imperial arts." DRYDEN.

Parcit Cognātis macŭlis simĭlis fera. JUV. Beasts of like kind will spare those of kindred spots.

> "Dog won't eat dog."
>
> "'Tis a hard winter when one wolf eats another."
>
> See "*Sævis inter se.*"

Pardi mortem adsimŭlat.—He feigns death like a panther.

Pardus macŭlas non deponit.—A leopard does not change his spots.

> "He who is born a fool is never cured."
>
> "Can the Ethiopian change his skin, or the leopard his spots."
>
> See "*Lupus pilum.*" "*Natūram expellas.*"

Parentes reverēre.—Revere your parents.

> "How sharper than a serpent's tooth it is,
> To have a thankless child." SHAKS.

Pares cum paribus facillimè congregantur. Cic.

> "Two of a kind, whate'er they be,
> Are forthwith certain to agree."
>
> See "*Æqualis æqualem.*"

Pariĕti loquĕris!—You talk to a wall!

Pario marmŏre purius. Hor.—Brighter than Parian marble.

Parĭter remum ducĕre.—To row together, or in time.

> [To act in unison.]
> "A long pull and a strong pull and a pull altogether."

Parĭtur pax bello. Cor. Nep.—Peace is obtained by war.

> "But civlyzation doos git forrid
> Sometimes upon a powder-cart." Biglow Papers.

Pars benĕficii est quod petĭtur si bene neges. Syr.—A favour is half granted, when graciously refused.

> "So sweetly she bade me adieu,
> I thought that she bade me return." Shenstone.

Pars mĭnĭma est ipsa puella sui. Ovid.—The girl is the smallest portion of herself.

> [The girl is all crinoline and chignon.]

Pars sanitātis velle sanāri fuit. Sen.—To wish to be cured is half way towards cure.

> "'Tis very certain the desire of life
> Prolongs it." Byron.
>
> "Despair of all recovery spoils longevity,
> And makes men's miseries of alarming brevity." Byron.

Parthis mendācior! HOR.—A greater liar than the Parthians.

Partŭriunt montes, nascētur rīdĭcŭlus mus. HOR.—The mountains are in labour, the birth will be an absurd little mouse.

> "Great cry and little wool, as the fellow said when he sheared his hogs."
>
> "Your windmill dwindles into a nutcrack."
>
> See "*Arcem ex.*" "*Murem pro.*"

Parva leves capiunt ănĭmos. OVID.—Small minds are captivated by trifles.

> "Little things attract light minds."
>
> "Pleased with a rattle, tickled with a straw." POPE.

Parva patĭtur, ut magis potiātur.—He puts up with small annoyances to gain great results.

> "I follow him, to serve my turn upon him." SHAKS.

Parvi sunt foris arma, nisi est consĭlium domi.—Arms are of little service abroad unless directed by the wisdom of counsellors at home.

> See "*Vis consilĭ.*"

Parvis imbūtus tentābis grandĭa tutus.—Having mastered the lesser difficulties, you will more safely venture on greater achievements.

> "He can carry the ox, who has carried the calf."

Parvum, non parvæ amicitiæ, pignus.—A trifling pledge of no small friendship.

Parvum parva decent. HOR.—Small things become the small.
> "A little bird wants but a little nest."
> "A small pack becomes a small pedler."

Pasce canes qui te lănĭent cătŭlosque lŭpōrum.—Rear dogs and wolves' cubs to rend you.
> See "*Ale lupōrum.*" "*Tigridis.*"

Patĕre legem quam ipse tŭlisti.—Submit to the rule you have yourself laid down.
> See "*Faber compĕdes.*"

Patiŏr ut potiăr.—I wince to win.
> "Hold a candle to the devil!"

Patrĭæ fumus igne aliēno luculentior.—The smoke of our own country is brighter than fire abroad.
> "Though you seat the frog on a golden stool,
> He'll soon jump off, and into the pool."
> See "*Bos alienus.*" "*Nescio quâ.*"

Pauca malè parta multa benè comparāta perdunt.—A few things gained by fraud destroy a fortune otherwise honestly won.
> "The unrighteous penny corrupts the righteous pound."
> "Dead flies cause the ointment of the apothecary to send forth a stinking savour.
> "One ill weed mars a whole pot of pottage."

Paucĭlŏquus sed erudītus.—A man of few words but learned withal.

"Still waters run deep."

Paucis carior est fides, quam pecunia. SALL.—But few prize honour more than money.

Paulātim, non impĕtu.—Gently, not by force.

"What raging rashly is begun,
Challengeth shame before half done."

"He that runs fast will not run long."

"'Tis best to pause, and think, ere you rush on." BYRON.

"Those, that with haste will make a mighty fire.
Begin it with weak straws." SHAKS.

See "*Nascĭtur.*" "*Vis consĭlĭ.*"

*Paulum sepultæ distat inertiæ
Celāta virtus.* HOR.
Hidden knowledge differs little from ignorance.

"A man knows no more to any purpose than he practises."

"A book that remains shut, is but a block."

"Concealed goodness is a sort of vice."

"Fair ladies mask'd are roses in their bud." SHAKS.

See "*Celāta virtus.*"

Pauper agat cautè.—If poor, act with caution.

"He who pitches too high won't get through his song."

Pauper enim non est, cui rerum suppĕtit usus. HOR.—He is not poor who has a competency.

> See "*Benè est cui.*" "*Præstat possidēre.*"

Paupertas mors altĕra.—Poverty is death in another form.

> "Hard toil can roughen form and face,
> And want can quench the eye's bright grace." SCOTT.

Peccāre humānum est.—To err is human.

> "Folly is the product of all countries and ages."
>
> See "*Unicuique.*" "*Vitiis nemo.*"

Pecuniam in loco negligĕre maximum interdum'st lucrum. TER.—To disregard money, on suitable occasions, is often a great profit.

> "Sometimes it is better to give your apple away, than eat it yourself."
>
> "He that repairs not a part, builds all."
>
> "A penny is sometimes better spent than spared."
>
> "He who greases his wheels, helps his oxen."
>
> "Don't spoil the ship for a halfpenny-worth of tar."

Pecuniōsus damnāri non potest.—A wealthy man can err with impunity.

> "A rich man's foolish sayings pass for wise ones."
>
> "Great men's vices are accounted sacred."
>
> "Through tattered clothes small vices do appear;
> Robes and furred gowns hide all." SHAKS.
>
> See "*Timĕat maledicĕre.*"

Pelle sub agninā lătĭtat mens sæpe lupīna.—A wolf often lies concealed in the skin of a lamb.

>["Yours truly," is not always true.]

>"I like not fair terms and a villain's mind." SHAKS.

>See "*Fronte polītus.*"

Pennas incīdĕre alicui.

>"To clip his wings."

>"To cut his comb off."

>"To take him down a peg."

Per angusta ad augusta.—Through dangers to distinction.

>"No cross, no crown."

>"The wind in one's face makes one wise."

>"The fire i' the flint
Shows not till it be struck." SHAKS.

>See "*Periisset.*"

Per fas et nefas.—By good means or bad.

>"By hook or by crook."

>"Either by might or by sleight."

>"By fair means or foul."

Per noctem plurĭma volvens.—Pondering over many things by night.

>"Darkness and night are mothers of thought."

>See "*Noctu.*"

Per risum multum possis cognoscĕre stultum.—By much laughter you detect the fool.

"Laughter is the hiccup of a fool."

See "*Risus abundat.*"

Per scelĕra scelĕribus certum est iter. Sen.—The sure way to wickedness is through wickedness.

Per varios casus, per tot discrīmĭna rerum Tendĭmus. Vir.

We journey on in life through varied hazards and misfortunes.

*Perăgit tranquilla potestas,
Quod violenta nequit.* Claud.

Power can achieve more by gentle means than by violence.

"Throwing your cap at a bird is not the way to catch it."

"Who overcomes
By force, hath overcome but half his foe." Milton.

See "*Potentia cautis.*"

Percontātōrem fŭgĭto; nam garrŭlus idem est. Hor.—Shun an inquisitive man, he is invariably a tell-tale.

"There's nothing makes me so much grieve,
As that abominable tittle-tattle,
Which is the cud eschew'd by human cattle." Byron.

Perdĭdisti vinum, infūsâ aquâ.—You have spoilt the wine by adding water to it.

"Too much water drowned the miller."

Perĕant, qui antĕ nos nostra dixērunt!—Confound those who have anticipated us in what we would have said!

Perfer, et obdūra. OVID.—Bear and forbear.

"Impatience does not diminish but augments the evil."

"Hope and strive is the way to thrive."

"Still achieving, still pursuing,
Learn to labour and to wait." LONGFELLOW.

See "*Levius fit.*"

Periculōsæ plenum opus āleæ. HOR.—An undertaking beset with danger.

"Doubtful the die, and dire the cast!"

Periculōsum est canem intestīna gustâsse.—There is danger when a dog has once tasted flesh.

"The tiger that has once tasted blood is never sated with the taste of it."

Perīculum ex aliis facĕre, tibi quod ex usu siet. TER.—To learn from other men's mistakes to prevent your own.

See "*Alienâ optĭmum.*"

Periērunt tempŏra longi Servitii. JUV.
To have slaved so many years for nothing!

Perii! plaustrum percŭli. Plaut.—I am undone! I have smashed the waggon.

[I have ruined all.]

Periisset, nisi periisset.—Had he not been visited by sickness, he would have perished utterly.

"The good are better made by ill,
As odours crushed are sweeter still." Rogers.

"There is some soul of goodness in things evil,
Would men observingly distil it out." Shaks.

See "*Deus quos.*" "*Per angusta.*" "*Tribulatio.*"

Perīmus lĭcĭtis.—We perish by permitted things.

"Seeming genial, venial fault." Tennyson.

Perit quod facis ingrāto. Sen.—What you do for an ungrateful man is thrown away.

—"To do good to the ungrateful is to throw rose-water into the sea."

"A favour ill placed is great waste."

"He that keeps another man's dog shall have nothing left him but the line."

See "*Ingrātus.*"

Perjuria ridet amantum
Jupiter. Ovid.

"And Jove but laughs at lovers' perjury." Dryden.

"At lovers' perjuries
They say Jove laughs." Shaks.

Permitte divis cætĕra. Hor.—Trust the rest to the gods.

Persuasione cape, non vi.—Win by persuasion not by force.

"The noisy fowler catches no birds."

"He that will take the bird must not scare it."

"Drumming is not the way to catch a hare."

"To a boiling pot flies come not."

"The fox barks not when he would steal the lamb." Shaks.

See "*Conciliat anĭmos.*" "*Pudōre.*"

Pervertunt officĭa noctis et lucis. Sen.

"They turn night into day."

Pessĭmum genus inimicōrum laudantes. Tac.—The most detestable race of enemies are flatterers.

"When the flatterer pipes, the devil dances."

"When flatterers meet the devil goes to dinner."

Petĭmusque damusque vicissim.—We give and take in turn.

"Open hand makes open hand."

"Mutually giving and receiving aid,
They set each other off, like light and shade." Churchill.

See "*Gratia gratiam.*" "*Manus manum.*"

Pica certat cum luscinĭâ!—The magpie is competing with the nightingale!

Pica Syrēnem imĭtans!—A magpie aping a Syren!

Pinguis aqualĭcŭlus propenso sesquipĕde exstet. Pers.—His bloated paunch stands forth projecting a good eighteen inches.

Piscātor ictus sapiet.*—A fisherman once stung will be wiser.

> "A burnt child dreads the fire."
>
> "He that hath been bitten by a serpent is afraid of a rope."
>
> "He who has once burnt his mouth always blows his soup."
> See "*Empta dolōre.*" "*Qui semel est.*"

Piscātur in aquâ turbĭdâ.—He fishes in troubled waters.

> [If you wish to catch gudgeons stir up the mud.]

Piscem natāre doces.—You are teaching a fish to swim.

> See "*Ante barbam.*"

Pisces magni parvŭlos cŏmĕdunt.—Great fish feed on the lesser.

> See "*Plus potest.*"

Piscis eget sale!—The fish requires salt! [Derisively, the sea abounding with salt.]

Pistillo calvior.—Balder than a pestle.

---

* In allusion to some fish with a prickly back fin.

Planta quæ sæpius transfertur non coalescit.—A tree often transplanted does not thrive.

> "I never saw an oft-removed tree,
> Nor yet an oft-removed family,
> That throve so well as one that settled be."
>
> See "*Saxum volūtum.*"

Plausuque petit clarescĕre vulgi.—He seeks renown by public applause.

Pleno modio verbōrum honor!—Honourable words by the bushel!

> "Leaves enough, but few grapes."
>
> "Promises may make friends, but 'tis performances that keep them."
>
> "He who gives fair words feeds you with an empty spoon."
>
> See "*Destināta tantum.*" "*Virtus in actione.*"

Pleno subit ostia velo. VIR.—He enters the port with a full sail.

> "Comes in at the end with a wet sail."

Plumbĕo jugulāre gladio.—To strike with a leaden sword.

[To use a useless argument.]

Plura sunt, quæ nos terrent, quam quæ premunt. SEN.—Our fears are always more numerous than our dangers.

> See "*Plus dolet.*" "*Timor mortis.*"

Plures adōrant solem orientem quàm occidentem.—Men worship the rising, not the setting sun.

> "The faded rose
> No suitor knows."

> "The rose is fairest when 'tis budding new." SCOTT.
>> See "*Amāre juvĕni.*" "*Turpe senex.*"

Plures crāpŭla quàm glădius.

> "Gluttony kills more than the sword."

> "Feasting is the physician's harvest."

> "Wine hath drowned more men than the sea."

> "Much meat, much maladies."

> "He, who is always drinking and stuffing,
> Will in time become a ragamuffin."

> "The drunkard and the glutton come to poverty, and drowsiness clothes a man with rags."
>> See "*Ense cadunt.*" "*Multo plures.*"

*Plures nimiâ congesta pecunia curâ
Strāngŭlat.* JUV.

An excess of hoarded wealth is the death of many.

Plures occīdit gula quàm gladius.

> "Gluttony kills more than the sword."

> "Feed sparingly and defy the physician."

> "Surfeits slay mae than swords."
>> See "*Plures crapŭla.*" "*Immodĭcis.*"

*Plurĭma sunt, quæ
Non audent homĭnes pertūsā dīcĕre lænā.* Juv.
There are many things which may not be uttered by men in threadbare coats.

"He that hath no honey in his pot, let him have it in his mouth."

Pluris est oculātus testis unus quàm aurīti decem. Plaut.
One eye-witness is better than ten hearsays.

"Seeing is believing."
"Give me the ocular proof." Shaks.
See "*Oculis magis.*"

Plus a medĭco quàm a morbo pericŭli.—There is more to be feared from the doctor than the disease.

Plus ălŏēs, quàm mellis habet. Juv.—There is more of bitterness than good nature in him.

Plus apud nos vera ratio vălĕat, quàm vulgi opīnio. Cic.
Sound conviction should influence us rather than public opinion.

Plus dat, qui tempŏre dat.—It doubles the value of a gift to be well-timed.

See "*Amĭcus certus.*" "*Nĭhil homĭni.*"

Plus dolet quam necesse est, qui ante dolet quàm necesse est.
Sen.—He grieves more than is necessary who grieves before any cause for sorrow has arisen.

"Let your trouble tarry till its own day comes."
See "*Calamitōsus.*" "*Carpe diem.*"

Plus in aliēno quàm in suo negotio vident homĭnes.—Men see more of the business of others than of their own.

"A looker on sees more of the game than a player."

Plus potest, qui plus valet. PLAUT.—He can do most who has most power.

"Might overcomes right."

"The weakest goes to the wall."

"The least boy always carries the biggest fiddle."

Plus salis quàm sumptûs. COR. NEP.—Tasteful rather than expensive.

"Rich not gaudy." SHAKS.

Plus sonat quàm valet. SEN.—He makes a great row but does nothing.

"More noise than wool."

Plus vident ŏcŭli quàm ŏcŭlus.—Two eyes can see more than one.

Pol! me occidistis, amīci! HOR.—By heaven you have destroyed me, my friends!

"God keep me from my friends, from my enemies I will keep myself."

"How sweet the task to shield an absent friend!
I ask but this of mine to—*not* defend." BYRON.

Pollĭcĭtus meliora.—One that promised better things.

Poma dat auctumnus.—The blossoms in the spring are the fruit in autumn.

Poma, ova, atque nuces, si det tibi sordĭda, gustes.
> "An apple, an egg, and a nut,
> You may eat after a slut."

*Popŭlus me sibĭlat, at mihi plaudo,
Ipse domi, quotĭes nummos contemplor in arcâ.* Hor.
The mob may hiss me, but I congratulate myself while I contemplate my treasures in their hoard.
> "Let him laugh who wins."
> "A fu' sack will tak a clout o' the side."
> "Let him laugh, who is on the right side of the hedge."
> "The fox never fares better than when he's bann'd."
> "They laugh that win." Shaks.

Poscentes varĭo multum diversa palāto. Hor.—Desiring things widely different for their various tastes.
> See "*Mores dispăres.*" "*Non omnes eadem.*"

Possunt quia posse videntur. Vir.—They succeed, because they think they can.
> "To believe a business impossible is the way to make it so."
> "Where there's a will there's a way."

Post acerba prudentior.—Losses make us more cautious.
> "What smarts teaches."
> See "*Piscātor ictus.*"

Post bellum auxilium.—When the war is over then comes help.

> "Baskets after the vintage."
>
> "When the dog is drowning every one brings him water."
>
> "When the friar's beaten, then comes James."
>
> See "*Machinas post.*" "*Mortuum unguento.*"

Post cinĕres gloria sera venit. MART.—Glory comes too late when we are nought but ashes.

> "He asked for bread and he received a *stone.*"
>
> EPIGRAM ON BUTLER.

Post festum venisti.—You have come too late for the feast.

> "Too late for the fair."

Post malam sĕgĕtem serendum est. SEN.—After a bad harvest sow again.

> [Yield not to difficulties.]

Post nubĭla Phœbus.—After clouds sunshine.

> "After clouds comes clear weather."
>
> "How calm, how beautiful comes on
> The stilly hour, when storms are gone." MOORE.
>
> See "*Forsan misĕros.*" "*Nondum omnium.*"

Post tenĕbras lux.—After darkness comes light.

Post rem devŏrātam, ratio!—The plan executed, reason comes to our assistance!

Potentia cautis, quam acribus consiliis, tutius habētur. TAC. Power is more safely maintained by cautious than by harsh counsels.
> See " *Peragit tranquilla.*" " *Pudōre.*"

Potentissimus est qui se habet in potestāte. SEN.—He is most powerful who governs himself.
> " Know, prudent cautious self-control
>   Is wisdom's root." BURNS.

Præcepta ducunt, exempla trahunt.—Precepts invite, but examples drag us to conclusions.
> See " *Longum est.*" " *Segnius.*"

Præmŏnĭtus, præmūnītus.
> " Forewarned, forearmed."
> " The candle that goes before, is better than that which comes after."
> " A man surprised is half beaten."
> " A danger foreseen is half avoided."
> " Good watch prevents misfortune."
> " A man that is warned is half armed."
>   See " *Monīti.*" " *Prævīsus.*" " *Turbinem.*"

Præsentemque refert quælĭbet herba Deum.—Every little blade of grass declares the presence of God.
> " To his tuned spirit the wild heather-bells
>   Ring Sabbath knells;
> The sod's a cushion for his pious want,
> And, consecrated by the heaven within it,
>   The sky-blue pool a font." HOOD.

Præstat aliquando quàm nunquam.
"Better late than never."

Præstat canem irrītāre quàm anum.—It is safer to irritate a dog than an old woman.

Præstat cautēla quàm medēla. COKE.—Prevention is better than cure.
"It is easier to prevent ill habits than to break them."
See "*Neglecta solent.*" "*Principiis obsta.*"

Præstat morāri.—Better take time.

Præstat otiōsum esse quàm malè agĕrĕ. PLINY.—Better do nothing than do ill.

Præstat possidēre, quàm persĕqui.—It is better to enjoy what we possess than to hanker after other things.
"If thou hast not a capon, feed on an onion."
"A man must plough with such oxen as he hath."
See "*Bene est.*" "*Is minĭmo.*" "*Ne te.*"

Præstat silēre quàm pauca dicĕre.—It is better to say nothing than not enough.

Prevīsum est levĭus quod fuit ante malum.—The evil is lessened when it is seen beforehand.
See "*Præmŏnitus.*"

Prævīsus ante mollĭor ictus venit.—The blow falls more lightly when it is anticipated.

"Good take heed doth surely speed."

"When clouds are seen wise men put on their cloaks;
When great leaves fall then winter is at hand." SHAKS.

See "*Monĭti.*" "*Præmŏnĭtus.*" "*Turbĭnem.*"

Pretĭo parāta, vincĭtur pretĭo fides. SEN.—Fidelity, purchased with money, money can destroy.

"A friend that you buy with presents, will be bought from you."

"He that is won with a nut, may be lost with an apple."

Prima cārĭtas incĭpit a seipso.

"Charity begins at home."

"Drown not thyself to save a drowning man."

See "*Heus! proxĭmus.*"

*Prima est hæc ultio, quod se
Jūdĭce nemo nocens absolvĭtur.* JUV.

The worst punishment of all is, that in the court of his own conscience no guilty man is acquitted.

Prima et maxĭma peccantium est pœna peccâsse. SEN.—The conviction of having committed a fault is its first and greatest punishment.

"The sting of a reproach is the truth of it."

"Conscience is the chamber of justice."

Prima feres hĕdĕræ victrīcis præmia.—You will wear the ivy wreath, the victor's meed.

Primas jactāre hastas.—To fire the first shot.

    [To throw down the gauntlet.]

    Princĭpĭis obsta ; sero medicīna parātur,
    Cum mala per longas convăluēre moras.   Ovid.

Check the beginning of evil; the remedy is too late when the disease by delay has increased in strength.

    "Small habits well pursued betimes
    May reach the dignity of crimes."   Hannah More.

    "Nip sin in the bud."

    "Counsel is irksome when the matter is past remedy."

    "Chasten thy son while there is hope."

    "A little fire is quickly trodden out;
    Which, being suffer'd, rivers cannot quench."   Shaks.

    See "*Adeo.*" "*Cui puer.*" "*Neglecta solent.*" "*Venienti.*" "*Præstat cautēla.*"

Princĭpium dīmĭdium totius.—The beginning is half of the whole.

    "Boldly ventured is half won."

    "The getting out of doors is the greatest part of the journey."
                                                    Cowley.

    See "*Cogenda mens.*" "*Dimidium facti.*"

Prius antĭdŏtum quam venēnum.—The antidote before the poison.

    [To offer excuses before an accusation.]

    "Call not a surgeon before you are wounded."

    "Never ask pardon before you are accused."

Prius ovem lupus ducat uxōrem.—Sooner will the wolf take the sheep for a wife.

"Mice care not to play with kittens."

Priusquam incipĭas consulto, et ubi consuluĕris maturè, facto opus est. SALL.—Deliberate before you begin; but, having carefully done so, execute with vigour.

"Speedy execution is the mother of good fortune."

Pro aris et focis.—For our altars and our hearths.

"For God and our country."

"How can man die better,
Than facing fearful odds
For the ashes of his fathers
And the temples of his gods?" MACAULAY.

Pro dignitāte cuique tribuātur. CIC.—Let each man have according to his deserts.

Pro incertâ spe præmia certa.—To sacrifice certain for speculative profit.

See "*Ne præsentem.*"

Pro percâ scorpium.—Instead of a fish he gives you a scorpion.

Pro re natâ.—To suit present circumstances.

Pro rege, lege, grege.—For the king, the laws and the people.

Pro thesauro carbōnes!—Instead of a treasure, coals!

> ["'Rum,' I hopes! 'Baccy,' I thinks! 'Tracts,' by jingo!" Sailor's remark on discovering that he had picked up a bottle of tracts.]

Proba merx facilè emptōrem repĕrit. PLAUT.—Good things soon find a purchaser.

> "Please the eye, and pick the purse."
> "Good wine needs no bush."

Prŏbĭtas laudātur et alget. JUV.—Integrity is praised and starves.

> "Desert and reward seldom keep company."

> "A life of honour and of worth
> Has no eternity on earth,—
> 'Tis but a name." LONGFELLOW.

> "Honesty's a fool
> And loses that it works for." SHAKS.

Procellæ, quantò plus habent vīrium, tantò minus tempŏris. SEN.—The more violent the storm the sooner it is over.

> "The more light a torch gives the shorter it lasts."

> "Small showers last long, but sudden storms are short." SHAKS.

> See "*Quod est violentum.*"

Procul a Jove, procul a fulmĭne.—Far from Jupiter, far from his thunder.

> "Those that eat cherries with great persons shall have their eyes squirted out with the stones."

Procul a pedĭbus equīnis.—Stand away from a horse's heels.

> "Take heed of an ox before, an ass behind, and a monk on all sides."

Prodĭgus est nātus de parco patre creātus.—A miser's son is generally a spendthrift.

Proditōres etiam iis, quos antepōnunt, invīsi sunt. TAC. Traitors are hated even by those whom they prefer.

> "The wicked even hate vice in others."

> "The treason is loved, but the traitor is hated."

> "Kings love the treason, but not the traitor."

> "A bad mother wishes for good children."

Prohibenda est ira in puniendo. CIC.—Anger should never appear in awarding punishment.

> "Rebukes ought not to have a grain more of salt than of sugar."

Propŏsĭto florem prætŭlit officio. PROP.

> "And neglected his task for the flowers on the way." MOORE.

Propositum perfĭce opus. OVID.—When you have set yourself a task finish it.

Propria domus omnium optĭma.—Our own house surpasses every other.

>"Dry bread at home is better than roast meat abroad."
>
>See "*Bos alienus.*" "*Patriæ fumus.*"

Proprio laus sordet in ore.—Self praise is odious.

>"Let another man praise thee, not thine own mouth."
>
>"God and man think him a fool who brags of his own great wisdom."
>
>"Self exaltation is the fool's paradise."
>
>"On their own merits modest men are dumb." G. COLMAN.
>
>See "*Multi te.*" "*Merx.*"

Proprium humāni ingenii est odisse quem læsĕris. TAC.—It is human nature to hate him whom you have injured.

>"He who is the offender is never the forgiver."
>
>"He who doth the injury never forgives the injured man."
>
>"Forgiveness to the injured does belong,
>But they ne'er pardon who have done the wrong." DRYDEN.
>
>See "*Odĭmus quem.*"

Propter vitam vivendi perdĕre causas. JUV.—To gain a livelihood at the expense of all that makes life worth the having.

Prospectandum vetŭlo latrante.—When an old dog barks, then look out.

>"When the old dog barks he giveth counsel."

Prospĕrum et felix scelus virtus vocātur. SEN.—Successful villany is called virtue.

> "A thief passes for a gentleman when stealing has made him rich."
>
> "Success consecrates the foulest crimes."
>
> "Treason never prospers: what's the reason?
> Why, when it prospers, none dare call it 'treason.'"
> SIR T. HARRINGTON.
>
> "It is a bad action that success cannot justify."
>
> See "*Honesta quædam.*"

Proteo mūtābĭlĭor.—More changeable than Proteus.

Protĭnus appāret quæ plantæ frugĭfĕræ futūræ.—It is soon known which trees will bear fruit.

> [A natural bent for good or evil is easily perceptible in youth.]
>
> "That that comes of a cat will catch mice."
>
> "The child is father of the man." WORDSWORTH.
>
> See "*Urit maturè.*"

Provŏcat et vincĭtur.—The challenger is beaten.

> *Prudens futūri tempŏris exĭtum*
> *Calīgĭnōsâ nocte premit Deus.* HOR.

Designedly God covers in dark night the issue of futurity.

> "Let no man seek
> Henceforth to be foretold what shall befall
> Him or his children." MILTON.
>
> "As to what is future, even a bird with a long neck cannot see it, but God only."

Prudentia cum vīrĭbus conjuncta.—Prudence and strength combined.

Pudīca non est, fama pudīcam quam negat.—She is not a modest woman whom common report condemns.

"Cæsar's wife should be above suspicion." LANGHORNE.

See "*Ad calamitatem.*" "*Invīso semel.*"

Pudor demissus nunquam rĕdit in gratĭam. SYR.—Modesty once lost, never returns into favour.

Pudōre et liberalitāte lībĕros
Retinēre, satius esse credo, quàm metu. TER.

It is, I believe, better to restrain the passions of youth by a sense of shame, and by conciliatory means, than by fear.

"There is great force hidden in a sweet command."

See "*Conciliat.*" "*Persuasione.*"

Puerōrum crepundia.—The baubles of children.

"Vain, froward child of empire, say,
Are all thy playthings snatched away?"
BYRON.

Pugna suum finem, cum jacet hostis, habet. OVID.—The battle is over when the foe has fallen.

"It is a base thing to tear a dead lion's beard off."

See "*De mortuis.*" "*Nullum cum.*"

Pulchrorum autumnus pulcher.—The autumn of beauty is still beautiful.

> "The sun is still beautiful, though ready to set."

> "As wither'd roses yield a late perfume." SHENSTONE.

Pulchrum est accusāri ab accusandis.—It is an honourable thing to be accused by those who are open to accusation.

Pulchrum est dĭgĭto monstrāri, et dicier "Hic est." PERS. It is a pleasant thing to be pointed at with the finger, and to hear it said, "That is he."

Pulchrum est vitam donāre minōri. STAT.—It is an honourable thing to be merciful to the vanquished.

> "Nature teaches us to love our friends, but religion our enemies."

> "Sweet mercy is nobility's true badge." SHAKS.

> See "*Bis vincit.*"

Pulchrum ornātum turpes mores pejus cœno collĭnunt. PLAUT.—Vulgarity of manners defiles fine garments more than mud.

Pullāta turba.—The rabble.

Pulvĕrem ŏcŭlis offundĕre.—To throw dust in one's eyes.

Pūnĭca fides.—Punic faith. [Treachery.]

Punītis ingeniis, gliscit auctorĭtas. TAC.—By punishing men of talent we confirm their authority.

Puras Deus non plenas adspĭcit manus. SYR.—Clean hands are better than full ones in the sight of God.

"Better poor with honour than rich with shame."

See "*Honesta paupertas.*"

Puris omnĭa pŭra.—To the pure all things are pure.

Puteus si hauriātur melior evādit.—A well which is drawn from is improved.

[Art is improved by practice.]

"Drawn wells have sweetest water."

See "*Doctrīna.*" "*Vitium capiunt.*"

QUA in re clarus quisque est, ad eam propĕrat.—
We all refer to that of which we know most.

Quâ vincit, victos protĕgit ille manu. OVID.—
With the arm which won the victory he protects the vanquished.

Quæ dĕdĕram suprà, rĕpĕto, funemque redūco. JUV.—That which I just now gave, I recall, and draw back the string.

"I would have thee gone,
And yet no further than a wanton's bird,
Who lets it hop a little from her hand,
Like a poor prisoner in his twisted gyves,
And with a silk thread plucks it back again." SHAKS.

Quæ dolent molestum est contīngĕre.—It is cruel to refer to those things which cause sorrow.

"When sorrow is asleep wake it not."

"Name not a rope in his house that hanged himself."

"A galled horse will not endure the comb."

See "*Malum benè.*" "*Quiēta non.*"

Quæ e longinquo magis placent.—Things coming from afar are most esteemed.

> "Rare commodities are worth more than good."
>
> "More cost, more worship."
>
> See "*Rarum.*"

Quæ fuĕrant vitia, mores sunt. SEN.—What were vices have become the fashion of the day.

Quæ fuit durum pati,
Meminisse dulce est. SEN.

That which has been endured with difficulty is remembered with delight.

> See "*Carius est.*" "*Jucunda est.*"

Quæ non prosunt singŭla, multa juvant. OVID.—Things which of themselves avail nothing, when united become powerful.

> See "*De parvis.*" "*Minūtŭla.*"

Quæ non ulla tulit, fertque, feretque dies. OVID.—That which never has been, never is, and never will be.

Quæ peccāmus jŭvĕnes, ea luĭmus senes.—We expiate in old age the follies of our youth.

> "Young men's knocks old men feel."
>
> "If you lie upon roses when young, you will lie upon thorns when old."

"Happy is he who knows his follies in his youth."

"The excesses of our youth are drafts upon our old age, payable with interest about thirty years after date." COLTON.

See "*Bonum servat.*" "*Maturè fias.*"

Quæ semel ancilla, nunquam hera.—Once a handmaid never a lady.

Quæ sua sors hodie est, cras fore vestra potest.—That which is his lot to-day may be yours to-morrow.

"Such as she is, who died to-day,
Such thou alas! mayst be to-morrow." PRIOR.

Quæ suprà nos, nihil ad nos.—Things beyond our reach are not worth our consideration.

"What is too high, that let fly."

Quæ venit ex tuto, minus est accepta voluptas. OVID.—That pleasure which can be safely indulged in is the least inviting.

"Danger and delight grow on one stock."

See "*Nitimur.*" "*Quicquid licet.*"

Quædam melius laudantur silentio, quàm oratione.—Some things are better praised by silence than by remark.

Quæque ipse miserrima vidi.
Et quorum pars magna fui. VIR.

Miseries of which I was an eye witness and in which I took a chief part.

Quærenda pecūnia primŭm est,
Virtus post nummos. HOR.

Riches are first to be sought for; after wealth, virtue.

"Get money, money still!
And then let Virtue follow, if she will." POPE.

See "*Rem facias.*"

Quales ex humĭli magna ad fastīgia rerum
Extollit, quoties voluit fortūna jocāri. JUV.

Such men as fortune raises from a mean estate to the highest elevation by way of a joke.

Qualis hera, talis pĕdissĕqua.—Like mistress, like maid.

"Like master, like man."

"Like priest, like people."

Qualis quisque est, tales existĭmat alios.—Every man judges of others by himself.

See "*Non soles.*" "*Qui sibi.*"

Qualis rex, talis grex.—Like prince, like people.

Qualis vir, talis oratio.—You may judge of a man by his remarks.

"Many a fool might pass for a wise man if he would only keep his mouth shut."

See "*Talis hominibus.*"

Qualis vita, finis ita.—As a man has lived, so will he die.
  "What is learnt in the cradle lasts to the grave."

Quàm apes, apum sĭmĭles.—As like as bees.
  "As like as two peas."

Quàm cito mortālibus beneficium perit!—How quickly with all is a kindness forgotten!
  "Nothing is more easily blotted out than a good turn."
  "Benefits please like flowers, when they are fresh."
      See "*Cui placet obliviscĭtur.*" "*Si quid juves.*"

Quàm curat testūdo muscas?—What does the tortoise care for flies?

Quàm multa injusta ac prava fiunt morĭbus! TER.—How much of injustice and depravity is sanctioned by custom!
  "That monster, custom, who all sense doth eat
  Of habit's devil." SHAKS.

Quam quisque novit artem, in hâc se exercĕat. CIC.—Let every man practise the trade which he best understands.
  "Every man to his trade."
      See "*Tractent.*"

Quam scit uterque libens, censēbo exercĕat artem. HOR.—Let every man find pleasure in practising the profession he has learnt.

Quàm seipsum amans sine rivali! CIC.—How much in love with himself, and that too without a rival!

Quamvis sublīmes debent humĭles metuĕre. PHAED.—However exalted our position, we should still not despise the powers of the humble.

"There is no such thing as an insignificant enemy."

"The least and weakest man can do some hurt."

"A little stone overturns a great cart."

"A mouse will put the finishing stroke to a castle wall."

See "*Nec asperandum.*"

Quando tumet venter, produntur facta latenter.—Conviviality reveals secrets.

"Thought when sober, said when drunk."

See "*In vino.*" "*Quod est in.*"

Quando ullum invĕniet parem? HOR.—When shall we find his equal?

"For Lycidas is dead, dead ere his prime,
Young Lycidas, and hath not left his peer." MILTON.

"We ne'er shall look upon his like again." SHAKS.

Quandōque bonus dormītat Homĕrus. HOR.—Even the good Homer is sometimes caught napping.

"But men are men; the best sometimes forget." SHAKS.

See "*Nemo mortalium.*"

Quandōquĭdem accepto claudenda est janŭa damno. JUV.
When the mischief is done the door is shut.

"Too late to grieve when the chance is past."

"When the steed is stolen, you shut the stable door."

See "*Machĭnas post.*" "*Post bellum.*"

Quanta pătĭmur!—How great the sufferings we endure.

"Sufferance is the badge of all our tribe." SHAKS.

Quanti casus humāna rotant!—How many accidents keep human life a rolling.

"Thus the whirligig of time
Brings in his revenges." SHAKS.

*Quanto quisque sibi plura negāverit,
A Dîs plura feret.* HOR.

The more a man denies himself the more will he receive from heaven.

Quantò superiōres sumus, tantò nos gerāmus submissius. CIC.—The higher our position the more modestly should we behave.

"The more noble, the more humble."

"An insolent lord is not a gentleman."

"Arrogance is a weed that grows mostly on a dunghill."

Quantum mutātus ab illo!—How changed from what he was!

> "How fallen, how changed
> From him, who, in the happy realms of light,
> Clothed with transcendent brightness, didst outshine
> Myriads, though bright." MILTON.

> *Quare vitia sua nemo confitētur?*
> *Quia etiam nunc in illis est. Somnium*
> *Narrāre vigilantis est.* SEN.

Why will no man confess his faults? Because he continues to indulge in them; a man cannot tell his dream till he wakes.

> "When we have what we like 'tis hard to miss it." BYRON.

Quem casus transit, aliquando invĕniet. SYR.—We may escape misfortune for a while, but the evil day will come.

> "The pitcher doth not go so often to the well, but it comes home broken at last."

Quem dī dilĭgunt, adolescens morĭtur. PLAUT.—He whom the gods love dies young.

> "The best go first, the bad remain to mend."

> "Perhaps the early grave
> Which men weep over may be meant to save." BYRON.

> "The less of this cold world the more of heaven." MILMAN.

> "Early, bright, transient, chaste as morning dew,
> She sparkled, was exhal'd, and went to heaven." YOUNG.

> See "*Mors optĭma.*" "*Optĭma citissimĕ.*"

Quem Jupiter vult perdĕre, prius dementat.—Him whom Jove would destroy he first deprives of his reason.

[Arrogant, insolent, and vainglorious people work out their own ruin.]

Quem pœnĭtet peccâsse, pœnè est innŏcens. SEN.—He who repents of his fault is almost guiltless.

"A fault confessed is half redressed."

"By penitence th' Eternal's wrath's appeas'd. SHAKS.

"Blest tears of soul-felt penitence!
In whose benign, redeeming flow
Is felt the first, the only sense
Of guiltless joy that guilt can know. MOORE.

See "*Lavant lacrymæ.*"

Quem sors diērum cunque dabit, lucro Appōne. HOR. Each day that fate adds to your life, put down as so much gain.

Quemvis hominem secum adtŭlit ad nos. JUV.—He is a Jack of all trades.

"A man so various, that he seemed to be
Not one, but all mankind's epitome. DRYDEN.

Quemcunque mĭsĕrum vidĕris, hominem scias. SEN.—Whenever you see a fellow-creature in trouble, remember that he is a man.

See "*Homo sum.*"

Qui altĕrum accusat probri, eum ipsum se intuēri oportet. Plaut.—He who accuses another of wrong should look well into his own conduct.

> "He who lives in a glass house should be the last to throw stones."
>
> See "*Clodius.*"

Qui amat me, amat et canem meum.

> "Love me love my dog.
> "He who loves me loves my dog too."

Qui amīcus est, amat, qui amat, non utĭque semper amīcus est. Sen.—A friend always loves, but he who loves is not always a friend.

Qui benè vult fari, debet benè præmĕditāri.—He who would speak well should well consider his subject beforehand.

> "Those who wade in unknown waters will be sure to be drowned."

Qui capit, capĭtur.—He who would catch is caught.

> "Biter bit."
>
> See "*Captantes capti.*"

Qui capit, ille facit.—He who takes it to himself, he it is who has done the act.

> "A guilty conscience needs no accuser."
> "He who feels himself scabby, let him scratch."
> "If the cap fits, wear it."
>
> See "*Heu! Quam.*"

Qui caret argento, frustrà utitur argumento.—He argues in vain who argues without means."

"Wealth makes worship."

See "*Nemo an.*" "*Tanti quantum.*"

Qui cavet, ne decipiātur, vix cavet cum etiam cavet. PLAUT.— He who tries to protect himself from deception is often cheated, even when most on his guard.

Qui celōcem regĕre nequit, onĕrāriam petit!—He who cannot even manage a yacht asks for a ship of burthen!

"Don't try to run before you can walk."

Qui cum contemptu vitæ invādunt.—Those who attack, though they die in the attempt.

"War to the knife."

Qui cum fortūnâ convĕnit, dives est.—A contented man is always rich.

"He is rich that is satisfied."

"We lessen our wants by lessening our desires."

See "*Is minimo.*"

Qui Curios sĭmŭlant, et Bacchanālia vivunt. JUV.—Men who ape the saint and play the sinner.

"They talk like angels but they live like men." JOHNSON.

See "*Fronte politus.*" "*Mel in ore.*"

Qui dedit benefĭcium, tacĕat; narret qui accēpit. SEN.—Let him who has granted a favour speak not of it; let him who has received one, proclaim it.

> "Do good by stealth, and blush to find it fame." POPE.

> "To John I owed great obligation:
> But John unhandsomely thought fit
> To publish it to all the nation;
> Sure John and I are more than quit." PRIOR.

Qui dĭgĭto scalpunt uno caput. JUV.—Those who scratch their hair with one finger. [Fearing to discompose their curls. Dandies.]

Qui e nuce nuclĕum esse vult, frangat nucem. PLAUT.—He who would have the kernel must crack the shell.

> See "*Dii laboribus.*" "*Nil sine.*"

Qui facit per altĕrum, facit per se. LAW MAX.—What a man does by the agency of another is his own act.

Qui fert malis auxilium, post tempus dolet. PHAED.—He who assists the wicked will in time rue it.

> "Save a thief from the gallows and he'll be the first shall cut your throat."

Qui festīnat ad divitias, non erit insons.—He who hastens to be rich will not be without fault.

Qui festīnis est, pĕdĭbus offendit.—He who hastens too much stumbles and falls.

> "A hasty man never wants woe."
>
> See "*Festīna lentè.*" "*Qui nimis.*"

Qui fortĭter emungit, elĭcit sanguinem.—He who blows his nose too hard makes it bleed.

Qui fugit molam, fugit farīnam.—Shirk work and you will want bread.

> "They must hunger in frost who will not work in heat."
>
> See "*Dii laborĭbus.*" "*Nil sine.*"

Qui gĕnus jactat suum, aliēna laudat. SEN.—He who boasts of his pedigree praises that which does not belong to him.

> "So yourself be good, a fig for your grandfather."
>
> See "*Nam genus.*"

Qui homo matūrè quæsīvit pecūniam,
Nisi eam matūrè parcit, matūrè ēsŭrit. PLAUT.
He who has in due season become rich, unless he saves in due season, will in due season starve.

> "A fat housekeeper makes lean executors."
>
> "Waste makes want."
>
> "He who spends more than he should
> "Shall not have to spend when he would."
>
> See "*Festo die.*"

Qui in amōrem
Præcĭpĭtāvit pejus perit quàm si saxo saliăt. PLAUT.
He who rushes headlong into love will fare worse than if he had cast himself from a precipice.

> "The man who wants his wedding garments to suit him must allow plenty of time for the measure." BULWER.

> Marry in haste, repent at leisure."

> See "*Fide sed.*" "*Nervi et.*"

Qui invĭdet, minor est.—He who envies us admits his inferiority.

> "Envy will merit as its shade pursue,
> But like a shadow, proves the substance true." POPE.

Qui jacet in terrâ, non habet undĕ cadat.—He who lies on the ground cannot fall.

> "He that is down need fear no fall." BUNYAN.

> "A dead mouse feels no cold."

> "I am not now in fortune's power,
> "He that is down can fall no lower." BUTLER.

> See "*Nondum incurvum.*" "*Forsan misĕros.*"

Qui luxuriōsus est, necesse est ut et avārus sit.—Spendthrifts are always of necessity greedy and covetous.

Qui malĕ agit, odit lucem.—An evil doer abhors the light of day.

> "Few love to hear the sins they love to act." SHAKS.

Qui maximè cavet, is sæpe cautor captus est. PLAUT.—He who is most on his guard is often himself taken in.

Qui medicè vivit, miserè vivit.—He who lives by medical treatment has but a wretched existence.

Qui multiplicat scientiam, multiplicat dolorem.—He who increases knowledge, increases sorrow.

"In much wisdom is much grief."

Qui nescit dissimulāre, nescit vivĕre.—He who cannot conceal his sentiments, knows not how to live.

"Innocence itself sometimes hath need of a mask."

"Truth should not always be revealed."

"Never fight an enemy whilst it is possible to cheat him."

"Craft against vice I must apply." SHAKS.
See "*Etiam illud.*" "*Qui simulat.*"

Qui nihil debet, lictōres non timet.—He who owes nothing fears not the sheriff's officer.

"Out of debt out of danger."

"Dreading that climax of all earthly ills,
"The inflammation of his weekly bills." BYRON.

"Let the galled jade wince; our withers are unwrung." SHAKS.

Qui nihil litigat, cœlebs est.—Who would avoid all strife, should be a bachelor.

"Wisely, I say, I am a bachelor." SHAKS.

Qui nimis propĕrè, minus prospĕrè.

> "Most haste, worst speed."

> "Discreet stops make speedy journeys."

> "Too swift arrives as tardy as too slow." SHAKS.

> See "*Da spatium.*" "*Festīna lentè.*"

Qui nimĭum propĕrat, serius absolvit.—He who makes too much haste gains his end later.

> "Haste makes waste and waste makes want."
> See "*Festīna lente.*"

Qui nocēre potest, et idem prodesse.—One who can do you a deal of good or a deal of harm.

Qui non est hodĭe, cras minus aptus erit. MART.—He who is not in readiness to-day, will be less prepared to-morrow.

> "Procrastination is the thief of time."
> "The man will surely fail, who dares delay,
> And lose to-morrow that has lost to-day."

> "Our yesterday's to-morrow now is gone,
> And still a new to-morrow does come on.
> We by to-morrow draw out all our store,
> Till the exhausted well can yield no more." COWLEY.

> See "*Deliberando.*" "*Dum deliberāmus.*"

Qui non liberè veritatem pronunciat, proditor est veritātīs.—He who does not fully speak the truth is a traitor to it.

Qui non potest quod vult, velle oportet quod potest.—He who cannot do what he wishes, must needs do as he can.

"If the mountain will not go to Mahomet, let Mahomet go to the mountain."

"Better play at small game than stand out."

See "*Præstat possidēre.*" "*Si bonem.*" "*Ut quimus.*"

Qui non prōfĭcit, dēfĭcit.—He who does not advance recedes.

See "*Non progrĕdi.*"

Qui non vetat peccāre cum possit, jubet. SEN.—He invites the commission of a crime who does not forbid it, when it is in his power to do so.

Qui non vult fĭĕri desidiōsus, amet. OVID.—He who would not be indolent, let him fall in love.

Qui parcit virgam, odit filium.—He who spares the rod hates his son.

"Spare the rod, spoil the child."

"A child may have too much of his mother's blessing."

"The devil was so fond of his children that he plucked out their eyes."

"He that spareth the rod hateth his son, but he that loveth him chasteneth betimes."

"Love well whip well."

"Woe to the house where there is no chiding."

"I must be cruel only to be kind." SHAKS.

"O ye who teach the ingenuous youth of nations—
　Holland, France, England, Germany or Spain;
I pray ye flog them upon all occasions,
　It mends their morals—never mind the pain." BYRON.

Qui peccat ebrius, luat sobrius. LAW MAX. He who sins when drunk will have to atone for it when sober.

Qui petit alta nimis, retrò lapsus ponĭtur imis.—Who aims at things beyond his reach, the greater will be his fall.

"The highest branch is not the safest roost."
See "*Feriunt.*" "*Sæpius ventis.*"

Qui pingit florem, non pingit floris odōrem.—He who paints the flower cannot paint its fragrance.

Qui prior est tempŏre, potior est jure. LAW MAX.—He who is first in time has the prior right.

"First come, first served."

Qui quæ vult dicit, quæ non vult audiet. TER.—He who says what he likes, must hear what he does not like.

Qui satur est, pleno laudat jejunĭa ventre.—When hunger is appeased we can preach the merits of fasting.

"The friar preached against stealing when he had a pudding in his sleeve."

*Qui se committit homĭni tutandum imprŏbo,
Auxĭlia dum requīrit, exĭtium invĕnit.* PHAED.

He who trusts himself for safety to the care of a wicked man, in seeking succour meets with ruin.

See "*Mali viri.*"

Qui seipsum laudat, citò derisōrem invĕniet. SYR.—He who sounds his own trumpet will soon find plenty to laugh at him.

"Where vain-glory reigns, folly is prime counsellor."

"Conceit in weakest bodies strongest works." SHAKS.

See "*Proprio laus.*"

*Qui semel aspexit quantum dimissa petītis
Præstent, matūrè redeat, rĕpĕtatque relicta.* HOR.

Let him who has once perceived how much that, which has been discarded, excels that which he has longed for, return at once, and seek again that which he despised.

"He told me once
The saddest thing that can befall the soul,
Is when it loses faith in God and woman,
For he had lost them both. Lost I those gems,
Though the world's throne stood open in my path,
I would go wandering back into my childhood,
Searching for them with tears."
ALEXANDER SMITH.

*Qui semel est læsus fallāci piscis ab hamo,
Omnĭbus unca cibis æra subesse putat.* Ovid.

The fish which has once felt the hook, suspects the crooked metal in every food which offers.

"A dog which has been beaten with a stick is afraid of its shadow."

See "*Empta dolōre.*" "*Mæsus timet.*"

Qui semel gustārit canis, a corio nunquam absterrētur.—A dog that has once tasted the flesh cannot be kept from the skin.

Qui semel scurra, nunquam paterfamilias.—Once a buffoon, never a good father of a family.

Qui sentit commŏdum, sentīre debet et onus. Law Max.—He who takes the profit ought also to take the labour.

"The sluggard will not plough by reason of the cold; therefore shall he beg in harvest, and have nothing."

See "*Dii laboribus.*" "*In sudōre.*"

Qui sibi mali conscii, alios suspicantur.—Those who are conscious of their own iniquity, suspect others.

"Ill-doers, ill-deemers."
"Whose nature is so far from doing harms,
That he suspects none." Shaks.

"Whose own hard dealings teaches them suspect
The thoughts of others." Ibid.

See "*Non soles.*"

Qui simŭlat verbis, nec corde est fidus amīcus,
Tu quoque fac simĭle, et sic ars deludĭtur arte. CATO.

Should any one attempt to deceive you by false expressions, and not be a true friend at heart, act in the same manner, and thus art will defeat art.

[If you would catch a man let him think he is catching you.]

"Deceiving a deceiver is no knavery."

"It is fair and just to cheat the cheater."

"Diamond cut diamond."

See "*Etiam illud.*" "*Qui nescit.*"

Qui sitĭunt, silentĭo bibunt.—They who are thirsty drink in silence.

"Asses that bray most eat least."

"Every time the sheep bleats it loseth a mouthful."

Qui spe aluntur, pendent, non vivunt.—Those who are nourished by hope live ever in suspense, and enjoy not life.

"Hopes delayed hang the heart upon tenter-hooks."

"The heart-sick faintness of the hope delayed!" SCOTT.

See "*Ināni spe.*"

Qui tacet, consentīre vidētur. LAW MAX.—From his silence a man's consent is inferred.

"Silence gives consent."

Qui tauros stimŭlent, multi, sed rarus arātor.—Many can drive oxen, few can plough.
> "Many can pack the cards that cannot play."
>> See "*Multi qui.*" "*Non est venātor.*"

Qui tempus præstolātur, tempus ei deest.—He who waits till an opportunity occurs may wait for ever.
> "A wise man will make more opportunities than he finds."
>> See "*Rusticus.*" "*Necessitāti.*"

Qui terret, plus ipse timet. CLAUD.—He who seeks to terrify others is more in fear himself.
> See "*Canes timidi.*"

Qui timidè rogat, docet negāre. SEN.—He who asks with timidity invites a refusal.
> "He that asketh faintly beggeth a denial."

Qui totum vult, totum perdit.—Want all lose all.
> "Grasp no more than thy hand will hold."
> "A greedy man God hates."
>> See "*Camēlus.*" "*Certa amittĭmus.*" "*Duos qui.*"

Qui vult cædĕre canem, facĭlè invĕnit fustem.
> "He who has a mind to beat a dog will easily find a stick."

Quibus in solo vivendi causa palāto est. JUV.—Men who only live to eat.
> See "*Fruges.*"

Quibus nec ara, neque fides.—Men who have no religion, no honour.

Quicquid agas, agĕre pro vīrĭbus.—Whatever you undertake let it be proportioned to your powers.

> "Learn to creep before you run."
>
> See "*Paulātim.*"

Quicquid calcavĕrit hic, rosa fiat! PERS.—May everything he treads upon become a rose!

> "You have but fed on the roses, and lain in the lilies of life."
> TENNYSON.

Quicquid delīrant reges, plectuntur Achīvi. HOR.—Kings play the fool, and the people suffer for it.

> "The pleasures of the mighty are the tears of the poor."

Quicquid erit, superanda omnis fortūna ferendo est. VIR. Come what may, all bad fortune is to be conquered by endurance.

> "Put a stout heart to a steep hill."

> "Wise men ne'er wail their present woes." SHAKS.

> See "*Levius fit.*" "*Tu ne cede.*"

Quicquid in buccam venĕrit, loquĭtur. MART.—He says anything that first comes into his mouth.

Quicquid licet, minus desiderātur.—What is permitted us we least desire.

> " Possession is the grave of pleasure."
>
> See " *Nitīmur.*"

Quicquid multis peccātur, inultum est. Luc.—A crime in which many are implicated goes unpunished.

> " A common blot is held no stain."

Quicquid præcĭpies, esto brevis. Hor.—Whatever you advise, be as brief as possible.

Quicquid vult, habēre nemo potest. Sen.—No one can have all he desires.

> *Quicunque turpi fraude semel innotuit,*
> *Etiam si verum dicit, amittit fidem.* Phaed.

He who has once made himself notorious as utterly unprincipled, is not credited even when he speaks the truth.

> " A liar is not believed when he speaks the truth."
>
> [Fable of boy and wolf.]
>
> See " *Invīso semel.*" " *Semel malus.*"

Quid ad Mercurium?—What has this to do with the matter?

Quid cæco cum specŭlo?—What need has a blind man of a looking glass?

"Blind men can judge no colours."

"What's the good of a sun-dial in the shade?"

Quid de quoque viro, et cui dicas, sæpe cavēto. Hor.—Be cautious as to what you say of men, and to whom you speak it.

"He that speaks without care shall remember with sorrow."

"Least said is soonest mended."

"A slip of the foot may soon be recovered; but that of the tongue perhaps never."

"A bridle for the tongue is a necessary piece of furniture."

"Give every man thine ear, but few thy voice." Shaks.

See "*Audīto multa.*" "*Non unquam.*"

Quid dŏmĭni facient, audent cum talia fures? Vir.—What will their masters not accomplish when low fellows are so presumptuous?

Quid dulcĭus homĭnum genĕri a naturâ datum est, quàm sui cuique libĕri? Cic.—What sweeter gift from nature has fallen to the lot of man than his children?

"Sweet to the father is his first-born's birth!" Byron.

Quid enim tentāre nocēbit?—What harm is there in making a trial?

"Nothing venture, nothing have."

See "*Audentes fortuna.*" "*Necesse est.*"

Quid est dignĭtas indigno, nisi circŭlus aurĕus in narĭbus suis?—What is an exalted position to a low fellow but a golden ring in a swine's snout?

"As a jewel of gold in a swine's snout, so is a fair woman that is without discretion."

Quid levius plumâ? Pulvis. Quid pulvĕre? Ventus. Quid vento? Mĕrĕtrix. Quid mĕrĕtrīce? Nihil.

What is lighter than a feather? Dust.
What lighter than dust? The wind.
What lighter than the wind? A harlot.
What lighter than a harlot? Nothing.

*Quid magis est durum saxo? Quid mollius undâ?
Dura tamen molli saxa cavantur aquâ.* Ovid.

What is harder than stone?
What more soft than water?
Nevertheless hard though the rock be, it is hollowed by the wave.

See "*Assidua stilla.*" "*Gutta cavat.*"

Quid non possit amor?—What is there that love will not achieve?

"Love grows with obstacles."

"Love rules the court, the camp, the grove,
All men below and saints above;
For love is heaven, and heaven is love." SCOTT.

See "*Nihil difficile.*"

Quid nostri philosophi? Nonne in his libris ipsis, quos scribunt de contemnendâ gloriâ, sua nōmĭna inscrībunt? CIC.—How do our philosophers act? Do they not inscribe their signatures to the very essays they write on the propriety of despising glory.

"Desire of glory is the last garment that even wise men put off."

Quid pro quo.

"Tit for tat."

See "*Par pari.*"

Quid quæque ferat regĭo et quid quæque recūset. VIR.—Consider what each soil will bear, and what each refuses.

*Quid quisque vitet, nunquam hŏmĭni satis
Cautum est in horas.* HOR.

No man ever properly calculates from time to time what it is his duty to avoid.

"That which one most forehets soonest comes to pass."

Quid sit futurum cras, fuge quærĕre. Hor.—Seek not to inquire what the morrow will bring with it.

> "He is miserable once, who feels it; but twice, who fears it before it comes."
>
> "Never cross a bridge till you come to it."
>
> "The mind flies back with a grand recoil
> From debts not due till to-morrow." Hood.
>
> "Love and life are for to-day." Prior.
>
> "To-night, at least, to-night be gay,
> Whate'er to-morrow brings." Moore.
>
> See "*Calamitosus.*" "*Carpe diem.*"

Quid te exempta juvat spinis de plurĭbus una? Hor. Wherein is the use of getting rid of one thorn out of many?

> "Or will you think, my friend, your bus'ness done
> When, of a hundred thorns, you pull out one." Pope.

Quid tandem non efficiant manus?—What will not perseverance achieve?

> See "*Audentes.*"

Quidquid excessit modum
Pendet instăbili loco. Sen.

Whatsoever has exceeded its proper limit is in an unstable position.

Quiēta non movēre.—Not to disturb that which is at rest.

"Stir not dying embers."

See "*Malum bene.*" "*Parcendum.*"

Quis custodĭet ipsos Custodes? Juv.

Who's to look after the keepers?"

Quis enim aut eum dilĭgit, quem metŭit, aut eum, a quo se metŭi putat. Cic.—Who can love the man he fears, or by whom he thinks he is himself feared?

"He that fears you present will hate you absent."

Quis enim læsos impūnè putāret Esse deos? Lucan.

Who will think that the gods can be insulted with impunity?

"The Baal-adorer bows on Sinai's steep;
Yet there, e'en there, O God, thy thunders sleep." Byron.

Quis enim modus adsit amōri?—What limit is there in love?

See "*Amantes amentes.*"

Quis enim virtūtem amplectĭtur ipsam Præmia si tollas. Juv.

Take away her rewards, and who will ever clasp naked Virtue to his bosom?

"Better sit idle than work for naught."

"He's an ill cook that cannot lick his own fingers."

"To take ambition from a soldier, is to rob him of his spurs."

"Though fame is smoke,
Its fumes are frankincense to human thought." BYRON.

See "*Dignæ canis.*" "*Honos alit.*" "*Rota.*"

Quis est enim, qui totum diem jaculans, non aliquando collineat. CIC.—Who is there that, shooting all day long, does not sometimes hit the mark?

"Often shooting hits the mark."

See "*Interdum stultus.*"

Quis fallere possit amantem? VIR.—Who can blind a lover's eyes?

Quis famulus amantior domini quàm canis?—By what servant is his master better loved than by his dog?

*Quis talia fando
Temperet a lacrymis?* VIR.
Who could tell such a story with dry eyes?

Quis tulerit Gracchos de seditione querentes? JUV.—Fancy the Gracchi complaining of treason!

See "*Clodius.*"

Quis tumidum guttur miratur in Alpibus? JUV.—Who thinks anything of goitre on the Alps?

Quisquis amat luscam, luscam putat esse venustam.—He who loves a one-eyed girl thinks that one-eyed girls are beautiful.

"He, whose mistress squints, says she ogles."

"Desire beautifies what is ugly."

See "*Turpia decipiunt.*"

Quisquis amat ranam, ranam putat esse Diānam.—If a man falls in love with a frog, he thinks his frog a very Diana.

"Love is blind."

"Fancy passes beauty."

See *above*.

Quisquis amat, servit; sequĭtur captīvus amātam.—Every lover is a slave: he follows captive at his mistress's heels.

"Fair tresses man's imperial race ensnare,
And beauty draws us with a single hair." POPE.

Quo me, Bacche, rapis tui Plenum? HOR.

Whither, O god of wine, art thou hurrying me, whilst under thy all-powerful influence?

Quo me vertam nescio. TER.—I know not which way to turn.

[I am in a quandary.]

Quo mihi fortūnas, si non concēdĭtur uti? Hor.—What is wealth to me if I cannot enjoy it?

> " A man that keeps riches and enjoys them not, is like an ass that carries gold and eats thistles."

> " The gown is hers that wears it; and the world is his who enjoys it."

> See " *Frustrà habet.*" " *Manifesta.*"

Quo more pyris vesci Călăber jubet hospes.* Hor.—In the same [hospitable] manner that a Calabrian would press you to eat his pears.

> " Thank'ee for nothing."

Quo moritūre ruis? Vir.—Whither art thou rushing to destruction?

Quo plus habent, eo plus cupiunt.—The more they have, the more they want.

> " Greedy fowk hae lang arms."

> " Avarice bursts the bag."

> " Much will always wanting be
> To him who much desires." Cowley.

> See " *Crescit amor.*"

---

* Pears were so plentiful in Calabria that they were given to pigs."

Quo plus sunt potæ, plus sitiuntur aquæ. Ovid.—The more they drink the more they thirst.
>"Thirst comes from drinking."
>"Ever drunk, ever dry."

Quo quisque est major, magis est placabĭlis ira. Ovid.—The more highminded a man is the more easily is his anger appeased.
>"The noble mind has no resentments." Shaks.
>"In taking revenge, a man is but even with his enemy; but in passing it over, he is superior."
>See "*Infirmi est.*" "*Ne malōrum.*"

Quo quisque peccat, in eo puniētur.—According to the nature of his sin shall a man be punished.
>"An eye for an eye, and a tooth for a tooth."
>See "*Par pari.*"

Quo quisque stultĭor, eò magis insolescit.—The greater the fool, the greater his insolence.
>"Presumption first blinds a man, and then sets him a running."

Quo semel est imbūta recens, servābit odōrem
Testa diu. Hor.

The cask will long retain the flavour of the wine with which it was first seasoned.
>"You may break, you may shatter the vase, as you will,
>But the scent of the roses will hang round it still." Moore.
>See "*Cui puer.*" "*Quod nova.*"

Quo tandem pacto deceat majoribus uti. Hor.—How to conduct yourself properly before your superiors.

Quo teneam vultus mutantem Protea nodo? Hor.—With what knot shall I bind this Proteus, who is ever shifting his ground?

> "Breaking his oath and resolution, like
> A twist of rotten silk." Shaks.
>
> See "*Aliud stans.*" "*Versutior.*"

Quocunque trahunt fata, sequamur.—Let us go, where fate directs us.

Quod alibi diminutum, exæquatur alibi.—That which is wanting in some respects, may be made up for in others.

Quod caret alternâ requie, durabile non est. Ovid.—That, which has not its alternation of rest, will not last long.

> "Double charging will break a cannon."
>
> See "*Iocandum.*" "*Misce.*" "*Stare diu.*"

Quod certaminibus ortum, ultra metam durat.—Things hatched in discord are not speedily terminated.

Quod cessat ex reditu, frugalitate suppleatur. Plin.—Let that which is wanting in income be supplied by economy.

> "Frae saving comes having."
>
> See "*Magnum est.*"

Quod cibus est aliis, aliis est acre venenum.

 "What's one man's meat's another man's poison."

 "Ill blows the wind that profits nobody." SHAKS.

  See "*Nam quod.*" "*Quod suave.*"

Quod contemnitur, sæpe utilissimum est.—That which is despised is often most useful.

 "Nought so vile, that on the earth doth live,
 But to the earth some special good doth give." SHAKS.

  See "*Inest sua.*" "*Rem Carendo.*"

Quod datur ex facili, longum male nutrit amorem.—Love for those too easily won does not last long."

 "But this swift business
 I must uneasy make, lest too light winning
 Make the prize light. SHAKS.

  See "*Magis illa.*"

Quod dedi, datum nollem.—I regret that I have given what I have.

Quod defertur, non aufertur.—That which is deferred is not abandoned.

 "Omittance is no quittance." SHAKS.

Quod dubites, ne feceris.—Don't do that of which you doubt the propriety.

Quod est in corde sobrii, est in ore ebrii.—What the sober man has in his heart, the drunkard has on his lips.

 "What soberness conceals, drunkenness reveals."

  See "*In vino.*" "*Quando tumet.*"

Quod est violentum, non est durābĭle.—That which is violent never lasts long.

> "For violent fires soon burn out themselves." SHAKS.

> See "*Procellæ, quanto.*"

Quod factum est, infectum fĭĕri non potest. TER.

> "What's done can't be mended."

Quod latet ignōtum est, ignōti nulla cupīdo. OVID.—What lies concealed is unknown; there can be no desire for what is not known.

> See "*Amissum quod.*"

Quod licet ingrātum est; quod non licet acrius urit. OVID. What we can have as a matter of course, is not valued; what is denied we eagerly covet.

> "Think you if Laura had been Petrarch's wife
> He would have written sonnets all his life?" BYRON.

> See "*Nitĭmur in.*" "*Quæ venit.*"

Quod nimis mĭsĕri volunt, hoc făcĭlĕ credunt.—What people in distress most wish for, they most readily believe.

Quod non est opus, asse carum est.—That which we really require not is dear at a farthing.

> "A good bargain is a pick-purse."

> "At a great pennyworth pause awhile."

Quod nova testa capit, invĕtĕrāta sapit.—The old cask tastes of what the new cask held.

"The child is father of the man." WORDSWORTH.

See "*Cui puer.*" "*Quo semel.*"

Quod nunc ratio est, impetus ante fuit. OVID.—What is now an act of reason, was but blind impulse.

Quod præstāre potes, ne bis promīsĕris ulli. CATO.—Don't promise twice what you can do at once.

"He that's long a giving, knows not how to give."

See "*Bis dat.*" "*Tardē benefacĕre.*"

Quod quisque sperat, facĭle credit.—We easily believe that which we hope for.

"Thy wish was father, Harry, to that thought." SHAKS.

See "*Ferè.*"

Quod rarò cernit ocŭli lux, cor citò spernit.—What the eye rarely sees, the heart soon despises.

See "*Multas amicitias.*"

Quod rarum carum, vilescit quotidiānum.—What is new is esteemed, but what is in every day use ceases to afford interest.

See "*Quo e longinquo.*"

Quod rătio nequiit, sæpe sanāvit mora. SEN.—Time hath often cured the wound which reason failed to heal.

"The slow, sweet hours that bring us all things good."
TENNYSON.

Quod satis est cui contingit, nihil amplius optet. Hor.—He who has enough for his wants should desire nothing more.

> See "*Is minimo.*"

Quod scis, nescis.—Keep your own counsel.

> "What one knows it is useful sometimes to forget."
>
> "Let not the bottom of your purse or of your mind be seen."
> See "*Qui nescit.*"

Quod sibi quis nolit fĭĕri, non inferat ulli.—Do as you would be done unto.

Quod sis, esse velis, nihilque malis. Mart.—Wish to be what you are, and wish for no other position.

Quod supra nos, nihil ad nos.—That which is beyond our reach is nothing to us.

> "What is too high, that let fly."

Quod suave est aliis, aliis fit amārum.—That which is sweet to some is bitter to others.

> "What's sport to you is death to us." [Fable of Boys and Frogs.]
> See "*Nam quod.*" "*Quod cibus.*"

Quod tegĭtur, majus credĭtur esse malum. Mart.—Hidden evils are most dreaded.

> "Mystery magnifies danger, as the fog does the sun." Colton.
> See "*Omne ignōtum.*"

Quod tibi fiĕri non vis, altĕri ne fecĕris. Prosp.—Do not unto another that which you would not he should do unto you.

Quod vos jus coget, id voluntāte impĕtret. Ter.—What the law will compel you to do, do of your own free will.

"Make a virtue of necessity."

Quorsum opus amīcis, si modo favĕat Deus.—We need not friends if Providence smiles on us.

"He that hath the grace of God, hath wealth enough." Shaks.

Quos vult, sors ditat, et quos vult, sub pĕdĕ tritat.—Fortune enriches or tramples on us at her will.

"Reputation is an idle and most false imposition, oft got without merit, and lost without deserving." Shaks.

Quot capĭtum vivunt, totidem studiorum Millia. Hor.

As many men as there are existing, so many are their different pursuits.

See "*Mores dispăres.*" "*Non omnes eădem.*"

Quot homĭnes, tot sententiæ. Ter.—As many men, so many opinions.

"And all may think which way their judgments lead 'em. Byron.
See "*Mores dispăres.*"

Quot īlĭcis folia,
Quot fluctus insŭlæ.

As numerous as the leaves of the oak, or the waves which wash the island.

Quot servi, tot hostes. SEN.—As many servants so many enemies.

Quum adsit via, semĭtam quæris.—You ask the path when the high road is before your eyes.

See "*Juxta fluvium.*"

Quum infirmi sumus, optĭmi sumus.—In time of sickness man is ever on his best behaviour.

"When the pirate prays, there is great danger."

See "*Ægrōtat dæmon.*" "*In morbo.*"

Quum licet fugĕre, ne quære litem.—When you can avoid it, never seek strife.

"Beware
Of entrance to a quarrel." SHAKS.

See "*Felix qui non.*" "*Nescis tu.*"

Radit usque ad cutem.—He shaves close to the skin.

"He would skin a flint."

See "*Aquam plorat.*

Rami correcti rectificantur; trabs minimè.—Branches may be trained; not the trunk.

See "*Obsta.*"

Ranæ aquam.—Would you take water to the frog?

See "*Athēnas noctuas.*"

Ranārum more bibĕre.—To drink like frogs.

Rancĭdŭlum quiddam balbâ de nare locŭtus. Pers.—Snuffling through his nose some stale joke.

*Rara est adeò concordia formæ
Atque pudicitiæ.* Juv.
Rare is the union of beauty and modesty.

"If half thy outward graces had been placed
About the thoughts and counsels of thy heart." Shaks.

*Rarò antecēdentem scelestum
Desĕruit pede pœna claudo.* Hor.

Get what start the sinner may, Retribution, for all her lame leg, never quits his track.

> "Limping justice ne'er will fail
> To hunt out the longest trail."
> See "*Habet deus.*"

Rarò vaga virgo pudīca est.—A gadding girl is rarely coy.

Rarum carum.—Scarce things are prized.

> "New things are most looked at."
> See "*Est natura.*" "*Quæ e longinquo.*"

Re opĭtulandum, non verbis.—Help by actions, not by words.

> "Many words will not fill a bushel."
> "Words butter no parsnips."
> "Words are but sands; 'tis money buys lands."
> See "*Destināta tantum.*" "*Ne verbis.*"

Rebus non me trado, sed commŏdo. Sen.—I do not sacrifice, but lend myself to business.

> "Don't make a toil of a pleasure."

Reddĭte cuique suum.—Give to each man that which is his due.

> See "*Suum cuique.*"

Redīre, cum perit, nescit pudor. Sen.—When modesty has once perished, it will never revive.

> "And Modesty, who, when she goes,
> Is gone for ever." W. S. Landor.

Refricāre cǐcātrīcem.—To re-open a wound.
>See "*Malum benè.*"

Regia, crede mihi, res est succurrĕre lapsis. Ovid.—It is a kingly act to help the fallen.
>"The monarch drank that happy hour
>The sweetest, noblest draught of power." Scott.

>"The peasants thanked her with their tears,
>When food and clothes were given ;
>'This is a joy,' the lady said,
>'Saints cannot taste in heaven.'" A. Smith.

Relāta rĕfĕro.—I simply state what I have heard.
>"I tell the tale as it was told to me." Byron.

Religentem esse oportet, religiōsum nefas. Gell.—A man should be religious, not superstitious.

Relĭgio docenda, non coercenda.—Religion must be taught, not forced.
>"Fire and faggot are but sad reformers."

Relĭgio pĕpĕrit scelerōsa atque impia facta. Lucr.—Religious questions have often led to wicked and impious actions.
>"Christians have burned each other, quite persuaded
>That all the Apostles would have done as they did." Byron.
>See "*Tantum religio.*"

Rem acu tĕtĭgisti.—You have hit the point exactly.
>"You have hit the nail on the head."

Rem carendo, non fruendo, cognoscĭmus.—We learn the value of things more in their loss than in their enjoyment.
> "The worth of a thing is best known by the want."
>> See "*Bonum, magis.*" "*Nostra intellĭgimus.*" "*Quod contemnĭtur.*"

*Rem facias; rem,
Si possis, rectè; si non, quocunque modo rem.* HOR.—Get money; by just means, if you can; if not, still get money.
> "Get wealth and power, if possible with grace,
> If not, by any means, get wealth and place." POPE.
>> See "*Quærenda.*"

Remis velisque.—With oars and sails.
> "Tooth and nail."

Repentè, tanquam procella.—Suddenly as a storm.
> "Just then, as by the tumult riven,
> Poured down at once the lowering heaven." SCOTT.

Res ad restim redĭit.—It is all over: I may as well go and hang myself.

Res ad triarios redĭit.—The reserve are engaged.
> "Up, guards, and at 'em."

Res adversæ consilium ădĭmunt. TAC.—Adversity deprives us of our judgment.
> "Our wisdom is no less at Fortune's mercy than our wealth."

Res age; tutus eris. OVID.—Occupy yourself, and you will be out of harm's way.
> "Constant occupation prevents temptation."
>   See "*Dæmon te.*" "*Facito aliquid.*" "*Nihil agendo.*"

Res angusta domi.—Straitened circumstances.
> "Chill penury repressed their noble rage,
> And froze the genial current of the soul." GRAY.

Res in cardĭne est.—The matter is under consideration.

Res non parta labōre, sed relicta.—Wealth not acquired by our own labours, but inherited.
> "He comes to the world, as a gentleman comes
>   To a lodging ready furnished." HOOD.

Res satis est nota, plus fœtent stercŏra mota.—It's a well-known fact, dirt stinks more when stirred.
> "Let that flea stick in the wa', when the dirt's dry, it'll rub out."
>   SCOTT.

Respĭce finem.—Keep your eye upon the goal.

Rete non tendĭtur accĭpĭtri neque milvio. TER.—The net is not spread for the hawk or the kite.
> "Sue a beggar and get a louse."

Rex aut asĭnus!—A king or a donkey.
>   See "*Aut Cæsar.*"

Rex eris, si rectè facies.—If your conduct be noble, you will be a king.
> "Howe'er it be, it seems to me,
>   'Tis only noble to be good;
> Kind hearts are more than coronets,
>   And simple faith than Norman blood." TENNYSON.

Ride, si sapis. Mart.—Be cheerful, if you are wise.

"Let me play the fool;
With mirth and laughter let old wrinkles come." Shaks.

See "*Itĕrum precor.*"

*Ridentem dīcĕre verum
Quid vetat?* Hor.

What prevents a man's speaking good sense with a smile on his face?

"But may not truth in laughing guise be dressed?"

"There is mony a true tale tauld in jest."

Ridentibus arrīde.—Laugh with those that laugh.

Ridētur, chordâ qui semper oberrat eādem. Hor.—He makes himself ridiculous who is for ever repeating the same mistake.

*Ridicŭlum acri
Fortius ac melius magnas plerumque secat res.* Hor.
Ridicule often cuts the knot, where severity fails.

Risu emorīri.—To die of laughing.

"Laughter holding both his sides." Milton.

Risu inepto res ineptĭor nulla est. Mart.—Nothing is more ill-timed than an ill-timed laugh.

Risum teneātis amici? Hor.—Can you restrain your laughter, my friends?

Risus abundat in ore stultōrum.—Laughter abounds in the mouths of fools.

    "The more fools, the more laughter."

    "And gentle Dulness ever loves a joke." Pope.

    See "*Per risum.*"

Risus profundior lachrymas parit.—The excess of mirth leads to tears.

    "They laugh till they cry."

    "Joy surfeited turns to sorrow."

Rixātor de lanā caprinā.—One who would quarrel about goats' wool.

    [A most captious person.]

    "To quarrel with his little finger."

Rōbŏri prudentia præstat.—Prudence availeth more than strength.

    "Zeal without knowledge is the sister of folly."

    See "*Vis consili.*"

Romæ Tibur amem ventōsus, Tibŭre Romam. Hor.—At Rome I love Tibur; then, like a weathercock, at Tibur Rome.

Romānus sedendo vincit.—The Roman conquered by delay.

    [Fabius Cunctator.]

    "Prudent pauses forward business."

    See "*Mora omnis.*" "*Velōcem tardus.*"

Rosam cum anĕmōnā confers.—You are comparing a rose to an anemone.

Rosam, quæ prætĕriit, ne quæras itĕrum.—Seek not the rose which is once lost.

  See " *De re amissâ.*" " *Non luctu.*"

Rota plaustri malè uncta stridet.—A wheel not greased will creak.

 [Those who are not properly paid will not work without grumbling.]

 "The sweat of industry would dry and die,
 But for the end it works to." SHAKS.

  See " *Digna canis.*" " *Quis enim.*"

Rudens omnis disruptus.—Every sheet has parted.

 [Every hope has vanished.]

Rūri sibi quisque mĕtit.—Every man for himself.

Rusticus expectat, dum deflŭat amnis. HOR.—The clown waits for the river to run itself dry.

 [Crossing Cheapside.]

Sæpe caput scăbĕret, vīvos et rōdĕret ungues. Hor.—He will often have to scratch his head, and bite his nails to the quick.
[To succeed he will have to puzzle his brains and work hard.]
See "*Dii laboribus.*"

Sæpe est sub sordĭdo pallĭolo sapientia. Cic.—Wisdom often exists under a shabby coat.

"A pearl may in a toad's head dwell,
And may be found too in an oyster shell." Bunyan.

Sæpe in conjugĭis fit noxia, cum nĭmia est dos. Auson.—It often happens, that misery will follow a marriage when the dowry is too large.

"A great dowry, a bed full of brambles."

Sæpe in magistrum scĕlĕra rĕdiērunt sua. Sen.—Crime oft recoils upon the author's head.

"Revenge and wrong bring forth their kind;
The foul cubs like their parents are." Shelley.

"We but teach
Bloody instructions, which, being taught, return
To plague the inventor." SHAKS.

    See "*Nostris.*" "*Sibi quisque.*"

Sæpe intĕreunt aliis mĕdĭtantes necem. PHAED.—Those who plot the destruction of others often perish in the attempt.

    See "*Qui capit.*"

Sæpe tacens vocem verbaque vultus habet. OVID.—The silent countenance often speaks with expressive eloquence.

"Her very silence, and her patience,
Speak to the people, and they pity her." SHAKS.

    See "*Dum tacent.*"

Sæpe tulit lassis succus amārus opem. OVID.—A bitter drug oft brings relief.

"Bitter pills may have wholesome effects."

    See "*Periisset.*" "*Tribulatio.*"

Sæpe viâ oblīquâ præstat, quàm tendĕre recta.—It is often better to go by a circuitous than by a direct path.

"The furthest way about is the nearest way home."

Sæpius opiniōne quàm re laborāmus. SEN.—We suffer more in imagination than in reality.

*Sæpius ventis agitātur ingens
Pinus, et celsæ graviōre casu
Dēcĭdunt turres.* HOR.

The lofty pine is most easily brought low by the force of the wind, and the higher the tower the greater the fall thereof.

"The higher flood hath always the lower ebb."
See "*Qui petit.*"

Sævis inter se convĕnit ursis. JUV.—Savage bears agree with one another.

"Bear won't bite bear."
See "*Parcit cognatis.*"

Sale nihil utilius.—There is nothing more telling than wit.

Salus, ubi multi consiliārii. COKE.—Where there are many counsellors there is safety.

Sapiens nihil facit invītus. CIC.—A wise man does nothing by constraint.

"What! upon compulsion? No!" SHAKS.

Sapientem pascĕre barbam. HOR.—To grow a philosopher's beard.

Sapientes tyrānni sapientium congressu.—Kings learn wisdom from associating with wise men.

Sapientia in exĭtu canĭtur.—The test of merit is success.

"At the end of the game you'll see who's the winner."
See "*Exĭtus acta.*" "*Finis corōnat.*"

Sardonius risus.*—A sardonic laugh.
> [An unnatural laugh.]

Sat cito, si sat tuto.—Quick enough, if safe enough.
> "Bustle is not industry."
>> See "*Festina.*"

Satiĕtas ferociam parit.—Full feasting breeds ferocity.
> "Then wander forth the sons
> Of Belial, flown with insolence and wine." MILTON.

Satis eloquentiæ, sapientiæ parum. SALL. — Eloquence enough, but little wisdom.

Satis est, quod sufficit.—That which satisfies is enough.
> "Enough is as good as a feast."
>> See "*Is minimo.*"

Satis in ipsâ conscientiâ pulcherrĭmi facti fructus est. CIC. There is sufficient reward in the mere consciousness of a good action.
> "Virtue is its own reward."

Satis superque.—Enough and to spare.

Satius est initiis medēri, quàm fine.—Early, not late remedies are the most effective.
> "Prevention is better than cure."
>> See "*Principiis obsta.*"

---

* *Sardōa herba.* An herb like smallage growing in Sardinia, which being bitten, causes great laughing and grinning, and afterwards death.

Satius est recurrĕre quàm malĕ currĕre.—It is better to turn back than to persevere in an evil course.

Satius fugĕre quàm malĕ manēre.—It is better to fly than to remain in disgrace.
> "Better a fair pair of heels than a halter."

Saxum volūtum non obducĭtur musco.
> "A rolling stone gathers no moss."
> "Three removes are as bad as a fire."
> See "*Planta quæ.*"

Scărăbæus citius faciet mel.—Sooner will a beetle make honey.

Scĕlĕre velandum est scelus. SEN.—Crime requires further crime to conceal it.
> "Things bad begun make strong themselves by ill." SHAKS.

Scīlĭcet ut fulvum spectātur in ignĭbus aurum,
Tempŏre sic duro est inspicienda fides. OVID.
As the yellow gold is tried in the fire, so is sincerity tested in adversity.

Scīlĭcet uxōrem cum dote, fidemque, et amīcos,
Et genus, et formam regīna pecunia donat. HOR.
For well-dowered wife, credit, friends, birth and beauty, all-powerful money gives them all.

Scindĕre glaciĕm.—To break the ice.

Scintilla etiam exigua in tenĕbris micat.—Even the smallest spark shines brightly in darkness.

Scire tuum nihil est, nisi te scire hoc sciat alter. PERS. Your knowing a thing is nothing, unless another knows you know it.

>See "*Paulum sepultæ.*"

Scribātur portis, mĕrĕtrix est jānŭa mortis.—Let it be well recorded that a harlot is a gate which leads to death.

>"One of Satan's shepherdesses caught
>And meant to stamp him with her master's mark." TENNYSON.
>See "*Vina Venusque.*"

Scribendi căcoēthes. JUV.—The itch of scribbling.

>"Let him be kept from paper, pen, and ink;
>So may he cease to write, and learn to think." PRIOR.

Scribendo disces scribĕre.—By writing you learn to write.

>"By working in the smithy one becomes a smith."
>See "*Doctrina.*" "*Fabricando.*"

Scribĭmus indocti doctique. HOR.—Learned or unlearned we all must be scribbling.

>"'Tis pleasant sure, to see one's name in print;
>A book's a book, although there's nothing in 't." BYRON.
>See "*Tenet insanābile.*"

Scriptōrum chorus omnis amat nemus, et fugit urbes. HOR. The whole race of scribblers flies from the town and yearns for country life.

Scruta laudat scrutarius.—A dealer in rubbish sounds the praises of rubbish.

"Let every man praise the bridge he goes over."

Secrētè amīcos admŏne, laudā palam. SYR.—Admonish your friends in private; praise them in public.

Securus abi. JUV.—You may safely leave that matter to take care of itself.

Sed mulier cupĭdo quod dicit amanti,
In vento et rapĭdâ scrībĕre oportet aquâ. OVID.

What a lady says to an eager lover he may write in the wind, or in running water.

"She can change her
Mind like the wind : whatever she has said
Or done, is light to what she'll say or do." BYRON.

Sed quàm continuis et quantis longa senectus
Plena malis! JUV.

But with what incessant and grievous ills is old age surrounded!

"For the air of youth,
Hopeful and cheerful, in thy blood will reign
A melancholy damp of cold and dry
To weigh thy spirits down, and last consume
The balm of life." MILTON.

3 F

Segniùs irritant ănĭmos demissa per aures,
Quam quæ sunt ocŭlis subjecta fidēlibus. HOR.

What we hear strikes the mind with less force than what we see.

> "Seeing is believing."
>
> See "*Longum est.*" "*Præcepta.*"

Semel in omni vitâ cuique arrīdet fortūna.—Once in each man's life fortune smiles.

> "Men at some time are masters of their fates." SHAKS.
>
> "There is a tide in the affairs of men,
> Which, taken at the flood, leads on to fortune:
> Omitted, all the voyage of their life
> Is bound in shallows and in miseries." SHAKS.

Semel insanīvĭmus omnes.—We have all been fools in our time.

Semel malus, semper præsumĭtur esse malus.—Those who are once found to be bad are presumed to be so for ever.

> "Give a dog an ill name, and you may as well hang him."
>
> See "*Ad calamitatem.*" "*Invīso semel.*"

Semper avārus eget. HOR.—The miser is ever in want.

> "He wants for ever, who would more acquire."
>
> See "*Crescit amor.*" "*Multa petentibus.*"

Semper bonus homo tiro est. MART.—A novice always behaves with propriety.

> "New brooms sweep clean."

Semper ego audītor tantum? nunquamne repōnam? Juv.— Am I always to be a mere listener? Shall I never reply?

Semper assĭdet grăcŭlus grăcūlo.—Jackdaw always perches by jackdaw.
> See " *Asĭnus asino.*" " *Simĭles simili.*"

*Semper tibi pendeat hamus;
Quo mĭnĭmè credis gurgĭte piscis erit.* Ovid.
Always keep your hook in the water: where you least expect one, the fish will be found.

Senecta leōnis præstantĭor hinnulōrum juventa.—An old lion is better than a young ass.

Senem juventus pigra mendīcum creat.—An idle youth becomes in age a beggar.
> "An idle youth, a needy age."

Senex psittăcus negligit fĕrŭlam.—The old parrot does not mind the stick.
> "An old dog will learn no tricks."
> "There is no fool like an old fool."

Senīlis stultĭtia, quæ delirātio appellāri solet, senum levium est, non omnĭum. Cic.—That folly of old age which is called dotage is peculiar to silly old men, not to age itself.

Sensim amor sensus occŭpat.—Love steals on us imperceptibly.

Sensim, sine sensu, ætas senescit. Cic.—Slowly and imperceptibly old age comes creeping on.

> "While I plan, and plan, my hair
> Is gray before I know it." Tennyson.
>
> See "*Tempora labuntur.*"

Senum consilia juvĕnum lanceæ.—The warnings of age are the weapons of youth.

Sepes calcātur, quâ pronĭor esse putātur.—The hedge is trodden down where it seems to lean.

> [*Viz.*, at its weakest point.]

Septem horas dormisse sat est juvĕnique senique.—Seven hours of sleep is enough for the young and the aged.

Sepulcri
Immĕmor struis domos. Hor.
Forgetful of thy tomb thou buildest houses.

> "Shows that we build, when we should but entomb us." Byron.

Sequentem fugit, fugientem sequitur.—It flies at our approach but follows us as we retire. [A Shadow, Glory, or Love.]

> "Follow Love and it will flee,
> Flee love and it will follow thee."

Sequitur fortūnæ lūmĭna vulgus. Ovid.—The vulgar follow Fortune's glances.

Sequĭtur sua pœna nocentem.—Punishment awaits crime.
> "The gallows will have its own at last."
>> See "*Culpam pœna.*"

Sequĭtur ver hyĕmem.—Spring succeeds to winter.
> See "*Nondum incurvam!*"

Sequĭturque patrem non passĭbus æquis. Vir.—He follows his father, but with shorter strides.

Sera in fundo parsimonia. Sen.—Saving comes too late when you get to the bottom.
> "Tis too late to spare,
> When the bottom is bare."

Sera nunquam est ad bonos mores via. Sen.—The way to good conduct is never too late.
> "Tis never too late to mend."

Serenĭtati nubem indūcit.—He throws a cloud over happiness.
> [A kill-joy; a mar-feast.]

Sermōnes blandi non radunt ora loquentis.—Soft speeches injure not the mouth of the speaker.
> "Soft words scald not the tongue."
>> See "*Frangĭtur ira.*" "*Ignis non.*"

Sermōnis prolixĭtas fastidiōsa.—A lengthy sermon is intolerable.

Serò clypĕum post vulnĕra sumo. OVID.—Too late do I take up the shield after the wound.

> "Every ditch is full of your after-wits."
> See "*Serum est.*"

Serò dat, qui roganti dat.—He gives too late who waits to be asked.

> "Love sought is good, but given unsought is better." SHAKS.

Serò venientibus ossa.—The bones for those who come late!

> "First come first served."
> "The late comer is ill lodged."
> See "*Ante molam.*"

Serum est cavendi tempus in mediis malis. SEN.—Caution comes too late when we are in the midst of evils.

> "When his head is broken he puts on his helmet."
> See "*Machĭnas post.*" "*Post bellum.*" "*Sero clypeum.*"

Serva modum.

> "Keep within compass."

Servus servo præstat, dominus domino.—Servants differ as their masters.

Si albus capillus hic vidētur, neutĭquam ingenio est senex.—What though his hair be gray, his mind is no less vigorous than ever.

> "The silver livery of advised age." SHAKS.

Si ad natūram vivas, nunquam eris pauper; si ad opinionem, nunquam dives. SEN.—If you live according to the requirements of nature, you will never be in want; if according to the fashions of the world you will never be rich.

Si bene barbātum făcĕret sua barba beātum,
Nullus in hoc circo queat esse beātior hirco.
If being well bearded brings happiness, a he-goat must be happier than any of us.

Si bovem non possis asĭnum agas.—If you cannot drive an ox, drive a donkey.

"If thou hast not a capon, feed on an onion."
See "*Qui non potest.*"

Si caput dolet, omnĭa membra languent.—If the head aches all the members of the body suffer.

Si curam curas, parĭet tibi curĭa curas.—If you care for the court, the court will bring cares for you.

"Uneasy lies the head that wears a crown." SHAKS.
"A crown
Golden in show, is but a wreath of thorns." MILTON.
See "*Beatus ille.*" "*Nec otia.*" "*Non enim.*"

Si damnōsa senem juvat alea, ludit et hæres. JUV.—If the destructive dice-box has pleasures for the father, the son will be a gambler.

"Gambling sire, gambling son."

"If gaming does an aged sire entice,
Then my young master swiftly learns the vice." DRYDEN.

Si fortūna juvat, cavēto tolli;
Si fortūna tonat, cavēto mergi. Auson.
Be not arrogant when fortune smiles, or dejected when she frowns.

Si juxta claudum habĭtes, subclaudicāre disces.—Live near a lame man, and you will soon learn to limp.

"Who keeps company with a wolf will learn to howl."

"He who goes to the mill gets befloured."

"Harm watch, harm catch."

See "*Corrumpunt.*" "*Dum spectant.*" "*Grex totus.*"

Si leonīna pellis non satis est, assuenda vulpina.—If the lion's skin falls short, piece it out with that of the fox.

"Policy goes beyond strength."

See "*Ars compensābit.*" "*Dolus an.*"

Si non adsint carnes, tarīcho contentos esse oportet.—If flesh is not to be had, fish must content us.

"Half a loaf is better than no bread."

Si possis, suavĭter; si non, quocunque modo.—Quietly, if you can; if not, by any means.

Si qua, metu dempto, casta est, ea denĭque casta est.
Quæ, quia non licĕat, non facit, illa facit. Ovid.
She only is chaste, who is chaste where there is no danger of detection: she who does not, because she may not, does.

*Si quâ sede sedes, et sit tibi commŏda sedes,
Illâ sede sede, nec ab illâ, sede recēde.*

If you sit on a seat, and that seat is a comfortable seat, sit on that seat, and do not leave that seat.

"Who is well seated, let him not budge."

"Striving to better, oft we mar what's well." SHAKS.

*Si quid dictum est per jocum,
Non æquum est id te serio prævortier.* PLAUT.

It is not fair to treat as serious that which is only said in joke.

Si quid juves, plumâ levior gratia: si quid offendas, plumbeas iras gerunt. PLAUT.—Give assistance, and receive thanks lighter than a feather: injure a man, and his wrath will be like lead.

"Eaten bread is soon forgotten."

"Men's evil manners live in brass; their virtues
We write in water." SHAKS.

See "*Cui placet.*" "*Quàm citò.*"

Si quis dat mannos, ne quære in dentĭbus annos.

"Look not a gift horse in the mouth."

Si Romæ fuĕris, Romāno vivĭto more. ST. AMBROSE.

When you are at Rome, live as Romans live.

"It is hard to live in Rome and strive against the Pope."

Si stĭmŭlos pugnis cædis, manus plus dolet.—If you strike a goad with your fist, your hand will suffer most.

> "Who spits against the wind spits in his own face."
> See "*Nunquam direxit.*"

Si succĭderit, de genu pugnat.   SEN.

> "If his legs fail him, he fights on his knees."
> "His fore feet though you sever, his grip he'll make good."
> PUNCH.

Si tibi amīcum, nec mihi inimīcum.—If it pleases you, it does not displease me.

> *Si tibi dēfĭciant mĕdĭci, medici tibi fiant*
> *Hæc tria; mens læta, rĕquies, mŏderāta diæta.*

If doctors fail thee, be these three thy doctors—Rest, cheerfulness, and moderate diet.

> "The best physicians are Dr. Diet, Dr. Quiet, and Dr. Merryman."

Si tibi machæra est, et nobis vĕruīna est domi.   PLAUT.—If you have a sword, we have a toasting-fork at home.

> "Two can play at that game."

Si vinum postŭlet, pugnos illi dato.—If he should ask for wine, box his ears.

Si vis pacem, para bellum.—If you desire peace, be ever prepared for war.

> "Arms carry peace."
> See "*Paritur.*"

Si vultur es, expecta cadāver.—If you would resemble the vulture, look out for a carcase.
   [Wait for dead men's shoes.]

Sibi malum repĕrit.—He is his own enemy.

Sibi nequam, cui bonus ?—To whom is he any good, if he is no good to himself?

Sibi non cavēre, et aliis consilĭum dare, stultum est.   PHAED.
   To counsel others, and to disregard one's own safety, is folly.
   See "*Nequicquam sapit.*"

Sibi parat malum, qui altĕri parat.—He prepares evil for himself who plots mischief for others.
   "Heat not a furnace for your foe so hot
   That it doth singe yourself."   SHAKS.
   See "*Captantes capti.*"

Sibi quisque peccat.—Every man's sin falls on his own head.
   "Curses, like chickens, always come home to roost."
   See "*Sæpe in.*" "*Nostris ipsōrum.*"

Sibi uni fortūnam debet.—He is the architect of his own fortunes.
   "The mould of a man's fortune is in his own hands."   BACON.

Sic cum inferiōre vivas, quemadmŏdum tecum superiōrem velis vivĕre.   SEN.—So live with an inferior as you would wish a superior to live with you.

Sic est ad pugnæ partes, re peractâ, veniendum.—When the battle is over you make your appearance.

See "*Machĭnas post.*" "*Post bellum.*"

*Sic omnia fatis
In pejus ruĕre.* VIR.

All things deteriorate in time.

Sic præsentĭbus utāris voluptătĭbus, ut futūris non nocĕas. SEN.—So enjoy the pleasures of the hour as not to spoil those that are to follow."

"Reckless youth makes rueful age."

See "*Festo die.*"

*Sic reus ille ferè est, de quo victoria lucro
Esse potest: inŏpis vindĭce facta carent.* OVID.

Bring a lawsuit against a man who can pay; the poor man's acts are not worth the expence.

"Sue a beggar and get a louse."

*Sic timet insĭdĭas, qui scit se ferre viātor,
Cur tīmĕat; tutum carpit inānis iter.* OVID.

A wealthy traveller fears an ambush, while one with empty pockets journeys on in safety.

See "*Cantābit.*"

Sic transit gloria mundi.—So ends all earthly glory.

"All that's bright must fade." MOORE.

Sic utĕre tuo, ut aliēno non lædas. Coke.—So use your own property as not to injure that of another.

Sidĕra cœlo addĕre.—To add stars to the firmament.
> See "*Athēnas noctuas.*"

Silentii tutum præmium.—The reward of silence is certain.
> "Never was a mewing cat a good mouser."
> See "*Audīto multa.*"

Simia non capĭtur laqueo.—A monkey is not to be caught in a trap.

Sīmĭa, quàm simĭlis, turpissĭma bestia, nobis!—How much do we resemble that filthy brute the ape!
> "Do chattering monkeys mimic men,
> Or we, turned apes, out-monkey them?"

Sīmĭa sīmia est, etiamsi aurĕa gestet insignĭa.—An ape is an ape, though decked with gold.
> "An ape's an ape, a varlet's a varlet,
> Though they be clad in silk or scarlet."
>> See "*In vestimentis.*" "*Licet superbus.*" "*Nihil fortunāto.*"

Simul et dictum et factum.
> "No sooner said than done."

Simul et jucunda et idōnea dīcĕre. Hor.—To say that which is instructive and also pleasing.

Simulātio amōris pejor odĭo est.—Feigned love is worse than hatred.

> "God keep me from false friends!" SHAKS.

*Simĭles aliōrum respĭce casus,
Mīlĭus ista feres.* OVID.

Consider the misfortunes of others, and you will be the better able to bear your own.

> "When we our betters see bearing our woes,
> We scarcely think our miseries our foes." SHAKS.

Simĭles simĭli gaudent.—Like likes like.

> "Like will to like, as the devil said to the collier."
> See "*Æquālĭs æquālem.*"

Sincērum est nisi vas, quodcunque infundis, acescit. HOR.—Unless the vessel be pure, everything which is poured into it will turn sour.

Sine Cĕrĕre et Baccho friget Venus.— Love would soon perish, unless nourished by Ceres and Bacchus.

> "When Want comes in at the door, Love flies out at the window."
>
> "Some good lessons
> Are also learnt from Ceres and from Bacchus,
> Without whom Venus will not long attack us." BYRON.

Sine ope dīvinâ nihil valēmus.—Without divine assistance we can achieve nothing.

> "Man proposes, God disposes."

Sine ore loquens, domĭnātum in anĭmum exercet.—Speaking, though speechless, it exercises dominion over the mind.
[The power of music.]

Sine pennis volāre haud facĭle est. PLAUT.—It is difficult to fly without wings.
See "*Haud facĭle.*"

Sint sales sine vīlitāte.—Never descend to vulgarity even in joking.
"Immodest words admit of no defence,
For want of decency is want of sense." ROSCOMMON.
See "*Ludĭte sed.*" "*Nimĭum risûs.*"

Sirēnibus ad persuadendum aptior.—More persuasive than the Syrens.

Sŏlāmen misĕris socios habuisse doloris.—It is a solace to the miserable to have a companion in their grief.
"Two in distress makes sorrow the less."
See "*Commūne naufragium.*"

Solem adjuvāre facĭbus.—To help the sun by torches.
See "*Ebur.*" "*Lucernam adhĭbes.*"

Solent mendāces luĕre pœnas malĕfĭcii. PHÆD.—Liars pay the penalty of their own misdeeds.
"Falsehood, like a nettle, stings those who meddle with it."

Soli lumen inferre.—To add light to the sun.
"With taper-light
To seek the beauteous eye of heaven to garnish." SHAKS.
See "*Athenas.*"

Solitūdĭnem facĭunt, pacem appellant.   TAC.—They make a desert and they call it peace.

"He makes a solitude, and calls it peace." BYRON.

Somnus suprā modum prodest.—Sleep is all important.

Sonus excĭtat omnis.   VIR.—Every sound alarms.

[A guilty conscience.]

"Whence is that knocking?
How is't with me, when every noise appals me?" SHAKS.

See "*Hi sunt.*"

*Spargĕre voces
In vulgum ambiguas.*   VIR.

To whisper insidious accusations in the ear of the mob.

Species virtutĭbus simĭlis—Outward appearances assuming the form of virtues.

"Oh what a goodly outside falsehood hath!" SHAKS.

See "*Habent insidias.*"

Spectātum veniunt, veniunt spectentur ut ipsæ.   OVID.—They come to see and be seen.

Spectēmur agendo.—Let us be judged of by our actions.

See "*Ne verba.*"

Spem pretio non emo.   TER.—I give not gold for mere expectations.

Spem vultu simŭlat, premit altum corde dolōrem.—He assumes a cheerful countenance suppressing the grief which weighs heavily on his heart.

Sperant omnes, quæ cupiunt nimis.—However extravagant men's desires, they hope to see them gratified.

*Spes bona dat vires, ănĭmum quoque spes bona firmat,
Vivĕre spe vidi, qui mŏrĭtūrus erat.*
Hope gives strength and courage, and saves an otherwise dying man from his grave.

> "Hope springs eternal in the human breast,
> Man never is, but always to be blest." POPE.

Spes est vigilantis somnium. COKE.—Hope is a waking dream.

> "A man he seems of cheerful yesterdays,
> And confident to-morrows." WORDSWORTH.

Spes servat afflictos.—Hope supports men in distress.

> "And sanguine hope through every storm of life,
> Shoots her bright beams, and calms the internal strife."
> KIRKE WHITE.

Spes sola homĭnem in miseriis solātur.—Hope is our only comfort in adversity.

> "The miserable have no other medicine,
> But only hope." SHAKS.

Sphingis ænigmăta dissolvit.—He unravels the enigmas of the Sphinx.

Spīrĭtus promptus, caro autem infirma.—The spirit is willing, but the flesh is weak.

Splendĭdĕ mendax. Hor.—Gloriously false.

[Like Rahab.]

Spretâ conscientiâ.—Deaf to the voice of conscience.

Stantis convīcia mandræ. Juv.—The abuse of cabmen in a block.

Stare diu nescit, quod non ălĭquando quiescit.—Nothing can exist long without occasional rest.

See "*Jocandum.*" "*Otia corpus.*"

Stat magni nōmĭnis umbra. Lucan.—He stands the shadow of a mighty name.

Statuâ taciturnior.—More silent than a statue.

Status, quo ante bellum.—The position in which we were before the war.

Stemmăta quid faciunt? Juv.—Of what avail are pedigrees?

"Great birth is a very poor dish at table."

See "*Nam genus.*" "*Nobilitas sine.*"

Stĕrĭlem fundum ne colas.—Cultivate not a barren soil.

Strangŭlat inclusus dolor atque exæstuat intus. Ovid.—Concealed sorrow bursts the heart, and rages within us as an internal fire.

"He is miserable indeed that must lock up his miseries."

See "*Illa dolet.*" "*Magis exūrunt.*"

Stratus humi palmes vidŭas desīdĕrat ulmos. Juv.—Drooping along the ground the vine misses its widowed elm.

Studiōrum dissĭmĭlitudo dissociat amicitias.—A dissimilarity of pursuits dissolves friendship.

Studium genĕrat studium, ignavia ignaviam.—Study invites study, idleness produces idleness.

Stulta maritāli jam porrĭgit ora capistro. Juv.—He deliberately thrusts his silly head into the matrimonial halter.

> "Marriage is a feast where the grace is sometimes better than the dinner." Colton.

> See "*Libĕro lecto.*"

Stulti est compĕdes licet aureas amāre.—'Tis folly to love fetters, though they be of gold.

> "Lean liberty is better than fat slavery."

> "Fetters of gold are still fetters, and silken cords pinch."

Stultĭtia est venātum ducĕre invītos canes. Plaut.—It is sheer folly to take unwilling hounds to the chase.

Stultĭtiam patiuntur opes. Hor.—He can afford to be a fool.

Stultĭtiam simulare in loco, sapientia summa est.—'Tis wisdom sometimes to seem a fool.

> See "*Qui nescit.*"

Stultōrum adjŭmenta, nocŭmenta.—The assistance of fools only brings injury.

Stultum est in luctu capillum sibi evellĕre, quasi calvitio mœror levētur. CIC.—It is sheer folly to tear the hair in grief, as if sorrow could be cured by baldness.

Stultum est timēre, quod vitāri non potest. SYR.—It is folly to fear what cannot be avoided.
> See "*Levius fit.*"

Stultus, ab oblīquo qui cùm discedĕre possit,
Pugnat inadversas ire natātor aquas. OVID.
He is a foolish swimmer who swims against the stream, when he might take the current sideways.
> See "*Contra torrentem.*"

Stultus labor est ineptiārum. MART.—It is folly to waste labour about trifles.

Stultus, qui, patre occīso, lībĕros relinquat.—He is a fool who spares the children after having killed the father.

Stultus stulta loquĭtur.—A fool talks of folly.
> "A fools speech is a bubble of air."
> See "*Inanium.*"

Stylo ferreo scribit.—He writes with an iron pen.
> [That which he writes will not be easily altered.]

Sua cuique deus fit dira cupīdo. VIR.—Every man makes a god of his own desire.
> "Every man hath his hobby-horse."

Sua cuique rei tempestīvĭtas.—There is a season for all things.

Sua cuique voluptas.—Each man has his peculiar hobby.

Sua munĕra mittit cum hamo.—His presents conceal a baited hook.
"Set a sprat to catch a mackerel."

Suadeo, quod ipse factūrus essem.—I am recommending you to do what I should do myself.

Suadetque lĭcentia luxum. CLAUD.—Liberty begets license.
"Give him an inch, he'll take an ell."

Suam quisque homo rem mĕmĭnit.—Every man looks well after his own interests.
"Every cock scratches towards himself."
See "*Heus! proxĭmus.*"

Suave, mari magno turbantibus æquora ventis,
Sterrâ magnum alterius spectare laborem. LUCR.
'Tis pleasant to stand on shore and watch others labouring in a stormy sea.

Suave me suffōcat.—He suffocates me with kindness.
"Even too much praise is a burden."
See "*Mel satietātem.*"

Suavĭter in modo, fortĭter in re.—Gently but firmly.

Sub aliēnâ arbŏre fructum.—Enjoying the fruits of the labour of others.

    See "*Ego apros.*"

Sub nutrīce puĕlla velut si ludĕret infans,
Quod cupĭdè petĭĭt, matūrè plena reliquit.   HOR.

As with a little girl playing with her nurse, the toy which she eagerly sought she soon tires of and discards.

Sub ŏcŭlis posĭta neglĭgĭmus, proxĭmōrum incuriōsi, longinqua sectāmur.   PLIN.—We neglect those things which are under our very eyes, and heedless of things within our grasp, pursue those which are afar off.

    "A shoemaker's wife and a smith's mare are always the worst shod."

    "Abroad to see wonders the traveller goes,
    And neglects the fine things which lie under his nose."

Sub omni lapĭde scorpiŭs dormit.—Every stone conceals a lurking scorpion.

    See "*Incēdis per.*" "*Latet anguis.*"

Sub pallĭo condĕre.—To hide under a cloak.

Sub rosâ.—Under the rose.*

    [That which is said sub rosâ is not intended to be repeated.]

---

    * Amongst the ancients the rose was dedicated to Harpocrates, the god of silence. On this account it was usual for the host to hang it up over his table, to intimate to his guests that nothing there spoken should be repeated.

Sub tecto imbrem exaudīre.—Safely housed to listen to the storm outside.

[To contemplate danger from a safe place.]

See "*Jucundissima.*"

Subitò crevit fungi instar.—He has sprung up like a mushroom.

Sublātâ causâ, tollĭtur effectus.—The cause at an end, the effect is removed.

See "*Cessante causâ.*"

Subrepti potāre Falerni. Juv.—To drink Falernian wine, the sweeter for being stolen.

Successus ad pernĭciem multos devŏcat. Phaed.—Success brings many to ruin.

Successus improbōrum plures allĭcit. Phaed.—The success of the wicked tempts many to sin.

See "*Impunĭtas semper.*"

Succōsior est virgo, quæ serpyllum, quàm quæ moschum olet.—The girl is more inviting who smells of wild thyme than she who smells of musk.

"A simple maiden in her flower
Is worth a hundred coats of arms." Tennyson.

Sudandum est iis, qui magistrātum gerunt.—Men in office must work hard.

Sui amans sine rivāli.—He who is in love with himself need fear no rival.

Sum quod eris, fui quod es.—I am what you will be, I was what you now are.

Summa sedes non capit duos.—The highest seat will not hold more than one.
>See " *Omnis potestas.*"

Summis uti vēlis.—To cram on every stitch of canvas.

Summum jus summa injuria. Cic.—Strict law is often great injustice.
>" Much law, but little justice."

Sumptus censum ne sŭpĕret. Plaut.—Let not your expenditure exceed your income.
>" Ask thy purse what thou should'st buy."
>>See " *Infra tuam.*" " *Messe tenus.*"

Sunt ăsĭni multi solum bino pede fulti.—Many asses have only two legs.

Sunt bona, sunt quædam mediocrĭa, sunt mala plura. Mart. Some things are good, some middling, more bad.

Sunt delicta tamen, quibus ignōvisse velīmus. Hor.—There are faults we would fain pardon.
>" A creature not too bright nor good
>For human nature's daily food." Wordsworth.
>" Not perfect, nay, but full of tender wants." Tennyson.

*Sunt verba et voces, quibus hunc lenīre dolōrem
Possis, et magnam morbi depĕllĕre partem.* Hor.

There are words and accents by which this grief can be assuaged, and the disease in a great measure removed.

Suo ipsius indicio periit sorex.—The rat betrayed by his own track perishes.

Suo ipsīus laquĕo captus est.—He is caught in his own snare.
> See "*Qui capit.*"

Suo jumento malum accersĕre.—To use his own beast to fetch home evil.
> [To be the author of his own misery.]

Suo quisque studĭo gaudet.—Every man rejoices in his peculiar study.
> See "*Sua cuique voluptas.*"

Suo sibi hunc glădio jugŭlo. Ter.—With his own weapon do I stab him.
> "I thank thee, Jew, for teaching me that word." Shaks.

Superanda omnis fortūna ferendo. Vir.—Every calamity is to be overcome by endurance.
> See "*Levius fit.*" "*Perfer.*"

Surdo fabulam narras.—You talk to a deaf man.

Sus magis in cœno gaudet quàm fonte serēno.—The pig prefers mud to clean water.

Sus Minervam!—The fool would teach the learned!
>See "*Ante barbam.*"

Sus saltāvit!—A dancing pig.

Sus tubam audīvit.—The sow has been greeted with music.
>"Cast not pearls to swine."

Suum cuique.—Let every man have his due.
>"Give the devil his due."
>See "*Reddĭte.*"

Suum cuique incommŏdum ferendum est potius quàm de altĕrius commŏdis detrahendum. Cic.—We should all endure our own grievances rather than detract from the comforts of others.
>"Let every pedlar carry his own pack."
>
>"Every man must go to the mill with his own sack."
>
>"Let every tub stand on its own bottom."
>
>"Let ilka herring hing by his ain head."

Suum cuique pulchrum.—What we possess is always beautiful.
>"Every man thinks his own geese swans."
>
>"What bird so white as mine, says the crow!"

Suum quemque scelus agĭtat. Cic.—Every one has his besetting sin.

Suus cuique mos.—Every man has his peculiar habit.

TABULÂ distinguĭtur undâ.—He is separated from the water by a plank.

"With but a plank between them and their fate."
                                                            BYRON.

Tăbŭla in naufrăgio.—A plank in a wreck.

"Any port in a storm."

"A drowning man will catch at a straw."

Tacĭta bona est mulier, quàm loquens.—A silent woman is always more admired than a noisy one.

"Her voice was ever soft,
Gentle, and low, an excellent thing in woman." SHAKS.

Tacĭtâ sudant præcordia culpâ. JUV.—Their hearts sweat with undivulged guilt.

"O coward conscience, how dost thou afflict me." SHAKS.

See "*Hi sunt.*"

Tacĭto mala vota susurro
Concipĭmus. LUCAN.
With bated breath we offer wicked vows.

Tacĭtum vivit sub pectŏre vulnus. VIR.—The secret wound still lives within the breast.

> "The Queen, who sat
> With lips severely placid felt the knot
> Climb in her throat, and with her feet unseen
> Crushed the wild passion out against the floor." TENNYSON.

See "*Illa dolet.*" "*Strangŭlat.*"

*Tacĭtus pasci si corvus posset, habēret
Plus dapis, et rixæ multò minus invidiæque.* HOR.
Had the crow only fed without cawing she would have had more to eat, and much less of strife and envy to contend with.

[To noise abroad our success is to invite envy and competition.]

"If the hen had not cackled, we should not know she had laid an egg."

See "*Jactantiæ.*"

Tædium vitæ.—Weary of life.

> "She only said, My life is dreary,
> He cometh not, she said;
> She said I am aweary, aweary,
> Oh God, that I were dead." TENNYSON.

Talis homĭnĭbus est oratio, qualis vita. SEN.—Men's language is as their lives.

Tam deest avāro quod habet quàm quod non habet. SYR. What he has is of no more use to the miser than that which he has not.

See "*Frustra habet.*" "*Quo mihi.*"

Tam Marte quàm Minervâ.—As much by strength as by skill.

[Brute force.]

Tangĕre ulcus. TER.—To touch a sore place.

[A tender point.]

Tangor, non frangor, ab undis.—I am touched but not broken by the waves.

"Every suitor is not a heart breaker."

Tanquam conchȳlium discerpĕre.—To open, as you would an oyster.

"Why, then the world's mine oyster,
Which I with sword will open." SHAKS.

Tanquam in tabŭlâ.—As in a picture.

Tanquam pavo, circumspectans se.—Admiring himself like a peacock.

"Behold him in conceited circles sail,
Strutting and dancing and now planted stiff,
In all his pomp of pageantry, as if
He felt the eyes of Europe on his tail." HOOD.

Tanta est quærendi cura decōris. JUV.—Such pains they take to look pretty.

Tantæne anĭmis cælestĭbus iræ? VIR.—Can heavenly breasts such stormy passions feel?

Tanti quantum habĕas sis. HOR.—You are judged of by what you possess.

> "O, what a world of vile, ill-favoured faults
> Looks handsome in three hundred pounds a year." SHAKS.
>
> See "*Nemo an.*" "*Ubi opes.*"

Tanto major famæ sitis est, quàm Virtūtis. JUV.
So much greater is our thirst for glory than for virtue.

Tantum bona valent, quantum vendi possunt. COKE.—Things are worth what they will fetch at a sale.

> "The worth of a thing
> Is what it will bring."

Tantum, quantum quisque potest, nitātur.—Let each man do his best.

> "A man can't do more than he can do.
> What says Don Ferdinando?"

Tantum religio potuit suadere malorum. LUCR.—Such crimes has superstition caused.

> See "*Religio peperit.*"

Tardè benefacere nolla est; vel tardè velle nolentis est.—To do a favour slowly is to begrudge it; to consent slowly shows unwillingness.

> "Lang tarrying taks a' the thanks awa'."
> See "*Bis dat.*" "*Gratia est.*"

Tardè, quæ credita lædunt,
   Credimus.   OVID.
We are slow to believe that which, if true, would grieve us.

Taurum tollit, qui vitulum sustulerit.*—He can carry the ox who has carried the calf.
   See "*Parvis imbutus.*"

Tecum habita.—Live not beyond your means.
   "Fond pride of dress is sure a very curse;
   Ere fancy you consult, consult your purse."
   See "*Infra tuam.*" "*Sumptus sensum.*"

Teipsum non alens, canes alis.—Unable to keep yourself, you are keeping dogs.
   "He that has not bread to spare should not keep a dog."

Telum imbelle sine ictu.   VIR.—A feeble dart short of its mark.

Temeritas est videlicet florentis ætatis, prudentia senectutis. CIC.—Rashness is the companion of youth, prudence of old age.
   See "*Juvenile.*"

---

* In allusion to Milo of Crotona, who is said to have begun by carrying a calf, and ended by carrying an ox.

Temperātæ suaves sunt argūtiæ,
Immŏdĭcæ offendunt. PHAED.

Witty remarks are all very well when spoken at a proper time: when out of place they are offensive.

"Of all the griefs that harass the distress'd,
Sure, the most bitter is a scornful jest." JOHNSON.

See "*Adhibenda.*" "*Cum jocus.*" "*Ludus enim.*"

Tempestas minātur antĕquam surgat;
Crepant ædifĭcia antĕquàm corrŭant. SEN.

The tempest threatens before it comes; houses creak before they fall.

"Coming events cast their shadows before." CAMPBELL.
"Often do the spirits
Of great events stride on before the events,
And in to-day already walks to-morrow." COLERIDGE.

Tempestas rerum.—Utter confusion.

Tempŏra labūntur, tacĭtisque senescimus annis. OVID.—Time rolls on, and we grow old with silent years.

"So still we glide down to the sea
Of fathomless eternity." SCOTT.
See "*Tensim, sine.*"

Tempŏra mutantur nos et mutāmur in illis.—The times are changing; we too are changing with them.

"Manners with fortunes, humours turn with climes,
Tenets with books, and principles with times." POPE.

"Foes, friends, men, women, now are nought to me
But dreams of what has been, no more to be." BYRON.

Tempŏra sic fugiunt.—Thus years glide by.
> See "*Fugit irrevocābile.*"

Tempŏre pacis cogĭtandum de bello.—In times of peace we should think of war.
> "Though the sun shines, leave not your cloak at home."
> See "*Pacem orāre.*" "*Turbinem.*"

Tempus erit, quo vos specŭlum vīdisse pigēbit. OVID.—The time will come when you will hate the sight of a mirror.
> "The roses in thy lips and cheeks shall fade
> To paly ashes." SHAKS.

Tempus fugit.—Time flies.
> "Time rolls his ceaseless course." SCOTT.
> "Like as waves make towards the pebbled shore,
> So do our minutes hasten to their end."

Tempus lenit odium.—Time softens animosity.
> "Time is anger's medicine.

Tempus omnia revēlat.—Time reveals all things.
> "The slow, sweet hours that bring us all things good."
> TENNYSON.
> "Time shall unfold what plaited cunning hides." SHAKS.

Temulentus dormiens non est excitandus.—A drunken man, when asleep, is better left alone.
> [Let a slumbering evil rest where it is.]
> "Stir not dying embers."

Tenĕbras inducĕre rebus.—To confuse matters.

*Tenet insanābĭle multos
Scribendi căcŏēthes.* JUV.
Many have an irresistible itch for writing.
See "*Scribĭmus.*"

Tentando ad Trojam venēre Pelasgi.—By perseverance the Greeks reached Troy.

"We have not wings, we cannot soar,
But we have feet to scale and climb
By slow degrees, by more and more,
The cloudy summits of our time." LONGFELLOW.
See "*Tu ne cede.*"

Terēdo ossium cor sollĭcĭtum.—A troubled heart is a worm to the bones.

"Care brings on grey hairs
And age without years."

Terram cœlo miscĕre.—To mingle heaven and earth.

[Inextricably to confuse matters.]

"Confusion's cure lives not
In these confusions." SHAKS.

Tertius e cœlo cĕcĭdit Cato. JUV.—A third Cato has dropped from the skies.

"A Daniel come to judgment!" SHAKS.

Teruncium addĕre Crœsi pecūniæ.—To add a farthing to the wealth of Crœsus.

    "Every little helps."

        See "*Athenas.*"

Testis nemo in suâ causâ esse debet.—No man should be a witness in his own cause.

Testudineus gradus. PLAUT.—Snail pace.

    "A snail's gallop."

Tetrum ante omnĭa vultum. JUV.—A countenance inconceivably forbidding.

Theātrum simul apĕrit et claudit.—He opens the theatre, and immediately closes it.

    [He raises expectation, and crushes it at the same time.]

    "The cow gives good milk, but kicks over the pail."

Thesaurus est mulier malōrum, si mala est.—A store-house of evil is a woman if she is depraved.

    "Beauty without virtue is a curse."

    "For men, at most, differ as heaven and earth;
    But women, worst and best, as heaven and hell." TENNYSON.

Thymo nemo vescĭtur, ubi adest caro.—No man will feed on herbs when meat is to be had.

Tigrĭdis evītā sodalitātem.—Court not companionship with tigers.

    "All those must such delights expect to share,
    Who for their friend think fit to take a bear." GAY.

        See "*Ale lupōrum.*" "*Pasce canes.*"

Tĭmĕat mălĕdĭcere pauper. Ovid.—Let the poor man mind his tongue.

> "He that has no silver in his purse, should have silver on his tongue."

> "That in the captain's but a choleric word,
> Which in the soldier is flat blasphemy." Shaks.

> See "*Pecuniōsus.*"

Tĭmĕo Danăos et dona ferentes. Vir.—I fear the Greeks even when they are offering presents.

> "Trust not a new friend or an old enemy."

> See "*Hostium munĕra.*"

Tĭmĭdi nunquam statuēre tropæum.—Cowards win no laurels.

> "None but the brave deserve the fair." Dryden.

> See "*Audentes fortuna.*" "*Fortes fortūna.*"

Tĭmĭdus se vocat cautum sordidus parcum. Sen.—A coward calls himself cautious, a miser thrifty.

Timor mortis morte pejor.—The fear of death is worse than death itself.

> "The sense of death is most in apprehension." Shaks.

> "Cowards die many times before their deaths,
> The valiant never taste of death but once." Shaks.

> See "*Calamitōsus.*" "*Plus dolet.*"

Tinnit; ināne est.—It rings, it is empty.

"As sounding brass or a tinkling cymbal."

See "*Vacuum vas.*"

Tolle cupīdĭnem Immītis uvæ. HOR. Don't long for the unripe grape.

"Who like sour fruit to stir their veins' salt tides." BYRON.

Tolle jocos, non est jocus esse malignum.—Cease your jests, there is no joke in being ill-natured.

"The generous heart
Should scorn a pleasure which gives others pain." THOMSON.

See "*Cum jocus.*"

Tolle moras: semper nocuit differe. LUC.—Avoid delays: procrastination always does harm.

"*Mer.* Come, we burn daylight, ho!
Rom. Nay, that's not so.
Mer. I mean, sir, in delay." SHAKS.

See "*Deliberando.*"

Tollenti onus auxiliāre, deponenti nequāquam.—Help him who is willing to work, not him who shrinks from it.

"Who has a mouth, let him not say to another, 'Blow!'"

See "*Dii facientes.*" "*Otiōsis.*"

Tollĕre cristas. JUV.—To become proud.

"Cock up your beaver." BURNS.

"I saw young Harry with his visor up. SHAKS.

Tolluntur in altum,
Ut lapsu graviōre ruant. CLAUD.
They are raised on high that their fall may be the greater.

> "With diadem and sceptre high advanced,
> The lower still I fall; only supreme
> In misery; such joy ambition finds." MILTON.
>
> See "*Feriunt.*"

Tota domus rhedā componĭtur unā. JUV.—The whole family is packed into one trap.

> "My sister and my sister's child,
> Myself and children three,
> Will fill the chaise: so you must ride
> On horseback after me." COWPER.

Toto cœlo.—By the whole heavens.

> [As wide asunder as the poles.]

Totus mundus agit histriōnem.

> "All the world's a stage."

Tractent fabrīlia fabri.—The cobbler to his last.

> See "*Quam quisque.*"

Tranquillo quilibet gubernātor est.—Any man can steer in a calm.

> "Easy to keep the castle that was never besieged."

Tres muliĕres nundĭnas faciunt.—Three women will make as much noise as a market.

> "Many women, many words."

Tribulatio ditat.—We benefit by affliction.

"Sweet are the uses of adversity,
Which like a toad ugly and venomous
Wears yet a precious jewel in his head." SHAKS.

See "*Est ipsis.*" "*Deus, quos.*" "*Periisset.*"

Tristis eris, si solus eris. OVID.—You will be melancholy, if you are solitary.

"And there is a worm in the lonely wood,
That pierces the liver and blackens the blood,
And makes it a sorrow to be." TENNYSON.

*Trudĭtur dies die,
Novæque pergunt interīre Lunæ.* HOR.

Day treads upon the heels of day, and the new moons hasten to their waning.

"The goal of yesterday will be our starting-point to-morrow."
CARLYLE.

See "*Fugit irrevocabĭle.*" "*Nec quæ.*"

Tu ne cede malis, sed contra audentior ito. VIR.—Yield not to calamity, but face her boldly.

"Set hard heart against hard hap."

"Courage mounteth with occasion." SHAKS.

See "*Audentes fortuna.*" "*Vincit qui.*" "*Quicquid erit.*"

Tu, quamcunque Deus tibi fortunaverit horam,
Gratû sume manu ; nec dulcia differ in annum.   HOR.
Enjoy thankfully any happy hour heaven may send you, nor think that your delights will keep till another year.

> "Take the goods the gods provide thee."   DRYDEN.

> "Take all the swift advantage of the hours."   SHAKS.
> See "*Carpe diem.*" "*Quid sit.*"

Tua res ăgĭtur, părĭes cum proxĭmus ardet.   HOR.—Your property is in danger when your neighbour's house is on fire.

> See "*Alienâ in.*"

Tuam ipsīus terram calca.—Walk on your own lands.

> "Mind your own business."

Tuēri pertināciter culpam, culpa altĕra est.—Obstinately to justify a fault is a second fault.

> "And, oftentimes, excusing of a fault
> Doth make the fault the worse by the excuse."   SHAKS.

Tuis te pingam colorĭbus.—I shall paint you in your own colours.

> [Take you according to your own showing.]
> "Out of thine own mouth will I judge thee."

Tunc canent cygni, quum tacēbunt grăcŭli.—The swans will not sing till the jackdaws are quiet.

> "For night owls shriek where mounting larks should sing."
> SHAKS.

Tŭnĭca pallĭo propĭor.—The shirt is nearer than the coat.
"Every miller draws the water to his own mill."
See "*Heus! proximus.*"

Turba—sequitur Fortunam, ut semper, et odit damnatos.—The rabble, as of old, truckles to success, and hates a favourite in disgrace.
"Sweep on, you fat and greasy citizens;
'Tis just the fashion. Wherefore do you look
Upon that poor and broken bankrupt there?" SHAKS.
See "*Ad calamitatem.*" "*Dejectâ arbore.*"

Turbĭne versatilior.—A perfect whipping-top for changing sides.
"Sir, she can turn, and turn, and yet go on,
And turn again." SHAKS.

Turbĭnem felix perspecta.—In prosperity look out for squalls.
See "*Tempore.*"

Turpe est alĭud loqui, alĭud sentīre; quantò turpĭus alĭud scribĕre, aliud sentīre! SEN.—It is a disgrace to say one thing and think another; but how much more disgraceful to write one thing and think another!

Turpe est laudāri ab illaudātis.—It is a disgrace to be praised by those who deserve no praise.
"The praise of fools is censure in disguise."

Turpe senex miles, turpe senīlis amor. OVID.—A soldier when aged is not appreciated; the love of an old man sickens.
"Bees touch no fading flowers."
"O doul on the day that gae me an old man." BURNS.
See "*Amāre juvĕni.*" "*Plures adōrant.*"

Turpia decipiunt cœcum vitia. Hor.—The faults of his adored escape the notice of the blind admirer.

> "So lovers, to their fair one fondly blind,
> E'en on her ugliness with transport gaze."
>
> See "*Quisquis amat.*"

Turpis et ridicula res est elementarius senex. Sen.—An old man at school is a contemptible and ridiculous object.

Turpis in reum omnis exprobatio.—Every reproach against an accused man is contemptible.

> "When a man's coat is threadbare, it is easy to pick a hole in it."
>
> See "*Captivum.*"

Turpius ejicitur, quàm non admittitur hospes. Ovid.—To dismiss a guest is a more ungracious act than not to admit him at all.

Tute hoc intristi, omne tibi exedendum est. Ter.—You made this mess yourself, and now you must eat it all up.

> "This even-handed Justice
> Commends the ingredients of our poison'd chalice
> To our own lips." Shaks.
>
> See "*Colo quod.*" "*Faber quisque.*"

Tute lepus es, et pulpamentum quæris!—What! you a hare, and ask for hare-pie!

> See "*Parcit cognatis.*"

*UBERIBUS semper lacrўmis semperque parātis
In statiōne suâ.* JUV.

Tears ready to do duty at a minute's notice.

"Two other tender drops, which ready stood,
Each in their crystal sluice." MILTON.
See "*Mærent omnes.*"

Ubi amor, ibi ocŭlus.—Where the love is, thither turns the eye.

"The eye will often wander
The road that love has taught."

"Yestreen, when to the trembling string
The dance gaed thro' the lighted ha',
To thee my fancy took its wing;
I sat, but neither heard nor saw." BURNS.

"His eyes
Were with his heart, and that was far away." BYRON.
See "*Ubi quis dolet.*"

Ubi cadāver, ĭbĭ erunt et ăquĭlæ.—Where the carcase is, there will the vultures be.

Ubi lapsus? quid feci?—Wherein have I erred? What have I done?

> "Alas! sir,
> In what have I offended you? What cause
> Hath my behaviour given to your displeasure?" SHAKS.

Ubi lībertas, ibi patrĭa.—Where freedom is, there shall my country be.

> "Should banded unions persecute
>   Opinions, and induce a time
>   When single thought is civil crime,
> And individual freedom mute,
> * * * * *
> Then waft me from the harbour's mouth,
> Wild wind, I seek a warmer sky." TENNYSON.

Ubi mel, ibi apes.—Where the honey, there the bees.

Ubi mens plurĭma, ibi minĭma fortūna; ubi plurĭma fortūna, ibi mens perexigua.—Talent and poverty, wealth and stupidity generally dwell together.

> "Fortune favours fools."

Ubi opes, ibi amīci.—Where there is wealth, friends abound.

> "I wot well how the world wags,
> He is most loved that hath most bags."

> See "*Fervet olla.*" "*Tanti quantum.*"

Ubi quis dolet, ibi et manum frequens habet.—The hand often travels to the part where the pain is.

> "The tongue ever turns to the aching tooth."

> See "*Ubi amor.*"

Ubi velis, nolunt, ubi nolis, cupiunt ultro. TERENCE.—When you will, they wont; when you wont they will.

*Ubi vincere apertè
Non datur, insidias armaque tecta parant.* OVID.
When they can't win in fair fight, they resort to all sorts of sly tricks.

Ubicunque ars ostentātur, verĭtas abesse vidētur.—Where art is displayed truth does not appear.

"Truth's best ornament is nakedness."

"But thy true lovers more admire by far
Thy naked beauties; give me a cigar." BYRON.

"An honest tale speeds best being plainly told." SHAKS.

See "*Veritatis.*"

Ultĭma ratio regum.—The last argument of kings.

[The sword.]

Ultĭmus ærumnæ cumŭlus. JUV.—The finishing stroke of all sorrow.

"And last, the crown of a' my grief." BURNS.

Ultra peram sapĕre.—To be wise beyond the scrip.

[Have a care for the morrow.]

Ultra septa transĭlīre.—To go beyond the bounds.

[To digress from the subject of discussion.]

Ultra vires nihil aggrediendum.—Attempt nothing beyond your strength.

Ulŭlas Athēnas portas.—You are carrying owls to Athens.
> See "*Athenas.*"

Umbra pro corpŏre.—The shadow for the substance.

Umbram suam metuens.—Fearing his own shadow.

Una avis in dextrâ melĭor, quàm quatuor extra.—One bird in the hand is worth four in the air.
> "One to-day is worth two to-morrows."
>> See "*Ad præsens.*" "*Capta avis.*"

Una dies aperit, conficit una dies. AUSON.—One day unfolds it and one day destroys.
> "Quick come, quick go."
>> See "*Citò matūrum.*"

Una domus non alit duos canes.—One house cannot keep two dogs.
> "Two of a trade never agree."
>> See "*Etiam mendīcus.*"

Una hirundo non facit ver.—One swallow does not make spring.

Undas numĕras!—You count the waves. [Labour in vain.]

Unde habeas, quærit nemo; sed oportet habere.—How you come by it no one asks; but wealth you must have.
> See "*Nemo an.*" "*Qui caret.*"

Ungentem pungit, pungentem rusticus ungit.—A fool repays a salve by a stab, and a stab by a salve.

[He mistakes friends for foes and foes for friends.]

"Save a thief from the gallows, and he'll be the first shall cut your throat.

"Don't pick a wasp out of a cream-jug."

Unguibus et rostro.—With beak and claw.

See "*Manibus.*"

Unguis in ulcĕre. CIC.—A nail in the wound.

"You rub the sore
When you should bring the plaster." SHAKS.

Uni cum duobus non est pugnandum.—One man must not fight with two.

See "*Ne Hercules.*"

Uni navi ne committas omnia.—Trust not your all in one ship.

"Have not all your eggs in one nest."

"Don't carry all your eggs in one basket."

"My ventures are not in one bottom trusted. SHAKS.

Unĭca prava pecus infĭcit omne pecus.

"One rotten sheepe will marre a whole flocke."

"One ill weed mars a whole pot of pottage."

"One rotten egg spoileth the whole pudding."

See "*Grex totus.*"

Unicuique dedit vitium natura creato. Prop.—To each man at his birth nature has given some fault.

> "Then gently scan your brother man,
>   Still gentler sister woman;
> Though they may gang a' kennin' wrang
>   To step aside is human."

See "*Peccare.*" "*Vitiis nemo.*"

Unicum arbustum non alit duos erithacos.—One tree won't hold two robins.

> "Two sparrows upon one ear of corn make ill agreement."

See "*Etiam mendicus.*"

Unius dementia dementes efficit multos.—The madness of one makes many mad.

> "Fools go in throngs."

> "Customs,
> Though they be never so ridiculous,
> Nay, let them be unmanly, still are followed." Shaks.

See "*Oscitante.*"

Unius dispendium alterius est compendium.—One man's loss is another man's gain.

> "It is an ill wind that blows nobody good."

See "*Nam quod uni.*"

Unus homo nobis cunctando restituit rem. Ennius.—One man restored our fortunes by delay.

> [By skilfully avoiding an engagement, Fabius exhausted the resources of the enemy.]

See "*Romanus.*"

Unus lanius non timet multas oves.—One butcher fears not many sheep.

> "When like an eagle in a dovecot, I
> Fluttered your Volces in Corioli." SHAKS.

Unus vir nullus vir.—One man is no man.

> [A man is nothing without the aid of others.]

> "Two heads are better than one."

> See "*Mutua defensio.*" "*Vis unīta.*"

Urbem latericiam invēnit, marmoream relīquit. SUET.—He found a city of bricks, he left one of marble.

Urit enim fulgore suo. HOR.—He burns us by his brightness.

> [We are vexed at his manifest superiority.]

> "Why, man, he doth bestride the narrow world
> Like a colossus, and we petty men
> Walk under his huge legs, and peep about
> To find ourselves dishonourable graves." SHAKS.

Urit matūrè urtīca.—The real nettle will sting early.

> "It early pricks that will be a thorn."

> "Soon crooks the tree
> That good gambrel would be."

> "What! can so young a thorn begin to prick?" SHAKS.

> See "*Protinus.*"

Ursa caret cauda, non queat esse leo.—The bear wants a tail and cannot be a lion.

> "The bear, he never can prevail
> To lion it for want of tail."

Urticæ proxima sæpe rosa est. Ovid.—The rose is often found near the nettle.

> "Where God hath his church the Devil will have his chapel."

> "Now out of this nettle, danger, will I pluck the flower, safety."
> Shaks.

Usque ad aras amicus.—A friend that will go to the scaffold with you.

Usque ad nauseam.—Enough, even to loathing.

Usque ad ravim.—Till you are hoarse with bawling.

Usus est altera natura.—Habit is second nature.

> "Custom in infancy becomes nature in old age."

> "The fools of habit." Tennyson.

> See "*Abeunt.*" "*Est in nobis.*"

Usus est optimus magister.—Experience is the best teacher.

> "Others' follies teach us not,
>   Nor much their wisdom teaches:
> And most of sterling worth is what
>   Our own experience preaches." Tennyson.

> See "*Experientia docet.*" "*Nocumenta.*"

Usus promptum facit.—Habit gives readiness.

Ut ameris, amabilis esto. Ovid.—To be loved, be loveable.

Ut desint vires, tamen est laudanda voluntas. Ovid. Though the power be wanting, the will deserves praise.
>"Take the will for the deed."

Ut dicunt multi, citò transit lancea stulti.
>"A fool's bolt is soon shot."

Ut in Velābro olearii.—Acting in concert, like the oil-merchants in the Velabrum.*

Ut lupus ovem.—As the wolf loves the lamb.
>"As the cat loves mustard."
>"As the devil loves holy-water."

Ut quimus, quando ut volŭmus non licet. Ter.—If we cannot do what we want, we must do what we can.
>"He that may not as he wad, maun do as he may."
>See "*Qui non.*" "*Si bovem.*"

Ut sæpe summa ingenia in occulto latent. Plaut.—How often the highest talent lurks in obscurity.
>"Some mute, inglorious Milton here may rest." Gray.

Ut sementem feceris, ita et metes. Cic.—As you sow, so shall you also reap.
>See "*Colo, quod.*"

---

* Velabrum. A place in Rome where oil-merchants dwelt, who never undersold each other.

Ut vidi, ut perii. Virg.—When I saw her I was undone.

> "It is engendered in the eyes;
> By gazing fed; and fancy dies
> In the cradle where it lies." Shaks.

Utendum est ætate: cito pede labitur ætas. Ovid.—Make good use of your time, it flies fast.

> "And we must take the current when it serves;
> Or lose our venture." Shaks.
> See "*Fugit irrevocabile.*"

Uter est insanior horum? Hor.—Which of these two is the greater fool?

Utile cum dulci.—The agreeable and the useful combined.

Utinam domi sim!—I wish I were at home.

> [Oh! that I were out of this mess and in safety.]
> "Now would I give a thousand furlongs of sea for an acre of barren ground; long heath, brown furze, anything." Shaks.

Uvaque conspectâ livorem ducit ab uvâ. Juv.—The grape becomes tinted from the grape it comes in contact with.

> "The rotten apple injures its neighbour."

Utrumque vitium est, et omnibus credere et nulli. Sen.—It is equally a fault to believe all men or to believe none.

> "Trust, beware whom!"
> See "*Fide, sed.*"

Uxori nubere nolo meæ. Mart.—I wont let a wife lead me to the altar.

> [I will not have a wife that shall be my master.]

VACUUM vas altĭus pleno vase resŏnat.—An empty vessel makes the most sound.

"The full cask makes no noise."

"Shallow waters mak' maist din."

See "*Canes timĭdi.*" "*Minĭma possunt.*" "*Tinnit inane est.*"

Væ victis!—Alas for those that get the worst of it!

Valeat, quantum valēre potest.—Let it go for what it is worth.

Valĭdior vox ŏpĕris, quàm oris.—Works have a stronger voice than words.

See "*Ne verba.*"

Variam semper dant otia mentem. Luc.—Idleness induces caprice.

Vario Marte pugnātum est.—They fought with varying success.

Varĭum et mutābĭle semper Fœmĭna. Vir.
A fickle and capricious woman.

> "A woman sometimes scorns what best contents her." Shaks.

> "Oh, woman! in our hours of ease,
> Uncertain, coy, and hard to please." Scott.

Vel cæco appăreat.—It would be clear enough even to a blind man.

Vel capillus habet umbram suam.—Even a hair hath its shadow.

> "No tree so small but it can cast a shade."

Vel hosti miserandus.—An object of pity even to a foe.

Vel muscas metuit prætervolitantes.—He fears the very flies.

Velis et remis.—With sails and oars.

> See "*Manĭbus.*"

Velle suum cuique est, nec voto vivĭtur uno. Pers.—Each man has his fancy.

> "We must every one be a man of his own fancy." Shaks.
> See "*De gustibus.*"

Velōcem tardus assĕquĭtur.—The swift are overtaken by the slow.

> "Slow and sure."
> "The race is not always to the swift."
> See "*Mora omnis.*" "*Romānus.*"

Velox consilĭum sĕquĭtur pœnitentia. SYR.—Repentance follows hasty counsel.

> "Marry in haste, repent at leisure." SCOTT.
>
> See "*Festīna lentè.*"

*Velut inter ignes
Luna minores.* HOR.
As shines the moon amid the lesser fires.

> "A lady with her daughters or her nieces,
> Shines like a guinea and seven shilling pieces." BYRON.

Velut umbra sequi.—To follow a man like his shadow.

Velŭti in specŭlo.—As in a mirror.

Veni, vidi, vici.—I came, I saw, I won.

Venĭa necessitāti datur. CIC.—We make allowance for necessity.

> "Necessity has no law."
>
> "It is hard for an empty bag to stand upright."
>
> "My poverty, but not my will consents." SHAKS.
>
> See "*Necessitas cogit.*"

Venĭa primum expĕrienti.—Consideration should be shown to a novice.

> "No man is his craft's master the first day."
>
> See "*Indulge.*"

Venienti occurrĭte morbo. PERS.—Check disease in its approach.

> "A stitch in time saves nine."
>
> "Disease is soon shaken
> By physic soon taken."
>
> See "*Principiis obsta.*"

Veniunt a dote sagittæ. JUV.—The arrows are from her dowry.

> "Not from Cupid's quiver."
>
> "But, oh! the love that gold must crown!" HOOD.
>
> See "*Dos non.*"

Ventre pleno, melĭor consultatio.—A good dinner helps deliberation.

Ventus neque manēre sinit, neque navigāre.—The wind will let us neither sail nor stay.

> See "*A fronte.*"

Vera incessu pătuit Dea. VIR.—The goddess was discovered by her gait.

Verba fiunt mortŭo. TER.—You tell a tale to a dead man.

Verba ligant homines, taurorum cornŭa funes.—Men are bound by words, bulls' horns by ropes.

> "My word is my bond."

Verba satis celant mores eădemque revēlant.—Words may either conceal character or reveal it.

Verberare lapidem.—To flog a stone.

Verbis aliud prodit quàm mente volūtat.—He utters in his language something different from what he ponders in his mind.

Verbis non solvendum est quidquam. TER.—Words pay no debts.

"Praise without profit puts little in the pocket."

"Fine words butter no parsnips."

Verbis pugnans, non re.—Differing in words, not in reality.

[A verbal, not an actual difference.]

Verbum sapienti sat.—A word is sufficient for the wise.

"To a quick ear half a word."

"A nod for a wise man, and a rod for a fool.".

Verecundia inūtĭlis egenti.—Bashfulness will not avail a beggar.

"Bashfulness is an enemy to poverty."

"A close mouth catcheth no flies."

Verĭtas premĭtur, non opprĭmĭtur.—Truth may be suppressed, but not strangled.

"In the end truth will out." SHAKS.

See "*Magna est.*"

Verĭtas vel mendācio corrumpĭtur vel silentio.—Truth is violated by a lie or by silence.

Veritātem qui non ūbĕrĕ pronunitiat, prodĭtor est veritātis.— He who does not speak the whole truth is a traitor to truth.

Veritātis simplex oratio est. SEN.—Simple is the language of truth.

> "When the hand is clean,
> It needs no screen."

> "The silence often of pure innocence
> Persuades, when speaking fails." SHAKS.

*Versāte diu, quid ferre recūsent,
Quid vălĕant hŭmĕri.* HOR.

Consider well what your shoulders are able to bear.

> "He that takes too great a leap falls into the ditch."
> See "*Infra tuam.*"

*Vesāna cupīdo.
Plurĭma cùm tĕnŭit, plura tenēre cupit.* OVID.

Mad desire, when it has the most, longs for more.

> See "*Crescit amor.*"

Versūtior es quàm rota fĭgŭlāris.—You are more shifting than a potter's wheel.

> See "*Quo teneam.*" "*Turbĭne.*"

Vestālium thoro purĭor.—More chaste than vestal's couch.

Vestīgia . . nulla retrorsum. Hor.—There is no retracing our steps.

"Marry in haste, repent at leisure."

Vestis virum facit.—A man is judged by his clothes.

"Fine feathers make fine birds."

"Let never maiden think, however fair,
"She is not fairer in new clothes than old." Tennyson.

See "*Nitĭdæ vestes.*"

Vĕtĕra extollĭmus recentium incuriōsi. Tac.—We praise old times, but show no curiosity about modern events.

Vetĕrem ferendo injuriam, invītas novam.—By submitting to an old insult you invite a new one.

"Make yourself an ass, and you'll have every man's sack on your shoulders."

See "*Omnia ferre.*"

Vĕtĕris vestīgia flammæ.—The traces of the old flame.

[Second love.]

Vĕtŭla vulpes lăquĕo haud capĭtur.—An old fox is not to be caught in a trap.

"An old ape hath an old eye."

See "*Annōsa vulpes.*"

Vexāre ocŭlos humōre coacto. Juv.—To vex the eyes with forced tears.

[Crocodile's tears.]

"Trust not those cunning waters of his eyes,
For villany is not without such rheum." Shaks.

Vi et armis.—By main force.

Via trita, via tuta.—A beaten track is a safe one.

"Keep the common road, and thou'rt safe."

Vicīnia damno est. OVID.—We suffer by our proximity.

[Who get a blow intended for another.]

"Shoot at a pigeon and kill a crow."

"Some innocents 'scape not the thunderbolt." SHAKS.

Vias novit, quibus effūgit.—He knows the roads by which he has escaped before.

"Find you without an excuse, and find a hare without a meuse."

Victi non audent hiscĕre.—The conquered dare not open their mouths.

"In a bondsman's key,
With bated breath and whispering humbleness." SHAKS.

Victrix fortunæ sapientia. JUV.—Wisdom triumphs over chance.

"For man is man, and master of his fate." TENNYSON.
"Men at some times are masters of their fates." SHAKS.

Vĭdeo mĕliōra probōque;
Detĕriōra sequor! OVID.

I see the better course and approve of it; I follow, alas! the worse!

"Breathes there a man, whose judgment clear
Can others teach their course to steer,
Yet run himself life's mad career
    Wild as the wave?" BURNS.

"I make a declaration every spring,
Of reformation ere the year run out,
But somehow this my vestal vow takes wing." BYRON.

Vigilanti stertĕre naso. JUV.—To snore with wakeful nose.

[To pretend to be asleep.]

Vile donum, vilis gratia.—For a paltry gift, little thanks.

"Thank 'ee for nothing."

Vilis sæpe cadus nōbĭle nectar habet.—A poor cask often holds good wine.

"So honour peereth in the meanest habit." SHAKS.

"As shines the moon in clouded skies,
She in her poor attire was seen." TENNYSON.

Vīlius argentum est auro, virtūtibus aurum. HOR.—Silver is of less value than gold, gold than virtue.

Vim vi repellĕre.—To repel force by force.

See "*Amāra bilis.*"

Vina Venusque nocent. MART.—Wine and women bring misery.

"Women and wine, game and deceit,
Make the wealth small and the wants great."

See "*Dives cram.*" "*Nox et amor.*" "*Scribātur.*"

Vīnāria angīna.—An aching for wine—a wine-ache.

Vincit omnia veritas.—Truth conquers all things.

> "Though malice may darken truth, it cannot put it out."
>
> See "*Veritas premitur.*" "*Magna est.*"

Vincit, qui patitur.—He who endures with patience is a conqueror.

> "Know how sublime a thing it is
> To suffer and be strong." LONGFELLOW.
>
> "To take up arms against a sea of troubles,
> And, by opposing end them." SHAKS.
>
> See "*Tu ne.*"

Vincit qui se vincit.—He is indeed a conqueror who conquers himself.

> "Who reigns within himself, and rules
> Passions, desires, and fears, is more a king." MILTON.
>
> See "*Potentissimus.*"

Vindicta bonum vitâ jucundius ipsâ. JUV.—Revenge is sweeter than life itself.

> "O, a kiss
> Long as my exile, sweet as my revenge!" SHAKS.
>
> See "*Implacabiles.*"

Vindictâ
Nemo magis gaudet, quàm femina. JUV.
No one delights more in revenge than a woman.

> "Sweet is revenge, especially to women." BYRON.
>
> See "*Implacabiles.*" "*Mulier sævissima.*"

Vindicta tarda, sed gravis.—Vengeance is slow, but stern.
> See "*Habet deus.*" "*Raro antecedentem.*"

Vino forma perit, vino corrumpĭtur ætas.—Wine mars beauty and destroys the freshness of youth.
> "Intemperance is the doctor's wet nurse."

> "Hundreds of men were turned into beasts,
> Like the guests at Circe's horrible feasts,
> By the magic of ale and cider." HOOD.

> See "*Nox et amor.*" "*Vina Venusque.*"

Vino vendĭbĭli suspensâ hedĕrâ nihil est opus.
> "Good wine needs no bush."

Vinum anĭmi specŭlum.—Wine is the mirror of the mind.
> "What the sober man keeps in his heart, is on the tongue of the drunkard."

> See "*In vino.*" "*Quando tumet.*" "*Quod est in.*"

Vinum caret clavo.—Wine carries no rudder.

Vir fugĭens et denuò pugnābit.—He that flies may fight another day.
> "He that fights and runs away,
> Will live to fight another day;
> For he that runs may fight again,
> Which he can never do that's slain."

> "Deeper to wound she shuns the fight;
>   She drops her arms, to gain the field:
> Secures her conquest by her flight:
>   And triumphs when she seems to yield." PRIOR.

Vir sapit, qui pauca loquĭtur.—He acts wisely who says little.

> "A still tongue maketh a wise head."
>> See "*Audīto multa.*" "*Non unquam.*"

Viresque acquīrit eundo. VIR.—She acquires momentum as she advances.

> [The progress of Fame or Rumour.]

Vīrgŭla divīna.—A divining rod.

> "Fortunes, heaven-born gifts."

Viri infelīcis procul amīci. SEN.—The friends of the unfortunate live a long way off.

>> See "*Fervet olla.*" "*Horrea formīcæ.*"

Viro laudatiōne labēculam aspergĕre. CIC.—To throw a blot on a man's reputation by praising him.

> "Damn with faint praise, assent with civil leer,
> And without sneering teach the rest to sneer." POPE.

Virtus est medĭum vitiōrum, et utrinque reductum. HOR. Virtue lies half way between two opposite vices.

> "Reason lies between the spur and the bridle."

Virtus in actiōne consistit.—Merit consists in action.

> "Words are good, but fowls lay eggs."

> "Talkers are no doers." SHAKS.
>> See "*Destinata.*" "*Ne verba.*"

Virtus, quæ facilem pravo præbet aurem, non ægrè cedit.—Virtue, which parleys, is near a surrender.

> "The woman that deliberates is lost." ADDISON.

> " But why pursue the common tale?
> Or wherefore show how knights prevail,
> When ladies dare to hear?" SCOTT.

Virtus unīta fortior.—Valour acquires strength by union.

> " Union is strength."
>> See "*Dum singuli.*" "*Vis unita.*"

Virtus, vel in hoste, laudātur.—Valour even in an enemy is worthy of praise.

> "God grant me to contend with those that understand me."

> "The stern delight that warriors feel
> In foemen worthy of their steel." SCOTT.
>> See "*Gaudet tentāmine.*"

Virtūte duce, comīte fortūnâ.—Virtue our leader, fortune our companion.

> *Virtūtem incŏlumem odĭmus,*
> *Sublātam ex ocŭlis quærĭmus invidi.* HOR.

We hate merit while it is with us; when taken away from our gaze, we long for it jealously.

> "What our contempts do often hurl from us,
> We wish it ours again. SHAKS.

Virtūtem infortunātam despĭcĕre mĭsĕrum.—It is a mean thing to despise unsuccessful merit.

Virtūtem primam esse puta compescĕre linguam. CATO. Consider it the greatest of all virtues to restrain the tongue.

Vis consĭlĭ expers mole ruit suâ. HOR.—Strength without judgment falls by its own weight.

> "Mettle is dangerous in a blind horse."
> See "*Paulātim.*" "*Rōbŏri.*"

Vis inertiæ.—The force which a body at rest exercises on a body in motion impinging upon it.

> [Stolid immobility or masterly inactivity.]

Vis unīta fortior.—Power is strengthened by union.

> "Union is strength."
> "The fast faggot is not easily broken."
> See "*Dum singŭli.*" "*Mutua defensio.*" "*Unus vir.*"

Visus fidelĭor audītu.—We trust what we see rather than what we hear.

> "Let every eye negotiate for itself
> And trust no agents." SHAKS.
> See "*Pluris est.*" "*Segnius irrītant.*"

Vitâ didicēre magistrâ. JUV.—They have learnt life's lessons.

Vita hŏmĭnis pĕrĕgrīnātio.—Man's life is a sojourn in a strange land.

Vitam impendĕre vero. Juv.—To lay down one's life for the truth.

"That father perished at the stake
For tenets he would not forsake." Byron.

Vĭtia otii negotio discutienda sunt. Sen.—The vices of idleness are only to be shaken off by active employment.

See "*Res age.*"

Vĭtiant artus ægræ contāgia mentis. Ovid.—The mind ill at ease, the body suffers also.

"When the head acheth, all the body is the worse."

See "*Dum caput.*"

Vĭtiat lăpĭdem longum tempus.—Length of time rots a stone.

See "*Gutta cavat.*"

Vitiis nemo sine nascĭtur. Hor.—No man is born without faults.

Vitiosâ nuce non emam.—I would not purchase it at the price of a rotten nut.

"It is not worth a button."

Vĭtĭum capiunt ni moveantur aquæ.—Stagnant waters putrefy.

"Standing pools gather filth."

See "*Ærūgo.*" "*Doctrina sed.*"

Vive bidentis amans. Juv.—Be a gentleman farmer.

"Are not these woods
More free from peril than the envious court?" Shaks.

See "*Beatus ille.*"

Vivĕre si rectè nescis, decēde perītis. Hor.—If you cannot conduct yourself with propriety, give place to those who can.

Vivĭmus aliēnâ fiduciâ. Plin.—We live by reposing trust in each other.

Vivĭmus ambitiōsâ Paupertāte omnes. Juv.
Poor and proud.
"It is a bad thing to be poor, and seem poor."

Vīvis fama negātur.—Renown is denied to the living.

Vīvĭtur exĭguo melĭus.—A small competence is best.
See "*Is minĭmo.*"

Vivum cadāver; vivum sepulchrum.—Though living, dead for all useful purposes.

Vixit, dum vixit, benè.—He took care to enjoy himself as long as life lasted.
[N.B. A good epitaph for an alderman.]

Volenti non fit injuria. Law Max.—No injury can be complained of by a consenting party.

Voces jactat inērtes.—He makes idle boasting.
"Foul-spoken coward, that thunder'st with thy tongue,
And with thy weapon nothing dar'st perform." Shaks.

Volam pedis ostendĕre.—To show the sole of the foot.
"To show a clean pair of heels."

Volcellis pugnant, non gladiis.—They fight with tweezers, not swords.

Volens nolente animo.—Consenting against his inclination.
"A man convinced against his will
Is of the same opinion still." BUTLER.

Volo, non valeo.—I am willing but unable.
See "*Ut desint.*"

Voluptas malōrum esca.—Pleasure is the bait of evil.
"Pleasures, while they flatter, sting."

Voluptates commendat rarior usus. JUV.—Pleasures are enhanced by a moderate indulgence.
See "*Mel satietātem.*"

Voluptātem mœror sequitur.—Sorrow follows pleasure.
"Joy and sorrow are next door neighbours."
See "*Invicem cedunt.*"

Vos inŏpes noscis, quis amīcus quisve sit hostis.—Poverty shows us who are our friends and who our enemies.
See "*Fervet olla.*"

Vox, et prætĕrea nihil.—A mere voice, and nothing more.
"As sounding brass, or a tinkling cymbal."
"Words, words, words." SHAKS.
See "*Dat sine.*"

Vulnus alit venis, et cæco carpĭtur igni. VIR.—She nourishes the poison in her veins and is consumed by a secret fire.
"Grief pent up will burst the heart."
See "*Illa dolet.*" "*Strangŭlat.*"

Vulpināri non decet, nec utrīque parti illudĕre.—It is not becoming to play the fox, or to play up on both sides.

> "May the man be damned and never grow fat,
> Who wears two faces under one hat."

Vulpes haud corrumpĭtur munĕrĭbus.—You cannot catch a fox with a bait.

Vulpes non itĕrum capĭtur laquĕo.—A fox is not caught twice in the same trap.

Vulpes vult fraudem, lupus agnum, fæmĭna laudem.—The fox loves cunning, the wolf covets the lamb, and a woman longs for praise.

Vulpīna lingua.—A foxy tongue.

[Cunning speech. Crafty arguments.]

Vultu sæpe lædĭtur piĕtas.—Merit is often belied by the countenance.

"His face would hang him."

Vultus index ănĭmi.—The face is the index to the mind.

"A man is known by the eye, and the face discovers wisdom."

> "In the forehead and the eye
> The lecture of the mind doth lie."

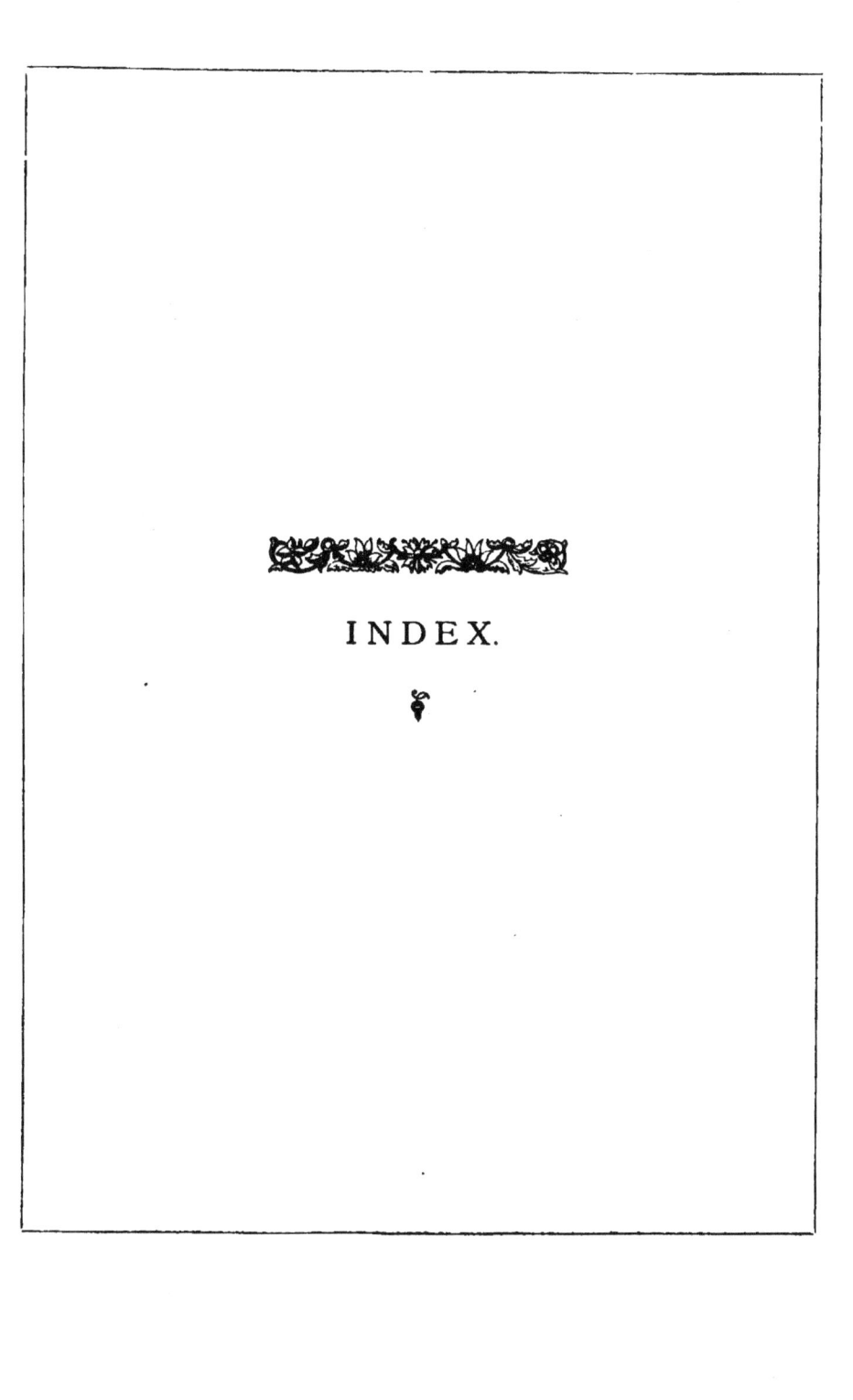

INDEX.

INDEX.

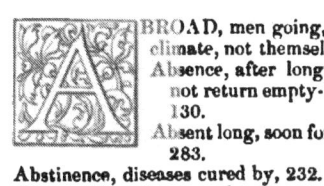

ABROAD, men going, change climate, not themselves, 57.
Absence, after long, should not return empty-handed, 130.
Absent long, soon forgotten, 283.
Abstinence, diseases cured by, 232.
Abuse of best things makes the worst, 63.
 of thing does not prove it useless, 109.
Abusing others, look at home, 283.
Accident often fortune of many, 51.
Accusations, do not listen to, 85.
 doubtful, leave stain, 46.
 lend not too easy ear to, 85.
Accused, before, to justify is to confess guilt, 111.
 cry not out before, 243.
Accuser of another, look well to himself, 356.
Acerra drinks till dawn, 168.
Acquaintance, a man judged by his, 287.
Acquires impetus as it advances, 464.
Act done against will, no act, 5.
 is judged of by event, 112.
 last, not equal to first, 58.
 not criminal, unless intent criminal, 5.
Acting, forte of race, 239.
Action, her pretty, did outsell her gift, 8.
 merit consists in, 958.
Actions from youth, advice from middle-aged, prayers from aged, 118.
 great, not always true sons, &c., 51.
 outward, reveal intentions, 5.
Actors, the nation a company of, 239.
Adamant, harder than, 96.

Adder, bright day brings forth, 29.
Admire, where none, useless, &c. 156.
Admonish a friend privately, 401.
Advance, not to, is to recede, 280.
Adversary, to checkmate, 6.
Adversity, true friends tested in, 166.
Adversity's sweet milk, philosophy, 96.
Advice, most reluctantly received, 259.
 should be brief, 370.
 we easily give to others, 116.
 when in health we easily give to sick, 116.
Æthiopian, to wash, 11.
 to whiten, 12.
Affairs of others, interfere not in, 166.
Affectation injures face more than small-pox, 180.
Affliction, we benefit by, 439.
After a storm comes a calm, 348.
 rain comes fair weather, 334.
 the battle you appear, 412.
 the vintage, baskets, 334.
 the wound, shield too late, 141.
Afterwits, every ditch full of, 406.
Age brings with it companions, 222.
 changes the inclinations, 273.
 entitled to respect, 24.
 has many griefs, 231.
 old, piety stays not, 247.
 save for, 58, 125.
 counsel of, sound, 60.
Ages, different, different pursuits suit, 14.
Agreeable combined with the useful, 452.
Amiable, be, that you may be loved, 451.
Air, to fish in, 166.
 to hunt for water in, 168.
 to whip, 245.

3 P

INDEX

Alarmed, to be needlessly, 222.
Alexander the Great, small man, 211.
All can't do all things, 279.
   covet, all lose, 96.
   his strength, with, 308.
   in danger, not lost, 130.
   none can like, or be liked by, 137.
   not pleased in same way, 14.
   saint without, all devil within, 146.
   things deteriorate in time, 412.
   things not good for all, 279.
   things, we cannot know, 248.
   we wish, we cannot have, 279.
All's well that ends well, 128.
   well, if suit be won, 112.
   we want we cannot have, 281.
Alone, who, happy or good? 155.
Altar, not at the, course to be considered, 30.
Alterations startle us more by novelty than profit us by their use, 308.
Altered, what can't be, endure, 201.
Always ready, 296.
Ambassadors with authority, 199.
Ancestors, our names from, but from virtues our honours, 237.
Ancestors, our names from, our virtue from ourselves, 269.
Anchors, best to trust to two, 41.
Ancient custom, 277.
   we praise, disregarding the modern, 459.
Anger begins with folly, ends with repentance, 187.
   concealed to be dreaded more than open, 186.
   denounced, 275.
   harms more than injury causing it, 140.
   is a transient madness, 186.
   its force broken by a soft answer, 134.
   like not horse, &c. 187.
   not appeased by anger, 160.
   of kings always weighty, 144.
   only ends with life, 187.
   short-lived in the good, 177.
   should never dictate punishment, 341.
   without power is folly, 34, 211.
   who subdues, conquers his greatest enemy, 187.
Angler, hasty, loses fish, 125.
Angry man, he that can reply to is too hard for, 134.
   man, when appeased, angry with himself, 187.
Animals have spirit of sires, 103.
Annoy, he only does it to, 152.

Annoyances, many surround an old man 231.
Another man's plate, to live off, 15.
   what we do by, our own act, 358.
Another's call, to live at, 15.
   crop, to reap, 15.
Answer, a soft, makes a furioso sheathe his sword, 131.
Ant, even, shows anger, 176.
Antidote before the poison, 338.
   use not before the poison, 243.
Antiquity entitled to respect, 24.
Ants, don't go to empty board, 157.
Anvil, a great, fears not noise, 175.
Anxiety, like the worm, consumes to the bone, 484.
Apes, we are much like, 413,
Apella, let the Jew believe it! 64.
Apelles, no painter first day, 175.
Apollo, it would puzzle even, 240.
   not always bend his bow, 256.
Appearance, no reliance to be placed on, 79.
Appearances assume the form of virtue, 416.
Appetite, poor, tastes many things, 120.
Apple, rotten, injures its neighbour, 144.
   tree, better in, than bad in distress, 215.
Apples, sooner will tamarisk bear, 236.
Apprehension of evil brings danger, 234.
Approve better course, I follow the worse, 460.
Architect, man, of own fortune, 115.
Argument, last, of kings, 445.
Arm, stretch no further than sleeve, 222.
Arms should give place to peace, 52.
Armour, when on, too late to retreat, 141.
Arm which won the victory, protects the fallen, 347.
Arms abroad useless without counsel at home, 319.
   let, give place to eloquence, 53.
Arrogance, a weed mostly on dunghill, 27.
   is intolerable, 27.
Arrow, a powerless, 431.
   is from her downy, 456.
   not always hits mark intended, 249.
Art, every one should have credit of being master of his particular, 67.
   perfection of, where no trace of artist, 27.
   long, life short, 27.
   man skilled in own, trust, 67.
   perfect, when no trace of artist, 27.
   practise not, and 'twill depart, 10.
As many opinions as men, 385.

INDEX.

Ass, beautiful in eyes of ass, 28.
    even will not fall twice in the same quicksand, 165.
    for stubborn, stubborn driver, 114.
    hay more acceptable to, than gold, 28.
    he hangs his ears like an, 82.
    hungry, heeds not blow, 28.
    in skin of lion, 28.
    to give bones to! 47.
    to sing to, 166.
    travelling, will not come home a horse, 57.
    only knows value of tail by loss, 42.
Asses, milk of, sustains her, 162.
    many, only two legs to rely upon, 424.
    that bray most eat least, 367.
Assistance most valued when most needed, 331.
    opportune benefit of, 262.
    unseasonable, as bad as an injury, 181.
Assurance often mistaken for confidence, 70.
Athens, you carry owls to, 446.
Attack by every available means, to, 306.
Attempt nothing beyond your strength, 445.
    not, either, or carry out, 244.
Authority, against those in, use not coercive measures, 4.
Author of own misery, 425.
Avarice, against, 137.
    increases with wealth, 64, 231, 402.
    never satisfied, 64, 165.
    folly of, 428.
Avaricious cannot have friends, 19.
Avenging gods come noiselessly, 86.

BABBIES, where God sends, he sends penny loaves, 83.
Bacchus hath drowned more men than Neptune, 163.
Bachelor is free from strife, 361.
Bachelor's bed most pleasant, 202.
Back, better go, than astray, 154.
    door robs the house, 112.
Backs, we see not our, 285.
Backwards, no going, 459.
Bad beginnings lead to bad results, 214.
    day, a bad night, 214.
    luck, 214.
    counsel, who gives, suffers, 215.
    crow, bad egg, 99.
    fowl, bad egg, 214.
    head, bad heart, 212.
    nor good, some things neither, 274.
    thing never dies, 215.
Bagpipe, bring not, to a man in trouble, 182.

Bait not hook, catch nothing, 69.
Bale, when hext, boot next, 69.
Ball striking wall, leaves mark, 46.
Banbury tinkers, in mending one hole, make two, 44.
Barber, learns by shaving fools, 126.
Bard, none to sing praises, 49.
Bark, struck, avoids place, 106.
Barkers, greatest, not bite sorest, 47.
Battle, after, bring weapons, 209.
Baubles of children, 84.
Bawling, avoid, 3.
Bay, he has nibbled at the, 199.
Be what you appear to be, 105.
Beads about neck, devil in heart, 146.
Beam, to cast out from another's eye, 126.
Bear, who shares honey with, gets least, 200.
    must, what can't be altered, 122.
    wants a tail, and can't be a lion, 450.
Bear's skin, sell not before caught, 23.
Beard, not make philosopher, 66.
Beards, sages, so far as, 36.
Beard, trim my, 217.
    washed, half shaved, 87.
Beast, one knows another, 39.
    not attack those of same kind, 317.
Beating, walnut-tree, donkey and woman require, 297.
Beautiful, everything, is loveable, 305.
    is the autumn of beauty, 345.
    neither, nor young, 245.
    things secured with difficulty, 85.
Beauty, a silent recommendation, 130.
    fades, 188.
    hangs on face of night, &c., 62.
    is potent, money omnipotent, 61.
    is transitory, 188.
    pride innate in, 120.
    without virtue a curse, 435.
Beck and call, to live at, of another, 15.
Bed, as you make, so lie on it, 58.
Bee, from industry in summer, eats honey in winter, 172.
    where, sucks honey, spider poison, 238.
    would you compare, to grasshopper? 55.
Beef, ill, ne'er made good broo, 202.
Beer, small, not think himself, 79.
Bees, boys stung avoid, 101.
    have honey and stings, 164.
    no, no honey, 256.
Beetle, blinder than, 158.
Before, who looks not, finds himself behind, 172.

476   INDEX.

Beg better than borrow, 38.
  buy rather than, 101.
Beggar, bashfulness not avail a, 457.
  enriched, no pride like that of, 29.
  even envies beggar, 108.
  has no friends, 221.
  on horseback, 29, 133.
  may sing before robber, 48, 929.
Begging a courtesy, selling liberty, 38.
Begin a task, easier than to finish, 174.
Beginning bad, ending bad, 41.
  of evil, check the, 338.
Begin well, good; end well, better, 128.
Believe evil, men unwilling to, 430.
  men, what they wish true, 123.
  not a liar when speaking the truth, 221.
  that you have it, and it is yours, 64.
Believers, quick, suffer, 257.
Bell, cracked, never sounds well, 119.
Beloved, when no more, 113.
Benefit, small, obtained, better than great in expectation, 48.
Benefited one, what has, destroys others, 238.
Benefits, old early, injuries not, 66.
Better half, 21.
Best things perish first, 310.
Better I approve, worse I follow, 460.
  a fair pair of heels than a halter, 399.
  enjoy what we have, than hanker after other things, 336.
  late than never, 336.
  times await us, 130.
Bird, early, catcheth worm, 23.
  in hand worth two in bush, 7, 48.
  in net may get off, 230.
  known by its note, 98.
  limed, misdoubts bush, 195.
  to frighten, not the way to catch her, 327.
Birds fly not into mouth ready roasted, 285.
  of a feather flock together, 10.
  old, not caught with chaff, 22.
  to kill two, with one stone, 96, 171.
Birth, not changed by wealth, 202.
Bitch, in her haste, blind puppies, 47.
Biter bitten, 48.
Bitter past, more welcome sweet, 132.
  rather than good-natured, 331.
  things, sweet, when soul hungers, 21.
  to endure, sweet to remember, 191.
Black man, to make white, 11.
  take no other hue, 196.
  white, they will swear, 258.
Blackamoor, let white laugh at, 205.

Blacksmith, let the, wear his own chains, 115.
Blind, among, one-eyed, king, 182.
  as the cast-off skin of a serpent, 199.
  in light of sun even, 45.
  lead blind, 44.
  man, clear enough to a, 454.
  man, no need of a mirror, 371.
  men are, when thoughts riveted, 44.
  men not judges of colours, 244.
  none so bold as the, 92.
  regard one-eyed man as lucky, 36.
  to be in light of sun, 45.
Blinder than skin of serpent, 199.
Blockhead, dolt, &c., described, 52.
Blood, human, all one colour, 155.
  you can't take, from stone, 25.
Blot, cleaning, with blotted fingers, 44.
Blow, blow, thou winter wind, &c., 38.
  from frying-pan, if it hurts not, smuts, 46.
  first, sip after, 128.
  not against the hurricane, 188.
  repeated, oak falls, 233.
  second, makes the fray, 160.
  the wind never so fast, lower at last, 286.
Blows, we get, and return, 44.
Blunder twice, not allowable in war, 278.
Boar, I kill, another eats the flesh, 100.
Boars, to take two in one thicket, 171.
Boast loudest, do least, 223.
  to, is one thing; to fight another, 16.
Boaster, idle, 468.
Boasting denounced, 232.
  envy waits on, 190.
Boat, to sail in same, 101.
Body, a little, often harbours a great soul, 211.
Bold in design, timid in execution, 179.
  man, fortune gives hand to, 31.
  resolution, the favourite of Providence, 171.
Bolt a door with a boiled carrot, 13.
Bombast, 43.
Bondage, vile, away with! 102.
Bone, gnaw the, fallen to thy lot, 144.
  what's bred, never out of the flesh, 240.
Bones snatched from mouth of hungry dog, 312.
  the, for last comer, 23.
Booby, mother won't give hers for another, 28.
Book, cursory perusal, useless, 261.
Boot on the head and foot in helmet, 136.

Boots, wear not too big for feet, 244.
Born, of a white hen, 13.
   misery to be, &c., 239.
   not, for selves alone, 278.
   with silver spoon in his mouth, 13.
Borrowing, who goes, goes sorrowing, 38.
Bought wit is best, 270.
Bounds, to go beyond, 113.
Bow, Apollo bends not, always, 256.
   as ruined by being strained, so mind ruined by indolence, 26.
   draw not, till arrow fixed, 30.
   have two strings to, 41.
   long bent, weak, 191.
   long bent, at length wax weak, 206.
   too much bent, broken, 26.
Bowl, fill the, &c., 50.
Boy, beardless, would teach old men! 23.
Boys stung, avoid bees, 101.
Boyhood's days, praises of, 198.
Brag, good dog, Holdfast better, 16.
Brain that sows not corn, plants thistles, 117, 252.
Brave, be, not ferocious, 131.
   born from brave, 131.
   helped by Fortune, 131.
   laugh at envy, 185.
   man owns every soil as his country, 305.
   never say "die," 131.
Bread, give not to dogs, 315.
   let him who earns, eat it, 83.
   to put, in cold oven, 168.
Breath, one man's, another man's death, 238.
   out of, to no purpose, 144.
   while there is, there is hope, 95.
   to waste, 170.
Bred in the bone, what is, will out in the flesh, 129.
Breeches, he shows to all, 164.
Brevity is the soul of wit, 143.
Brew, as you, so bake, 58.
Briar, nip, in bud, 251.
Bribes enter without knocking, 33.
Bricks, tale of, when doubled, then Moses comes, 69.
Brothers, their quarrels most bitter, 135.
   their wrath fierce and devilish, 4.
Brute, a, without a single redeeming point, 227.
Buffoon, once a, never a good Paterfamilias, 366.
Bull, flying from, he fell into river, 95.
Burden, cheerfully borne, light, 200.

Burdens light, far heavy, 205.
   let every man bear, 426.
Burnt child dreads fire, 195, 328.
   who has been once, blows his soup, 328.
Bush, he who fears every, should not go to the woods, 384.
Business of others men see, more than own, 332.
   none of mine, 275.
Bust of Mercury cannot be carved from every wood, 110.
Busy, he that is, is tempted by one devil— he that is idle, by a legion, 259.
Busy-bodies are also malevolent, 72.
Busy-body [described], 14.
Busy-body, 202.
   old, nothing worse than, 80.
Buy him not at his own price, 11.
I would rather than beg, 101.
Buyer should be on his guard, 53.
Bye-and-bye, street of, &c., 94.

CA' ME, ca' thee, 105.
Cæsar, either, or nobody, 34, 391.
Cake, good, more of the make, 184.
Cake in peace best, 281.
Calamity the touchstone of a brave mind, 439.
Calamities, rush to, by flying, 138.
Calends, Greek, 6.
Calm, only can steer in a, 438.
Calumny, denounced, 276.
Calumny, prevalence of, 261.
Camel coveting horns, lost ears, 46.
   mangy, will carry more than herd of asses, 46.
Can, do as you, if wishes thwarted, 451.
Candle under a bushel, 205.
Candour breeds hatred, 99.
Capon, if you have not, feed on an onion, 336.
Captive, insulted with impunity, 48.
Carcase, where, there ravens, 443.
Care and toil, man wakes to, 86.
Care brings grey hairs, 484.
   enemy to life, 96.
   free from, far from court, 37.
   hovering over roofs of wealthy, 72.
   mad to see a man sae happy, 71.
Cares are comforts, 132.
   deny rest, 248.
   fluttering, bat-like, 72.
   light, cry out, great dumb, 72.
Carrion, left by eagle, feeds crow, 63.

INDEX.

Cart, putting the, before horse, 72.
Carthage must be destroyed, 81.
Cask easy to set rolling, 89.
   poor, often holds good wine, 461.
   retains the flavour of the wine, 379.
Cat loves mustard, as the, 451.
   when away, mouse will play, 235.
   would eat fish, but will not wet feet, 51.
Catch, while we, we are caught, 44.
Cats, keep no more than catch mice, 137.
Caught in own snare, 425.
Cause at an end, effect removed, 423.
   hidden, effect notorious, 52.
Causes, happy is he who can trace, 122.
   trivial, greatness overthrown by, 100.
Caution, excess of, does no harm, 4.
   illustrations of, 52.
   from excess of, 108.
Cautious man observes character of others, 52.
Censure pardons ravens, rebukes doves, 76.
Certain issue, aim at, 55.
   signs forerun events, 55.
Certainty, leave not, for chance, 7.
   to sacrifice, for uncertainty, 339.
Chaff even weighty on a long journey, 205.
   from mass of, little grain, 98.
   no wheat without, 276.
Chair unsound finds ground, 166.
Chameleon, more changeable than, 58.
Chance decides fate of monarchs, 51.
Changed, I am, 283.
Changing his ground constantly, 380.
Changing weather described, 295.
Chaos, more ancient than, 24.
Character, evil of losing one's, 127.
   try to deserve the one you possess, 71.
   watch from natural signs, 52.
Changed from what he was, 354.
Charity begins at home, 337.
Charming, be, 107.
Charybdis, in avoiding, we fall into Scylla, 174.
Chaste, more, than Vestal's couch, 458.
Chasteneth, whom Lord loves he, 83.
Chatter, in, river, talent, drop, 168.
Chatterbox, greater than raven, 62.
Cheer, good, lacking, friends off, 121.
Cheerful habit, cultivate, 171.
   look makes dish a feast, 234.
Cheerfulness enjoined, 94.
   makes burthen light, 200.
   recommended, 189.
Cheese, I speak of, you chalk, 100.

Chicken, count not before hatched, 23.
Child may beat a man that is bound, 48.
   train up in the way he should go, &c., 8.
   pig, father's pork, 100.
Children a source of happiness, 371.
   and fools have merry lives, 169.
   have wide ears, long tongues, 218.
   married life without, 60.
   notice everything, 218.
   old men's, rarely live long, 128.
Chimney-sweep, wrestle with, and covered with soot, 153.
Chip of old block, 131.
Choleric men are blind and mad, 186.
Christmas festivities enjoined, 12.
Churl! drink all, &c., 244.
Cinders, avoiding, step not on coals, 240.
Circumstances, mould to self, 106.
Cities, far from gay, &c., 37.
City, a great, a great desert, 209.
Claw me, and I'll claw thee, 18.
Clean hands better than full in God's sight, 346.
Climate, men going abroad change, not themselves, 57.
Climb not too high, lest the fall greater, 438.
Cloak at home, leave not, when sun shines, 49.
Clodius impeaches the adulterer, 57.
Clothes, fine, hide not clown, 202.
   showy, attract most, 269.
Clouds, after, sunshine, 334.
   all, not rain-clouds, 283.
   behind the, sun shines, 195.
Clown, fine clothes hide not, 173.
Club law, 27.
Coals, glowing, sparkle oft, 5.
Coals to Newcastle, 66.
Coat, cut your, according to cloth, 222.
   great, not for summer, 11.
   in a shabby, no one treated with respect, 173.
   threadbare, armour against robbers, 48.
Cobbler, not go beyond his last, 244.
Cock, as old crows, so crows young, 1.
   barley corn better to, than a diamond, 28.
   every, fights best on his own dunghill, 141.
Coin, much, much care, 64.
Colander, to drink from, 98.
Cold, dispel the, 88.
Colt, you may break, not horse, 67.
Combined defence is safest, 236.
Comforts, only known by loss, 287.
Coming events cast shadows before, 432.

Commence, to, requires effort, 58.
Commencement, to make, requires mental effort, 58.
zealous in, careless in end, 4.
Commentators ridiculed, 205.
Commerce, see effect of, 29.
Common fame, seldom to blame, 150.
Commonplace things difficult to say pleasantly, 84.
sense, a man of, 3.
to all, is, death, 228.
Companion, wicked, invites to hell, 63.
as good as carriage, 59.
Companions in grief, 102.
man judged by, 287.
Compare moorhen to swan! 138.
Compassion, none like the penny, 82.
Complain, when we cannot, wretched to suffer, 225.
Complete the work designed, 341.
Compliment, soft spoken, poison, 220.
Concealment, fault fostered by, 16.
of fraud, a fraud in itself, 135.
Conceit. A conceited fellow, 11.
Concert, fight in, 94.
Concise, to try to be, and become obscure, 43.
Conclusions, hasty, lead to repentance, 7.
Concord recommended, 60.
Condemn, many do, what they cannot understand, 74.
Confess our faults, why we do not, 354.
Confesses his fault, who, is almost guiltless, 365.
Confidence, caution necessary in placing, 127.
never safe, 297.
Confuse matters inextricably, to, 484.
matters, to, 484.
Confusion worse confounded, 160.
utter, 432.
Confuted, and yet not convinced, 469.
Conquer self, conquer worst enemy, 187.
she stoops to, 51.
we, and are conquered, 45.
Conquered must hold their tongues, 460.
Conqueror, go forth as, 159.
he is truly a, who conquers himself, 40.
weeps, the conquered ruined, 129.
Conscience, a guilty, needs no accuser, 22.
a thousand witnesses, 60.
at bar of one's own, 168.
betrays guilt, 60.
clear, wall of brass, 152, 235.

Conscience, deaf to voice of, 418.
evil, breaks many necks, 150.
free from reproach, a brazen wall, 235.
guilty, needs no accuser, 60.
is a thousand witnesses, 60.
let, check flattery, 241.
makes cowards, 151.
Consenting against his inclination, 469.
Consider well before resolve, 81.
your powers and their limit, 458.
what it will become you to do, 249.
Consideration gets as many victories as rashness loses, 53.
parent of wisdom, 53.
the matter is under, 391.
Constant dropping wears the stone, 123.
Constitution, preserve your, 42.
Content advocated, 244.
more than a kingdom, 188.
recommended, 196.
where is, there abundance, 261.
Contented mind, a continual feast, 188.
Contented, no man is, with his lot, 275.
Contention, result of all, uncertain, 104.
Contentment with little, greatest wealth, 37.
Contrariness described, 271.
Contrasts commend each other, 62.
Conversation ministers to mind diseased, 21.
reveals character, 428.
Correction of wise man and fool compared, 27.
Conviviality reveals secrets, 352.
Cooks, too many, spoil broth, 137.
Corinth, all can't go to, 272.
not every one sees, 272.
Corn, brain that sows not, plants thistles, 117.
Corruption of best things, worst, 63.
Costs little, what, little esteemed, 383.
Cough a, assists a hesitating musician, 148.
Counsel, bad, who gives, suffers, 215.
give not, till asked for, 253.
keep, thyself first, 257.
of age, armour of youth, 404.
of aged sound, 60.
others, and disregard one's self, 411.
Counsellor, pillow should be, 169.
Counsellors, where many, there safety, 397.
Countenance betrays guilt, 150.
man judged by, 102.
Counterfeit, nothing, lasts, 265.
Country girl preferable to town, 423.
God made, man town, 240.
life, pleasures of, 247.

INDEX.

Country, mine which feeds me, not which gave me birth, 161.
   pleasures of, praised, 298.
   to die for, meritorious, 92.
Course, to change for better, 169.
Court, far from, free from care, 247.
   favours of, uncertain, 75.
   how favours granted by, 75.
Courtesy begging, selling liberty, 101.
   entreated, half returned, 143.
   in conferring favours enhances them, 8.
   less of, more of purse, 245.
   much entreated, is half recompensed, 143.
   on one side never lasts, 38.
Cousin germans, quite removed, 4.
Covet not property of others, 14.
   we cannot, that of which ignorant, 160.
Covetous, ever in want, 402.
   man no good till he dies, 35.
   men's chests full, not they, 64.
   of another's, prodigal of own, 15.
   the least, the least in want, 188.
   world too small for the, 35.
Covetousness, advice against, 244.
Cow gives milk, and kicks over the pail, 17.
Coward calls himself cautious, 436.
   if driven to it will fight the devil, 178.
Cowardice, often hidden by bluster of daring, 31.
Cowards win no laurels, 436.
Cowl does not make monk, 66.
Cows, cursed, have short horns, 75.
Coyly resisting, 92.
Crab-tree, wherever planted, will not bear pippins, 240.
Crab would catch the hare! 46.
Cracked pitcher, rarely broken, 215.
Cradle, what learnt in, lasts to grave, 8.
Craft, not great in, but arms, 149.
Credit, he who loses, dead to the world, 127.
Crime, disgrace of others deters from, 14.
   betrays itself, 186.
   he who profits by commits it, 67.
   no one revels in long, 121.
   often recoils on author, 395.
   power won by, never turned to good purpose, 164.
   punish to prevent, 254.
   requires further crime to conceal it, 399.
   success in, leads to worse deeds, 166.
   who meditates, commits, 238.
Crimes in which many are implicated, unpunished, 370.
Crimes may be secret, but not secure, 186.

Crocodile's tears, 65.
Crœsus, to add to wealth of, 66.
   to add a farthing to wealth of, 435.
Crooked logs not to be straightened, 202.
   stick will have crooked shadow, 214.
Crop, to reap another's, 15.
Cross, behind the, stands devil, 146.
   on breast, devil in heart, 146.
   one gets, another crown, 161.
Crosses are ladders that lead to heaven, 90.
Crow, breed up a, and he'll pick out your eyes, 13.
   has seized a scorpion, 62.
   more noisy than, 62.
   one, not pick out another's eyes, 317.
   pretty bird when jackdaw's away, 63.
   silent, eats most, 428.
   thinks her own bird fairest, 28.
Crowd, not company, 210.
Crown rewards crime of one, gibbet that of another, 161.
Crows are not whiter for washing, 12.
Cruel to refer to what grieves hearer, 347.
Cruelty, with winsome, she refuses, 116.
Cry, don't, before out of wood, 23.
Cuisine, to keep up as good as father, 1.
Cunning speech, 470.
Cup concealed under dress, rarely honestly carried, 21.
   every inordinate, unblessed, 6.
   full, must be carried steadily, 10.
   to drink from same, 101.
Cupid some kills with arrows, some traps, 90.
Cur, biting, wears torn skin, 72.
Cured, what can't be, must be endured, 122.
Curiosity and detraction, 72.
Current, to struggle against, 295.
Cursed cows have short horns, 75.
Curs, snapping, never want sore ears, 72.
Custom in infancy, becomes nature in old age, 450.
   makes all things easy, 103.
   second nature, 61.
   something allowed to, 16.
Cut coat according to cloth, 458.
   leg, with own adze, to, 186.

DAINTIES, who love, beggars, 177.
Dance, to, out of time, 113.
Dancer, mask of, with toga, 172.
Danger comes most speedily when treated with contempt, 56.
   foreseen is half avoided, 335.
   furthest from, when on guard, 49.

INDEX. 481

Danger, he that fears seldom feels, 49.
  next neighbour to security, 56.
  out of, 113.
  past, God forgotten, 9.
  to contemplate from a distance, 99.
  seldom felt when feared, 220.
Dangers of others, wisdom from, 122.
  past, sweet to remember, 191.
  through, to distinction, 323.
  of others, wise to learn from, 121.
Dark, bright in, dull in day, 270.
Dark, when all, light comes, 286.
Daughter, judge of, by mother, 109.
Daw, a-cawing on steeple, &c., 216.
Day, every, hath a night, 184.
Day, evil thereof, sufficient, 45.
Day, praise a fair, at night, 128.
  rainy, put by for, 58.
  what will bring, not known, 258.
Dead, even when, he will be beloved, 113.
  flies cause ointment of apothecary to stink, 320.
  for all useful purposes, though living, 468.
  immoderate grief for, unwise, 272.
  lion, little birds may pick, 228.
  man, he talks to, 229.
  men cannot bite, 228.
  men's shoes, look not for, 169.
  men, you anoint with salve, 229.
  speak not against, 77.
  the best counsellors, 311.
  the, to exact offering from, 1.
  the, to stab, 192.
Deaf man, you talk to a, 425.
  to entreaty, 31.
Death, after the doctor, 229.
  better than disgrace, 215.
  common to all, 228.
  falls heavily on man, known to all, unknown to self, 162.
  fear of, dispelled by music, 222.
  fear of, worse than itself, 436.
  in the pot, 227.
  is preferable, 227.
  levels sceptres and spades, 228.
  no herb will protect against, 62.
  sense of, most in apprehension, 201.
  takes good, leaves the wicked, 228.
  to the wolf—life to the lambs, 227.
  who plots, perishes, 255.
  will have his day, 247.
Debauchery denounced, 88.
Debt, happy who is out of, 122.

Debt, little, makes debtor, great one an enemy, 11.
  out of, out of danger, 122.
Deceit, all that, should steal, &c., 146.
  in guise of duty most deceptive, 291.
Deceived, who has, deceives again, 16.
Deception increases, 118.
  leads to deception, 118.
  who has used, will deceive again, 16.
Decorum, observe, in sport, 206.
Deeds, not words, are required, 285.
Deep rivers are silent, 241.
Defence uncalled for makes us our own accusers, 171.
  combined, safest, 236.
Dependent on others, to be, miserable position, 225.
Defer not till to-morrow, &c., 50.
Delay, by, occasion lost, 94.
  heightens desire of knowledge, 175.
  irksome, but teaches wisdom, 227.
  is folly, 259.
  let there be no, 259.
  sweet reluctant, &c., 92.
Delays nourish desires, 175.
Deliberate before you act, 30.
  carefully, execute promptly, 57.
Deliberation, imitate snail in, bird in execution, 57.
  recommended, 81.
Delight, excess of, palls the appetite, 114.
Demons in act, gods in face, 219.
Denial, civil, better than rude grant, 8.
Depend, to, on others, wretched, 225.
Depth, go not out of your, 17.
Descend, easy to, 117.
Design, bold in, timid in execution, 179.
Desires, nourished by delays, 175.
  set bounds to, 165.
Despair gives coward courage, 178.
Desperate cuts, desperate cures, 19.
  steps, beware of, &c., 195.
Despise enemy, soon beaten, 242.
Destroy, whom Jove would, he renders mad, 15.
Devil can assume pleasing form, 135.
  can cite Scripture, 147.
  drive out by devil, 74.
  happy the man, whose father went to, 15.
  he that shippeth, must make best of him, 58.
  let him always find you occupied, 117.
  rebukes sin, 15.

Devil sick, a monk would be, 9.
   who has shipped, must carry him over the sound, 115.
Devil's back, what gotten, &c., 77.
Diamond cut diamond, 288.
Dice, best throw of, to throw away, 13.
Die is cast, 190.
   never say, 264.
Dies young, he whom gods love, 354.
Diet cures more than lancet, 232.
Different men, different tastes, 14.
Difficulties between two, 456.
   embolden the brave, 160.
   give way to diligence, 484.
   past, sweet to think of, 192.
Difficulty, man conquers, 266.
Dignity, position of, easier improved than acquired, 117.
Dilemma, to be in same, 167.
Diligent man always finds something to do, 154.
   man ever occupied, 154.
Disasters, authors of own, 287.
Discontent, worst evil, 244.
Discord wears torn mantle, 107.
Discretion, want of, leads us in avoiding one evil to fall into another, 173.
Discourse, fair, as sugar, &c., 59.
Disease, he suffers from same, 102.
   check, in its approach, 456.
   remedy worse than the, 9.
Diseases desperate grown, &c., 114.
Disgrace, desire nothing which brings, 245.
   of others prevents crime, 14.
   what brings, avoid, 245.
Dish, in riven, all lost, 179.
Disposition not changed abroad, 57.
Dissembler described, 68.
Dissemblers deceive themselves, 48.
Divide and rule, 89.
Divine power, yield to, 53.
Do thoroughly what you are doing, 12.
   what becomes you, 249.
   what you should, not what you may, 159.
Doctor, more to be feared from, than from the disease, 331.
Dog, all bite the bitten, 5.
   beware of the, 52.
   does the moon care for the barking of, 197.
   easy to find stick to beat, 213.
   give a bad name to, as well hang him, 185.
   hunts in sleep, 106.

Dog, living, better than dead lion, 7.
   into mouth of bad, falls good bone, 61.
   lame, help over stile, 73.
   man may cause his to bite him, 140.
   old, won't learn new tricks, 81.
   one, barking, another barks too, 197.
   returned to his vomit, 47.
   silent, and still water avoid, 18.
   that means to bite don't bark, 31.
   valiant in own kennel, 141.
Dogs that bark at distance bite not at hand, 47.
Dolphin, he paints, in woods! 81.
   to teach, to swim, 81.
Dominion, love of, engrossing passion, 71.
Done, nothing, when aught remains to do, 264.
   what is, can't be undone, 5.
Donkey known by his ears, 109.
Door, client watching, go out at back, 30.
   creaking, hangs long, 215.
   is shut when mischief done, 353.
   where one shuts, another opens, 286.
Doves, censure rebukes, &c., 76.
   eagles produce not, 246.
Dowry, a great, destroys happiness, 395.
   not wife, attraction, 91.
Downy, the arrow is from her, 456.
Draw, while we, we are drawn, 95.
Dreaded by many, beware of many, 233.
Dress keeps cellar dry, &c., 180.
   wisdom consists not in, 173.
Drink makes men wits, 129.
Dripping, constant, wears rock, 29.
Drop, a, not even, left, 244.
   by drop fills the tub, 78.
   by drop, lake drained, 52.
   last, makes cup run over, 107.
Dropping waters wear away rocks, 145.
Drunkard convicted by praises of wine, 198.
Drunken man asleep, leave alone, 433.
Drunken man mad, 266.
   night makes cloudy morning, 62.
Drunkenness discloses every secret, 26.
Duck not always dabble in same gutter, 192.
Dunce, travelling, becomes greater, 133.
Dust in the eyes, to throw, 142.

EAGLE, leavings of, feed crow, 63.
   does not catch flies, 25.
   breeds not dove, 246.
   suffers little birds to sing, 25.
   teach to fly! 25.
Eagle's fate and mine, &c., 39.

INDEX.   483

Early bird catcheth worm, 23.
  habits second nature, 67.
  remedies most effective, 398.
  ripe, early rotten, 188.
  rising best, 86.
  training, importance of, 8.
Ears, listen to man with four, 108.
Earth, between, and heaven, 168.
Earthquake, he fears not the, 256.
Ease combined with dignity, 313.
Easy thing to find a staff to beat a dog, 213.
Eat, men born only to, 136.
  to live, not live to eat, 99.
Eating, mode of, a good deal in, 104.
Economy the surest source of gain, 294.
Education, poor man's haven, 27.
  polishes the manners, 178.
Eel, held by tail, not taken, 277.
Eels become accustomed to skinning, 74.
Effects to causes, 122.
Egg, from, to apple, 2.
  to-day, better than hen to-morrow, 7.
  to give, to get ox, 69.
Eggs, as like as, 283.
  hatched from unlucky, 286.
  who would have, must endure hens' cackling, 249.
Either a deity or a devil, 34.
  a man or a mouse, 34.
  Cæsar or nobody, 34.
Elephant, as quickly hide under your armpit, 56.
  cares not for a gnat, 175.
  will not catch mice, 100.
Eloquence, let out on hire, 187.
  one great in, other arms, 151.
Empty expressions. Bombast, 43.
  granary, ants won't go to, 157.
  vessel most sound, 223.
Emulation begets emulation, 9.
  hath thousand sons, 9.
  whetstone of wit, 9.
End, an, of the matter, 44.
Enchantments to Egypt! 30.
  in, things mend, 282.
Endurance conquers evils, 132.
Endure, all must, what is the common lot. 123.
  the present and hope, 96.
  what is painful to secure advantage, 122.
Enemy, despise, and be beaten, 242.
  do not dally with, 56.
  learn from, 120.
  may become friend, 109.

Enemy, miserable lot to have, 224.
Enemies, gifts from dangerous, 436.
Energy without reason fails, 466.
Enjoyment, one to share necessary, 292.
Enough and to spare, 398.
  as good as a feast, 243.
Enter not, or pass through, 277.
Entreaty, deaf to, 31.
Envious man waxes lean at fatness of neighbour, 98.
Envy, brave, laugh at, 185.
  has no holiday, 184.
  is blind, and depreciates virtues of others, 44.
  no man, 241.
  produced by relationship, 58.
Epigram should resemble a bee, 304.
Equal, when shall we see his, 283.
Err, human to, 65.
  to, on same string, 99.
Errors caused by necessity, pardonable, 455.
Ethiopian, to wash the, 12.
Evening crowns the day, 112.
  what will bring, not known, 258.
Events, coming, cast their shadows before, 54.
Ever drunk, ever dry, 379.
Everybody, Jupiter even cannot please, 242.
Every man his due, 426.
  man to his trade, 351.
  may-be hath a may-be not, 134.
  one to his liking, 77.
Everything, about, and something more, 77.
  affect not to know, 247.
Evil, a necessary, 249.
  approaching, brings danger, 234.
  avoiding, find good, 99.
  bear with, and expect good, 96.
  by evil, to cure, 215.
  comes from neighbouring evil, 16.
  communications corrupt good manners, 63.
  deeds, penalty, think of, 172.
  deeds, you bring to light, 172.
  gain equal to loss, 206.
  gotten, evil spent, 213.
  impending, ignorance better than knowledge of, 54.
  speaking as bad as doing, 213.
  to do, pretext soon found, 213.
Evils, best forgotten, 178.
  endurance conquers, 132.
  follow each other, 214.
  of two, choose the least, 77.

INDEX.

Evils, lessened when foreseen, 336.
   to which used, hurt less, 74.
Example, good, best sermon, 68.
   profit by good, 1.
Expect not everything, everywhere, from everybody, 247.
Expensive things please most, 209.
Experience learnt by suffering not forgotten, 101.
   teaches, 112.
Experienced man, trust, 113.
Experiment on worthless subject, 126.
Explain by difficulty, useless to, 264.
Extremes, to make, meet, 142.
Eye ever wanders to object of regard, 443.
   for eye, &c., 201.
   sees not, when mind engaged, 44.
   the best channel of instruction, 402.
   what, sees not, heart rues not, 54.
Eyes, far from, far from heart, 283.
   he has in back of head, 170.
   to throw dust in, 142.
Eyesight to be trusted more than ears, 301.

FACE, his, would hang him, 102.
   not woman, attracts, 116.
   the index to the mind, 470.
   a very forbidding, 435.
Faces, two, under one hood, 91.
Failings, all have not same, 180.
   e'en his, lean to virtue's side, 4.
Faint heart never won fair lady, 131.
Fair face may hide foul heart, 79.
   feathers, fair fowls, 269.
   means, if, cannot, foul shall, 129.
   without, foul within, 135.
Faith, good, necessity of keeping, 127.
   old, he goes back to, &c., 67.
Fallen, a kingly act to help, 389.
   the crowd despises the, 441.
False, all was, &c., 146.
   friends worse than open enemies, 414.
   in one respect, never trusted, 119.
Falsehood never long hidden, 210.
   one, leads to another, 118.
Falsehoods border on truths, 119.
Fame, by public applause, he seeks, 329.
Familiarity breeds contempt, 267.
   of master spoils servant, 120.
   too much, breeds contempt, 267.
Famine followed by pestilence, 119.
Fancy, long observed, retained, 84.
Fare hard, to, 196.
Farming, too high, does not answer, 262.

Farthing, to lose last, 5.
Fascinating, be not too, 71.
Fashion dictates mode of living, 111.
   more powerful than tyrant, 61.
   its rule all-powerful, 144.
   we live by, not common sense, 111.
Fat kitchen, lean will, 125.
Fates will not permit, 120.
Father, his, you are by nature, I by counsel, 240.
Father's arts in vain you try! 257.
Fault condemn, not the actor, 37.
   denied, doubled, 281.
   every clown cap find, 104.
   fostered by concealment, 16.
   unpunished invites crime, 185.
Faults on both sides, 160.
   small, indulged in let in greater, 289.
   sweet, he is full of, 4.
   we pardon, in youth, 170.
   we see not our own, 65.
Faultless, no man is, 65.
Favour enriched by courtesy, 8.
   of great not lasting, 43.
   out of place an injury, 38.
   who will not give has no right to ask, 38.
Favours, force not on the unwilling, 253.
   small, conciliate, great gifts make enemies, 11.
Fear, he must many, whom many fear, 250.
   not what must be endured, 420.
Fears, present, worse than reality, 224.
   vanish at approach of danger, 201.
Fearing his own shadow, 446.
Feast, too late for, 334.
Feather by feather, goose plucked, 52.
   to cut throat with, 192.
Feet, all, tread not in one shoe, 14.
Feigned love worse than hatred, 414.
Fellow, a noisy, useless, 154.
Fellow-men, to help, godlike, 153.
Fellowship, love and lordship have no, 308.
Fern grows in neglected land, 252.
Fetters of gold, still fetters, 419.
Fiction should resemble truth, 126.
Fiddle, let him play second, who can't play first, 32.
Field, for talent, a fine, 152.
   should be poorer than the farmer, 309.
Fig he calls a fig, 27.
   he is looking out for a, 126.
Fight with tweezers, not swords, they, 469.
Fine feathers make fine birds, 459.
Finger, not worth snap of, 246.

INDEX.

Firtrees to Norway! 30.
Fire, add not fire to, 159.
  all rake, to own pot, 151.
  and water, to mix, 25.
  closest kept, burns most, 186.
  he carries, in one hand, water in another, 17.
  neglected, gains strength, 251.
  nourished by its ashes, 160.
  one burns out another's, &c., 74.
  hidden by deceitful cinders, you walk on, 174.
  sea, woman, three ills, 160.
  to quench with oil, 303.
  will not put out fire, 160.
  when next house is on, look to own, 440.
Firm, be, or mild on occasion, 61.
First come, first served, 23.
  to mill, first grind, 23.
Fish, don't cry, before caught, 23.
  fears hook concealed, 52.
  if would catch, mind not wet, 122.
  good, still in sea, 184.
  in troubled waters, 328.
  to swim, you are teaching, 328.
  venture small, for big, 69.
  who would catch, must not mind getting wet, 172.
Fix, to be in a, 172.
Flame, breeze helps, blast kills, 239.
  gnat allured by, perishes, 68.
  traces of the old, 459.
Flames acquire strength, 107.
Flatterer, when, pipes, the devil dances, 327.
Flattery, warning against, 241.
  in parlour, plain dealing kicked out of doors, 299.
Flies, more taken by honey than vinegar, 161.
Flint, in coldest, hot fire, 241.
Flock, diseased from one, 144.
Flog a stone, to, 357.
Flowers, fair, not long by way, 84.
  gather while sun lasts, 93.
Fly before eye, elephant, 151.
  better, than remain in disgrace, 399.
  even can be spiteful, 147.
  lose, to catch trout, 250.
  to, when no one pursues, 138.
Folly of one man, fortune of another, 15.
  of others, best to learn wisdom from, 15.
  this the reward of! 102.
  to throw the helve after the hatchet, 140.

Food, more die of, than famine, 233.
Fool and money soon part, 211.
  cannot see his own faults, 104.
  carves his heart to all, 257.
  fortunate, intolerable, 262.
  habit of, to find faults, 104.
  observations of, sometimes of value, 183.
  one, makes many, 197.
  send to market, and fool he will return, 57.
  sometimes speaks to point, 183.
Fool's heart dances on his lips, 203.
Fools, advice of, worthless, 174.
  favoured by fortune, 132.
Fools' help injures, 419.
  names always on walls, 272.
  speech, many an injury comes from, 109.
Foot, judge of statue by, 110.
Forbidden things are most desired, 142.
  what not, not permitted, 249.
Force, to repel, by force, 461.
Forced merchandise is offensive, 222.
Forelock, time has, 135.
Forest, to carry wood to, 172.
Forewarned, forearmed, 335.
Forgets himself, 258.
Fortunate to learn caution from others' misfortunes, 122.
Fortune, a great, enslaves us, 132.
  and arts assist each other, 27.
  ever changes, 134.
  favours fools, 132.
  favours the bold, 31.
  gifts of, not all good, 82.
  good, not last for ever, 133.
  good, falls to lot of base, 61.
  great, enslaves owner, 132.
  her capriciousness and cruelty, 134.
  rarely brings good or evil singly, 214.
  smiles on every one once, 402.
  wearies with carrying the same man always, 186.
Forward, go, and fall, &c., 1.
Fortune's favour uncertain, 186.
  gifts not always beneficial, 133.
Fortunate man may be anywhere, 145.
Foundation, weak, destroys work, 79.
Fountains, even, thirst, 130.
Fox grows grey, not good, 208.
  in bargain with, expect tricks, 71.
  known by his tail, 51.
  let every, guard own tail, 151.
  not caught twice in same trap, 470.
  not to be caught with a bait, 470.
  old, not caught in snare, 22.

486 INDEX.

Fox thrives best when most cursed, 224.
Fraud, to connive at fraud, 135.
Free horse, spur not, 280.
Freedom, seek! 102.
Fresh feres will dry, &c., 131.
Friend, bear with fault of, 19.
  compete not with, 68.
  every man's, no man's, 20.
  he makes no, who never made a foe, 20.
  in need, friend indeed, 262.
  must bear friend's infirmities, 19.
  no worse, than brought from home, 201.
  second self, 17.
  to abuse absent, denounced, 3.
  true tested in adversity, 20.
Friends tie purses with spider's web, 59.
  ask not from what you yourself can do, 243.
  become foes, foes friends, 50.
  fly away when cask dry, 85.
  have all things in common, 59.
  heaven preserve me from, 181.
  like fiddle-strings, not to be screwed too tight, 40.
  old, forget not, in making new, 288.
  proved by acts, not words, 109.
  quarrels of, renewal of love, 50.
  they cease to be, who dwell far off, 283.
  treat, as if about to be enemies; enemies treat as if about to be friends, 18.
Friendship last as long as pot boils, 124.
  of the great, warning against, 93.
  sudden, sure repentance, 127.
Frog cannot out of her bog, 42.
Frogs, to drink like, 387.
Frugality a great revenue, 211.
Fruit, all soils bear not same, 280.
  forbidden, coveted, 162.
  if you will have, must climb the tree, 122.
  ripest, first falls, 56.
  to seek for in garden of Tantalus, 98.
Frying-pan, out of, into the fire, 173.
Fuel, take away, take away fire, 55.
Full cup must be carried steadily, 10.
  of courtesy, full of craft, 323.
Funeral pile, to pick meat from, 98.
Fury supplies arms, 140.
Future concealed from us, wisely, 343.
  mind anxious about, wretched, 45.

GAIN acquired by many soon accumulates, 128.
  at cost of reputation, a loss, 75.
  for outlay required, 250.

Gain, smell of, is good wherever from, 206.
  to make, some outlay necessary, 250.
Gambler, the more skilful, the more depraved, 13.
Gambling, avoid, 13.
  sire, gambling son, 407.
Game, good sportsman kills much, not all, 41.
Garlands, not for every brow, 272.
Garlic, I speak of, you reply about onions, 100.
Garments, borrowed, fit not, 157.
  showy, attract, 269.
Garners, fill while you can, 58.
Gay coat makes not gentleman, 173.
Geese, all his are swans! 234.
Gems, fairest, lie deepest, 85.
General, good, and soldier, 164.
Generalities, fraud lurks in, 90.
Gently, but firmly, 421.
Gentleman, he is the best, who is son of his own deserts, 237.
Gentleness, more effected by, than violence, 324.
Gently not by force, 321.
Ghosts, to fight with, 70.
Giant among pigmies, 36.
Gift, long waited for, is sold, not given, 143.
  a small, nevertheless acceptable, 234.
  goodwill of, best part of, 234.
  he doubles, who gives in time, 430.
  -horse, look not in mouth, 409.
Gifts from enemy must be received with caution, 158.
  from enemies dangerous, 436.
  gods conciliated by, 234.
  great, make enemies, 11.
  made with cheerful countenance acceptable, 75.
  of the wicked unprofitable, 214.
Gilt, try skill in, then gold, 167.
Give and take, 124.
  and take in turn, 327.
  each his due, 388.
  neither counsel nor salt till asked for, 253.
  to, pretext for asking, 69.
  way, and you conquer, 53.
Gives twice, he that gives in a trice, 39.
Giving is fishing, 69.
Gladiator asks advice in the arena, 142.
Glass houses, who live in, not throw stones, 356.
Gloriously deceitful, 418.

Glory, desire of, last garment wise men put off, 373.
  immortal, waits on talent, 178.
  more desired than merit, 430.
Glove, a white, often conceals a dirty hand, 136.
Gluttony brutalizes us, 398.
  kills more than sword, 101.
Gnat allured by flame perishes, 68.
Goad, you kick against, 61.
Goat must browse where tied, 222.
God and mammon, you can't serve, 80.
  and our country, for, 339.
  comes with leaden feet, &c. 147.
  forgotten, when danger past, 9.
  made country, man town, 28.
  made first garden, first city, Cain, 240.
  helps those who help themselves, 437.
  permits the wicked, but not for ever, 23.
Gods, avenging, are shod with wool, 86.
Gold, accursed hunger for, 32.
  all is not, that glitters, 136.
  eloquence no avail against voice of, 33.
  fetters of, 32.
  is proved by fire, 33.
  no lock holds against, 33.
  ring of, in sow's nostril, 22.
  to gild, 99.
  walks through the midst of guards, 33.
Golden hook, to fish with, 32.
  key opens all doors, 33.
  spades, to dig with, 202.
Good and evil are united, 274.
  and evil from same hour, 40.
  and quickly seldom meet, 124.
  debts become bad unless called in, 40.
  die first, &c. 228.
  do, if you expect to receive, 217.
  luck lasts not, 133.
  luck easier lost than one, 134.
  luck, with, 41.
  name, as sweet ointment, 271.
  no, to self or others, 249.
  thing can be twice said, 39.
  thing, often abused, 266.
  thing is soon caught up, 84.
  things best known by loss, 42.
  time coming, 208.
  too late, good as nothing, 143.
  turn deserves another, 143.
  watch prevents misfortune, 335.
Goods lost by not demanding, 40.
Goose, sauce for, what's &c., 201.

Goslings teach goose to swim, 23.
Gossiping, evils result from, 148.
Govern well, they only who have obeyed discipline, 252.
Grace, unbought, 79.
Grain by grain hen fills crop, 223.
Grammar dry, but fruits of sweet, 204.
Granary empty, at, no ants, 157.
Grand eloquence, little conscience, 42.
Grand-dame, teach to suck eggs, 25.
Grant, civil denial better than rude, 8.
Grapes, sour, won't make sweet wine, 196.
Grasp all, lose all, 46, 54.
Grasshopper dear to grasshopper, 55.
Grasshoppers, wait for the, 96.
Gratitude, if not openly expressed, ingratitude, 179.
  least of virtues, ingratitude worst of vices, 179.
Grey and green make worst medley, 19.
  hair, yet mind vigorous, 406.
Grease, let him fry in his own, 115.
Great coat, wear not in summer, 11.
  favour of, not lasting, 43.
  fear, favour of, 93.
  gifts make enemies, 11.
  houses full of saucy servants, 218.
  men have reaching hands, 21.
  men's vices counted sacred, 322.
  some born, &c. 51.
  talkers, little doers, 231.
  things made up of small, 260.
Greatest talkers, least doers, 453.
Greek Calends, at, 6.
Greeks bring presents, I fear, 436.
Grief, all can master one, but he who has it, 116.
  away with effeminate! 229.
  beauty's canker, 212.
  brims itself, 113.
  day of, to make birthday, 110.
  is dispelled by wine, 71.
  light, that seeks counsel, 200.
  never long, except our own fault, 254.
  only fit for women, 229.
  pent up bursts the heart, 209.
  proves to be a blessing, 90.
  secret, real grief, 161.
  secret, the greatest, 209.
  to lay up one in store for self, 45.
  vanishes when cause removed, 89.
Grieve, all men, cannot tell the reason, 226.
  not before there is need, 331.
Grieving, away with! 229.

INDEX.

Grind with every wind, 287.
Grove, one, not satisfy two robins, 448.
Guard, you trust, to an unarmed man, 289.
Guards themselves, who shall guard? 375.
Gudgeons, to swallow, before catched, 23.
Guest, a constant, is never welcome, 280.
Guest should not remain long, 292.
Guilt betrayed by the countenance, 150.
Guilty acquitted, judge condemned, 192.
   conscience needs no accuser, 356.
   thunder alarms, 151.

HABIT, second nature, 3.
Habitual prosperity injurious, 40.
Hail, as thick as, 169.
Hair, it hangs by a, 78.
   take, from dog that has bitten, 74.
Half a loaf better than no bread, 408.
Hallucination, a delightful, 221.
Hammer, between, and anvil, 182.
Hand and foot, 216.
   one, washes the other, 217.
   which gives gathers, 143.
Handmaid, once a, never a lady, 349.
Hands, I have washed my, of it, 199.
   many, make light work, 231.
Handsome looks recommend, 130.
Hanging and wiving go by destiny, 288.
Happen, best not know what will, 244.
Happiness better than luxury, 281.
   in our own power, 239.
   invites envy, 98.
   no such thing as perfect, 260.
   realize your, 274.
   to remember in misery, greatest grief, 225.
Hard knot, hard wedge for, 215.
   life, but a healthy one, 29.
   things alone will not make a wall, 97.
   things, if said, must be expected, 62.
Hardest step over threshold, 87.
Hare alarmed at rustling of leaves, 200.
   he lives life of, 200.
   hindmost dog may get, 130.
   to run with, hold with hounds, 91.
   you a, and ask for hare-pie! 442.
   you compare tortoise to, 46.
Hares, following two, lose both, 96.
Harlot, the gate of death, 400.
Harm watch, harm catch, 36.
Harms, their, our arms, 121.
Harp dispels care, 55.
   to, on same string, 48.
   you, perpetually, on same string, 48.

Harping, still, on my daughter, 48.
Harvest lasts not for ever, 58.
Haste, dangers of, 125.
   denounced, 268.
   make no more, than good speed, 124.
   marry in, repent at leisure, 7.
   more, less speed, 125.
   trips up its own heels, 73.
Hastiness, beginning of wrath, 84.
Hasty conclusions, speedy repentance, 7.
   counsel, followed by repentance, 455.
   hand catches no frogs, 73.
Hate, greatest, springs from greatest love, 4.
   so that they fear me, let them, 301.
   men, those they have injured, 342.
Hatred, kind in, more harmful, 186.
   of relations bitter, 4.
   undying, 163.
Haughtiness denounced, 180.
Hay, he has on horn, 130.
   make, when sun shines, 93.
   you give, to dog, bones to ass, 47.
Head aches, when, body ill, 93.
   neither, nor tail, 245.
   to carry on, love dearly, 48.
   without a tongue, 49.
Headstrong man and fool alike, 166.
Healer of others, himself diseased, 15.
Health, to give to men, is to resemble the gods, 153.
Hear all, say nothing, 32.
   see, and be silent! 31.
   to, is to heed, 31.
Heart, as thinketh in, so is he, 149.
   fell down to his heels, 22.
   if, fail thee, climb not, 34.
   out of fulness of, mouth speaks, 5.
   sick, can't bear annoyance, 221.
Heaven, sins against, leave to, 82.
   spit not against, 53.
   to war against, 167.
Heaviness endure a night, joy come in the morning, 131.
   may endure for night, &c., 195.
Heavy meals invite not study, 165.
Heed, take, of an ox before, horse behind, and a monk on all sides, 341.
Heir, absent one will not be, 3.
   follows heir, 148.
   grief of, only masked laughter, 148.
   ill-gotten wealth helps not, 77.
   to make one's physician, 213.
Hell and chancery always open, 122.
   paved with good intentions, 82.

Helmet, worn bare by, 30.
Help, slow, no help, 39.
 those who strive, 437.
Helve, to throw, after hatchet, 7.
Here, or nowhere, what we seek, 151.
Hesitation, chance lost by, 81.
Hidden evils most dreaded, 384.
High, who aspires, must down, &c., 123.
 winds on high hills, 123.
Higher the tower, greater the fall, 54.
Himself, he is planning for, 126.
Hindmost, plague seize, 301.
Hog, fat, all baste, 67.
Hole, to make, by stopping another, 264.
Holidays last not for ever, 282.
Home, farthest way about, nearest way to, 59.
 is home, be it never so homely, 320.
 no place like, 42.
 to begin at, 2.
Homer sometimes nods, 352.
Honesty praised, but starves, 340.
 with poverty better than ill-gotten wealth, 156.
Honey catches most flies, 60.
 cloys, 219.
 -comb in lion's mouth, 170.
 no use in ass's mouth, 28.
 sweet, but bee stings, 147.
 sword anointed with, 220.
 tongue, heart of gall, 219.
 wears sting, 164.
 where bee sucks, spider sucks poison, 238.
Honied tongue has its poison, 147.
Honour and ease unite not, 274.
 or blame undeserved affect only the base and liar, 119.
 shines in mean habit, 173.
Hook, or by crook, 323.
Hope, a last, 427.
 and chance adieu! 184.
 and fear, betwixt, 183.
 deferred, heart sick, 173.
 doubtful, hope denied, 92.
 good, often beguiled, 118.
 he is consumed by a vain, 173.
 of escape, incentive to vice, 218.
 shall brighten days, &c., 50.
 still left, 286.
 the dream of the waking, 417.
Horned animal, you attack, 62.
Hornets, to worry, 188.
Horns, I gave you credit for having, 24.

Horse, gift, to look into mouth, 102.
 one may steal, another not look over hedge, 76.
 taken to water, won't drink, 181.
 urge, to turning post, 174.
 without food, won't work, 102.
Horse's heels, avoid, 2.
 tail, to remove hairs, take one by one, 52.
Hot and cold, to blow, in same breath, 109.
Hot sup, hot swallow, 45.
Hour brings good and evil, 40.
 enjoy pleasures of, 91.
 is passing, 157.
 one to-day, worth two to-morrow, 48.
House, in own, man king, 91.
 last to know disgrace of, 79.
 should be honoured by owner, not owner by house, 246.
Houses, to build, and not to inhabit, 9.
Human blood is all of one colour, 155.
Hunchback sees not own hump, 126.
Hunger and delay raise up anger, 20.
 best cook, 119.
 best sauce, 115.
 better to satisfy, than dress fine, 119.
 despises not rough food, 191.
 makes raw beans relish, 115.
 raises up anger, 120.
 relishes raw beans, 115.
 sharpens anger, 119.
 sweetens all but itself, 120.
 teaches many a lesson, 230.
Hungry bellies have no ears, 191.
 dog eats dirty pudding, 191.
 horse, clean manger, 191.
 man, angry man, 119.
 man listens to nothing, 191.
 man, oppose not, 106.
Huntsmen, all not, who blow horn, 232.
Hurry, never speak in a, 242.
Hurt, cry not out before, 243.
Hypocrisy, description of, 261.

I AM not what I once was, 283.
Idiot, revenge of, without mercy, 177.
 tale of, sound and fury, 43.
Idle, better to be, than ill-occupied, 336.
 brain, devil's workshop, 74.
 hands, for, Satan finds work, 74.
 man always excuse for holiday, 159.
 man full of cares, 313.
 men, devil's playfellows, 74.
Idleness brings destruction, 63.
 favourable to love, 313.

Idleness ruins the constitution, 63.
   sepulchre of living man, 63.
   the root of all evil, 259.
Ignorance, a strong remedy for evils, 178.
   fallen man's best friend, 178.
   of impending evil better than knowledge, 54.
   where bliss, folly to be wise, 54.
Ignorant, let, learn, and learned refresh memory, 175.
Ill-gotten goods seldom prosper, 213.
   luck asleep, wake not, 215.
   name, who hath, is half hanged, 5.
   weeds grow apace, 252.
   yoked, 212.
Impossible, nothing to man, 266.
Impossibility, to attempt an, 142.
Impotent desires avoid, 244.
   fury, 211.
Imprudent patient makes harsh doctor, 66.
Impulse conquers reason, 275.
   influence of, 166.
Inclination, to be forced to act against, 299.
Income, live according to, 222.
   to live with false show of, 116.
Inconsistent, nothing so, 265.
Indignation, this secret of! 152.
Indulgence for offences, who requires, must give, 10.
   to Rome, 30.
Industrious, the gods help, 85.
Infection, take some new, &c., 74.
Ingratitude, worst of vices, 179.
Injure one, threaten many, 233.
Injuries destroy affection, 179.
   prove blessings, 103.
   put us on our guard, 270.
   should be treated with contempt, 210.
Injury for injury, 201.
   it has done, and will, 270.
   pretext to do, soon found, 213.
   to meditate, is to commit, 180.
Innocence the best security, 152.
Innocents, some, 'scape not thunderbolt, 174.
Inquisitive man, a gossip, 72.
   man always ill-natured, 274.
Inside and out, turn it, 184.
Instruct by praise, 197.
Insults, by submitting to old, invite new, 459.
Integrity, I'll wrap myself in, 218.
Intemperate die young, 163.
Intention, not act, constitutes crime, 5.
Interest, whose, was it? 66.
Invention, easy to improve on, 116.

Iron, strike, while it is hot, 123.
   you teach to swim! 124.
Irons in the fire, he that hath many, some will cool, 262.
Irrelevant things, he says, 238.
Issue, aim at certain, 55.
   of all contention uncertain, 104.
Ivory, to whiten with ink! 99.

JACK, every, has his Jill, 28.
   good, makes good Jill, 42.
Jackdaw among muses, 143.
   stripped of stolen feathers, ridiculous, 229.
Jest on sacred matters, to, 206.
John Barleycorn, inspiring, &c., 71.
Joke, driven too far, brings hate, 8.
   to, amidst mourners, 182.
Jokes, true, never please, 70.
Joking apart, let us be serious, 21.
   must have proper limit, 8.
Joy, from springs of, misery, 182.
   greatest grief to remember, in misery, 225.
   holidays of, vigils of sorrow, 184.
   surfeited, turns to sorrow, 164.
   to turn, to sorrow, 110.
Joys, think, we may buy too dear, &c., 51.
Judge condemned, when guilty acquitted, 192.
   of a man by his remarks, 350.
Judged by our actions, 416.
June, month of, who would scorn, &c., 50.
Just, learn to be, 87.
   to obtain what is, ask for what is unjust, 310.
Justice, from unjust, to expect, folly, 192.
   let, be done, though heavens fall, 126.
Justify, to, before accused, is to confess guilt, 111.

KERNEL, if you wish, must crack the shell, 122.
Key, used, always bright, 10.
Kick not against the pricks, 167.
Kill, power to, not wish, 107.
Kindness, forgotten, injuries not, 66.
   long deferred, not to be thanked, 143.
   spontaneously offered, doubly gratifying, 39.
   to kill by, 267.
   to forget, 59.
   unusual, suspicious, 283.
   which we can return, agreeable, 38.
Kings have long arms, 21.
   play fool, people suffer, 369.

INDEX. 491

Kiss, connubial, nothing wrong in, 269.
Kisses, stolen, sweeter, 92.
Kissing goes by favour, 75.
Knocks, not words, 280.
Knot, to untie, 270.
Knotty timber requires sharp wodges, 19.
Knowledge is power, 186.
    to have a smattering, 195.

LABOUR conquers all things, 195.
    division of, lessens task, 89.
    gods sell everything for, 86.
    in vain, 26.
    itself a pleasure, 195.
    long, deserves sleep, 309.
    nothing done without, 266.
Labourer worthy of hire, 85.
Ladder, who holds, as bad as thief, 12.
Lamb, to snatch from wolf, 13.
Lamp, it smells of, 206.
Lane, a long one without a turning, 131.
Languages, many on earth, one in heaven, 232.
Lantern, to use, at noonday, 205.
Large heap, pleasant to take from, 29.
Last act not equal to first, 58.
Late, bones for those who come, 406.
Laugh, at the wrong moment, 392.
    let him who wins, 333.
    to-day, cry to-morrow, 114.
    with those who laugh, 392.
Laughs ill who laughs himself to death, 2.
Laughing, to burst with, 392.
Laughter abounds in fools, 393.
    can you restrain? 392.
    leaves us serious, 114.
Laurel branch, I bear, 199.
Laurels, to seek, from bride-cake, 198.
Lava, walk over, hidden by ashes, 174.
Law, avoid, 122.
    of requital, 201.
    strain the, and injustice follows, 424.
Laws, good, offspring of bad actions, 40.
Lawsuit, one, begets another, 204.
Leaden feet, but iron hands, God uses, 147.
Leader, good, makes good follower, 42.
Leaf, to turn over a new, 169.
Learning, no royal road to, 227.
    sour roots, sweet fruits, 204.
Least said is soonest mended, 371.
Leather, liberal of another's, 76.
    nothing like, 401.
    raw, will stretch, 89.

Leave well alone, 90.
Leech never satisfied, 278.
Legs, stretch, according to coverlet, 177.
Leisure, not even, to scratch ears, 240.
Leopard not change his spots, 317.
Let well alone, 375.
Letter once written, can't be recalled, 204.
Liar, not believed when he speaks truth, 16.
Liars should have good memories, 221.
Liberal enough of another's leather, 76.
Liberality shouldn't exceed means, 242.
Lie, half truth, worst lie, 119.
    one, makes many, 118.
Life, enjoy, while it lasts, 96.
    not all beer and skittles, 243.
    while, hope, 95.
Light burdens, far, heavy, 205.
    comes when all dark, 286.
Lightning harmless, 43.
    strikes one, alarms many, 69.
Like likes like, 10.
    master, like man, 218.
    will to like, 28.
Likeness the mother of love, 10.
Lilies whitest in blackamoor's hand, 62.
Lily, to paint the, 99.
Lion, dead, little birds may pick, 48.
    destroy, when but a whelp, 251.
    he makes, of a mouse, 234.
    hungry, to wrest prey from, 106.
    may be beholden to mouse, 176.
    not so fierce as painted, 224.
    partnership with, 200.
    to frighten with a mask, 199.
    you may know by claw, 110.
Lions at home, 90.
    in peace, deer in war, 170.
Lion's way of sharing, 200.
    whelp, nourish not, 200.
Lips, he moistens, but leaves palate dry, 195.
Listeners hear no good, &c., 285.
Little birds may pick dead lion, 48.
    body often has great soul, 211.
    drops produce shower, 223.
    enjoy your, &c., 196.
    neglect, lose greater, 211.
    pitchers, long ears, 218.
    presents maintain friendships, 38.
    sticks kindle fire, 239.
    stream drives great mill, 110.
    things are pretty, 176.

Little strokes fell oaks, 233.
   things, many, make great, 260.
Live according to your means, 177.
Loaf, give, beg shieve, 69.
Lofty tree soonest falls, 397.
Lone sheep in danger of wolf, 236.
Long absent, soon forgotten, 232.
   absent, and empty-handed! 130.
   lane, no turning, 130.
Look before you leap, 81.
   high, and fall low, 54.
Looker on sees most of the game, 332.
Loss, comforts only known by, 287.
   not felt, lost nothing, 178.
   of which we are ignorant, no loss, 20.
   sometimes better than to win, 102.
Losses, often gains, 102.
Lost, what is, grieve not for, 78.
Lot, no man contented with, 255.
   of others pleases, not our own, 67.
Lotus, he has tasted, 205.
Louse, he'd skin, for market, 25.
Love, a pleasure in youth, sin in age, 19.
   advocated, 63.
   and a cough cannot be hidden, 20.
   and be wise, Jove cannot, 19.
   and dignity dwell apart, 272
   and lordship, no fellowship, 171.
   be in, and wise, a god cannot, 19.
   brooks no delay, 20.
   credulous thing, 64.
   flee, and it will follow thee, 404.
   fruit of love, 136.
   good to be off with old, &c., 254.
   in, and war, all fair, 90.
   laughs at locksmiths, 259.
   let him, none, and be loved by none, 245.
   like a shuttlecock, 20.
   making and dance, despise not, 246.
   me, love my dog, 356.
   old, good to be off with, &c., 80.
   pleasures of, enhanced by injury, 192.
   quarrels end in concord, 50.
   remedy for, land between, 232.
   she never told her, &c., 161.
   to, as wolf, lamb, 207.
   to hatred, &c., 164.
   who can, and be wise, 18.
Lov'd me for dangers passed, &c., 136.
Lover, nothing difficult to, 259.
   one, lost, another comes, 184.
   you'll soon find new, 131.
Lovers are madmen, 18.

Lovers, quarrels of, lead to love, 18.
Loves, man who, easy of belief, 64.
Low person, raised, obnoxious, 29.
Luck, good, lasts not, 133.
Luck, sly, good, delightful, 117.
Luxuries bring sorrow, 243.
   of life, seek not, 243.

MADMAN or poet, he is either, 34.
   thinks others mad, 181.
Main force, 460.
Malady, to add malady to, 227.
Malevolence, less, or more power, 34.
Malice, bear no, 242.
   injury measured by, 180.
   drinks own poison, 187.
Man, alone, god or demon, 155.
   and woman, fire and chaff, 154.
   architect of own fortune, 115.
   at five, fool at fifteen, 56.
   at sixteen, child at sixty, 56.
   author of our misery, 287.
   black, to make white, 11.
   bound, boy may beat, 139.
   bound, child may beat, 48.
   brings worst enemy from home, 253.
   down, all tread on, 80.
   drunk, gone from home, 3.
   every, for himself, 151.
   fallen, all tread on, 5.
   forget not that you are, 220.
   from naked, you can't take shirt, 254.
   give every, his due, 157.
   his own enemy, 201.
   I am, &c., 155.
   I dare do all that may become a, 34.
   inconstant, described, 226.
   not liked, does all amiss, 185.
   no, wise at all times, 253.
   of refined taste, 101.
   of three letters, F. U. R., 155.
   old at thirty, or young at eighty, 163.
   once obnoxious, all he does, bad, 185.
   outwardly angel, &c., 135.
   perfect to finger tips, 7.
   proposes, God disposes, 155.
   prosperous, should remain at home, 91.
   son of own works, 115.
   to kick, when down, 47.
   to man, demon, 155.
   to man, god or wolf, 154.
   to save, against his will, 185.
Man's extremity, God's opportunity, 69.
   most dark extremity, in, &c., 69.

INDEX. 493

Mandrabulus, manner of, 216.
Many a slip between cup and lip, 230.
   hands, light work, 231, 233.
   if dreaded by, beware of many, 233.
   littles make a mickle, 78.
   men, many minds, 227.
   vain to do by, what few can, 137.
   words, little credit, 231.
Marines, tell it to, 64.
Marketing, want of pence stops, 163.
Mark intended, arrow hits not, 249.
   to miss his, 3.
   to overshoot, 113.
Marriage, inopportune, 211.
Marry, honest men soon, wise never, 202.
   in haste, repent at leisure, 7, 158.
   to, in month of May, unlucky, 221.
   to, well, marry not, better, 202.
Mask, no one can wear, long, 254.
Master's eye makes the mule fat, 301.
Masters, none can serve two, 80, 128, 254.
Mastiff, gentle, but don't vex, 140.
Matter, yet undecided, 8.
May and December never agree, 19.
   we frolic, while 'tis, 50.
Meal dangerously seasoned, 45.
   not from own sack, 275.
Means, live according to, 177.
   wanting, not will, 273.
Measures, extreme, avoid, 246.
Meat, after, comes mustard, 209.
   from funeral pile, 98.
Medal, every, has reverse, 184.
Meditate injury, is to commit, 180.
Meditates a crime, who, commits one, 238.
Medium in all things, 103.
Memory, treasure of mind, 152.
Men would be angels, angels gods, 67.
Mercury, not made of all wood, 110, 273.
Mercy, sweet, nobility's true badge, 242.
   to him who gives, the rule, 255.
Merit, poverty keeps down, 149.
Merry and wise, 392.
Mice have taken themselves off, 234.
   the, are off, 234.
Middle course, best, 218.
Might, if not by, by sleight, 27.
Mildness governs more than anger, 161.
Milk, spilt, grieve not over, 78.
Mill, can't grind with water past, 135.
   can a, go with water past? 22.
   first come to, first grind, 23.
Miller, sees not every wave, 278.
Mind, best taught by whip, 96.

Mind, conscious of own rectitude, 221.
   diseases of, caused or cured by music, 21.
   grows and decays with body, 69.
   longs for occupation, 22.
   longs for what it has missed, 22.
   makes body rich, 178.
   must have relaxation, 206.
   rust of, destruction of genius, 10.
   that broods o'er guilty woes, &c., 22.
   uncertain, described, 158.
Minds, so many, so many men, 278.
Mine, be, I will be thine, 105.
Minnow lose, to catch salmon, 69.
Minute, catch good, 287.
Mire, you have got out of, 113.
   you stick in same, 167.
Mirth, amidst, misery rises, 182.
   in midst of, sorrow, 218.
   indulge not in boisterous, 2.
   pennyworth of, worth pound of sorrow, 189.
Mischief, let them call it, &c., 156.
Miser, does nothing good till he dies, 35.
Miseries of others, from, he fears for his own, 14.
Misery, highest, help nighest, 69.
Misfortune of fool, warning to wise, 51.
   to smile at, hurts, 166.
Misfortunes, grieve not for, 278.
   make friends, 59.
   of others, profit by, 41.
   sweeten happiness, 50.
Mistakes, pardon, 75.
Mob, sometimes right, 183.
Mocking is catching, 95.
Moderation recommended, 225.
Modesty should accompany youth, 8.
Molehill, to make mountain of, 26.
Money conquers all things, 264.
   loss of, stings, 248.
   love of, grows with money, 64.
   makes the man, 430.
   makes the mare to go, 61.
   master or slave of owner, 163.
   more than lord's letter, 26.
   nothing stings so bitterly as loss of, 248.
   ready, is Aladdin's lamp, 33.
   smell of, good always, 206.
Monk, cowl does not make, 66.
Monkey, every, has gambols, 92.
   higher he goes, more shows tail, 29.
   old, caught at last, 24.
Monument, paper best, 111.
Mony sma's mak a great, 223.

Moon cares not for dog's bark, 197.
  gazing, he fell into gutter! 197.
  rays of, won't ripen grape, 207.
More we have, more we want, 65.
Morn described, 87.
  early, favours study, 33.
Morning air hath gold in mouth, 86.
Most haste, worst speed, 73.
  who doth, doth least, 128.
Mote, in brother's eye, see, 104.
Mountain, of molehill! 100.
  to make, of molehill, 26.
Mountains never unite, 227.
Mouse, after fashion of, 234.
  caught in trap, 79.
  drown'd, to pour water on, 47.
  in pitch, 235.
  may bite in two cable, 145.
  relies not on one hole, 235.
  will not love cat, 207.
  you make elephant, 100.
Much coin, much care, 37.
  to him having, much given, 67.
  would have more, lost all, 46.
Mules scratch each other, 236.
  when, breed, 70.
Murder, one, made villain, 161.
  will out, 186.
Murderer, hate, pity victim, 187.
Mushroom, sprung up like as, 423.
Music causes or cures disease of mind, 21.
  cures sorrow, 235.
  dispels fear of death, 222.
  handmaid of divinity, 235.
  helps not toothache, 182.
  induces madness, 235.
  power of, 55.
  provokes love, 175.
Musician, cough assists, 148.
Musk, all smell not of, 280.
Myself, liberate me from, 201.

NAIL, drive, that will go, 185.
Name, change, you are spoken of, 236.
  good, valued, 271.
  luck in a, 307.
  the shadow of mighty, 210.
Naming one, exclusion of another, 113.
Nathan to David, "Thou art the man," 236.
Native land attracts us, 257.
Natural bent suppressed, not cured, 240.
Nature, crooked by, not altered, 202.
  surpasses art, 28.
Necessity, even gods yield to, 251.

Necessity has no law, 251.
  make virtue of, 116, 284.
  makes coward fight, 178.
  mother of invention, 217.
  obey, 144.
  strong weapon, 97, 178.
Need makes old wife trot, 97.
Negation proves nothing, 251.
Neighbour's crop, always best, 124.
Nero at home, Cato abroad, 184.
Nest, hatched in same, 101.
Net, spread in vain before bird, 137.
Nettle, grasp, or it will sting, 131.
  dishes, new appetites, 104.
New brooms sweep clean, 404.
  nothing, under sun, 263, 265.
News, evil, rides post, 119.
Night and day, work at it, 270.
  when darkest, dawn nearest, 69.
Nile, fling him into, &c., 145.
Nobility of conduct best, 269.
  without wealth useless, 269.
No gains without pains, 285.
  joy without alloy, 182.
  means, no market, 163.
No mill, no meal, 86.
  song, no supper, 256.
  sweet without sweat, 172.
Nonsense, a little, relished, 191.
  he talks, 76.
  it is all, 286.
  leave, to boys, 267.
Note, bird known by, 98.
Nothing, by doing, we learn evil, 259.
  comes from nothing, 110.
  doing, men do ill, 154.
  stake, nothing draw, 250.
  to know, best, 263.
  wholly bad, 183.
Nought never in danger, 215.
Novelty always handsome, 143.
  is charming, 35, 105.
  man yearns for, 104.
Novice, make allowance for, 455.
Numbers, safety in, 80.
Nutmeg, what should cow do with, 28.

OAK, old, you can't straighten, 80.
Oaks, great, from little acorns, 110.
Oar, with one touch water, with other sand, 17.
Oats, sow wild, 169, 246.
Obligation received, sell liberty, 38.
Obligations, be not unmindful of, 38.

INDEX.   495

Obligations, excess of, may lose friend, 11, 38.
Obscurity, to dispel, not make, 277.
Occasion, wise to consider, 251.
Occupation, mind longs for, 22.
Ocean, to add water to, 217.
Offence, for one, try not man twice, 253.
   in act of committing, 168.
Offender never pardons, 342.
Offer, good, refuse not, 263.
Office tests the man, 209.
Ointment, to cure all with same, 101.
Old age, a disease in itself, 186.
   age comes unawares, 93.
   age creeps on us, 194.
   age, fear, and companions of, 222.
   be, betimes, to be old long, 42.
   birds, not caught with chaff, 22.
   block, chip of, 25.
   fox not caught in snare, 22.
   foxes want no tutors, 11.
   head can't be on young shoulders, 193.
   love, good to be off with, &c., 80.
   man's eye, care keeps watch in, 231.
   men's children rarely live, 128.
   wives' tales, he tells well, 141.
   woman dancing makes dust, 24.
   woman would dance! 24.
   young, old long, 163, 217.
Olive, nothing hard in! 265.
Once bit, twice shy, 195.
One beats bush, another gets bird, 15, 100.
   eyed men happy among the blind, 36.
   bird in hand worth two in bush, 7.
   child, loss of, 132.
   enemy, flying from, to another, 158.
   excels in one thing, another in another, 17.
   fire burns out, another's burning, &c., 74.
   fool makes many, 448.
   from, judge whole, 111.
   good turn deserves another, 143.
   hand, with, he scratches, with other strikes, 18.
   hour to-day, worth two to-morrow, 48.
   man's breath, another's death, 238.
   nest, build, in one tree, 116.
   poison is cured by another, 19.
   scabbed sheep infects flock, 16.
   thing requires aid from another, 18.
   thing to boast, another to fight, 16.
   thinks one thing best, another another, 16.
   to-day worth two to-morrows, 50.
   uses his tongue, another his teeth, 15.
   way he looks, rows another, 17.
Open countenance conceals thoughts, 135.

Opinion, change of, not inconstancy, 253.
   give not, till asked for, 5.
   good, of self, to have, 79.
   varying, illustrated, 17.
   wise change, fools never, 253.
Opportune time for speaking, 226.
Opportunity, catch the, 287.
   lost by delay, 94.
Oppression causes rebellion, 181.
Orange, too hard squeezed, gives bitter juice, 40.
Orator, good, bad man, 42.
Orphans, surgeon experiments on, 167.
Others' affairs, to interfere in, 166.
Others, do unto, as you would be done unto, wretched to depend on, 225.
   wretched to rest on fame of, 225.
Out of breath to no purpose, 144.
   of frying-pan to fire, 173.
   of sight, out of mind, 3, 232.
Outlaw, an, 49.
Oven, mother, who has been in, suspects daughter in, 283.
   sooty mocks black chimney, 57.
Over-burden kills beast, 107.
   doing is doing nothing to the purpose, 5.
   warmth false, worse than truth, 220.
Owl has one note, crow another, 16.
   sings to nightingale! 43.
Owls to Athens! 30.
Owner's foot, best manure, 281.
Ox, carriage draws the! 72.
   (eating head off) in stall, 43.
   fallen, all help to kill, 5.
   fierce, has short horns, 75.
   in strange stall looks to door, 42.
   many can drive, few plough, 232.
   muzzle not the, 85.
   sacrifice of, won't bring all things, 279.
   to hunt hare with, 43.
   weary, most sure-footed, 43.
Oxen, unwilling, to harness, 185.

PAIN and pleasure succeed, 184.
   comes with pleasure, 218.
   from, pleasure comes, 93.
   is forgotten when gain comes, 50.
   mingles with pleasure, 224.
   past, is pleasure, 50.
Pains, without, no gains, 86.
Palates, no dish pleases all, 227.
Pap, boil not, before baby born, 23.
Pardon, ask not, before accused, 243.
   others, 255.

Parings of nails, he won't lose, 25.
Parrot utters one cry, quail another, 14.
Passage-money, to lose even! 140.
Passion and shame torment, &c., 11.
   bows down mind, 140.
   lead by bridle, 187.
Past, from, judge present, 110.
   from the, we judge of the future, 2.
   perils, look back on! 131.
   pleasure, to live again, 152.
   to remember, live twice, 105.
Patience enjoined, 84.
   lightens burthens, 201.
   overtaxed, rage, 140.
   plaister for all sores, 67.
   revels in misfortunes, 142.
   sorrow's salve, 171.
   who have not, poor, &c., 171.
Patient, intemperate, harsh doctor, 66.
   man, beware fury of, 140.
Peace advocated, 46.
   assumed, hides warfare, 217.
   egg in, better than ox in war, 281.
   valuable from discord, 87.
Pearls to swine, 166.
Pedigree, no merit from, 237.
   what does it avail? 237.
Penny and penny will be many, 211.
   wise, pound foolish, 169.
Pepper to Hindostan! 50.
   who has much, may use much, 66.
Perfect, none, all at once, 254.
Peril, in time of, sleep not, 170.
Pestilence follows famine, 119.
Petticoat near, smock nearer, 151.
Philosophers, as far as beard, 36.
Physician, heal thyself, 15.
   make not heir, 213.
Physicians won't take medicine, 122.
Picture, poem without words, 236.
Pie, to put finger in another's, 166.
Pigeons, taken, when crows escape, 76.
Pig, from, a grunt, 192.
   we don't kill every day, 58.
   worst, gets best pear, 61.
Pigstye, to make a palace of, 26.
Pillow should be counsellor, 169.
   take counsel of, 270.
Pious texts, man may repeat, &c., 79.
Pipe, no longer, no longer dance, 121.
Pit, he has made, he falls in, 174.
   he falls into his own, 255.
Pitch, touch, defiled, 153.
Pitcher, useless, not broken, 215.

Place, give, to superiors, 73.
Places, all wise man's ports, 161.
Planet, three-halfpenny, 149.
Play often ends in anger, 207.
Please all, nobody can, 137.
   all, no one can, 198.
Pleases least, what most urged, 223.
Pleasing, while we instruct, 80.
Pleasure and action make hours short, 22.
   and pain succeed, 184.
   bought with pain, bad, 270.
   diseases interest of, 217.
   in midst of, sorrow, 218.
   leads to pain, 142.
   mix, with grave designs, 224.
   rills of, not sincere, 164.
   sweet after pain, 50.
   none perfect, 260.
   remembrance of, misery, 225.
   swiftly glide away. &c., 190.
Ploughman on legs, better than gentleman on knees, 228.
Ploughs, he, land of others, &c., 138.
Pluck, want of, shows want of blood, 80.
Poets, we are born: orators, we become, 239.
Point, nothing to the, 258.
   you have hit, 168.
Poison beneath honey, 164.
   in, there is physic, 90.
   quells poison, 215.
   take not antidote before, 243.
Politeness recommended, 60.
   veils craft, 135.
Ponder before you act, 88.
Poor and proud, 468.
Poor man aping rich ruined, 180.
Popularity, love of, all powerful, 197.
Position, act consistently with, 49.
   to rise to a higher, 2.
Pot boiling over cools itself, 113.
   boils, while, friendship, 124.
   your broken, better than my whole one, 255.
Pottage, old, sooner heated than new made, 18.
Poverty coming away goes love, 124.
   from, to renown path hard, 2.
   keeps down merit, 149.
   makes men mean, 250.
   needs much, avarice more, 83.
   parts friends, 124.
   speak not of your, 78.
   tries friends, 166.

Power won by crime, no good, 164.
Powerless, I am not, 107.
Practice better than theory, 112.
 makes perfect, 84.
Practise what you preach, 68.
Praise encourages science, 156.
 from successful man, 197.
 hire of virtue, 156.
 is not pudding, 245.
 undeserved, satire in disguise, 38.
Praised by some, blamed by others, 198.
Praises are our wages, 156.
 he sings his own, 186.
Preach, what you, practise, 68.
Precepts lead, examples draw, 205.
Precipice is in front, wolf behind, 1.
Prepared, be, always, 220
Present, receive, with approval, 91.
Presents, burdensome, 45.
 regard for donor make, most acceptable, 4.
Prevention better than cure, 220.
Price, buy him not at his own, 11.
Pricks, hard to kick against, 61.
Pride innate in beauty, 120.
 will fall, 153.
Prince, if fight with, no scabbard, 71.
Princely mind undoes family, 180.
Princes' favours, wretched to hang on, 43.
 trust not in, 93.
Prize, we do not, things till lost, 42.
Prodigal of property of others, sparing of own, 76.
Proffered service stinks, 181.
Profit, no, where no pleasure, 200.
Promises are not gifts, 245.
 worth nothing, 82.
Prosperity discovers vices, &c., 33.
 has many friends, 157.
 in, expect adversity, 172.
 tries man, 277.
Proud man who won't bend knee, 154.
Proverb, it has become a, 55.
Providence helping, no barrier, 82.
 tempers wind to lamb, 132.
 without, all vain, 268.
Providential aid, 83.
Provisions get, journey over! 111.
Prudence, charioteer of all virtues, 33.
 in action avails most, 12.
Prying person described, 202.
Pudding, proof of, in eating, 112.
 handle, while hot, 93.
Puffed goods, putrid, 222.

Punishment awaits offences, 23.
 delayed, comes, 147.
 follows crime, 68.
 hope of escaping, invites vice, 218.
 must not exceed offence, 53.
Pupil will eclipse tutor, 220.
Pure source, from, pure water, 2.
Purse, empty, frights friends, 70.
 let your, be your master, 177.
 proud, 202.
 who steals, steals trash, &c., 127.

QUALITY, without any good, 275.
Quarrels enhance pleasures of love, 20.
 interfere not in, 241.
Question, hear both sides of, 31.
 the, is before the court, 8.
Quoit attracts more than philosophy, 87.

RABBLE, not influenced by reason, 233.
 obeys impulse, 233.
Rack makes innocent confess, 108.
Rain, after, fair weather, 282.
 out of, under spout, 95
 to see, better than feel, 99.
Rains, it never, but it pours, 214.
Ram may kill butcher, 245.
Rat, one hole, easily caught, 235.
Rats, caught, receive no mercy, 255.
 wise, run from falling house, 234.
Raven, bring up, and he'll pick out your eyes, 59.
 chides starling, 57.
Razor against grindstone, 288.
 to cut whetstone with, 63.
Reader, bad, no audience, 175.
Rebukes, no more salt than sugar, 161.
Receiver bad as thief, 67, 135.
Reckless youth makes rueful age, 42.
Red-haired, black-lipped, &c., 65.
Red-handed, taken, 168.
Reed, blow from, hurts not, 43.
 every, won't make a pipe, 110.
Rejoice with those who do, 141.
Relating it, I shudder, 157.
Relations, hatred of, most bitter, 4.
Relationship produces envy, 58.
Relaxation, mind must have, 206.
Religion, jest not with, 206.
Remedies worse than disease, 144.
Remembrance of friend, cherished, 150.
Remind me, you need not, 221.
Reminding a man makes him forget, 221.
Report, common, not all wrong, 150.

3 S

INDEX.

Report, false, rides post, 119.
Repose, from, to tumult, 77.
Reproach, recoiling, humbles, 264.
Reputation, difficult to preserve, 150.
   try and serve your, 71.
Rest for the weary, 89.
Restive horses roughly dealt with, 114.
Results mostly unexpected, 181.
Retirement, thanks to God for, 83.
Revenge in cold blood, devil's act, 177.
   old, still sucking teeth, 187.
   proof of weak mind, 177.
Rich, all ask if man be, none if good, 21.
   for self, poor for friends, 88.
   gifts wax poor, &c., 75.
   man, rogue, or rogue's heir, 88.
   men wish to be, suddenly, 88.
   mouthful, heavy groan, 227.
   not gaudy, 268.
   pleasures not made for, alone, 237.
   to die, folly to live poor, 216.
Riches bring misery, 233.
   increase, 65.
   more, greater fool, 29.
   not always for deserving, 89.
   serve wise men, command fool, 163.
Riding, more belongs to, than boots, 232.
Ripest fruit falls first, 56.
River, to dig a well by, 193.
   runs for ever, 194.
River's course not to be changed, 129.
Rivers, deepest, flow with least sound, 18.
Roast meat, he gives, beats with spit, 17.
   meat, you cry, faring well, 190.
Robin Hood, many talk of, &c., 279.
Rock aground, on same, 148.
   unmoved, like a, 162.
Rod, in time, mocked, not feared, 74.
   spare, spoil child, 185.
Rogue, none like godly rogue, 216.
   says, "Yes" to what rogue says, 13.
   that I am, &c., 146.
Rogues fall out, when secrets out, 139.
Rolling stone gathers no moss, 399.
Roman, now dressed as, now Greek, 226.
Rome, at, do as Rome does, 61.
   not built in a day, 254.
Root worthless, tree bad, 214.
Rope broken, by straining, 139.
   he cannot buy, to hang himself, 247.
   not a farthing left to buy, 247.
   to throw, after bucket, 140.
   triple, not easily broken, 139.
Rosamund, epitaph of, 147.

Roses found near nettles, 450.
   may nauseate, 219.
   sleep on, repent on thorns, 164.
Rosebuds, gather ye, while ye may, 91.
   let us crown ourselves, &c., 50.
Round, round, while thus we go, &c., 45.
Ruin of others, to rejoice to win by, 142.
Rule others, he cannot, who commands not self, 4.
Rumour grows easily, &c., 110.
   public, not all false, 279.
Rural life advocated, 37.
Rust of mind, destruction of genius, 10.

SACRED, you mix, with profane, 224.
Sadness follows gladness, &c., 282.
Safe bind, safe find, 4.
   to be, never be secure, 49.
Sage, sweet at times to drop, 92.
Saint, bad man worst when aping, 216.
   without, devil within, 146.
Saints, not all who seem, 279.
Salt, with grain of, 70.
Sand, rope of, 109.
   sow not in, 272.
   to plough the!, 204.
   you are sowing in, 26.
   you count the, 26.
   you weave rope of, 109.
Sands make mountain, &c., 260.
Sarcasm, you indulge in, 268.
Satiety kills more than hunger, 233.
Satire, difficult not to write, 84.
Sauce for goose, &c., 201.
Saying and doing, two things, 245.
Scamps, a precious pair of, 25.
Scandal, all add to, 32.
   denounced, 203.
   nothing moves quicker than, 119.
Scars, he jests at, &c., 116.
Sceptre one thing, ladle another, 14.
Sceptres, death levels, and spades, 228.
School despise, remain fool, 116.
   taught in same, 101.
Science, praise encourages, 156.
Scribblers, self-conceited, 141.
Sea, best to avoid, 192.
   great fish caught in, 168.
   once at, wish not for shore, 217.
   to hunt in, 166.
   urchin, more prickly than, 99.
Season, not soil, brings crop, 23.
Seats, to sit on two, 91.
Seclusion, life of, good, 249.

INDEX.

Seclusion, who lives in, lives not in vain, 249.
Secret, betray not, 59.
   tell to no one, 252.
Secrets, keep, 26.
   they who gape after, cannot retain them, 248.
Secure, to be safe, never be, 49.
   too, not safe, 49.
Security, danger next neighbour to, 56.
See and to be seen, 416.
Seeing is believing, 402.
Self conceit, 262.
   control, greatest rule, 163.
   every one loves, 255.
   love denounced, 232.
   master of, master of others, 163.
   nearest to self, 151.
   praise, no recommendation, 222.
Serpent, head of, to bruise, 49.
   to nourish, 59.
   would you have sting twice! 189.
Servant, bad, tongue worst part of, 203.
   be not, if you can be master, 18.
   good, makes good master, 252.
Servants, saucy, in large houses, 218.
   who fears, less than servant, 223.
Service to unwilling, no service, 39.
Set a sprat to catch mackerel, 421.
Shade, fruit won't ripen in, 149.
Shadow, catch not, lose substance, 54.
   to dispute about, 76.
Shame, borne easier than worry, 267.
Shear sheep, don't flay them, 40.
Sheep, lone, in danger of wolf, 236.
   one scabbed, infects flock, 16.
Shepherd should shear, not flay sheep, 40.
Shilling, never without a, 273.
Ship, trust not your all in one, 447.
Shipwreck, common, a consolation, 59.
   to watch, from shore, 99.
   who suffers twice, must not blame Neptune, 165.
Shirt, close, skin closer, 151.
Shoe, anxious for, not foot, 76.
   same, not for all feet, 280.
Shore, hug the, 204.
Short cuts, long ways round, 59.
Shot, always in locker, 273.
   to fire the first, 338.
Sickness brings reproof, 284.
   chamber of, chapel, 169.
   his, increases from remedies, 9.

Sieve, to catch shower in, 162.
Sighs subside, tears shrink, 130.
Silence advocated, 257.
   a woman's greatest ornament, 230.
   cries aloud, 95.
   enjoined, 105, 111, 284.
   no wisdom like, 32.
Silent dog and still water, avoid, 18.
Silk, not from sow's ear, 273.
Silks put out kitchen fire, 177.
Silver spears conquer everything, 26.
   the, has become dross, 27.
Simon, I know, Simon me, 288.
Sin, by that, angels fell, 71.
   not wilful, no sin, 149.
   some rise by, &c., 89.
   strange, strange punishment, 288.
   to love, worse than to commit, 144.
   to meditate, is to commit, 238.
   wages of, death, 23.
Sincerity gives wings to power, 46.
Sinful heart, feeble hand, 151.
Sinning, habit of, takes away sense of sin, 61.
Sir Positives, two, won't agree, 171.
   Robert, gallant, &c., 168.
Six one, half dozen the other, 160.
Skill helps, where force fails, 27.
Skin, even, he won't give us, 240.
Skins may differ, &c., 155.
Slander comes from depraved mind, 203.
   denounced, 276.
   flies gently, &c., 199.
   leaves a score behind it, 46.
   strongly, and some will stick, 46.
   to be angry at, makes true, 179.
Slanderers, devil's bellows, 203.
Slave of men, or things, same thing, 259.
Sleep, men mutter affairs in, 106.
Sleeping pilot, reward not, 145.
Sleeps well, who knows not sleep broken, 37.
Sleeve, broken, holdeth arm back, 2.
Slip, many, 'twixt cup and lip, 230.
Sloth, mother of poverty, 189.
Slothful, way of, hedge of thorns, 189.
Slow help, no help, 39.
Slut, you may eat egg after, 333.
Small matters, unequalled in, 218.
Small rain lays dust, 176.
   spark, great fire, 107.
   things, cautious in, &c., 169.
   things have their charm, 176.
   things, imitate not, 245.
   things make heap, 78.

INDEX.

Sma' winnings mak heavy purse, 78.
Smarts, what, teaches, 96.
Smattering of knowledge, 195.
Smile on lip, tear in eye, 104.
Smoke, avoiding, fall into fire, 138.
    from, to flame, 77.
    to dispute about, 77.
    where, fire, 128.
Smooth words make smooth ways, 121.
Snapping curs have sore ears, 72.
Snare for others, caught in, 148.
Snow, boil or pound, only water, 240.
    gone at last, 85.
    whiter than, 269.
Soft and fair goes far, 60.
    answer turneth away wrath, 121.
    remonstrance succeeds, 161.
    spoken compliment, poison, 220.
    thinking it, find it hard, 134.
    words, hard arguments, 160.
Soils, all, are not fertile, 13.
Solitude, nurse of wisdom, 249.
Some sow, others reap, 15.
Soon ripe, things, perish, 54.
Sooner will earth mount to heaven, 56.
Sooty chimney costs many a beef-steak, 6.
Sore, rub not, but bring plaister, 215.
Sorrow brings premature age, 212.
    feel for others', 277.
    man author of his, 253.
    pays no debt, 278.
    to drink away, 93.
Sorrows come not single spies, 133.
    come uninvited, 212.
    dwell near pleasure, 114.
    succeed each other, 214.
Sow, some, others reap, 15.
Sow, washed, returns to mire, 47.
Sowre apple-tree, tied to, 212.
Spare the rod, spoil the child, 185.
Spark, a small, may yet remain, 197.
    produces great flame, 78.
Sparrow in hand worth pheasant flying, 48.
Speak, or be kicked, 34.
    the whole truth, 458.
    when you are spoken to, 5.
Speaks, who, sows; hears, who, reaps, 32.
Speaking, practice in, makes eloquent, 84.
Spears, fight with silver, &c., 26.
Speech, given to disguise thought, 108.
    silvern, silence golden, 105.
    unguarded, reveals truth, 203.
Speed, like delay to anxious, 107.

Speedy, not slow, measures, 56.
Spigot, to save at, and let out of bunghole, 6.
Spilt milk, grieve not over, 78.
Sprat, set, to catch mackerel, 250.
Springes to catch woodcocks! 79.
Squinting, catching, 95.
Staff, leave not at home, 3.
Stage, all the world is a, 438.
Stammer, you should, to understand stammerer, 36.
Staring, no time for, 277.
Stark naked, 170.
Steel whets steel, 124.
Step by step, ladder ascended, 145.
Stepmother, to weep at tomb of, 129.
Still water breeds vermin, 10.
    waters run deep, 53.
Stirrup, difficult thing to get foot in, 58.
Stolen fruit is sweet, 92.
    waters sweet, 92.
Stomach full, heart glad, 119.
Stone in one hand, bread in the other, 17.
    no, left unturned, 265.
    to draw blood from, 1.
    you seek water from, 25.
    you talk to! 196.
Stools, between two, ground, 96.
Stoop, he must, who has low door, 250.
Storm, after, a calm, 282.
Storms, vows made in, forgotten, 9.
Story, change name, and you are subject of, 236.
Straining breaks the bow, &c., 26.
Stratagem, to oppose by, 71.
Straw, last, breaks camel's back, 107.
Straws in air, from, we judge of wind, 2.
Stream, smooth, deep, 241.
Streams, muddy, from muddy springs, 212.
Strife with powerful, avoid, 71.
Strike when iron hot, 123.
Strings, have two to bow, 128.
Strong of hands, &c., still of tongue, 203.
Study, no, after heavy meals, 165.
Stumble, may prevent fall, 103.
    take heed not to, 53.
    to, twice over same stone, 189.
Stumbles, who, twice, deserves harm, 165.
Subtlety, set trap, caught itself, 48.
Success alters manners, 156.
    leads to insolence, 134.
    makes fool look wise, 156.
    or ruin, 34.
    seems honesty, 156.

INDEX.

Sudden trust, sudden repentance, 241.
Suffering teaches wisdom, 101.
Sugar, even, may spoil dish, 219.
Suit, best, that best fits me, 49.
Summer lasts not for ever, 263, 282.
Sundays, when two meet, 6.
Sun even has its spots, 260.
Sun, gnats dim not, 197.
    shines, when, leave not your cloak at home, 49.
Sunshine, no, without shadow, 224.
Sup ill, if eat all at dinner, 125.
Supper, light, beneficial, 57.
    take light, 109.
Suspicion haunts guilty mind, 238.
Suspicious mind sees everything on dark side, 7.
    virtuous are not, 238.
Swallow, one, does not make a summer, 446.
Sweetest wine, sharpest vinegar, 63.
Swift, race not always to, &c., 51.
Sword, draw not for every one, 241.
    laid by, rusts ingloriously, 10.
    let not idiot have, 102.
    of lead, to cut with, 192.
    of lead, scabbard of ivory, 167.
    robber and traveller wear, 106.
    trust not to boy, 243.
Swords, turn then your, on me, 9.

TAIL, make not, broader than wings, 137.
    to put, between legs, 52.
Take heed is a good reed, 4.
Tale, good, may be twice told, 79.
    honest, speeds best, 210.
    marred in telling, 212.
    of bricks, doubled, 69.
    one, good till another told, 31.
    told by idiot, &c., 43, 76.
Talent wins glory, 178.
Talk much, err much, 112.
    to sea-shore! 204.
Tamarisk sooner will bear apples, 236.
Tantalus, fruit from garden of! 98.
Tartar, catching a, 134.
    I have caught, 32.
Task, easier to begin, than finish, 174.
Taste much, poor appetite, 120.
Tastes, no accounting for, 77.
Tattle, all can, away from battle, 170.
Teaching, you learn by, &c., 89.
Tear, nothing dries more quickly, 195.
    relieves sorrow, 113.

Tears avail not, &c., 221.
    eloquence of, 183.
    far off, interest of, 90.
    like summer tempest, 104.
    power of, 183.
    repentant, wash our guilt, 199.
    you kiss away her, 129.
Teeth, men dig graves with, 101.
Temper, govern your, 22.
Tempest drear, little we heed, &c., 55.
Thanks when none present, no thanks, 179.
Thief honest when it thunders, 9.
    knows thief, 139.
    to tread softly like, 139.
Thieves dread commotion, 139.
    great, we take off hats to, 139.
    not all, dogs bark at, 174.
    like, they know each other, 181.
    poor, in halters, &c., 139.
Thistles, gather, expect prickles, 68.
Thorns, who sows, must not go barefoot, 215.
Thread, as arranged, weave, 58.
    one weaves, other draws, 152.
    to cut, 204.
Threatened folk live long, 223, 249.
Threatens, he, who is afraid, 47.
Threats, he terrifies by, or wheedles, 35.
Threshold, hardest step over, 87.
    most difficult pass, 58.
Thunder, in, thief honest, 9.
Tide fetches away what ebb brings, 15.
    there is, in the affairs of men, 402.
Time and tide wait not, 248.
    bald behind, 135.
    flies, 138.
    good, coming, 208.
    lost, never found, 138.
    no note of, save by loss, 176.
    rolls on, 109.
    stoops to no man's lure, 138.
    take when time is, &c., 50, 81.
    tries a', 74.
Time's swiftness proved by retrospect, 176.
    who neglects, time will, 138.
Timid dogs bark most, 31.
Tit for tat, 44.
Title one thing, contents another, 16.
To-day, he fell, I may to-morrow, 153.
    layman, to-morrow clerk, 226.
    nobody, prince to-morrow, 153.
Told ten times, it will please, 79.
To-morrow, and to-morrow, &c., 94.

To-morrow, care not for, 50.
  let, take care of, &c., 45.
  pupil of to-day, 87.
  we will believe it, not to-day! 64.
Tongue, hard to bridle, 203.
  honied, hath poison, 147.
  long, sign of short hand, 223.
  says little, arm strong, 203.
Tools, edged, you play with, 62.
Too little, nor too much, give not, 255.
  much care bad, 267.
  much of a thing bad, 243.
  secure, who is, not safe, 49.
  to will in two, 26.
Tooth and nail, 216.
Toothless man, envies those who eat, 99.
Tortoise, you compare hare to, 46.
Tower, the higher, greater fall, 54.
Trace, not even, left, 245.
Trade, two of, never agree, 127.
Transportation, do something worthy of, if you would be somebody, 30.
Treachery betrays itself, 186.
Treasures, to brood over, 57.
Tree, as known by fruit, so man by deeds, 25.
  fallen, all go to with axe, 80.
  gives its nature to fruit, 25.
Trial, fly from, confess guilt, 120.
Trickery comes back to its master, 48.
Tried it, who has, fears it, 113.
Trifles, contend not about, 272.
  light as air, confirmations strong, 7.
Trifling causes, great results! 110.
Triumph, sing not of, before victory, 23.
Trivial things, mighty contests, 100.
Trouble, all have, in this life, 239.
  man in, help, 73.
Troy, faults within and without, 160.
  thing of the past, 138.
True, what all men say, 150.
Trumpeter, his own, 186.
Trust, but beware whom, 127.
  not too much, 252, 257.
  sudden, sudden repentance, 241.
Trout, not caught in dry breeches, 172.
Truth and oil get uppermost, 210.
  in things much talked of, 183.
  lost in arguments, 268.
  stranger than fiction, 118.
  unguarded speech reveals, 203.
  will prevail, 210.
Tub, he tells tale of, 238.
Turn, one good, deserves another, 327.

Twice, he dies, if by own weapons, 39.
  he gives, who gives in a trice, 39.
  over, do nothing, 5.
Twig, as bent, tree inclined, 8.
Two can play at that game, 107.
  can't quarrel, if one won't, 134.
  Hercules cannot cope with, 242.
  pigeons, catch, with one bean, 96.
  to one, odds, 242.
Tyrant, hard to see an old, 121.
Tyrants, few, die natural death, 6.

UNADORN'D, adorn'd the most, 79.
Uncertainties, seek not, &c., 54.
Underling, if, don't dress too fine, 26.
Understand, what not, condemn, 74.
Understood, what not, explained by what not! 160.
Unfortunate are spiteful, 103.
Ungrateful man, tub with holes, 179.
  man, one, injures many, 179.
Union is strength, 139.
Uniting, by, we stand, 94.
Unknown, because no bard, &c., 49.
Unlearn, difficult to, what learnt, 80.
Unoccupied, let not devil find you, 74.
Unsaid, let it be, 175.
Untried, no means left, 265.
Unwilling hounds, to hunt with, 185.
Upside down, things turned, 162.
Use can change nature, 103.
Used key, always bright, 10.
  plough shines, 252.

VAIN glory brings hatred, 232.
Valour, hidden, as bad as cowardice, 54.
  rejoices in test, 142.
Variety, its charms, 192.
  spice of life, 105.
  want of, brings satiety, 105.
Vase, it was intended for, it is a pot, 21.
Vasty deep, swimming in, they appear, 24.
Vengeance, noblest, to forgive, 40.
Venison, all flesh not, 278.
Venture not from shore, 204.
Verbiage, mere, not worth carrot, &c., 62.
Verses, I wrote, another had merit, 157.
Vessel, cracked, small force breaks, 107.
  steer, talk not, 275.
Vessels, large, may venture, &c., 204.
Vexations are trials, 90.
Vice, avoiding, fools find another, 95.
  from, to fly to other, vain, 137.

INDEX.

Vice, height of, slowly reached, 254.
  in garb of virtue deceives, 118.
  where vengeance follows, 68.
  who spares, wrongs virtue, 41.
  worst, in garb of virtue, 79.
Victory, or Westminster Abbey, 34.
  this, ruin, 148.
Villain, conscientious, worst, 216.
  none like conscientious, 146.
Villany reduces to level, 117.
  thus I clothe, &c., 147.
  vengeance follows, 68.
Vinegar from sweet wine, fear, 140.
Viper produces viper, 99.
  smallest, hath venom, 176.
Virtue, affable, dignified, 152.
  increased by praise, 198.
  its own reward, 398.
  rejoices in test, 142.
  to vice easy, 117.
  won't walk far without vanity, 199.
Virtuous suspect not others, 238.
Voice, harsh, dismissing, welcome sweet, 29.
Vote, to pay off a grudge by, 45.
Vows made in storms are forgotten, 9.
Vulgar, manners of, contagious, 36.

WALL, hard things only won't make, 97.
  tottering to, lean on, 166.
Walls, fools write on, 272.
  to whiten two, from one pot, 96.
Want least, they, who least covet, 188.
Wants, to have no, money, 274.
  to satisfy, at small cost, 71.
War, fear of, worse than war, 224.
  in, blunder not twice, 278.
  neither fear nor provoke, 37.
  pleasant to inexperienced, 92.
  raging, laws dumb, 182.
  to prepare for, battle over, 209.
  with vices, peace with persons, 37.
Warning, he was slain who had, not who took, 226.
  take, 226.
  who had, was slain, not who took, 53.
Wash a blackamoor white, 11.
  a dog, comb a dog, still a dog remains a dog, 11.
Wasps, irritate not, 271.
Waste not, want not, 125.
Watch, good, prevents misfortune, 56.
Water, dropping wears rock, 145.
  he begrudges, to wash with, 25.

Water, hunting for, in sea, 168.
  past, can mill go with? 22.
  still, breeds vermin, 10.
  to draw in a sieve, 65.
  to pound, in a mortar, 25.
  unknown, wade not in, 197.
Wave, as one leaves, another succeeds, 15.
Way of slothful, hedge of thorns, 189.
Weak, despise not the, 242.
  even, may attack, 263.
Wealth, and means of enjoying, 84.
  care follows increase of, 64.
  changes not birth, 202.
  changes not, ends troubles, 233.
  command, or it commands you, 163.
  goes not to Acheron, 150.
  his who enjoys it, 137.
  little, little care, 233.
  love of, makes him old, 163.
  nothing prevails against, 61.
  poor in midst of, 210.
Weariness can snore upon the flint, &c., 29.
Weaver's shuttle, days swifter than, 56.
Web, for, begun, God sends thread, 85.
  tangled, we weave, &c., 118.
Weeds, frost hurts not, 76.
  want no sowing, 252.
Weep not too much, 272.
Weeping hath a voice, 183.
  pleasure in, 104.
Weigh matter well, 33.
Welcome, best cheer, 234.
Well begun is half done, 41.
What bird so fair as mine? says Crow, 28.
Wheat, none without chaff, 276.
Whetstone to cut, with razor, 63.
Whispering she would ne'er consent, &c., 92.
Whist owes to Hoyle, &c., 49.
Whistle and drink, none can, 128.
White glove hides dirty hand, 136.
  hen, born of a, 13.
  robed in, at funeral, at wedding in mourning, 13.
Wicked dread good conduct in others, 165.
  flee when none pursue, 151.
  gifts of, profit not, 214.
  hatred better than company of, 220.
  know not happiness, 253.
  speeches of, deceit, 146.
  who spares, injures good, 41.
Wickedness with beauty, devils hook, baited, 118.
Wider ears, and a short tongue, 31.

INDEX.

Wife, chose from equals, 10.
  commands, by obeying, 51.
  faithless, shipwreck to house, 240.
  unwillingly married, enemy, 158.
Wild days, having had, sow wild oats, 246.
Wilful fault, no pardon, 154.
  man maun hae his way, 39.
Will, take, for deed, 273.
Willingly, things done, easy, 200.
Willow, bend the, while young, 8.
Willows, weak, bind other wood, 176.
Willy nilly, 271.
Wind, not serving, take to oars, 82.
  sow, reap whirlwind, 204.
Windmills, to fight with, 70.
Wine and love lead to no good, 288.
  brings out the truth, 173.
  dispels grief, 71.
  given for mirth, not drunkenness, 6.
  good, familiar creature, 71.
  good, needs no bush, 222.
  he cries, sells vinegar, 234.
  in bottle, won't quench thirst, 137.
  makes sane man mad, 181.
  one thing, drunkenness another, 17.
  sweetest, makes sharpest vinegar, 4.
  unlocks the breast, 24.
  wears no breeches, 173.
  wears no mask, 24.
  when, sinks, words swim, 26.
  women, and dice, avoid, 88.
Wings he covers with, bites with bill, 17.
Winter, calculate length of, 58.
Winter, summer's heir, 95.
  will re-appear, 229.
Wisdom, best learnt from folly of others, 15.
Wisdom consists not in dress, 173.
  none to silence, 105.
  rides on ruins of folly, 121.
  to be used, 274.
Wise head keeps close mouth, 111.
  man makes opportunity, 251.
  men learn by other men's mistakes, 15.
  not, unless wise for self, 213, 256.
Wiser, we become, as older, 11.
Wish, father to thought, 123.
  this my, and command, 153.
Wit, bought, best, 112.
  folly, unless man keeps it, 8.
  not bought, till paid for, 96.
With or without you, I can't get on, 249.
Woe succeeds woe, 133.

Woes cluster, &c., 214.
Wolf changes hair, not nature, 208.
  dances round well, 207.
  death to, life to lamb, 227.
  fears pit, hawk, snare, 52.
  I hold by the ears, 32.
  in sheep's clothing, 118.
  looking for wings in! 207.
  nourish whelps of a, 13.
  to hold by ears, 207.
  to love, as, loves lamb, 207.
  to snatch lamb from, 13.
  wants not pretext against lamb, 213.
Wolves head. An outlaw, 49.
  who kennels with, must howl, 250.
  you must howl with, &c., 61.
Woman either loves or hates, 33.
  a general, women soldiers, 229.
  being a, raise not sword, 242.
  jealous, set house on fire, 174.
  laughter, tears deceive, 130.
  leader of enterprize, 97.
  once fallen, past hope, 256.
  piqued, fierce as hell, 164.
  rich, intolerable, 184.
  scorned, merciless, 230.
  silence greatest ornament in, 230.
  to lust after, adultery, 238.
  trust not, when dead even, 230.
  undisguisedly bad, then good, 24.
Woman's obstinacy described, 271.
  tears, power of, 183.
Women, detected, assume anger, 260.
  injured, not appeased, 164.
  worst and best, &c., 63.
Won, as, so spent, 213.
Woods, let timid avoid, 284.
Wooers, too many, bad, 262.
Wool, you seek, from a donkey, 28.
Words, spoken, not recalled, 258.
Words and no deeds, rushes, &c., 109.
  fair, butter no parsnips, 82.
  fair, won't feed cat, 245.
  for women, actions for men, 203.
  high-sounding, fear not, 243.
Work, all, and no play, &c., 191.
  at end of judge workman, 128.
  grumblingly done, bad, 200.
  while you can, 95.
Workmanship surpass'd material, 217.
Worm, to snatch from the trap, 3.
  tread on, it turns, 176.
Worst, best to know, 288.
  things at, mend, 69.

Worthy most, give to, 83.
Wound, bleeding inwardly, worst, 72.
 healed, scar remains, 108.
 small, despise not, 78.
 their own death accompanies the, 21.
Wounds, healed, open not, 215.
 self-inflicted, 150.
 wept o'er, &c., 191.
Wrang, if ye do, mak amends, 199.
Wrath, let not sun go down on, 242.
Writing, by, we learn to write, 116.
Wrong-doers and assenting parties, equally punishable, 12.
 to forget, best revenge, 177.

YEARS, how they roll! 100.
Years know more than books, 112.
Yesterday, slave, to-day free, 150.
Yesterday will not return, 138.
Young in limbs, old in judgment, 258.
Young old, old long, 217.
Young, so, and wise, ne'er live long, 188.
Youth, be careful before, 265.
 consideration, due to, 218.
 control not, correct not age, 67.
 habits of, accompany age, 67.
 impetuosity of, 193.
 mistakes of, pardon, 175.
 spirits riot in, 193.

PRINTED BY WHITTINGHAM AND WILKINS,
TOOKS COURT, CHANCERY LANE.

THE UNIVERSITY OF MICHIGAN

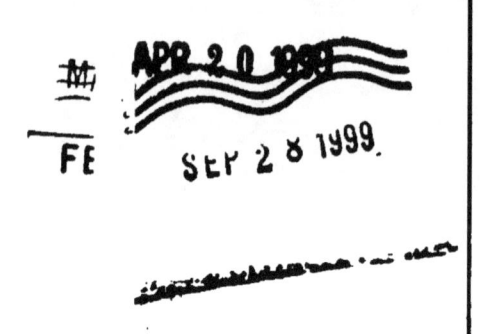

DATE DUE
APR 2 0 1999
SEP 2 8 1999

**DO NOT REMOVE
OR
MUTILATE CARD**

THE UNIVERSITY OF MICHIGAN

DATE DUE

APR 20 1999

SEP 28 1999